PENGUIN BOOKS

GAME DAY

Thomas Boswell is a sportswriter and columnist for *The Washington Post*, where he has
worked since 1969. He is also the columnist
for *Golf* magazine, a frequent contributor to
GQ and *Inside Sports*, and a guest commentator on National Public Radio. He lives outside Annapolis with his wife Wendy and son
Russell.

GAME DAY

THOMAS BOSWELL

GAME DAY

Sports Writings
1970–1990

PENGUIN BOOKS

PENGUIN BOOKS
Published by the Penguin Group
Viking Penguin, a division of Penguin Books USA Inc.,
375 Hudson Street, New York, New York 10014, U.S.A.
Penguin Books Ltd, 27 Wrights Lane,
London W8 5TZ, England
Penguin Books Australia Ltd, Ringwood,
Victoria, Australia
Penguin Books Canada Ltd, 10 Alcorn Avenue, Suite 300,
Toronto, Ontario, Canada M4V 3B2
Penguin Books (N.Z.) Ltd, 182–190 Wairau Road,
Auckland 10, New Zealand

Penguin Books Ltd, Registered Offices:
Harmondsworth, Middlesex, England

First published in the United States of America by
Doubleday, a division of Bantam Doubleday Dell Publishing Group, Inc., 1990
Published in Penguin Books 1992

1   3   5   7   9   10   8   6   4   2

Articles appearing herein have previously appeared in *The Washington Post* and *Golf*.
Excerpt from "My Back Pages" (Bob Dylan) © 1964 Warner Bros. Inc. All Rights Reserved.
Used By Permission.
Excerpt from "Choruses from 'The Rock'" in *Collected Poems 1909–1962* by T. S. Eliot,
copyright 1936 by Harcourt Brace Jovanovich, Inc., copyright © 1964 by T. S. Eliot,
reprinted by permission of the publisher.

THE LIBRARY OF CONGRESS HAS CATALOGUED THE HARDCOVER AS FOLLOWS:
Boswell, Thomas, 1948–
Game day: sports writings 1970–1990/Thomas Boswell—1st ed.
p.   cm.
ISBN 0-385-41617-2 (hc.)
ISBN 0 14 01.5944 4 (pbk.)
A collection of columns originally published in the Washington
Post and Golf Magazine.
1. Sports.   2. Newspapers—Sections, columns, etc.—Sports.
3. Washington Post (Washington, D.C.: 1974)   4. Golf magazine
(New York, N.Y.)   I. Title
GV707.B63   1990
796—dc20   90–37335

Printed in the United States of America

CONTENTS

INTRODUCTION

The fun of writing a column about sports is that, much of the time, you aren't really writing about sports at all. You're writing about what might be called the commonsense ethics of everyday living. Games are about who won, who lost and how. But they're also about what's right, what's wrong and why.

Was Billy Martin a victim or a perpetrator? What exactly is George Steinbrenner's main problem? And, be honest, do we really hope that he finds a cure?

These days, sports may be what Americans talk about best. With the most knowledge. The most passion. The most humor. The most distance. The most capacity for a cheerful change of mind. When we meet someone for the first time, it's no accident that sport becomes the subject so often and so quickly. Yes, it's an easy, superficial topic—if we want it to be. But talking about sports has also become one of our best ways of probing people, sounding their depth, listening for resonances, judging their values.

What do you think of Pete Rose now? Should he be banned? Jailed? Put in the Hall of Fame? All three? Would you still invite him to dinner?

Which sports or teams of athletes do you love? Or hate? And why? Mars Blackman knows he has to pretend to despise Larry Bird. President George Bush has followed the bedraggled Houston Astros for years; is that a tip-off that he's more Texan than preppie? What issues make you see red? Overpaid players? Or greedy owners? Strikes? Or franchise shifts? Be careful. You tip your hand every time you open your mouth. Are you generous or jealous, judgmental or broad-minded? Talk sports and it will slip out. Whose honor do you instinctively defend? Old Tom Landry, put out to pasture? Or those miserable choking-dog Broncos? Oooops.

Is Jack Nicklaus a genuine hero? If so, what can we learn from his thirty years in public life? Is it a hint that he jetted home between rounds to see his kids play in Little League?

What, if anything, moves you beyond self-consciousness, beyond hipness, beyond self-protective intelligence, and turns you into a vulnerable ventilating fan? Any woman who marries a man with no favorite team, no childhood hero, no incurable need to call Sportsphone at 1 A.M. (that's 212-976-1313), should consider herself fairly warned. She's probably hooked a cold fish.

With tens of millions of exceptions, sports are still more a fascination for men than women. That only underlines our point. Men can't find any other subject where they can reveal themselves so much, yet pretend that they have said so little.

Is John Thompson a highly principled leader, a true educator and an example to youth? Or is he a paranoid racist?

Because sports are a subject about which we feel deeply, yet usually pretend not to care too much ("it's only a game"), they have become perhaps our richest and most user-friendly topic of conversation. Especially when the subtext is moral. And how many conversations about sports lack a moral undertone? The question beneath every event, even for athletes, is: Who deserves to win? "Deserves," that is, in the broadest sense. To an athlete, this often means: Who has developed his available talent most fully? To a team, it can translate as: Who interacts best as a group? An individual or a team that has trouble perceiving itself as truly worthy of victory has great difficulty reaching its goals.

A large part of a sportswriter's job, although it is seldom acknowledged, is to present, as clearly as possible, the central characters and issues in what amounts to an ongoing national conversation about mores: How do we act and how should we act?

At what point does obsession with victory reduce an entire sport to absurdity? And has anyone seen Dennis Conner lately?

Given a concrete set of circumstances, what constitutes a reasonably wise or a spectacularly foolish course of action? Not so long ago, such discussions in this country were couched in specifically religious terms. The frame of reference was, more or less, the Bible with its commandments, allegories, cautionary tales and parables. The prodigal son, David and Goliath, doubting Thomas or the story of Ruth might be invoked at the dinner table. Today, where would we reach first for material or metaphor to make such points to our children? Probably to sports.

Why? Because millions of people in this country know more about the achievements, failures, embarrassments and private lives of athletes than they know about anyone on earth except their family and friends. Even national politicians and celebrity entertainers are not covered on an intense daily basis, sometimes for decades. Athletes and coaches take it for granted.

Do society's outcasts, like Satchel Paige, have insights and a capacity for joy that members of the mainstream lack?

Americans frequently talk about sports as though they were an extension of their own private lives—because it feels like they are. When fans meet famous athletes for the first time, the assumption of familiarity is so total that players are sometimes alarmed. No wonder fans feel so free to ask for autographs in restaurants. There's almost no sense of distance to break down.

Why, this is just butterfingered old Joe, the good-block, no-catch tight end. He fumbled in the Rose Bowl, went into drug rehab when he was with the Raiders, got traded to the Redskins during training camp and now picks up a few bucks by trading quips with the anchorman on the local evening news. We know him better than plenty of our cousins.

Many of us, perhaps unconsciously, are attracted to this peculiarly modern possibility—long-distance intimacy. Mass media have given us a chance to observe the essential behavior of other people in a core area of their lives for years on end.

Can one virtue excuse many vices? Say hello to Bobby Knight. And what do you think of John McEnroe? Jerk or genius?

Sports are the area where we can be philosophical without pretending to own a philosophy. Because sports congratulate themselves on being trivial, even creating the "trivia question," we allow ourselves the luxury of unsystematic insight. We welcome new evidence about complex personalities. For instance, we'll wait twenty years to form our final opinion of Kareem Abdul-Jabbar, allowing him to change, grow and finally reveal himself to us as an adult. For once, we care more about learning than judging.

Because sports are real, we don't ask them to make perfect sense. We just ask them to be alive in every detail. Sports lend themselves to moral musing because each situation is unique and specific; we all have the same facts on the table before us. And they *are* facts. Our discussions have hope of being grounded in reality.

Should Ray Leonard retire? Or keep fighting Tommy Hearns and Marvin Hagler until he ends up talking like Muhammad Ali? Must a man inevitably become the thing he does?

If you can't talk sports—national sports, local sports and even neighborhood sports—you may feel like a social outsider in many communities in this country. In fact, sports have become central to what remains of our American sense of community. In an age that is a political, religious, artistic and cultural kaleidoscope of relativist values, how can we feel united? What can we agree about? Or even discuss calmly, yet enthusiastically, with a sense of shared expertise and a glimpse of a shared ideal?

Sports have never had so profound a hold upon people because they have never been so desperately needed. In a century that has banished certainty in almost every corner of our life, in a time when, one after another, almost all our compasses have been demagnetized, there is an enormous collective yearning for a sense of orientation.

We're not expecting truth, doctrine or dogma, mind you. "Isms" have had a bad credit rating for a long time. Even Communism, this century's only new world religion, has already lost its faith. We'd just like to get our bearings occasionally, thank you very much. We've learned to make little things suffice. For instance, it is reassuring to know that as long as George III owns the Yankees, they will never be in another World Series.

What made Red Auerbach's Boston Celtics—first with Bill Russell, then with John Havlicek and finally with Bird—seem like more than a basketball team?

When we want to ask simple but embarrassing questions, we often turn to sports for analogies and limited practical insight. How should a person live? Or face tragedy? What constitutes a useful life? To many moderns, such topics might instantly run the risk of sounding more comic than cosmic. From the values of religion to the concepts of physics to the words of poetry, we are accustomed—almost resigned—to ambiguity.

Sports, with their artificial simplicity, their final scores, their winners and losers, prod us away from that sea of gray, at least for a while. We may not know how all men should live, but we know that Magic Johnson embodies unselfishness and a joy-in-task that we might see as a useful model. We may not know how we would cope with tragedy until we meet it. But the memory of speed skater Dan Jansen competing in the Olympics on the same day that his sister died might be of some use to us. Jansen fell, raced again three days later and fell once more, yet still seemed somehow ennobled by his effort.

In games, we often discover the implicit values and powerful preferences that we hold in common, even though we seldom express them. We all sense that Michael Jordan and Julius Erving have special qualities. When we try to find words for what those estimable qualities are, we educate ourselves about ourselves.

Whatever happened to humble heroes? Would we be better off without high fives, elbow bashes, touchdown spikes, Day-Glo batting gloves, inflatable sneakers, backboard smashing, Mohawk hairdos and 900 numbers?

When we want to focus on how *not* to live, when we want to isolate and understand what is destructive or unacceptable behavior, where do we turn? Not to our legal system certainly. There, the concept of an individual's responsibility for his actions is so attenuated as to be almost nonexistent. In sports, the individual still must answer for himself. Neither a broken home nor a bad hop helps you beat the rap.

Is playing high school football worth the risk of getting your neck broken?

Perhaps two hundred years ago the average American could have mentioned the latest doings of Samuel Adams or Thomas Jefferson and assumed that his neighbor would know all about these men, their lives and their ideas. Republican politics was a common ground on which Americans could meet. To what degree have sports supplanted politics and religion as the meeting ground where we argue about our values?

Before you laugh, fly over cities like Cincinnati, Pittsburgh, St. Louis, San Diego, Dallas, Detroit, Cleveland, Phoenix, Tampa, Miami, Seattle, Kansas City, Houston, Atlanta and many others. Look for the primary architectural symbols. Cathedrals, statehouses, ballparks. You'll see the ballparks and stadiums first. They're the structures that dwarf everything else.

Only when you come to America's "world" cities—New York, Chicago, Los Angeles, Washington, San Francisco—do you find skylines where the coliseums are on a common scale with other monuments and skyscrapers.

Let somebody else blow a brain lobe figuring out whether this is tragic news or encouraging. What's interesting is that in the last thirty years, thanks to TV and our whole mass-media explosion, America has become infatuated with a vast open-ended subject on which tens of millions of people are experts. As spectators, we all observe the same behavioral laboratory together.

Is it worth the risk of death to feel that you are completely alive? Ski jumpers, downhill racers and bobsledders think so.

The one paradoxical strength of our games is that, even when 100 million people watch the Super Bowl, nobody involved with our spectacles is allowed to take the event or themselves very seriously. For instance, sportswriters with even a hint of a political, religious, philosophical or even generational agenda tend to disappear quickly.

Sports are too specific, too detailed, too reality-tested and—above all—too thoroughly known by too many people for media pundits to get away with much. As soon as you start to overstate your case, you can hear the screams from the street. You can't fool many of the people much of the time about Ray Leonard's last fight. They saw it, by damn. Just like they've seen all his others since the 1976 Olympics. Some watched the replay, too.

It's ironic that a columnist writing on the editorial page about the Congress and a sportswriter holding forth on the affairs of the Washington Redskins are often held to different standards. A case can be made that greater accuracy, far more disclosure of sources, less appearance of conflict of interest, a less predictable pattern of partisan bias and crisper writing are generally expected of the sportswriter.

One of the charms of sportswriting is that it's bad form to admit what you're really talking about. The fans know the subject within the subject, even if it isn't named. Besides, it would be hard to start a column by saying, "Neo-Nazi sexual pervert Genghis Hitler, in a typical orgy of paranoiac lying, was at his manic-depressive best this afternoon as he tried to deny reports that he had firebombed the hotel room of his egomaniacal superstar."

Besides, you'd have guessed who Genghis Hitler was in a blink.

In keeping with the code of my craft, I have no intention of revealing the true deconstructed, textually critiqued semiotic "meanings" of the stories collected in this book. I had no such notions when I wrote them and I won't cook any up now.

For twenty-one years at *The Washington Post*, I have, like other sportswriters, had a great luxury. I've been allowed to report and write several thousand stories without ever being ordered to produce anything of lasting worth. If I couldn't figure out a person or a team, if I couldn't understand an issue, if I couldn't crack the case, nobody threatened to fire me. As long as I got the facts right, met the deadline, wrote to length and didn't get us sued, I was free to proceed to the next job. And hope for better luck.

Sooner or later, you get lucky. You hit a subject you grasp. Or a person who wants to talk. Or who likes talking to you. You're at the right place at the right time. Or the wrong time, depending on how you feel about earthquakes. Sometimes you revisit the same subjects, the same people, the same issues so often that, eventually, your vision comes into focus.

For instance, I've been interviewing John Thompson on "game day" since 1972; I covered his Hoyas as a beat man for years when Patrick Ewing still lived in Jamaica. I first talked to Ray Leonard as he taped his hands before he'd ever thrown a professional punch. I had lunch with Martina Navratilova when she was sixteen, long before she defected. When I met George Steinbrenner, he'd never fired Billy Martin. My first story on Moses Malone was written when he was in the eighth grade. On a summer playground, Red Auerbach once asked if I'd seen that kid at Northwestern High named Lenny Bias. I'd known Gene Mauch for five years as Minnesota Twins manager before he even began his saga with the California Angels.

The pieces here are, simply, my favorites. No thread could connect them all, I hope. But, by accident, I think a theme runs through many of them: our American predilection for talking about values when we talk about games. For example, every topic in italics in this introduction could serve as marginalia for a chapter of this book.

During my lifetime, sports have become one of the primary mediums through which Americans are able and willing to discuss the ethics of everyday life. Is this as pathetic as it sounds at first blush?

When decent behavior and self-expression collide, what should you do? How should we cope with utterly capricious failure? To what degree do political systems influence the development of the individual personality? Can a single hero work significant change on mass prejudice? How does a principled man keep from selling his soul, yet still succeed in the real world? Is an hour of glory and artistry worth a lifetime of brain damage?

Yes, these are sports questions. When we talk about John McEnroe and Greg Norman, Ivan Lendl and Joe Louis, John Thompson and Ray Leonard, we are forced to ask them.

Great athletes have, without knowing it or wanting it, been put in something akin to the position of mythic or religious characters in other cultures in other times. That is to say, they have taken on a symbolic quality. For them, no doubt, this is a mixed blessing—a kind of celebrity squared. But for the public, is the trade-off so bad?

Are the issues that our passion for sports help us to discuss—with knowledge, good cheer, honesty and without the weight of dogma—really as trivial as we like to pretend?

Football

NFL Coaching: American Roulette

January 11, 1981—"NFL coaches are getting to be like those Datsun cars—you can't tell 'em apart. Why don't I have a head coaching job? 'Cause they're afraid of me. If you're not a puppet, you're in trouble." —George Allen, ex-Super Bowl coach.

"We're in the era of the Charlie McCarthy coach. You're the dummy and somebody else pulls the strings. Vince Lombardi couldn't make it now. Some accountant would get the owner's ear and undermine him. The third man—the guy between you and the owner—is the franchise ruiner. The story's always the same. Just change the names from Stram to Allen to Bum Phillips to Jack Pardee." —Hank Stram, ex-Super Bowl coach.

"Hank said that? Well, is that any different than the rest of corporate America? It's executive-level politics. Our new NFL owners didn't grow up with the game like the old families—the Halases and Rooneys—so they frequently need advice. And, you know, the sources of that advice are sometimes unreliable. . . . I don't like the trend. I see too many old friends and good coaches who are out of work without sufficient reason." —Tom Landry, coach of the Dallas Cowboys.

"I can't think of any profession as insecure as being an NFL head coach. Your fate is never in your own hands. One injury, one bad call, one bad bounce, and a year's work can be burned up. They say the breaks all even up in the long run. But how many of us last that long?" —Chuck Knox, coach of the Buffalo Bills.

"They say, 'Nobody knows Bud Grant.' That's on purpose. In the NFL, visibility equals vulnerability. You're best off if you either haven't got a personality or know how to hide it. I admire Chuck Noll because he's won four Super Bowls and remained totally invisible. People like Stram and Allen can't get back in the game because they're too strong. As coaches, we have no union, no bargaining agent, no protection and no strength to deal from. We are purposely kept in that position by the league. We're resented because we have so much impact on the game; pro football is a coach's medium and always has been. So the league sees us as a necessary evil. We're muzzled . . . can't say, 'Boo.' Everybody'd be happier if we were clones, like the officials. Everything you say is supposed to be 'positive.' . . . If I'd known twenty-five years ago what I know now, I don't know if I'd have gotten into this profession." —Bud Grant, head coach of the Minnesota Vikings.

Perhaps the only job as insecure as coaching in the NFL is capping oil-well fires.

Last week, Jack Pardee, the NFC coach of the year in '79, was fired by the Washington Redskins. Two weeks before that, Bum Phillips, a coach so flamboyant and successful that his name was synonymous with Houston and the Oilers, was fired. Only a year ago, 50,000 people gathered to greet his team—after a loss.

These executions, so unthinkable before the '80 season, have made NFL insiders think long and hard about the nature of their profession and the directions in which it might be headed.

As Pardee sat dejectedly in his home in Unison, Virginia, Monday, he seemed dazed.

"The coach should be allowed to coach and not be shot down from other angles," Pardee said, after losing an internal power struggle with the team's general manager, Bobby Beathard, for the support of their liege lord, Jack Kent Cooke. "Let me do my job, not worry about jockeying for position. . . . I can't be a figurehead. Don't tell me to win, then say, 'But do it this way.'

"Without authority, I don't want the job."

Then, rather sadly, Pardee said, "It wasn't this way when I took the job."

Pardee is just the latest of many old-school coaches—men who took as their models the Vince Lombardis, Paul Browns and George Allens—who are discovering that their jobs, and, consequently, their entire sport, may be undergoing a fundamental shift.

The day of the colorful, all-powerful coach is apparently in full wane. The exceptions to the rule, ironically, are the few coaches who, at present, are the most successful in the NFL—Landry, Noll, Knox, Dick Vermeil, Don Shula. Even they worry that what has happened to others will befall them.

Knox, who this year rebuilt the Bills into an 11–5 playoff team, is one of that successful, but perhaps endangered, species.

"This is a very insecure, very fickle profession," says Knox, who was forced out by the Rams after the '77 season, despite winning five consecutive division titles. "If you win, you're asked to 'win bigger' or 'win it all.' You create your own great expectations, then you are judged by them. You can lose your job because you haven't satisfied the fans or the owner or the players. The last time I saw a figure, the average tenure of an NFL coach was 2.4 years. We make a running back's life expectancy look great by comparison. Usually, if you're fired once, that's it. No second chance. If you get fired twice, forget it.

"After twenty-seven years of coaching, eighteen in the pros, I've decided one thing: You have to have control over the acquisition of talent or your fate is almost entirely out of your own hands. You have to establish command. That's why I'm everything," says Knox, whose title is vice president in charge of football operations.

"Unfortunately, it takes unusually smart ownership to resist all the pressures to change coaches every time there's a problem. They know the devil they've got, but they forget to think about the devil they're going to bring in next. Buffalo is a perfect example. For twenty years, they had the worst record in the NFL under one owner. The reason was the constant changes of head coaches. They kept the people [executives] who were supplying the bad talent, but fired the poor guys who got stuck with it."

Several factors now work simultaneously against those charismatic figures who demand primary control over their team's destiny, and, thus, their own.

"When every team in the NFL gets six million [in network TV money] before they even pump up the balls for preseason camp, it changes people's priorities," says Stram, who, for his fifteen seasons with the Chiefs, had only four fewer victories than the top team in pro ball. "Once, the owner wanted

a strong coach who could win, because it might mean the difference between profit and loss. Now, he knows the bottom line will be black, so he
wants to be part of the fun so he can also get part of the credit. The issue
comes down to pride of authorship.

"Then the problems start. Watch out for the guy who sits next to the boss
at the game. He's the one 'explaining' it all to the owner—or his version of
it. Time after time, that guy's the organization ruiner. He becomes the
middleman. Here's how it goes:

"If you're the coach, you ask this guy—whether he's called the GM or a
vice president—for the things you need. As a simplified example, let's say I
ask him for a blocking sled. So he says, 'Buddy, I'll get you that sled if I have
to go to the wall for you.'

"Then he goes to the owner and says, 'That coach wants another sled.'

"Of course, the owner says, 'Well, does he need it?'

" 'Hell, no,' says the middleman, 'that guy's got more sleds than Spalding.'

"And that," concludes Stram, "is how you get fired. You feel like you're
surrounded by machine guns and piranha fish, but it's just memos and
meetings. Before I left the Chiefs, I said to [owner] Lamar Hunt, 'Sir, why
don't you just change the name of this team to the Kansas City Memos?' "

The emergence of this whole cult of middle-echelon executives is no
accident.

"It had to happen," says Grant, who has taken the Vikings to four Super
Bowls. "Years ago, I felt that we beat many teams before we ever took the
field, just because they were so poorly run in the front office. They had bad
judgment on trades, drafts, who to cut or keep. Their executives beat them
before their coach even drew up his game plan.

"It was inevitable that executives would get vastly better, and they have.
Dallas is a perfect example with their innovations in scouting and use of
computers. But Dallas is entirely atypical because nobody else has the harmony that they do between Tom [Landry], Gil Brandt [personnel vice presi-
dent], Tex Schramn [president-GM] and [owner] Clint Murchison."

So other teams copied the Cowboys' methods, but didn't have the good
fortune of ideal camaraderie. Start discussing the Cowboys' success with any
of those four executives, and they immediately start praising the other three.
"It's not entirely accidental," says Landry. "We suggest to each other, but we
don't encroach. They all have opinions about me, I'm sure . . . not all
flattering. I appreciate the fact that they never mention them."

Never?

"Well," Landry says, "not in the last twenty-one years."

In this era, then, of compulsively "involved" owners, such as St. Louis's

Bill Bidwill, New Orleans's John Mecom, Houston's Bud Adams and Washington's Cooke, plus the arrival of a generation of bright, ambitious front-office politicians, the NFL coach often finds it necessary to develop personal rules for survival, tricks of the trade that have nothing to do with a blitz or a man in motion.

The two most prevalent types are the absolute opposite. The coaches in one school—led by Vermeil and the Cardinals' Jim Hanifan (who follow the traditional example of men such as Sid Gillman and George Allen)—make a public relations show of letting the world know how hard they work. They sleep in their offices, make their wives into true football widows and are tough on their staffs. In the other school, exemplified by Grant, Landry and Noll, coaches try to efface themselves completely so that, if possible, no one will know what they do, or, if that is not feasible, at least won't know who they are.

Members of the former group are so transparent that they are amusing. "Most of 'em are just carrying over immature habits from college coaching days," says Knox. "You know, the head coach tells a couple of assistants to leave their cars parked by the gym and leave a light on in the office all night so it will look like somebody is working on beating State U. twenty-four hours a day.

"I've been in those [college] programs where the head coach says, 'You get four weeks vacation, but you're not actually going to take it all, are you?' If you take three weeks off a year, they make you feel guilty.

"I believe that the law of diminishing returns applies to work, too. You can work your assistants so hard that they just surrender to you so they can go home and have dinner. We have a rule that we never implement a decision that we make after the sun goes down. I just say, 'If it still looks this smart at eight A.M. tomorrow, then we'll do it.' "

"I think that the people in this league that I resent as much as anybody are the ones who try so hard to give the appearance that nobody ever really cared enough about football until they came along," says Schramm, whose Cowboys keep sane hours and a regular schedule. "This is a terribly stress-filled business and you don't have to make it worse."

Now that Phillips is temporarily gone, the NFL's only conspicuous nose-thumber at the workaholics is Grant, who has won eleven division titles in the last thirteen years. "Oh, I believe in the work ethic," says Grant. "I just don't believe in the work-work-work ethic."

To that end, the Vikings come to preseason camp at least two weeks later than any other team. Practice sessions get progressively shorter until they are only ninety minutes long in December. Occasionally, Grant gives a surprise day off, saying cryptically that he feels like going hunting. "Time does not represent work," Grant says. "People who think it does just show their insecurity."

Just as dangerous as the problem of emotional burnout is the less often mentioned danger of personality stultification. "It's very easy for an NFL coach to stop growing personally," Grant says. "It can stunt you. I would have no trouble thinking of names. I sometimes wonder what other work I would be prepared to do. We NFL coaches might have the temperament of the old-time military, you know, the first lieutenants in World War I going over the top. Our mortality rate is similar. . . . We're the one dispensable item on the team."

How does Grant insulate his psyche from the peculiarities of his job?

"I go duck hunting every morning, even during the season. I'm out there before daylight, usually for about an hour and a half. I'm back in the office by nine A.M."

What does this illustrate?

"First things first," says Grant mischievously.

"I sometimes feel sorry for NFL coaches," says one NFL front-office executive. "They seem so reined in. Just look at how much happier and more outgoing John Madden is now that he's quit coaching. Every time you see him on TV, you think: What a delightful person. What makes you sad is thinking about all the guys who never break free."

Often, that dour exterior is a defense mechanism.

"The worst thing you can do is talk yourself into a visible position," says Landry, one of the NFL's three stone-faces, along with Grant and Noll. "The fans hang on your statements, and remember them. We all live to eat our words. If you say enough of them, they can kill you."

Case in point: Phillips, who said last year, "We've knocked on the door to the Super Bowl, and now we've banged on it. Next year, we'll kick the damn thing down."

"Visibility killed Hank Stram," says Grant flatly.

"I've heard it said that, in Houston, Bum just became too much," says Landry. "I wouldn't know, but people say he sort of became what the Oilers were. Maybe Bud [Adams] didn't like that."

Certainly, the rule of thumb for survival is now simple: Keep your head down. "I don't do commercials," says Grant, referring to Phillips's larger-than-life size in Houston. "No billboards and no Bummerooski plays. There's enough credit to go around, but only if the coach makes sure of it."

To that end, the never-been-fired Grant has perfected a whole repertoire of self-deprecating one-liners, his favorite being: "To survive as a coach in this league, you have to have an understanding wife, a loyal dog and a great quarterback—not necessarily in that order."

As an added fillip, Grant occasionally picks his spots to fire off a salvo or two, dropping remarks about "When I write my book." What's the good of keeping your mouth shut for years on end if you don't every so often show the teeth inside?

Of all the coach's worries, perhaps the most insidious is the vicious cycle of success. "What the NFL has now," says Stram, "is a system that punishes excellence. All the rule changes, the drafting procedures, the new scheduling formula are directed toward helping the weak and defeating the strong. The more brilliant the coach, the more wins he gets out of the least talent, the worse it can catch up with him in the end."

In the NFL, this is called the coach-of-the-year curse. Schramm gives this illustration: "In '78, Atlanta used a lot of gimmicks, like the so-called grits blitz, and went 10–6. It was a fluke and Atlanta was smart enough to know it. In '79, they were 6–10. The Falcons [led by ex-Cowboy Eddie LeBaron as GM] didn't panic. They just kept building along the same lines. This year they were 12–4, and I think it's a solid 12–4, built on rock, not on sand.

"In '79, the Redskins went through the same progression. Pardee did some bright, innovative new things and went 10–6. It was a nice fluke. This year, their luck was bad; they were 6–10. But if they stick with Pardee's program, they may yet come out like the Falcons."

Schramm said this the day before Pardee was fired.

"Whenever a team jumps up suddenly, everybody studies them in the off-season," Schramm says. "Once you get everybody's attention, life's a lot tougher. Next year, Buffalo and Oakland will get a truer test. They've made some smart changes."

That's where the jinx comes in.

"The prerequisite for winning coach of the year seems to be that you do something brilliant with a bad team," Schramm says. "That lays you open the next year to being a big flop. You'll notice that neither Landry nor Noll has ever been coach of the year."

The reason is that both franchises built slowly, unspectacularly, patiently, then became long-running powers. The Cowboys, who shocked the NFL by giving Landry a ten-year contract in the midst of six consecutive losing seasons, and the Steelers, who stuck with Noll when he lost sixteen games in a row, have reaped the reward of nine Super Bowl appearances.

"The one key to success in the NFL is stability," says Landry without qualification. "Get somebody good and stick with him. Of course, that seems to be the opposite of what's happening now."

All the superficial motives lead franchises toward dramatic changes.

"Because coaches are supremely important in football, there's a temptation to change them," Schramm says. "In baseball, the best artists win. In football, the coach is the top artist, the number one creator."

Ted Marchibroda, who won three straight division titles with Baltimore, then was fired two years later, explains why those supreme football artists can suddenly become so expendable.

"A coach's most important responsibility is the emotional level of his team," says Marchibroda, who still has not found another job. "After material [raw talent], that's what wins the most games. But if your material is weak, whether through injury or whatever, then emotion isn't enough. What happens then is that, since nobody wants to face the weaknesses of his players, they blame the bad motivation on the coach. And the less secure the coach's job becomes, the less confidence the players have in him and the less able he is to motivate them. It's a vicious cycle."

Or as Pardee put it this week, after being reminded that Cooke had criticized him publicly at midseason for the Redskins' lack of emotion: "That's just a cover-all, scapegoat excuse made by every team that has deficiencies in material."

The familiar progression is inexorable. Often, as with Pardee, the downward vortex of poor material, dying morale and insufficient authority vested in the coach leads to a bitter firing.

It shocks the NFL's most consistent winning teams that so few franchises discover the escape hatch in this predicament. As Stram says, "Every good team cheers every time another team fires its coach and has to start over again."

"If your players aren't certain that the coach is making decisions for two or three years down the line, then you ain't got nothin'," Schramm says.

Landry takes the argument one step further, and perhaps gets to the crux of the issue.

"Football is still primarily emotional. Hitting comes first. Thinking comes second," says the supposedly emotionless coach. "So my job is to get men to do what they don't want to do—punish themselves. If you give them an out, a way to avoid the pain and not pay the price, they'll take it. Not consciously. But subconsciously, they'll take the out. How do you get them to pay that price in punishment to themselves?

"Well," says Landry, "one of the best ways is to make sure that they are concerned about keeping their jobs. And they won't be if they think that the coach may not keep his job."

Marchibroda embellishes the same idea: "Football is the ultimate team game. All eleven men are linked. If one lets down, he can sink the other ten. But it's also the game where it's hardest to tell—impossible, really—which men are only giving eighty or ninety percent. As a coach, you have to inspire them, make them willing to play like wild men. And as soon as they lose confidence in either your ability or your authority, how long do you think they're going to play for you with reckless abandon?"

These are bad days for coaches drawn larger than life, for those who see the football world as a canvas on which they will paint a grand mural and leave their signature—clear and solitary—in the corner.

"The life is draining out of the game," Stram grumbles. "Some super-rich guy buys the team and meddles in it. Some jock sniffer, who's not even a football guy, runs the front office. The assistant coaches are technicians who divide the team up into offense, defense, special teams and the kicking game. They're the theorists. And the players are big, strong, weight-trained mechanics who do exactly what they're told. The coach is just the guy standing in the middle holding a clipboard, with nothing to do.

"Where the hell is the humanity in the game? I remember when guys got into the game so they could express themselves. It was heroic."

For all his outward stoicism, those familiar inward fires burned in Pardee. Just hours after his firing, he was still stunned by the way reality was inter- fering with his coaching dream. "If I'm going to take the credit or the blame when we win or lose," he said plaintively, "then I want to control my own destiny."

That's not the way it works these days.

"The trend," Grant says, "is toward hiring pro assistants for the head jobs. They tend to be, let's say, more malleable."

When Bum Phillips, with his rattlesnake-skin boots, his ten-gallon hat, his cracker-barrel humor and his anachronistic crew cut, got the real boot, he told his friends, "Don't act so sad. I didn't die. I just got fired."

The sadness was not so much for Phillips as for the fascinating type of give-'em-hell NFL leader that he epitomized. Bum may not have died, but his stalwart breed looks far from healthy.

Cowboy in a Fedora

December 12, 1988—Outside the Dallas Cowboys' locker room in RFK Stadium, you could hear the players chanting, "TL, TL." Inside, Tom Landry could hear the words of center Tom Rafferty, who was speaking for every one of them.

"I said, 'This man has taken a lot of grief and unfair criticism. But he's stuck by us. And he's the guy who's going to get us back on top,'" said Rafferty, a Cowboy for thirteen seasons, including a chunk of the glory days of America's Team.

"And then I gave him the ball."

Rafferty said it as though he could hardly believe he had the audacity to give Landry a game ball. So what if the Cowboys had lost ten games in a row? So what if they'd just beaten the defending world champions in their own ballpark?

How do you hug a statue? How do you heal the hurt feelings of a computer?

Tom Landry, however, was not cold, calculating or made of stone yesterday. He was, and is, vulnerable these days. Aging a bit and beaten often, he's showing his heart and drawing forth gumption in his young team in response. They're down; in fact, they're awful. But he refuses to desert them. Tom Landry doesn't leave his wounded.

"We thought we'd won the Super Bowl. We were lookin' for the champagne," said Landry, his voice full of Texas twang, relief and merriment. "We're really delighted. Especially against my favorite group, the Washington Redskins. I'd say, under the circumstances, it was one of our greatest victories . . .

"I was really touched by the game ball and very surprised. What they said was important [to me]," Landry added, standing in the bowels of the stadium where he has suffered many of his most exasperating defeats. "Can't remember the last game ball I got. But, in twenty-nine years, somebody had to give me one sometime."

When the Redskins' final pass failed in the end zone, Landry threw his arms over his head in joy. "I don't know if I've ever showed that much emotion here," he admitted. "I doubt it." Linebacker Eugene Lockhart ran to Landry, hugged him and screamed, "We finally made it!" That seemed to free something in the sixty-four-year-old coach and he started looking for players to grab. First, Landry patted Jim Jeffcoat's big tummy, then he jogged to smack the rear of Michael Downs, who made the game-saving deflection.

Hard times have humanized the Cowboys, and Landry in particular. Redskins coach Joe Gibbs ran to midfield to shake hands. "Joe's the first Redskin coach in a long time who's been a friend of mine," said Landry. "You don't find better people or coaches than him."

The Cowboys insist the same is true of Landry, who, during the ten-game nightmare, heard himself described as senile and read polls where two-thirds of Dallas fans say he should retire immediately and not finish the year that remains on his contract. With the Cowboys up for sale, Landry's future could be in jeopardy. This week, a minority owner, Ed Smith, dared to say he'd buy the team and fire the coach.

Could this 24–17 Dallas win have saved Landry's job? "I don't know," said Landry, breaking his career record for smiles and quips in one day, "whether I want to save it or not."

Landry doesn't care what anybody thinks of his coaching. Except his players. And what they think, let Randy White speak for them all: "He deserves a game ball each week. If you're on the inside, you know this is one of the best coaching jobs he's ever done here. We've lost twelve games but nobody's quit. That comes from the top. He's still out there coaching every position. If they leave Tom Landry alone, he'll turn this team around. This guy's one of the greatest coaches who ever coached anything. And he still is.

"If he told me to stand over there and pour water," added White, "I'd probably go over and pour the water. That's the respect I have for the man."

From a distance, it is easy to wish that, after five Super Bowl trips, Landry would hang up his fedora with stoic dignity and amble away. But that denies the competitive fire in this man only those close to him can feel. With less than five minutes to play in frigid RFK, the Cowboys faced third and nine at the Redskins 12. Score tied, 17–17. Who called the game-winning play? Landry, of course. Three Jet, Y and X Cross, Wing Hank. That means Landry figured how to get his hot receiver, Michael Irvin (three touchdown catches) isolated on Dennis Woodberry, who'd replaced injured Darrell Green. Basic coaching, you say? If it's easy to get advantageous matchups in a crisis, how come, in the last minutes of play, Washington was throwing unsuccessfully to Mike Oliphant and Don Warren, not guys named Monk, Sanders and Clark?

Landry doesn't want the easy way out—the rocking chair and the engraved invitation to the Hall of Fame. Maybe the times have passed him by. Maybe he shouldn't come so close to being his own offensive and defensive coordinator. Maybe he doesn't delegate enough. Maybe the flex defense is passé. Maybe the linemen he's got now would be bad enough to doom any coach for years to come.

But that's not what Landry sees, or, at least, will allow himself to see. He's the only coach the Cowboys have ever had and, dogged as a real cowpoke rounding up strays, he's going to drag them back to the top. Then retire. If he feels like it. "Patience," Landry says, then repeats it a couple of more times. "You can't build anything without it."

Was this day a final small moment of modest glory for Landry—a match lit against a larger darkness? Or was it the symbolic beginning of a long road back for a bad team that had lost twenty-five of its previous thirty-three nonstrike games? Was this Landry's last trip to RFK? Or will he still be laughing last in the '90s?

One key may be whether the Cowboys pick first or second in the NFL draft. Who'll have the league's worst record, the Cowboys or the Packers, with whom they started the day tied at 2–12? In order to pick first (and tap UCLA quarterback Troy Aikman), it would have helped to lose this game.

"What happened to Green Bay [against the Vikings]?" Landry asked casually.

They won, he was told.

"That's incredible," he said, shaking his head. "That's amazing."

Slowly, a soft, sundown smile crossed Landry's face. Yes, another smile. "Now there'll be some people who'll say I shouldn't have coached so well today."

"Jesus Christ, This Is Tough"

TAMPA, January 6, 1980—

Jack Youngblood could not ignore his broken leg any longer. The tape, the splints—all the supports were gone. Tears came to his eyes and he began to whimper and pant and finally hyperventilate.

His breath came so rapidly and uncontrollably that he had to jab a finger into his stomach to stop the waves of cramps.

"Jesus Christ, this is tough," he muttered under his breath.

Jack Youngblood, you see, was putting on his socks.

This road to the Super Bowl doesn't go through Pittsburgh. It goes through hell.

Youngblood, the Rams All-Pro end, played every defensive minute of Los Angeles's 9–0 victory over Tampa Bay today on a broken left leg. Not a sprain or a twist; a real fracture. Unwrapped and naked, that leg looked swollen, bent, grotesque after this NFC championship game.

"It felt however a broken leg is supposed to feel," Youngblood said through gritted teeth as he dressed standing on one leg like a 6-foot-4, 243-pound crane. "I didn't know until just before the game that I could bear it and play.

"If I had a breath in my body, I swore I was going to play. I've known what it felt like to be a loser, felt it so many times. Now I know what it feels like to be a winner."

The Rams won an ugly, dull and brutally blunder-filled game for which they will probably be denigrated.

Don't tell Youngblood and his friends on the Ram defense that their ticket to the Super Bowl is homely. The price they have paid for it makes it inexpressibly beautiful to them.

"The mind is great," said 6-foot-6 defensive end Fred Dryer, an intellectual. "It has a tendency to forget all the crud that you endure in life. And I've shared a lot of it with these guys.

"I don't want any slaps on the back now. Words are cheap now. 'Great job' will be handed out for free.

"The only people who know what we did today are the people in this row," said Dryer, sweeping his hand across that corner of the Ram dressing room where the veterans, the heart of the defense, all had their lockers—Youngblood, Dryer, Jack (Hacksaw) Reynolds and Jim Youngblood, a quartet with thirty-seven years of Ram experience and never a Super Bowl trip.

"We just kept turning the screws and turning the screws until they had nowhere to go," said Jack Youngblood, sucking on a cigarette and relishing the thought of Tampa's pathetic seven first downs and 181 yards of offense.

"Some of us old guys got together back here in the corner before the game," Jim Youngblood related. "We said, 'Zero is the number.' When we scored our first field goal, we got together on the sideline and told each other, 'We just won the game. It's over. They don't score today.'"

Many Rams felt relief today, and vindication also after losing four of the last five NFC championship games.

"The boat's full again now," crowed quarterback Vince Ferragamo, who has taken heat much of the year. "All the people who jumped out will climb back in with us now.

"But I have no bad feelings toward people. This win is so overpowering," said this second-year med student, "that it wipes out everything else."

"I feel dizzy," said Georgia Rosenbloom, the team's owner and widow of Carroll Rosenbloom. "I can't believe it's over. Has the clock really run out?"

The old Rams felt no such dizziness. Their appreciation of reality is keen. A broken leg sharpens the senses.

"This man does things I can't understand," said Dryer, looking at Jack Youngblood.

Those who have known Youngblood all his life, however, feel no surprise. For instance, Van Collins from Youngblood's hometown of Monticello, Florida, knew three days ago that Youngblood would play.

"I called Jack up and said, 'How's the leg?' " recounted Collins, a hunting guide who takes care of Youngblood's bird dogs during the season. "He said, 'It's broke pretty good, Vandy. But I brought 'em this far. I can't quit on 'em now.' "

Late tonight, the other Rams had dressed. The team bus waited. No one complained. Youngblood was still battling to get dressed, fighting each sock and boot, muttering and groaning to himself. No one dared help him.

The ancient jeans, old shirt, faded corduroy jacket and Western belt were finally in place. The Red Man tobacco and the Ram game plan—covered with asterisks and stars—were stuffed away in a leather carrying bag as old as his career.

Left behind in his locker were a can of orange juice and a candy bar for energy that he had not eaten. An ashtray, however, was full of pregame cigarette butts.

Youngblood journeyed to the bus a step at a time, stopping for every autograph—perhaps as a rest. On his head was a cowboy hat with a rattlesnake headband—the rattles hanging down the back.

"Vandy, thanks for comin' down," said Youngblood, pumping Collins's hand and all the others in the band of Monticello friends outside Tampa Stadium. "Everybody sure enjoyed that venison and wild duck that you grilled up for us last night.

"Now, don't worry . . . I'll be ready for Pittsburgh," Youngblood reassured them—having no idea if he was speaking the truth.

Slowly, Jack Youngblood walked toward the waiting bus, toward the teammates he couldn't let down, toward the Super Bowl that had haunted and taunted them all so long.

He limped back toward Pasadena. One step at a time.

Endangered Species

December 10, 1989—Neal Olkewicz has a friendly smile in the middle of his big black beard and a large rattlesnake tattooed on his huge left biceps. Over the last eleven years he has been the most vicious hitter and the nicest guy on the Washington Redskins.

When he retires after this season, his body and his game still intact, the NFL will lose the best middle linebacker nobody ever knew. He's what the sport and the league used to be and what they always will be—at their best. If you knocked Olkewicz down, he'd laugh. If he knocked you down, he'd help you up.

That is unless you were Walter Payton, who loved to take your best lick, then jump back up. Olkewicz would wallow all over the great Payton, even hold him down, just to infuriate him. For them, the play did not stop until Payton escaped from Olky.

On Sunday, Redskins coach Joe Gibbs won his 100th game and wide receiver Art Monk caught his 650th pass—third best in NFL history. However, in the victorious locker room neither of these future Hall of Famers was hoisted on teammates' shoulders. Olkewicz was. In the final close minutes, nobody was yelling, "Win one for Joe" or "Win one for Art." All-Pro Jim Lachey and others yelled, "Win one for Olky."

Olkewicz, you see, isn't an athlete. He's a football player. He isn't a star. He's a leader. Sports celebrities are common. Olkewicz is rare. As Gibbs says: "He's the son you'd be proudest of. He's done so much with so little. Heck, we try to get rid of him every year. But he just battles and wins the job."

When the Redskins were introduced on Sunday, Olkewicz ran out last—in honor of his final home game. He tried to relish the ovation. "But I couldn't take my eyes off this chunk of ice in front of me. It's the first time I've been the last one out. I figured: I'll just fall on my face. That'd be great."

Olkewicz has spent his entire career laughing at himself, although nobody else ever would. "When we fell behind 14–0, I said, 'Just my luck, I had to pick this game. We'll lose. We'll get blown out. The defense will get blamed. And I'll be back on the kickoff team.'"

Growing up in a Pennsylvania steel town, Olkewicz dreamed of being a Marine. Then, after exposure to higher education at the University of Maryland, he decided being a state cop would be dangerous enough. Finally, "all mellowed out," his natural gentleness coming to the fore, Olkewicz settled for playing the most violent position in professional sports.

Olkewicz always has been such a cheerful contradiction: tough yet funny, studious yet wild, scary yet cuddly, slow yet everywhere at once, invaluable yet unappreciated. Olkewicz may be the ultimate Redskin of his period—a sort of missing link between the scruffy Over the Hill Gang of the '70s who were left behind by George Allen and the clean-cut, work-ethic, high-tech weightmen of Joe Gibbs in the '80s.

From his first training camp, Olky was identified as a throwback who loved the trenches and the hard knocks. "I like giving them and I like getting them if they aren't too bad," he says.

Diron Talbert, who was Texas-style tough with the brag and the cowboy boots, spotted the Pennsylvania ornery in Olkewicz, who kept his mouth shut but wore short sleeves in a snowstorm. Back then the Redskins closed their last practice before home games with a goofy game of volleyball over a crossbar. When he retired, Talbert left the old ball—symbol of rough-and-tumble camaraderie—in Olkewicz's custody, but never dreamed the squatty kid would last so long.

Recently, with so many old Redskins injured or extinct and so many young ones building a new framework, the volleyball games have disappeared. "We've almost become a new team," says Olkewicz. "Just when it looked like a total collapse around here really, we've started coming together real well."

A new team may need new rituals, so Olkewicz worries about the volley-ball. "Thought about giving it to [Greg] Manusky," Olkewicz says, referring to the free agent rookie linebacker from Colgate who wears a Mohawk haircut with razor-cut racing stripes around his head. "But I might keep it for my trophy case."

The trophy case probably needs it more since Olkewicz never has promoted himself and seldom has been celebrated. It's hard to make nearly 1,500 NFL tackles and not get noticed, but Olkewicz is so compact for his position at 6 feet, 230 pounds and so slow (no known time in the 40) that he deflects credit. Who else could lead a Super Bowl team in tackles (while also playing special teams) and still be a trivia question?

"He's been real good for a whole lot of years and still is," says linebacker Monte Coleman, another '79 arrival. "He's one tough sucker. . . . Every fight, he's the first guy in to help you. . . .

"When we were rookies, he'd say, 'Hear that train? It's coming for us, Shaky. I'm going back [getting cut].' He always listened for that train because he wasn't the most talented. . . . He never got the credit he deserved. I think he should've made the Pro Bowl a couple of times."

Olkewicz always has gotten his praise where it meant the most to him. From his teammates. "He's a devastating hitter," says 6-6, 290-pound Lachey, who has the physique Olkewicz must wish he could order from a catalogue. "The way he rolls his hips and snaps through a guy—it's just a knack of knowing when to strike."

Yes, like the rattlesnake in the tattoo.

This has been a rough year for Olkewicz. After missing only eight games in ten years, he had his fourth knee surgery in a season when Washington at one time had eleven starters out of action. Fittingly, the team bounced back with much the same toughness Olkewicz always exemplified, squeezing a pretty good season out of a pretty raw deal.

Olkewicz has played football for twenty-five years, from the rocky fields of Phoenixville, Pennsylvania, to the ice of Green Bay to the mud of Cleveland. He's loved them all. But he's glad to leave. The league has changed on him. "It's more of an athletic contest now—almost run-and-shoot," says a man who remembers the heyday of NFL defense, when the head slap and the bump-and-run were legit, before holding became legal and "in the grasp" was born.

"I just want to get out—knock on wood—while I'm in one piece, then smell the roses for a while. Maybe get into law enforcement [his college degree]," Olkewicz says. "I don't want to coach, except maybe kids. The stress of winning [in the pros] or the recruiting [in college]—not for me, I don't think. I just liked the fun part—the playing. I'd have done it in an empty field with no stands, no TV."

You'll notice he didn't say "no money." Olkewicz was the Redskins' player representative in the last strike. Just as in every other fight, he was the first to stand up in that one, too. "Oh, there could have been [blackball] consequences," he says. "Always possible when you stand up to somebody."

But that's never bothered Olkewicz.

"I already miss him," says Coleman. "All my dinosaurs are leaving."

Olkewicz, and perhaps even his breed, may be vanishing. But he won't leave without fond wishes. Like the song says, "God save the human cannonball."

Try That Hard, Risk That Much

September 16, 1987—The Jeb Stuart football program is as typical as the high school's colors—red, white and blue. The grass around the practice field is a bit long, the scoreboard a trifle old. Whistles blew at practice Monday and crickets still sang in the sticky air. This might have been any team anywhere in America. Except Stuart's players were in tears.

During special-team drills, which John Avila particularly loved, one player began crying. It spread. "Some kids were just bawling," said coach Tom Arehart.

Perhaps it was the sight, moments before, of co-captain Mark Maldonado leading calisthenics alone. Sometimes he would hesitate, it seemed, hoping for Avila to begin the next set of push-ups. But Avila—the other captain—was not there. He was in Alexandria Hospital in a coma.

As matters stand, it appears that Avila's life-threatening injury, suffered Friday in the third quarter against Edison High, was the definition of a football fluke. A 190-pound guard and linebacker, he was well conditioned and showed no signs of exhaustion. He had no history of injury and wasn't even hit hard. He was a typical kid having a typical game. He complained of cramps, told teammates he couldn't see properly, walked to the sideline, then lay down on the bench. As his father and coach stood over him, he lapsed into a coma.

Avila's father, Moises, said he thinks Arehart's decision to play his son on both offense and defense was a mistake. But many coaches do the same. "His father is angry," Arehart said. "My heart goes out to him. He has a right to say anything he wants. I don't blame him one bit. It's human nature to want something to point at. I coached my son for three years. If it'd happened to him, I'd have lashed out at something."

So far, there's no faulty helmet, no cruel coach, no dirty foe. We can't even blame "spearing"—tackling with the helmet. That dangerous and barred, but common, tactic causes most high school deaths. But apparently not this time. What befell Avila was just football. With good rules, equipment, coaching and conditioning, the best player on a team can still be seriously injured or killed. And you can't even find out why from the films.

Every autumn, millions of American parents face the question of whether to let their sons play high school football. And millions of boys, though they might not admit it, wonder if they really want to play. It's a generational issue.

My father played, against his parents' preferences. So did I. My wife is already against our son playing. Strange how mothers, long before they know what their infants will be, are certain they won't be footballers. Even I wouldn't care if he doesn't play.

After all, what value does football possess that makes it worth risks of injury that are greater than other school sports? Last year, two football players in northern Virginia died after being stricken on the field. Yesterday, the wire services carried reports of deaths of high school football players in Florida and Texas. Last year, seventeen deaths were reported at the high school level.

My own memories hardly make the case less ambivalent. I never enjoyed the game past the junior varsity level. Everybody has his own fear threshold. Varsity contact worried me from the first and I didn't have the talent or willpower to play above it. I got a letter but my memory is of running to practice wondering why I was there.

Yet, now, I'm glad I played the sport past the point of fun. Even to the point of fear. Because football is not a sport that is about pleasure. That's its paradox. And its power.

Sleepy Thompson at St. Stephen's School is the dean of northern Virginia football coaches. He's a friend of Arehart's and even coached the doctor, Gerard Engh, who first attended to Avila. High school ball is a small world. "It could have happened in our game or any game," said Thompson. "Our co-captain plays guard and linebacker, too. Goes both ways. And he's a doctor's son.

"Every year I ask myself how to keep parents from saying to their sons, 'You can't play football,'" he added. "It's very hard to express. There's an element of fear that a youngster has to learn to overcome. The contact, the hurting in the game, the soreness afterwards. It's different than any other sport. With the fatigue and the pounding, it's very easy to pack it in. When I see them stay with it and stay with it, I feel something I've never sensed any other place in coaching."

Thompson loved baseball first, then basketball, and football last. But he decided to coach football for twenty years after giving up the others.

"It's not a sport for everybody," he said. "But I think it's the best teaching tool of all. You have to be in a locker room after a defeat when the kids have laid out everything they have in a way they may not have done anywhere before. Then they come in Monday and put it back together, preparing to try that hard, risk that much, all over again."

What all football teams face, on a manageable scale, is fear and risk and deeply felt failure. And perhaps even a hint of tragedy, too. Occasionally, a team such as Stuart, through a terrible accident, must face a full dose of those things on an adult level.

It is tempting to buy into some of that ineffable mystique of risk-pain-failure-growth of which Thompson speaks so sincerely, at least for the millions of us who came through high school football with no serious scars.

However, that does not allow us to speak for the few who did not.

Jerry Smith: AIDS

August 27, 1986—In the fifty-year history of the Washington Redskins, only two men scored more touchdowns than Jerry Smith. Only two regulars ever played in more games. Only one receiver caught more passes. Many a Redskins All-Pro, even Bobby Mitchell or Larry Brown, never equaled Smith's sixty visits to the end zone. Yet, in his thirteen seasons, you never heard too much about Jerry Smith. He was shy and quiet. Though he didn't avoid publicity, he was lukewarm toward it.

You'll hear plenty about him now. And you should.

In a career full of brave performances, Smith never had a more courageous play than the one he made on Tuesday when he became the first well-known American to say he had AIDS at a time when the public was unaware of it. It was an act of heroism. And a significant one.

Smith, who is hospitalized and has lost sixty pounds, could have just said nothing. He'd have been remembered as the star who caught more passes in a season (67 in '67) than any tight end previously. He'd have been recalled as handsome, popular, gifted and clutch. To the huge majority of those who'd met him—who only knew his famous face, not his private self—it would all have been pure and simple. Most gravely ill men would leave it that way. Why add pain to pain?

Instead, Smith thought his honesty might help somebody else. He's right. His story helps further at least three worthy goals. It helps keep acquired immune deficiency syndrome and AIDS research in the public eye at a time when it needs to be kept there. It helps reduce the social stigma of the disease for those who have it and for the people who care for them. If Rock Hudson and Jerry Smith can get AIDS, then anybody—somebody in our own lives—can get it. It's not shameful and remote; it's a real and present danger. Perhaps most important, Smith's candor, with the weight of his estimable life and career behind it, attacks and undermines the stereotyping in our society.

Smith's mother told *The Washington Post* that she wondered whether her son still would be inducted into the Washington Hall of Stars at RFK Stadium this fall after news of his disease became known.

Smith told her not to worry. He would be. Because, as he's discovered increasingly in the last awful year, when people are faced with issues of sufficient seriousness and immediacy, they often are able to step beyond clichéd thinking and personal biases. They are capable of understanding.

What the whole AIDS discussion may help us grasp is that gays—whom this disease primarily affects—are basically like everybody else. They range from saintly to murderous, from artist to All-Pro, the same as people of any race, creed, color or sex. Well-known and well-liked AIDS victims force the population to realize that gays are individuals who have to be dealt with one at a time, judged on their overall merits, like anybody else.

For many of the Redskins of 1965 to 1977, Smith offered a life lesson. "If you love a guy, you love him. That's all there is to it. 'Jerry G' has been a very dear friend almost twenty years," said Redskins assistant general manager and NFL Hall of Famer Bobby Mitchell. "I don't remember too many days in all that time when I didn't think about the guy. Jerry was always a very private person, and everybody respected his privacy, but he had a lot of friends. One of the highlights in our house for Gwen and me was having him over to dinner. Around the people he knew well, he was a very fun guy."

Mitchell was not surprised at Smith's courage this week. "He could have left it like it was, not said anything, and ninety-nine percent of the people would always have remembered him as a great All-Pro. . . . But this is just like him. He was always our Mr. Clutch, the guy who'd make the tough third-down catch over the middle in traffic and just never drop the ball.

"Maybe this will help people understand some things better. This guy is such a great guy, he deserves any decent response he gets."

Is that what Mitchell really believes will happen? "You got to show me. In my life, I haven't seen anything bad that goes away very fast," said Mitchell. "Progress is slow. About the only thing that ever unites us quickly is war. . . .

"I don't know how pro athletes will react to this," said Mitchell. "It scares jocks more. It takes a little longer because we grow up so wrapped in macho and it takes a long time to strip it away."

Redskins fans will remember Smith sliding on his knees in the end zone to catch a grass-high bullet from Sonny Jurgensen or balancing on the sideline stripe by his toes to snag a Billy Kilmer pass on his fingertips. Smith's teammates will remember his foolishness, like taking Jurgensen out to drink a few "milk shakes" so the redhead would throw him more passes. Mitchell sums him up for many when he says, "Jerry's just a real super dude."

In the long run, however, Smith will probably not be remembered best for his many catches or his many friends. Now, he will be remembered most vividly for two other things. He had AIDS and he had the courage to say so.

eXquIsIte eXcess

MIAMI, January 21, 1989—

If the only good excess is wretched excess, then the Super Bowl is art. Born in the '60s, far ahead of its time, the Super Bowl may now be the perfect '80s event: morally ambiguous but great fun while it lasts.

This Sunday's Super Bowl XXIII for the National Football League championship is not a game. Like its self-parodying forebears, it is a week of guiltless, gaudy Bunyanesque Americana that dwarfs any mere athletic contest. Long before Trump and Reaganomics, there was the Super Bowl—a leveraged buyout of dull good taste, predicated on absolute faith that conspicuous consumption begat growth.

Perhaps no Super Bowl has been set in such bold relief as this one— because of Overtown and Liberty City. This is an event so big, so sure of its place, that it remained largely untouched by three days of urban riots here this week that included deaths, arson and hundreds of arrests.

"It never reached the point where we thought there was a chance of

improving the situation. . . . It ill-served [the problem] to inject ourselves," NFL commissioner Pete Rozelle said Friday. Three days earlier,
Rozelle had said, "The one big plus is that it's early in the week." And he
was right. Before the biggest parties began this weekend, the last fires were
out.

Players from the Cincinnati and San Francisco teams talked of little else.
Forty-Niners quarterback Joe Montana wore a Miami-Dade police hat and
said police and firemen were the week's real heroes: "They're going through
a lot tougher times than we are." Bengals tackle Anthony Munoz said he and
others would walk the riot corridor if asked. And the Bengals' Solomon
Wilcots uttered the line that may be remembered longer than Sunday's final
score: "Some of us went out to see [the movie] *Mississippi Burning* and came
back to see Miami burning."

In almost inescapable contrast, Rozelle, asked to define the NFL's "social
responsibilities" in this tense time, answered that any "excess food" from his
Spice and Salsa gala for 3,000 would be donated to the homeless. Let them
eat stone crabs. And whole roast pig, lobster, sushi, sashimi, Peking duck
and guava banana shakes.

The commissioner, who is the man most responsible for creating the tone
of the Super Bowl, added that news of the riots had "ruined his week" but
said he assumed "an awful lot of money" from the extravaganza would "seep
down" through the Miami economy to the underclasses. As for scaling down
future Super Bowls, Rozelle added, "These things happen in the world. We
can't stop them."

Nothing stops, or even deflects, the NFL—which did not cancel a single
game the week President Kennedy was shot—from fulfilling its self-ap-
pointed role as national purveyor of bread and circuses. As San Francisco's
retiring center Randy Cross put it: "If you're going to have a party, have a
great party. How could you put up a big enough tent or plan a proper
tailgate party in just ten days?"

The Super Bowl is to sport what the inauguration is to politics. The city
that is graced and burdened with the game feels much as Washington has
this week. The general population has little connection with its most glit-
tering events—isn't invited, may feel socially snubbed and may be inconvenienced by it. Yet that annoyance is coupled with civic pride at being seen as
important.

Both events have their parties and parades, fireworks and concerts, guilt
and hangovers. You never know who you'll see next, Frank Sinatra or a
three-story-high inflatable Spuds MacKenzie.

Hyperbole is a minimum Super Bowl requisite. Where else could you call a show with Liza Minnelli and Sammy Davis, Jr., the Ultimate Event? And what's playing at the Jackie Gleason Theatre just a few yards from Rozelle's blowout? *Les Misérables*. At least Joe Namath isn't Jean Valjean. If irony could be drawn and quartered, the Super Bowl would do it.

No wonder so many of these "ultimate" football games have been anticlimactic as sport; they're overshadowed as pop culture before they ever begin. The game itself has an inferiority complex that is well earned. The biggest, roughest, toughest jocks in sport come here and, by Sunday, have been diminished and frazzled by the weight of the event. Every team comes here fearing and protecting itself against the Week more than the Foe.

Above all, like any great, god-awful Mardi Gras or New Year's Eve, the Super Bowl is an excuse. For what? That's the hook: an excuse for anything. If days in the sun and surf and nights at Penrod's and the Club Nu don't numb your pleasure neurons, then your id is officially dead. Say, was that Michael Jordan leaving Deco's at 3 A.M.?

Everything that is best and worst about America's most self-congratulatory sports event has been on display here. The worst is common knowledge among football fans. To hype its product, the NFL long ago added this Extra Week to prepare. For a week, players are put on display like beauty queens competing in a Miss Congeniality competition. Every player sits at a table for an hour for three straight days for interviews. He's under orders not only to be there but to talk and to make it good. And, every year, the NFL arrives at the Super Bowl with a dozen new heroes whose life stories have been masticated coast to coast by 2,200 reporters.

For example, no two coaches ever have been such charming foils as the 49ers' Bill Walsh and his old buddy and pupil, Sam Wyche of the Bengals. "We really don't have a chance," said Wyche. "But they have to play the game anyway, 'cause they've already sold the TV ads. . . . They are Goliath. We're David in our sandals and leather wrap. . . . We've got our smooth stones and our slingshots in our pockets. We know we're very fortunate to have rooms at the Omni."

"I hate to see Sam talking that way," retorted Walsh. "Maybe I can call him and pep him up. . . . I never worry about Sam, because he's such a good businessman. There are so many Sam Wyche Sporting Goods signs in South Carolina that I worry about the environment. We are not talking about a gentleman business here. He can get you ten thousand pairs of shoes on twenty-four hours' notice."

The hype is invariably great. Case in point: 49ers defensive back Tim McKyer. Thanks to him, both teams have been screaming insults at each other the last three days.

Said Cross, "You know the line, 'Give me your huddled masses yearning to breathe free.' Well, the Super Bowl should have a logo that says, 'Give me your egos, yearning for attention.'"

The aptly named Boomer Esiason may be the quintessential Super Bowl week personality. "Smile," said the Bengals' white-haired, left-handed quarterback, pulling a camera from behind his back so he could photograph 500 reporters sitting before him. "Nobody is going to believe me in about twenty-five years that you are all listening to me."

No, not much has happened this week. Walsh has admitted he'll probably retire hours after the game. Wyche may replace him as 49ers coach. If the Miami papers aren't running diagrams of the Ickey Shuffle, then there's an explanation of the Bengals' controversial no-huddle offense, which Walsh says is "ethically, right on the edge of the rules." Jerry Rice, the most dangerous player in the game, is hurt too badly to practice but gets caught dancing in the early morning on his bad ankle. "I was only dancing straight ahead," the 49ers' wide receiver alibied.

Nothing is too weird for Super Bowl week. Near the Bengals' hotel you can buy Miss Ella's Lucky Pussy Cat Powder or find an arms store that's sold out two shipments of stun guns this week.

This is the place where supply meets demand—then shows a little more leg in hopes of striking an even better deal. Wyche joked that he thought of selling his team's audibles to corporations. "You know, we come up to the line and scream 'Toyota 22' into the sideline mike." With a straight face, Rozelle says the NFL has considered but rejected corporate sponsorship of the whole Super Bowl. "The Trump Castle Super Bowl," said Rozelle, kidding.

Perhaps Walsh has the best perspective on it all. "It's a happening. I don't know what I'd change about it," he said. "Football's an incredibly popular sport all across the country. It has to culminate in something. Why not this?"

The Super Bowl Jinx

January 28, 1987—Something in the nature of pro football doesn't love a close Super Bowl game and wants it blown open. Just as curious, there's also some perverse force that doesn't love the team that wins such a runaway.

What everyone has noticed for XXI years is that Super Bowl games seldom have a fourth quarter. The issue has been settled by then. Rival TV networks even anticipate this and schedule hot movies (Stephen King's *The Dead Zone)* to begin an hour before the Super Bowl's due to end. Grab the channel switchers.

Although we all know that fifteen Super Bowls have been decided by double-digit margins and that only four have been settled by fewer than seven points, there is an unknown Super Bowl corollary: the larger your margin of victory, the worse you perform the next season.

The New York Giants should enjoy their hour of inflated, perhaps even grossly exaggerated glory. Here's why.

The last ten teams who did what the Giants did—win a Super Bowl by more than two touchdowns—fizzled the next season. Not one of the ten (spread over the last twenty years) repeated as champion. Far more shocking, only one of the ten even reached its conference championship game. Two had losing records the next season. Another missed the playoffs. Four were eliminated in the first round as meek wild cards.

When you win the ultimate game in ultimate fantasy fashion, when you're not only the best but head-and-shoulders best, what do you do for an encore?

Usually, you rest on your laurels, become a multimedia celebrity, grow stagnant strategically and fall flat on your rich and famous face.

Was that Lawrence Taylor in a Superman suit in the Giants' locker room? Think that towel-waving Phil McConkey will get a few endorsement offers? He and Phil Simms already have signed deals to tell their life stories. What about those boogeying Giants at midfield after the final gun? Could they be talked into a "Super Bowl Shuffle II" video?

The Giants may live in Jersey now; they may shop at 7-Eleven and drive RVs. But they can see Manhattan, and perdition, on a clear day. Abandon hope, all ye who come under contract here.

Perhaps Chicago's William Perry is the best illustration of what Super Bowl success does to marginal players who attract attention because of quirks.

Perry did print advertisements for Alberto-Culver, Georgia-Pacific, Mr. Big Paper Towel, Long Underwear, Hair Care Products, Duke Manufacturing, Levi Strauss, Shakespeare, Drexel Burnham and Carrier Transicold. The 300-pound Bear banked $300,000 for an appearance in Wrestlemania 2, where he was—hold your breath, Bill Parcells, this could be LT—picked up and thrown out of the ring by Big John Studd (6 feet 10, 367 pounds).

The Refrigerator even got $7,500 for attending a bar mitzvah. They say everybody has his price. But the Fridge was a one-man closeout sale.

A whole team doesn't have to go for the greed to lose its collective edge. It's enough if a few key folks forget their diets or their weight lifting.

From the days of Hank Stram and the Kansas City Chiefs ("The I formation's the offense of the '70s") to Mike Ditka and the Chicago Bears (whose 46 was supposed to be the defense of the '80s), the NFL has followed this pattern.

"It's really tough to handle great success and come back with the same hunger," said Redskins general manager Bobby Beathard yesterday. "I picked the Giants to win big, and I'm glad they did. I've told myself they won't be able to handle it either. From what I saw Sunday, they might be the first team so good that they can. But I hope I'm wrong."

Coach Parcells is the man who kept the Giants' hat size in check all year. "I heard Parcells really laid into them the minute they got in the locker room after they beat us 17–0," Beathard said. "He chewed them for everything they did wrong. He's got a knack of knowing how to keep them on edge."

But how do you chew out a team that wins the postseason 105–23? Will these Giants among men listen when reminded that twelve of their regular season games were decided by ten points or fewer?

The only good excess is utter excess. And that's been the Super Bowl's calling card. The pregame hype is approached only by the postgame analysis. However, what we're just beginning to suspect is that these Super Bowl distortions may have a ripple effect.

Is it possible that huge buildups contribute to huge blowouts? And, in turn, can these routs lead teams down the primrose path of self-infatuation?

We'll never prove this, but let's pose it anyway. Good NFL teams show remarkable resiliency in crisis. They don't just give second effort. They give tenth or twelfth effort. Every time teams suffer any body blow—a turnover, a failed drive, a score by the foe—they must regroup and attack again.

Isn't it possible that two weeks of ballyhoo, plus the very real pressure of a championship game, leave teams with far less than their usual resiliency? When one team makes a strong midgame surge, the way the Giants came from a 10–7 deficit to a 16–10 lead, the other club is simply not able to respond as it usually would in the regular season.

Given two weeks to wind themselves into subliminal knots, Super Bowl teams play on the edge of emotional control like manic-depressives swinging between joy and despair. Our old football friend, momentum, becomes Mr. Momentum, Sir. Once an excellent team draws blood in such a setting, its ears just na'cherly lay back against its head.

This blowout-to-bust syndrome has been around for twenty-one Super Bowls. It's probably here to stay a while. So don't worry too much about the Giants next season. They probably took care of Denver, and themselves, too, on Sunday.

The Team
of the '80s

Average Joe

STANFORD, California, January 21, 1985—

For two weeks, they asked him about the kid. And Joe Montana just gave 'em that humble tellin'-no-secrets smile.

Montana could have snapped back, "Hey, look in the record book. I'm the highest-rated passer in the history of pro football. This guy Dan Marino has had one hot year. I've been the MVP of a Super Bowl; he's just here for the first time."

But Montana said nothing. Montana deflected the credit and the praise and the Super Bowl hype. He let the pressure build on the twenty-three-year-old Marino until the kid snapped at fans and reporters and showed his frayed nerves to everyone.

Montana waited until today in Stanford Stadium to have his say.

Then, in his understated way—scrambling and rolling out, dumping to his backs and flipping darts over the middle—Montana broke some of the records on the Super Bowl books.

The San Francisco 49ers' 38–16 demolition of the Miami Dolphins and their phenom, Marino, was one long testimonial to Montana's modest methods. Guiding an offense that amassed a Super Bowl record 537 yards, Montana made sure that the once-beaten 49ers won more games in a season (eighteen) than any NFL team ever.

Most passing yards, 331. Most yards rushing by a quarterback, 59. Most yards total offense, 385.

All of that goes into the books next to Montana's name, along with three touchdown passes today and 24-for-35 precision. Montana, who is both the most accurate passer in history (64 percent) and the hardest to intercept, has been the MVP of both Super Bowls he's been in—XVI and XIX.

From sunny afternoon to foggy dusk to chilly night, Montana lived up to the words that 49ers coach Bill Walsh laid on him afterward: "I think Joe Montana is clearly the best quarterback in football today, and he's the greatest to come along in some time."

If this keeps up, before long the capital of Montana may not be Helena. It'll be Joe.

"Deep down inside, when all you hear for two weeks is 'Miami, Miami,' I think that gives you something to prove," Montana said. "I thought that was the key [to the game]. . . . It just motivated us. . . . No one gave [this team] any credit. It didn't bother me, but I had something to prove as much as anyone. . . . We've been overlooked the last two weeks and most of the season, really.

"We wanted to show that they had to reckon with us."

Marino may have thrown his 56th touchdown pass of an unbelievable season today, but he'll spend the winter knowing that his statistics—29 of 50 for 318 yards and two interceptions—looked better than they were. While Montana was elusive in the pocket and crisp on every key pass, Marino couldn't move off a dime under pressure and underthrew many a pass.

"We thought Miami's defense fit into our offense almost perfectly," said Montana, whose career passing rating of 92 is eight points better than anyone else in NFL history. "They lay back and give up the short pass, and that's what we like to take."

All week, Montana hinted he thought the pressure might be getting to Marino. "It looks like he's about had it with what's going on," said Montana after frequent reports that Marino was testy. "I think he's getting sick of [the hype] already."

This evening, Montana grinned and said, "Everybody was asking me, 'What do you think of him?' He was taking all the heat."

Montana and Marino seem like foils created for each other. They are equally diligent about praising their linemen and being compulsively non-controversial, but Montana does it with a humility of bearing and speech that is as natural to him as a swagger is to Marino.

"We love him a lot," said halfback Roger Craig, who scored three touchdowns, two on passes from Montana of 8 and 16 yards. "If he's hurt, he'll still practice. Heck, he even lifts weights with us. If he has to give up his body to run the ball, he will."

Asked, "Do you know why you play so well in big games," Montana paused, then answered, "No."

"Well, could you make up a reason?"

"No, thanks," Montana said.

If that gentleman named Marino had not passed for more than 5,000 yards and 48 touchdowns during the regular season, Montana's year would have been acclaimed as fabulous: 279 for 432 passing for 3,630 yards and 28 touchdowns, with 10 interceptions.

In the end, Marino had to carry too much weight. Without a running game and facing one of the NFL's best defenses, the deck was stacked against him. Montana, on the other hand, had most of the edges—a quality running attack facing a defense that was weak against the rush.

As 49ers offensive lineman Randy Cross said, "It's a gratifying feeling when you can run at 'em and it works. You can run around 'em and it works. And you screw up and it works."

With a ground game that chewed up 211 yards, Montana could orchestrate an almost perfectly balanced offense.

Now, the light of celebrity will turn its fickle beam back to Montana—to his personal life and all that goes with being the MVP in the most important of all football games. But it probably won't come too close to nailing down the real Joe Montana.

The real Montana exists in those fragile microseconds when the pocket is crumbling around him and the secondary receivers in Walsh's pass pattern are just breaking into the open. Then, his quick feet, his quick arm and his quick eyes find solutions only the truly great ones can concoct.

As the final gun sounded here, the average Joe with the best football moniker anybody ever got handed, made one last excellent, split-second decision. He could search out Marino for a conciliatory handshake. Or he could beat the crowd to the locker room before it engulfed and mauled him.

Montana didn't think. "I just ran," he said, "and nobody could catch me."

"Rice Is God"

MIAMI, January 1989—

A generation ago, London subways bore the graffiti "Clapton Is God," as a sort of ultimate inarticulate tribute to that rock guitarist's transcendent riffs. A generation before that, jazz buffs paid the same homage to Charlie Parker, muttering, "Bird is God." What can't be described often gets deified.

Now, it is Jerry Rice who borders on sacrilege. As the San Francisco wideout received his MVP trophy after Sunday's Super Bowl, a 49ers fan who'd sneaked into the ceremony yelled, "Rice is God!"

In the best finish to the best Super Bowl, Rice was the best player. He had more yardage from scrimmage (220) than anyone other than the Redskins' Ricky Sanders (239) last year while saving his best work for the most critical times. "I did okay. . . . I was real lucky," Rice said, in the tradition of Unitas and DiMaggio. "I don't talk a game. I just play it."

And how.

"Rice is not a normal human being. I'm sorry, he's just not," said 49ers veteran Randy Cross. "In the movies, Arnold Schwarzenegger was made in a test tube as the perfect human being. But Jerry Rice is damn near it."

The way Rice moves while a ball is in the air, gliding like a hawk on an air current, and what he does after he grabs that ball, changing direction as suddenly as a snake in water, takes the breath from those who watch him and steals the heart from those who try to defend him.

The range of creative expression in Rice's performance went far beyond the Super Bowl records that he set with 11 catches for 215 yards in the 49ers' 20–16 last-minute victory over the Cincinnati Bengals.

Rice caught a pass entirely with one hand, never touching the ball with the other, as he tapped his feet in bounds. Not bad for a man who, six days ago, sprained his ankle so badly that he was listed as "questionable" for this game.

On another majestic solo, he kept from stepping out of bounds by an inch, then contorted his body and stretched his arm full-length to hook the ball over the goal-line flag for a touchdown. Not bad for a fellow the Bengals said they would intimidate.

Rice shagged posts in traffic, like a 27-yarder in the final minute to set up the winning score, and corners alone, like his touchdown that tied the game, 13–3. He shook deep up the sideline for 30 yards with a defender in his lap. He caught hitches when cornerbacks laid off him in fear and drags just over the middle when linebackers couldn't spin their heads fast enough to find him. He even ran a reverse to open the game.

However, Rice's best catch, and his most symbolic—the one that will be played forever on NFL highlights with a basso profundo announcer intoning —came on the 49ers' first play from scrimmage after Stanford Jennings's 93-yard kickoff return had given the Bengals a 13–6 lead. No team ever needed to announce its seriousness more urgently. So Rice went deep.

With Lewis Billups, the Bengal with the big mouth, on his hip, Rice shifted into his marvelous cruise control—the gear in which he seems to run as fast as anybody on the field, but with far more fluid grace and control of his body. Who knows if Rice jumped too soon or whether he simply decided to show a couple of hundred million people that gravity is not quite a universal law.

Billups and others returned to earth. Rice didn't. His fingertip catch for 31 yards lit the fire his teammates needed. It also gave Rice a moment of equality with his childhood hero, Lynn Swann.

"I saw Swann's catch against Dallas in the Super Bowl," said Rice. "The best I ever saw." Now Rice probably owns the second-most-spectacular.

What Rice did this windy evening—in fact, what he has done for the past month with 21 catches for 399 yards and 6 touchdown receptions in three playoff games—warps the imagination and redefines what is possible. "He's the best receiver ever to play this game," said San Francisco's Ronnie Lott, who often must cover Rice in practice. "I've never seen a guy with those tools have that dedication."

Though Rice looks so graceful that the term (or accusation) "Natural Athlete" seems stitched on his jersey, it is actually craftsmanship and toughness for which Rice is known.

"He had a legitimately badly sprained ankle," said Cross. "He's one of this game's tougher people."

"The technical parts of his game, how precisely he runs patterns, make him so special," said forlorn Bengals coach Sam Wyche. "The quarterback has to worry about the pass rush, but he never has to worry about where Rice will be. . . . Then he concentrates on the ball utterly."

"The responsibility of talent is hard work" is Rice's motto. In four years, it has taken him from the relative obscurity of Mississippi Valley State to 1,570 receiving yards with 15 touchdowns in 1986, then the NFL MVP award for his numbing 22 touchdowns in 1987. This season, his numbers seemed almost mortal (1,306 yards and 9 touchdowns) until his playoff eruption.

Before this game, the Bengals got cocky, perhaps because of the recurrent bad ankle that has annoyed Rice all season. They said all four of their defensive backs could outsprint him. They said they could beat him up, too.

"My speed is really deceiving," said Rice, his smooth face almost showing annoyance and his big smile fading. "But like I said all week, this is not a track meet. . . . They did a lot of talking earlier, but I try not to get intimidated."

Rice looked at the sea of cameras before him and the huge gold trophy of a football about to be put, securely, in his hands. *"Wheeew.* Great feeling."

At first, Rice tried to say that Joe Montana should have won his third Super Bowl MVP, although the vote was 10–1 in favor of Rice. "I'm a modest guy. I don't like to take credit."

But credit refused to go away. So, gradually, Rice cruised under the sweet emotion and let it settle in his arms. "Today is a day I will never forget," he said, holding his young daughter, with red ribbons in her hair, in his arms as his wife and his parents stood around him. "I know what I can do. I'm not out to prove anything to anybody. I'm out to prove something to Jerry Rice."

If he wants to prove to himself that he is the best receiver who ever chased a flying football, then he may have completed the job.

Lotta Lumps

NEW ORLEANS, January 1990—

When the great San Francisco 49ers teams are remembered in the future, only one defensive player's name will be recalled. Other great teams have had as many as half a dozen household names on their defense.

The 49ers have Ronnie Lott.

Unless you think Charles Haley, Keena Turner or Michael Carter is going to the Hall of Fame (and even they don't think so), it looks like Lott is going to be pretty lonely in Canton in the twenty-first century. Who's he going to scream at in the same way he's been going berserk in the 49ers huddle for nine years?

To the San Francisco defense, Lott isn't a lot. He's everything. He is the brains of the outfit—the signal caller, the film student, the Southern California grad, the philosophical voice on the team. But he's also—pound for pound—the team's hardest hitter.

On one hand, Lott is unselfish, totally team-oriented. He blends. But he also sticks out. As 49ers linebacker Matt Millen said: "Ronnie consistently makes more key plays than anybody I've ever seen. He's not the fastest or the best at any one thing—except making The Play.

"He causes the fumble. He makes the goal-line tackle. He runs the interception back for a touchdown, like he did against the Vikings. He bats away the sure touchdown pass, like he did against the Rams. . . . He does the inspiring thing when needed. It's unteachable."

When Super Bowl XXIV begins, you can be sure that Denver quarterback John Elway will be looking for Lott. When they first met, USC *v.* Stanford, Lott intercepted Elway's first pitchout—*intercepted a pitchout*—and ran it in for a touchdown. Stanford never recovered.

As an NFL rookie in 1981, Lott was moved from his natural safety spot to cornerback. Never a speedster, Lott was picked on by everybody, Lott picked back, returning three interceptions for touchdowns and being named All-Pro. Along the way, the rookie read the riot act to 49ers veterans, telling them, "Nobody's going to take advantage of me because I'm playing with [you] wimps."

Now back at safety, Lott is the central stable personality on this San Francisco defense—its leader, role model, tone setter and disciplinarian. The son of a soldier, he's punctual, clean-cut and the first volunteer for every Bay Area charity. "I like to be ten minutes early to everything," said Lott, who may use the word "responsibility" more often than he says the word "I."

Yet, Lott is also San Francisco's central unstable temperament. He's a legendary wild man, exploding into inspirational tirades and reaching ridiculous heights of combat readiness. "He's such a nice guy off the field that you wouldn't expect him to be so devastating on it," said Dennis Smith, who was Lott's roommate at USC and now is the Broncos' star safety. "Ronnie talks to everybody. I mean he'll have a thirty-minute conversation with a total stranger on any subject. I'd say, 'Can we go now?' "

At USC, Smith once delivered an enormous hit on 230-pound Heisman Trophy winner George Rogers. "Best lick I ever saw in college. Knocked Rogers five yards backward," says Lott. What Lott doesn't mention is how he himself reacted.

"As soon as I turned around," said Smith, "here comes Ronnie running at me full-speed. He damn near hit me as hard as I hit Rogers."

That's how Lott congratulates his best buddy—by trying to knock them both unconscious. Maybe that makes it easier to understand the famous finger story. In 1985, when doctors told Lott it would take eight weeks for surgery to repair the tip of his little finger, Lott told them to cut it off instead so he could be back in three weeks. Good-bye first joint.

Toughness is the quality that the 6-foot, 200-pounder respects most. You see, he claims he does not really love violence. It is simply part of his sense of commitment to his team. As a result, Lott, who turns thirty-one in May, must reach whatever pitch of emotional craziness his job requires. If he could have reached the NBA, "you'd never see me playing football. You don't have to be mean in basketball. . . .

"In this sport, you need to have a nasty. . . . I want a Matt Millen, a Tim McKyer on my team. Personalities make the game. Not blasé robots with talent. That doesn't get it. It doesn't mesh. You need people with flair and a good feeling for each other."

The players Lott doesn't respect are those with talent but not commitment. "Maybe I'm popping off a little bit, but I think Bo Jackson should have taken the Raiders to the playoffs. . . . When you [only] play six games, you would expect [that person] to *play* all six games. You look at somebody for results, not how great an athlete they are. I'm biased [by friendship] but I think [the Raiders'] Marcus Allen is the guy who plays hurt, who goes through adversity, to get respect."

Lott thinks Bo knows self-promotion. Or maybe Lott just doesn't like the way Jackson tried to bowl him over, instead of angling out of bounds, when they last met. "I don't remember Bo Jackson running over me," said Lott. "You might have been watching the wrong game film. He ran *into* me. He ran *over* Mike Harden [the previous week]. That's getting run *over*. . . . I made sure at least to stay [standing] up so it wouldn't look bad because I knew the first person to call me [to tease] would be [Dennis] Smith."

The fulcrum of this Super Bowl will probably be the confrontation between Denver's offense and the group that Rams quarterback Jim Everett called "The Ronnie Lott Gang." As San Francisco quarterback Joe Montana acknowledged: "Our offense didn't play that well this year until recently. We sputtered. The defense was the mainstay of this team."

And the mainstay of that defense is Lott, whom Everett called "the best defensive player I've ever seen. . . . Anyone who underrates the 49ers' defense, one, has to be very stupid, and I don't have a two or three."

At the moment, Lott has a groin pull and has missed practice time. If he's slowed, or leaves the game, the 49ers are not the same. With Lott, San Francisco has a swarming defense that's better than its individual stars. Broncos coach Dan Reeves said, "Look at the films and they always have nine guys around the ball." Maybe that's why they're 'Niners.

In the locker room, just minutes after the last Super Bowl, Lott was leading a team pep talk about trying to repeat as world champs. "I talked to some of the [Los Angeles] Lakers about how they approached it," said Lott. "We decided to talk about it. We didn't hide it."

That's one side of Lott, the man of athletic intensity and commitment.

On the other hand, why has Lott been wearing a Cleveland Indians cap everywhere for weeks as a lucky charm?

"I'm a Tom Candiotti fan," said Lott, meaning the Indians' knuckleballer.

Any hidden meaning there? Some new source of jock inspiration befitting the usual tone of Super Bowl week? Maybe an incurable disease or a boyhood pact? "No," said Ronnie Lott. "He's just a good person and a friend. Life's much deeper than this game."

"Get Out Your Thesaurus"

NEW ORLEANS, January 28, 1990—

Before this month, the San Francisco 49ers were the reigning world champs of football and the NFL team of the 1980s. Now, that's small potatoes. Now, the 49ers are full-blown legends. Now, after a 55–10 coronation in Super Bowl XXIV, they should be nominated by acclamation as a legitimate contender for the title of Best Team Ever.

That's what happens when you meet three teams in the playoffs and beat them by exactly 100 points.

"After this game, I'd like to match this team up in a dream Super Bowl with any team that ever played," said 49ers defensive captain Ronnie Lott. "This has got to be the best of the four [49ers' Super Bowl championships]. . . . We don't play to the other team's level. We rise to our own standard."

Before this month, Joe Montana was one of the best quarterbacks who ever lived. Now, if he's not actually viewed as the best, it seems only common decency to say that no one has ever been better. For sure, Montana is the January Man, the best postseason passer ever.

Montana threw five touchdown passes on Sunday and has now created a stat that may never be challenged. Over the past two postseasons, he's thrown nineteen touchdown passes with one interception.

"Get out your thesaurus and look up 'great,' said 49ers linebacker Matt Millen. "Then list every word behind it. Montana's even more than that. . . . I have yet to see anybody completely dominate not just every game but an entire season like he has. Name anybody you want in any sport—that's the greatest season I've ever seen anyone play."

Sometimes a team needs a showcase to make the world understand just how great it truly is. After this cold-blooded evisceration of the benumbed and befuddled Denver Broncos, they will never be forgotten or defrauded of one iota of their due respect.

How good are these 49ers? Probably better than we think, no matter how high we aim. What the Chicago Bears once did to the Washington Redskins for a game (73–0), the 49ers have now done to their whole league for an entire postseason. Total score against Minnesota (41–13), Los Angeles (30–3) and Denver: 126–26.

"They are playing as well as anybody ever has. They're at a level that's incredible. . . . And when they get up on you, they'll stomp you right into the ground," said Denver coach Dan Reeves, who obliged San Francisco with a conservative game plan that, ironically, almost seemed designed to hold down the score. "It's going to be very difficult for someone to say that they're not one of the great teams of all time. . . .

"When you come up [short] like this, life is awful cruel."

Cruel as a 49er. "They are executioners," said rookie Broncos safety Steve Atwater. He would know. San Francisco attacked the strength of the Broncos' defense all day—its crunching safeties, Atwater and Dennis Smith. "They are so aggressive that, with play action, we thought we could sneak somebody behind them," said Montana, whose 22-for-29 day for 297 yards, including 13 consecutive completions, was built on long, daring, soul-devouring scoring passes of 38, 28 and 35 yards. All came after play fakes and embarrassed Denver safeties.

The 49ers have a way of finding insults everywhere—so long as it helps them slay their foes. "Some things happened out in the streets [between Broncos and 49ers]," said Montana. "They weren't talking to us and I think that helped motivate our team."

How can you win? The Rams talked and the 49ers got mad about that and vowed to take no prisoners.

Are these 49ers on a par with the Pittsburgh Steelers of the '70s who won four Super Bowls? Don't be silly. Of course they are. In the past two postseasons, San Francisco won all six of its playoff games by a combined score of 208–54. In those games, the 49ers' defense allowed only four touchdowns.

"I felt sorry for John Elway," said Millen. "We just took everything away from them. Everything they tried, we were right there." Elway did not complete a pass beyond the line of scrimmage until 2:30 was left in the first half.

"Our defense focuses on detail," said Lott. "We're not intimidating, like the [old] Bears. We play intelligent football—every man in the right spot on every play. It's a team sport. You don't need a bunch of household names to play defense."

After this shellacking, the most one-sided game in Super Bowl history, a lot of people owe Terry Bradshaw an apology. The former Steeler said, half kidding, that the 49ers might be ahead of Denver 55–3 at halftime. And he added, not kidding at all, that he didn't think Elway was tough enough mentally to handle what would face him.

If it hadn't been for a call that negated a San Francisco end zone interception (and gave Denver a touchdown), the score would have been 55–3. "Boy, was Bradshaw off," said Millen. "He doesn't know anything."

Next in the 49ers' sights? The Green Bay Packers of Vince Lombardi, the team that won five NFL titles in the '60s.

"We're a young team," said Millen, almost in disbelief. "Montana's the only guy on the team over thirty-one. And he can play for years."

The ink in the record book was still fresh when the 49ers began planning their next foray. "Let's go back again," Lott told his teammates.

"For the last three months, I've kept a picture in my locker that my wife gave me. It's of our three kids, each one wearing one of my Super Bowl rings," said Montana, whose otherworldly statistics for this month include 65 completions in 83 attempts for 800 yards, 11 touchdowns and no interceptions. "Underneath the picture, it says, 'Okay, Daddy. The next ring is yours.'

"Well, she can have this one. I'll take the next one."

To the rest of the NFL, that sounds suspiciously like a threat.

Broncos: Ready till the Game Starts

NEW ORLEANS, January 1990—

Who says it's better to have loved and lost than never to have loved at all? Not the Denver Broncos.

The Broncos have visited the Super Bowl three times in four years and lost by 19, 32 and 45 points. That's some arithmetic progression. If they make it back to the Dud Bowl next year, what's the opening line? Fifty-eight?

A certain sympathy attends the Broncos at this hour. Poor John Elway. Poor Dan Reeves. They deserve better, we say. But do they really? Some doubt exists as to how much empathy they've earned. If we should give credit where credit is due, then surely it's only fair to give discredit where it is due, too. The Broncos are the worst big-game team since the Red Sox. At least when the Red Sox lose, it's close.

Even the Broncos are getting tired of excusing themselves for these midwinter fiascoes. It's all right to lose. It's even all right to get kicked around some. But shouldn't any outfit that calls itself "professional" (not to mention "a champion") give a better account of itself than these guys did? The Broncos' own fans knew best when they said, "Lose to Cleveland. Stay home."

Part of the problem is that the Broncos come from the finesse AFC and aren't ready for top NFC teams when they get geared up to full big-game hostility. Also, Denver is largely a product of its home field—Mile High Stadium—where the team, under Reeves, is 54–15, as opposed to 31–35 on the road. Meet the Broncos on the level and they're not too imposing. Finally, the Broncos look slow on artificial turf.

However, even when you've discounted the Broncos' ability as much as possible, you still can't excuse a team that gets beaten 136–40 in three title games. They're ready till the game starts.

"I don't know why in Super Bowls we completely fall apart," said nose guard Greg Kragen. "If we'd played this game in San Francisco or Denver [in the regular season], I'm not saying we'd have won the game, but it would not have been this kind of score."

"You start questioning why we can't play better in the Super Bowl," said Elway. "At least Fran [Tarkenton, the ex-Vikings quarterback] was in a couple of those [three] Super Bowls he lost. I've never been in one. We've been manhandled every time. . . . On a scale of one to ten, with ten as the worst, we've come up with three tens."

Elway and Reeves have gotten most of the praise for Denver's success—and it's deserved. But they also deserve the raspberry for their work Sunday. "Elway won't have any harder time living this down than I will," said Reeves, who's a stand-up guy who owns eight Super Bowl rings as a player and coach.

This time, Reeves was outcoached by rookie George Seifert. The 49ers scored three touchdowns on long post patterns behind Denver's safeties. One is a coaching coup. Three is negligence.

"Once you've shown your cards, we've got it figured out," said San Francisco linebacker Matt Millen, meaning the 49ers make quick adjustments to an opponent's game plan. Either the Broncos' coaches never adjusted or their safeties never listened.

"We hadn't practiced for that. . . . They prepared better than we did for this game," said Denver rookie safety Steve Atwater. "We came out a little tight."

"We gave them the long pass and they took it," said Broncos linebacker Karl Mecklenburg. What was Denver's Plan B? Or was there one?

The 49ers thought they could run at the Broncos' left side. And they thought they could run counter plays against Denver's line slants on short-yardage downs. The Broncos never adjusted to either ploy.

Montana may have offered the worst indictment of Broncos thinking: "I was never touched." If the Broncos had, when the score reached 13–3 or 20–3, gone to blitzing, could San Francisco have scored more than 55 points? The only time Montana is human is when he's prone.

Given time, tempo and no Broncos rush, Montana hit a groove—thirteen completions in a row. Denver defensive coordinator Wade Phillips lamented, "Montana seemed to know what defense we were in." What a surprise. If you don't hide what you're holding, or knock Montana down, he's going to complete 80 percent.

Denver, despite being the underdog, displayed no new attacking ideas. None. The 49ers jammed the Broncos' wideouts on every possession. But Denver never ran a hitch-and-go or a deep fade. By contrast, 49er Tom Rathman said, "By halftime, we still hadn't used half our game plan." Maybe they still haven't.

Elway's work also was less than expected. "He didn't look like John Elway," said 49ers safety Ronnie Lott.

Elway said he fought a bug all week, perhaps explaining why he was so flat and uninspired. "We did not take charge. That's what a quarterback is supposed to do," said Denver linebacker Michael Brooks.

"John's a good man and a good player but he just didn't play well today," said Mecklenburg, adding, "I think anyone in the NFL could have beaten us today the way we played."

Fair or not, Elway gave weight to the arguments of former Steeler Terry Bradshaw, who says Elway has been babied and lacks mental toughness, and former Colt Johnny Unitas, who says Elway scrambles because he reads defenses poorly and plays best when he turns the game into streetball.

Even Seifert seemed to imply the same when he said, "For Denver, the play doesn't start until Elway begins to scramble." So the 49ers wouldn't let Elway out of the pocket. Pinned there, Elway twice misread the 49ers' coverage so badly that he threw interceptions directly at defenders.

Both Elway and Montana were at the center of controversies all week and were widely viewed as wronged men. The 49ers rallied around the humble Montana, even calling a team meeting in his support. Elway, the glamorous cover boy who monopolizes attention in Denver, got no such spontaneous show of loyalty.

Any 55–10 game produces an orgy of second-guessing, as it should. Why didn't the Denver coaching staff prime its team to withstand an early 49ers blitz, then counterattack? Instead, the Broncos repeated all week: "We can't get behind. We have to start fast."

So when the 49ers, with their scripted game plan, took their usual early lead, 13–3, the Broncos folded, acting beaten before they'd given themselves a fair chance for rebuttal. What the 49ers do best is start a game and finish it. That doesn't leave much in the middle. But you better take it.

"We might have started to panic," said Phillips.

Many teams in many sports have fallen apart after experiences less traumatic than what Denver has endured in the last four years. Hopefully, the Broncos will listen to their wiser voices, like Vance Johnson, who said, "Winners find a way to make something like this work and losers blame somebody else."

Mark Jackson, who's been in Denver for these four hexed years, put it best: "The people who shun the opportunity to be humiliated are the true losers."

Interlude

---

*The Hellhound
of Pool*

February 18, 1978—King James Rempe, the hellhound of pool, stalked the
table with a werewolf's hypnotic stare, his eyes at last alive, his mane bris-
tling as though a full moon had finally broken through the midnight clouds.

"What's the longest run of this tournament?" hissed King James, the
greatest pool shooter.

"Hundred balls," whispered Weenie Bean Staton, director of the World
Series of Pool that runs nightly through Sunday at Arlington's Jack & Jill
Cue Club.

"What's Wimpy got me by?"

"A bunch. You need a hundred and one to shoot the lights out."

"Yeah?" Rempe's eyes lighted. "What're the odds on that?"

"Ain't none, kid," said Staton, looking at the almost impossible safety shot
that Luther (Wimpy) Lassiter, seven times world champ, had left Rempe.
"You're not even on the board."

Rempe looked at the cue ball, nudged perfectly into the mouth of the pocket, a millimeter from the hole's edge, and far from the clustered balls at the opposite end.

"Looks like I better not let ol' Wimpy shoot again."

This was not a trick shot. It was harder than those cosmetic four-rail combos they rattle in on the talk shows.

This was a pool shot. Eight feet of green felt separated Rempe from the single striped ball at which he had a prayer. He would have to jack the back end of his ivory Palmer cue up to shoulder height to gouge the cue ball out of its hiding place. That would give the white ball not only a certain swerve because of the transfer of English but an element of unpredictable massé action as well. In addition, that exaggerated English also would make the object ball deviate.

Rempe ran his hand over an invisible spot at midtable. Every felt cloth has a nap, a grain. This one, he knew, ran counterclockwise around the rails and needed smoothing.

As he paced around his nine-by-four-and-a-half-foot universe, Rempe worried about the humidity. It was high. Lassiter liked that. "Wimpy wins when it's wet," they always said.

The damper the air, the tougher every shot became. "Throw shots" couldn't be thrown as much, soft cushions became harder, making each ricochet larger and harder to control. And, worst of all, the pockets tightened. Shots rattled and stayed out. Wimpy loved that. The tougher, the better. Knowledge . . . that was the name of straight pool . . . decades of minutiae.

Finally, Rempe, the most deliberate, meticulous and intense of players, fed the computer every germane detail that he had learned since he was age six.

Rempe set up vital break shots, straight balls after this one. He had been off his stick all night, his stroke as rusty after a three-month layoff as the color of his mustache. But he had felt the oil seeping back into his elbow for the last few racks.

"If I make this one," he said to Staton as he bent over, dusting talcum on his bridge hand, "Wimpy can break his stick and pack it."

It was bravado, but it was also prophecy. For the next silent hour Rempe ran. Lassiter looked. Despite his perfection, Rempe (half Lassiter's sixty years) was not himself. Sometimes the devil cue ball stayed on its imaginary string. Sometimes it wandered. Rempe set up vital break shots, then messed them up and had to manufacture others, always planning far ahead, often as much as fourteen shots.

Before Rempe missed, Lassiter had long since packed his ancient leather, tack-studded cue case, adjusted his black tuxedo and called it a night. The game was over. Rempe ran on.

When after 168 straight balls the 169th shot kicked out, Rempe gave a little look to Larry Lisciotti, one of the seven players in the tournament, that said, "We know I missed that on purpose. These people aren't going to go home until I do. And I'm tired."

"A run like that means nothing to me," said Rempe. "I'd rather run thirty and play every shot right. That was just willpower, improvisation, stubbornness. I decided it was time to stop playing like a dog."

A crowd of fewer than fifty people in the darkened two-hundred-seat pit had watched the match between Lassiter and Rempe, probably the two most dominant and colorful players in the last quarter century.

"Ninety percent of the people here had no idea what I was doing," said Rempe. "For an hour and a half I was in a trance. If a bomb had gone off, I wouldn't have heard it."

This virtuoso performance in the back room of a pool hall had been accomplished for the sake of perhaps a dozen knowing eyes, the two most important being his.

"There is only one weakness in my game," said Rempe with bitterness oceans deep. "Desire . . . mine is almost dead.

"I worked since I was a kid for one goal—to find the perfect stroke. I found it. I became the best in the world. I reached my goal. And no one cared.

"In the last six years I've won thirty-five tournaments, and nobody knows my name. People say, 'Rempe. Rempe. Never heard of you. Can you beat Minnesota Fats and Willie Mosconi?' I tell 'em, 'Sure. How 'bout with one hand?' And they look at me like I'm lying."

Rempe is fighting ghosts—wealthy ghosts who don't fight back. "Mosconi is an old man who hasn't played in twenty-five years and who still has the gall to say he's the best in the world. It's like Joe Louis saying he's still the champion. Mosconi has done more than any man to hold the game back. He won't play and he won't shut up. He just promotes his name and makes money off equipment endorsements. At the U.S. Open in 1969 he got twice as much to commentate for TV as the winner got for winning. Fats can't run two. Fats can't even make his simple trick shots anymore. He's a joke . . . a rich joke."

Pool's young lions are carnivores who rip each other's hides at every opportunity. There simply isn't enough flesh on the carcass of their wounded sport to go around.

"We're up against phantoms," said Lisciotti. "People hear about Mosconi running five hundred balls, back in the days when the tables were bigger [and easier], the pockets were bigger and the balls were clay [no transference of English to contend with]. People come to see us run our eighty or a hundred and they'd say, 'These guys are bums.'"

The years trickle past for the likes of Rempe and Lisciotti, and the pool bonanza they keep foreseeing never comes.

"All we have to do is look at Wimpy to know where we're all going," says Lisciotti. "His nerves are shot.

"Every pressure he ever swallowed within himself has come back out to the surface now. He's just a mass of tics and twitches."

That vision of a tissue-thin present and an unworthy future haunts all the turning-thirty studs in this tournament—Rempe, Lisciotti and their pro buddy Mike Carella.

"There's nothing in the game now," says Carella. "If you won every tournament, you'd make maybe thirty thousand dollars a year."

Once, when they were young, the game was simple for them all.

"We were the only kids in our high schools with a diamond ring, a car, a roll of hundred-dollar bills," says Rempe. "We said, 'This is it.'

"For two years I played ten hours a day, never missed a day. The story's almost identical for all of us. We all hit the road when we were sixteen."

"I thought I was Robin Hood," said Carella. "We followed each other through the small towns like a hustlers' caravan. When Rempe was sixteen, he went through the South like a cyclone. Everywhere I went people said, 'This kid Rempe just cleaned out the sheriff, the mayor and the judge. This town's empty.'"

"I once played the mayor of Winewood, Oklahoma, for three and a half days," says Rempe. "He tapped out [went broke] four times. But he wouldn't let me leave town until he got a fresh stake. He said if I left the pool hall with his money, he'd have me arrested for not gambling."

Now these old pirates of the highway are turning thirty and, like the song says, no sooner do they hit the road again than they find themselves "running on empty."

"You're out there two weeks," says Carella, "and you say, 'Please, somebody get me out of here.'

"You know that sooner or later, you'll book a loser."

That catchall phrase "booking a loser" can mean shipping yourself to Tap City by spotting a sucker too much weight (handicap). Or it can mean death.

"I had to hear that friends of mine like Cuba Joe and One-Eye Teddy had been killed in shoot-outs before I got the message," said Lisciotti.

"When you're a kid you don't believe that if a guy shoots you, you'll die," said Rempe. "Until you see it."

"I owned my pool room," says Lisciotti. "I had to sell it. I just got sick of being around it every day."

With the years, Rempe's dreams—and those of the handful of other players almost his equal—have changed. They fantasize about the old days —thirty, even a hundred years ago. Tournaments in hotel ballrooms with tuxedos, balconies, dead silence, the cream of society holding its breath. They mention the strange names of ancient pool lovers—Twain, Mozart.

"In England, in Japan, we're gentlemen," says Carella. "Here we're bums."

The scenario of the dream is always the same. A wealthy TV sponsor starts the ball rolling. An honest lawyer organizes the warring, factionalized players. A TV commentator coaches the public in the intricacies of the game.

"The boom's not coming. It's further away every year," says Carella.

"No," snaps Rempe. "I won't reach my peak until I'm thirty-five. I say it's coming. I wasn't born too soon."

For now, little affairs, like the one this week at Weenie Bean's, are an excuse for several of the best in the world—Irving Crane and Steve Miserak also are on hand—to take the cue out of mothballs.

It's 2 A.M. in the Jack & Jill, the hour things liven up, the hustlers' hour. The sharks eye one another.

"The game of pool among the general public has never been healthier," says Staton. "The table manufacturers say twenty-two million people a year play regularly. This parlor has been open twenty-four hours a day every day for the eleven years since we opened. We don't even have a front-door key.

"This pool hall has never been broken into."

Rempe, the king of a game that is in danger of withering on the vine, smiles to himself. "A pool hall," he says, "is harder to break out of."

John Thompson

That Championship Season

April 11, 1976—Monk Malloy's first mass in 1967 was a watershed day. Everybody was there, all the stars of the nonpareil Archbishop Carroll High basketball teams from 1958 to 1960, teams that had won fifty-five games in a row and had been ranked No. 1 in America.

Though Malloy was now a priest, it seemed strange to call him Father. Even Edward—his Christian name—seemed too formal for Malloy, and people always called him Monk, Mugsy or the Mayor.

The Mayor was short for "the Mayor of Turkey Thicket," since no one could get in a pickup game on that illustrious Northeast playground without the say-so of the deadliest outside shooter in all Washington.

It seemed even stranger that none of them had a basketball game to play that day.

From this one high school team had come a 6-foot-11 center for the Boston Celtics, a 6-9 forward for the New York Knicks, a two-time All-America for Boston College, and that didn't include the undisputed best player on the team or Malloy, the best shooter, or another Lion who played football for the professional Denver Broncos.

But by that spring day in 1967 at St. Anthony's Parish, the last of the old buddies had hung up their uniforms. Injuries, time and the limits of their talents and temperaments had ended the athletic careers of all of them before they reached twenty-six.

That day they were just tall men in their middle twenties with nothing glamorous in front of them—except the rest of their lives.

As Malloy looked around that day with the eye of a priest, if only a young one, he wondered where they would all be in a few years without basketball to stand between them and "the world, the flesh and the devil."

Suddenly Tom Hoover, 6-9, 260 pounds, came over and threw his arm around the smaller Malloy. He had arrived from New York in a long car and flashier clothes.

"I forgot to get you a present, Monk," said Hoover. "What do you need? I can afford anything."

"I don't need anything," said Malloy, smiling.

"That's all right," said Hoover. "I'll send you two hundred dollars anyway."

Malloy recounted the incident recently—"It's a parable, I suppose"—after being told that Hoover had been indicted, tried and acquitted three times in the last three years on major narcotics charges.

"I'm not surprised that Tom's had trouble," said Malloy, who is now Professor Malloy, second in charge of the University of Notre Dame's religion department. "We could all see long ago where the rest of us were headed."

After that day the young Lions scattered. As though to prove that sports is no better or worse inoculation for life than any other, they became almost everything.

Priest, lawyer, college professor, high school teacher, jet pilot, engineer, high school coach, college coach. The nine key Carroll players became all those things.

But from those nine lives—at one time or another—also came a thirty-four-year-old vagabond and transcontinental bicycle rider, a prison basketball coach, a nightclub stand-up comic, a used-car salesman, a prosperous shoe salesman, a New York fashion model, a TV-radio announcer, a bar owner and a rock-music promoter crying "The Ice Man Cometh."

Obviously some of the nine have tried on many lives and shed them again like shoppers picking over racks at a late-season clothes sale.

But they have been more than that. Sheet-metal worker, roofer, a janitor who listened to opera while he swept, telephone lineman. Amusement-park owner with over $1 million in assets, an IBM think-tank analyst and a continent-hopping troubleshooter who audits the books of a multinational corporation from Canada to Guatemala to Japan. And one who has been charged, and exonerated after long trials, with possession of 1,580 pounds of marijuana and with being part of a Harlem heroin ring.

Where are they now, those adventurous young men, stars of Washington's greatest schoolboy team at seventeen, who are now twice that age and still in some cases making the transition from being famous children to functioning adults?

Malloy made perhaps the most sedate adjustment. The top student in his Archbishop Carroll class, Malloy always saved his flamboyance for the basketball court, where his 6-4 frame, his quick release and his idiosyncratic way of cocking the ball far back behind his head gave him an almost unstoppable shot.

"I still say Monk was one of the two best shooters ever to come out of D.C.," says George Leftwich, the top all-around star of the record fifty-five-game skein. "Off the court he always fit the image of a country priest, very intelligent but still warm and down-to-earth."

Malloy's lead legs betrayed him at Notre Dame, where opponents discovered that he could not score if he could not get the ball. After an average basketball career at Notre Dame, Malloy stayed at the university and now teaches Christian ethics and runs the school's seminary program.

If Malloy's life has been a straight line of expectable achievement, then Doug Barnes—the sometime starter at guard—has drawn his life with the wide arcs of shifting fortune.

Barnes—bright, free-spirited and allergic to books—finished last academically in his class. For the last seventeen years he has been a city- and job-hopping vagabond, unmarried and unfettered. He toured the country coast to coast last summer by bicycle, listening to opera in public libraries along the way.

"I have the lightest-weight bike in the world—three pounds," glows Barnes. "It feels like flying."

Last winter he coached basketball at Attica prison. This year he is "a permanent substitute" at Bladensburg High teaching English, music and physical education.

His brother Billy Barnes, who played the same sixth-man role in 1959–60 after his brother graduated, now coaches the old Archbishop Carroll team they once played for.

"Every other Barnes stays home and works," said the stay-at-home Bill, "and the ones in between hit the open road."

Doug Barnes has "held so many jobs that his W-2 tax forms look like IBM's brochures," said Bill, who is married and a father. The roving Barnes has been a bartender on Tuxedo Road in Cheverly, a teacher, coach, telephone lineman, sheet-metal worker, roofer, messenger and janitor. "The only janitor who listens to opera while he sweeps the floor," said Bill.

"He's enjoying the hell out of life," said Maus Collins, the great shambling bear of an assistant coach on those old Carroll teams and now Carroll athletic director. "He gets along anywhere and with anybody. I'm a little envious."

Doug Barnes has also gone through the greatest physical and philosophical changes of the group. Despite his life of the open road, his capricious trips to Ireland to trace the family tree and find new pub companions, Barnes had his battles with a deep bitterness.

He tried to joke. He would return from job interviews and say, "I lucked out. They only asked me for my last ten places of employment," according to brother Bill.

Then "three years ago I took stock of myself," Barnes says. "I saw myself turning into one of those guys who sits at a bar every night reminiscing and plays in a slow-pitch softball league.

"That pride from athletics was still in me. It just had to be ignited."

He stopped hoping for luck and, in his own way, said what Walt Whitman had sworn before him: "I myself am good fortune."

He started a scrapbook: "Life Begins at 31."

Barnes has lost sixty-five pounds and discovered in himself an appetite for Solzhenitsyn and other serious novelists. "I'm educating myself now," he said, though he earned a B.A. long ago.

The years have soothed the bitterness that time is the only ointment for, and Doug has gradually amazed the Barnes clan by cheerfully staking out a political position well to the left of his brothers. "A little to the left of Attila the Hun," says Bill.

"I'm not very successful. I've never made more than six thousand dollars in a year," says Doug. "I've lived a Damon Runyon-type life, an interesting life. I certainly wouldn't change it. I'm less settled down now than I ever was. But that's the way I want it."

One might think that a more volatile topic than any mere political debate among ex-Carroll players might be the question: Who was the greatest of those Lions?

Not so. All say Leftwich.

The great streak was really two separate streaks, made by two drastically different teams and grafted together by two lifelong friends—Leftwich and 6-11 John Thompson, now basketball coach at Georgetown.

The 1958–59 team, after two early-season losses to college freshman teams, roared through its last twenty games with a bigger team than the present Bullets. Thompson, 6-9 Hoover ("People were not used to seeing a man constructed like that in those days," recalls Collins), defensive specialist Walt Skinner, 6-3, Malloy, 6-4, and 6-0 Leftwich won with sheer terror.

In 1959, sophomore John Austin and Ken Price replaced Hoover, the best rebounder, and Malloy. Carroll stopped bludgeoning and started running.

Leftwich moved from guard to forward. On a team with two future first-team college All-Americas, Thompson and Austin, he was both high scorer and high rebounder.

"Both years we had a bunch of guys who could have scored thirty points a game, but we all settled for fifteen," said Leftwich. Nevertheless, Leftwich took the biggest shots, like the corner jump shot at the buzzer that salvaged a one-point victory in the end-of-season Knights of Columbus tournament sixteen years ago this week. That shot saved a perfect 35–0 season and the No. 1 ranking in America.

Leftwich was supposed to be the great pro from that unmatched Carroll team. Thompson lacked Hoover's ruggedness, and Hoover lacked Thompson's touch. Austin lacked Malloy's size, and Malloy lacked Austin's speed. Leftwich had everything, including enormous confidence and poise under pressure.

He also had an auto accident his first year at Villanova. It left him with what athletes simply call "a knee." Leftwich's impatience to start playing again helped pave the way to seven operations. He still regrets that too short convalescence more than anything in his life. "Once those babies [knees] go," he says, "it's all over."

Playing on "one wheel," Leftwich was still considered one of the East's best college guards, but his backcourt mate Wally Jones became the pro standout.

Leftwich now sells shoes. Last summer he was a guest speaker at more than seventy basketball camps in his work in sales and promotion for Converse basketball shoes. "I'm still close to the game," he says proudly.

Leftwich is proudest that "we were no jock bums. Five of us got postgraduate degrees."

Now a bit paunchy, still pleasant, modest and "Mr. Popularity," as Malloy calls him, Leftwich no longer looks like a star athlete but like a prosperous, relaxed salesman.

But he is also one of those ghostlike figures who sit in the top row of gyms watching the latest generation of "superstar" children. Grown men point him out respectfully to their youngsters and say, "That's George Leftwich. You never heard of him, but he could have been one of the greats."

If one characteristic predominates in most of the ex-Carroll players, it is a self-confidence, a willingness to pull up roots and take chances, a self-reliant audacity that might seem almost self-destructive in others.

Austin, the baby of the team but the one who went furthest in basketball, making All-America twice and leading the nation in scoring for several weeks while at Boston College, epitomizes that self-reliance.

Like Sherlock Holmes, Austin invented his own profession. He runs a portable amusement park that operates in Anacostia Park in the summer but moves to Five Flags in Georgia in the winter. Austin, who calls himself the father of the Porta-Park and the only black in the amusement-park field, claims a setup with over $1 million in equipment.

"It's been a long road, but I'm making it," he says.

"I knew he would," said Leftwich. "He was so thrifty as a kid that even though his father owned a store I never got one free piece of candy out of him."

Austin, a man of maxims, mottoes and long working hours, claims one key to his self-improvement: "Read, read, read."

"At first I was considered a blockbuster in this field. I had to find out where to get help with federal funding; I had to prove that I was serious, that I could develop a track record. Sports helped me. That's when I learned that when it gets tougher, you fight harder."

When Thompson, Leftwich, Skinner, Price and Billy Barnes all graduated in 1960 and coach Bob Dwyer suddenly left Archbishop Carroll, Austin departed, too, transferring to De Matha. The balance of schoolboy basketball power, a matter of fierce concern to a surprising number of people, shifted with him and stayed at De Matha for fifteen years.

One integral member of those Carroll teams has dropped entirely out of sight in the last ten years. Skinner, a top student, a loner, the coach's pet for his unselfishness, is now simply called "the Phantom" when Lions meet.

His old teammates assumed he had stayed out of contact because he had little feeling for those heroes of adolescence, because he was too much "the brain" to care about basketball.

To find Skinner might tax Hercule Poirot. Skinner found basketball at Catholic University insufferably depressing after the excellence of Carroll and quit the team. He eventually got a master's degree in engineering at CU, then moved on to five years as a Navy pilot, then ten homes in the next eight years. "I didn't stay in one place long enough for anyone to catch up with me," says the enigmatic Skinner, who has now alighted in Snellville, Georgia, where he is an IBM computer analyst in a think-tank-type job.

Far from having left basketball behind him, Skinner is the last of the teammates to still play the game competitively—in adult summer leagues. He calls playing for Carroll "the best thing that's happened in my life. I've had people in Japan ask me if I was the Walt Skinner who played for Carroll.

"The only thing since that has matched the high of a Carroll victory was landing on an aircraft carrier," said Skinner. "They say that gets in your blood, too."

Even the memories from those days when they were famous long ago have not receded. "For a long time I threatened to break Hoover's leg with a baseball bat," said Skinner. "If I saw him today, I'd probably still want to."

The enormous Hoover always aroused emotions on the same outsized scale as his frame.

"Most people heard about Tom before they ever met him," said Thompson. "They approached him lightly and they were ready to break out running."

Hoover's modus operandi was established early. "He was too big," said Leftwich, who followed Hoover to Villanova. "Every joke he played would turn out detrimental to whoever he played it on. He was like the comic-book character Baby Huey." Hoover's jokes usually involved pain, or the threat of it.

"Tom always hung around older guys and they loved to make a fool of him," says Collins. "He was no ideal Charlie, but I was always partial to him." So was Thompson. "He wasn't a bully. He was personable, funny . . . anybody would love talking to him." Of course, Thompson has the reassurance of being one of the few people who could look down on Hoover.

"Hoover took incredible abuse," said head coach Dwyer, who built Washington's first integrated basketball powerhouse at Carroll. "He took crap from the whites for being black, and he took crap from the blacks for playing with whites."

Telephoned death threats came as no surprise.

"After games I've seen guys spit in his face and punch him in the groin and Hoover walked away," vows Collins. However, one fan went too far, following Hoover onto the Carroll bus, still screaming "nigger" insults.

"Hoover split the guy open with one blow," recalled Collins. "But the guy hadn't had enough. He came back a week later and claimed he had been drunk. So Hoover hit him again. They took him to Providence Hospital and sewed him up."

After flunking out of Villanova, Hoover had a short pro career with the Knicks, Nets and Lakers, usually playing the role of enforcer. As glib and swank off the court as he seemed paleolithic on it, Hoover was a TV basketball color man, a pro basketball radio announcer and a New York fashion model; he owned a bar called Mother's, sold used cars, appeared in nightclubs billed as "The World's Tallest Stand-up Comic" and worked for Mayor Lindsay's youth programs. He became an agent for rock singer Jerry (the Ice Man) Butler.

Above all, he found it necessary to live the life of the Big Man, the role that he always felt was expected of him.

"In high school twenty-five dollars would make Tom the kingpin," said Leftwich. "But when you get older you need a whole lot more."

According to New York special narcotics prosecutor Sterling Johnson, Jr., Hoover was charged in 1973 with possession of 1,580 pounds of marijuana (worth $1.8 million), which was allegedly found in the trunk of a car issued by the New York City government to Hoover.

The case was dismissed, according to Hoover's lawyer, William McGowan, because authorities "could not tie Hoover to the car."

Hoover's worst year was 1975. He made one paragraph of national news as the ex-athlete named in an indictment of a twenty-person conspiracy to violate narcotics laws pertaining to heroin.

According to special prosecutor Johnson, Hoover was charged with "delivering mannite," a substance used to dilute heroin. McGowan defended Hoover and won acquittal on grounds that Hoover "had only a nominal connection" with the other men charged in the indictment, one of whom was arrested with $288,000 in cash in the trunk of his car. Hoover was also acquitted on a smaller charge of possession of marijuana.

"Everybody walked [went free]," said McGowan. "The prosecutors were trying to use pressure on Tom because they thought he had information about others. It's guilt by association. He knows nothing. . . . Why, Tom has worked for Lindsay. . . . If Tom stays in New York, the police are ready to pick him up for spitting on the street. It's not fair."

A score of telephone calls over a six-month period and over a dozen messages left resulted in only one short interview with Hoover the day of his final acquittal. "I've been having some hard times," said Hoover. "I can't talk right now. I have to leave town right away."

Of all Carroll's starters, Hoover was certainly the most conspicuous, Kenny Price the most nearly invisible.

Yet in the trillionth proof that Aesop's Hare and Tortoise is based in truth, the low-profile Price finds himself at thirty-four in the sort of life that Hoover might have dreamed.

Price played football at Xavier and Howard universities, was a flanker–defensive back in the AFL for a year for the Denver Broncos "as the forty-sixth or forty-seventh man," then spent a grubby year in football's little-known minor leagues in Seattle.

That ended his athletic career. Price settled down to scratching out a master's in business and a law degree from Howard.

Many of Price's old teammates, who have not seen him in a couple of years and have lost track of him through the grapevine, still think of him as a rather sad, puzzling failure. "Jeez, I saw him fitting shoes in a men's shoe store a few years ago," said one old teammate. "I walked out so he wouldn't see me and be embarrassed."

Price was working his way through law school. He would be hard to recognize now. After starting near the bottom at IBM as a salesman, he has worked his way up, until in the last year he has reached the post of auditor and policy inspector for Canada, South America and the Far East. Or, as he says, "about two-thirds of the world. I fly everywhere. We audit books and see if our foreign offices are aware of company policy and are following it."

Price has the stamina and enthusiasm for the grueling, lucrative job. He stopped at a Carroll game this month, but sat inconspicuously in a top row. "Washington was on the way from Toronto to Barbados," he said with a sly smile.

Of all those shooting stars, only one has stayed in the basketball big time, making college All-America at Providence, playing two years with the Boston Celtics and now coaching the highly successful team at Georgetown University that threatens to be a top-twenty team next year.

On John Thompson's office shelf at Georgetown—to remind him of all that he has learned from his game so that he can pass on the central lesson to his players—is a deflated basketball. The air goes out of the basketball half a century before the breath goes out of the body.

Of all Carroll's players, Thompson was the straight arrow, perhaps the least complicated, a huge, gentle man without o'erweening ambition.

"John always worked hard," recalled Malloy. "His character came from his parents. They were the salt of the earth. His father was a railroad porter and his mother was a domestic, but they stressed the importance of education."

Thompson may not have invented any new full-court-zone-trap-blitz defenses, but he became the first coach in America to institute a full-time academic counselor for his basketball team. In a realm where recruiting and the dishonesty (or at least the tainted character) associated with that word are the rule, Thompson is viewed as a freak who puts principle first.

Archbishop Carroll is far behind them now. Only Thompson and Leftwich remain close friends. Since Malloy's first mass few have seen each other. But from South Bend to Snellville to Barbados, the memories do not go away.

The man with the most memories is Dwyer, the coach who quit big-time basketball suddenly and rather inexplicably after the fifty-fifth victory and before the first defeat of the next season. Dwyer turned down college coaching offers to concentrate on his insurance business and coach in a less harried world at tiny, highly academic, expensive St. Anselm's, a school with a graduating class of fifteen.

Dwyer voluntarily went from No. 1 in America to the very smallest school possible—what he lightly calls "the bottom of the tank-town circuit." He has now run his coaching victory total over 600, has no ulcer and is one of sixteen men to be voted on this year for a place in basketball's Hall of Fame in Springfield, Massachusetts.

He now no longer coaches rough-and-tumble young men who must go through the bends of learning that though they were feted athletes at eighteen, they will be anonymous grown men at twenty-five. Dwyer's players now "know they will probably be doctors, lawyers, teachers."

Yet Dwyer still keeps the pictures from that earlier, rougher, less certain world. A photo of Leftwich's last-second shot hangs over his desk and he has the old team pictures in his attic. He remembers every detail of those years, the team feuds, even the shot charts that proved that Skinner, he who threatened to hospitalize Hoover, had passed the ball to his nemesis more than any other player.

"We had all kinds on that team," said Dwyer. "I guess they didn't do too badly."

None of Dwyer's players had to change his self-evaluation as quickly or achieve wisdom as suddenly as Leftwich, the best of them all.

"I was asleep in the back seat of a car when we were sideswiped head-on by a gasoline truck," said Leftwich, recalling his injury. "The doors flew open and I was thrown out. When I came to, I started cursing. Then I said, 'Hold on. Maybe I better make sure I'm alive before I start swearing.'"

Leftwich knew he should be grateful for his life, but "even so, I really don't know how I ever kept that injury in perspective."

Leftwich somehow reordered his deepest priorities. "Lord, what a favor wisdom does for those whose desires she adjusts to their powers," wrote Montaigne.

Leftwich adjusted, but he gives the credit to his old Carroll teammates. "I guess I got through it because I never really took myself seriously. They wouldn't let you. You never looked in the mirror and said, 'Yes, I am great.'

"We acted silly together, not like stars. I remember a tournament in Rhode Island where we had a giant water-gun battle. Thompson and Hoover ran around like ten-year-olds. During the next year we all looked for the best water pistols to take back there.

"We hated being recruited [by colleges]. We helped each other duck out of those free dinners. But we got excited about those water fights.

"When I realized I would never be a pro, I knew I could cope with it, because I had lived basketball to the fullest during the streak.

"That sounds like a contradiction, because I wanted to be a pro so much. But somehow, I felt like I hadn't missed anything."

> Be not too curious of Good
> and Evil . . .
> But be . . . satisfied that
> you have light
> Enough to take your step
> and find your foothold.
>   T. S. ELIOT

The Door
with No Name

January 24, 1982—"Terrible, Dan, we're playing terrible, if you want to know the truth," said Georgetown coach John Thompson, sitting in his office talking to a caller. "We have the blahs. I need some of those wonder drugs to get everybody fired up.

"I gave 'em the day off today. Shocked 'em. They expected the slave master to start beating on 'em. Damnedest thing in the world . . . win thirteen in a row, then lose two, and you're the son of a gun who doesn't know what he's doing . . .

"Dan, I'd like your natural reaction. Did you hear Bucky Waters call Pat Ewing 'the Darth Vader of college basketball' on TV? How'd you take it? Should I have called NBC? Everybody here was very disturbed . . . more calls from alumni than anything for years. . . . No, I didn't do anything. Looks like I'm crying. Complain when you win," laughed Thompson, signing off.

So who was that?

"A fan who calls anytime he thinks I'm low," said Thompson. "Dan Rather."

The white door tucked in an obscure corner of Georgetown's old-shoe McDonough Arena has no nameplate. If you're like most who come here, you think you're lost. That's just what John Thompson wants when you knock on his door.

"I want to be hard to find for the people I don't want to find me. Everything here," he says of his inner sanctum, "has a purpose. Each little thing probably tells something about me."

In recent months, ever since the 7-foot schoolboy Center of the Century for this season—Patrick Ewing—enrolled at GU, the great inquisitive world has been wending its way to this door. Thompson is ready for the buzzing flies who sniff out the famous. Like the methodical 300-pound bear he is, Thompson has spent ten years in this gym booby-trapping his lair, building his shells within shells of self-defense and preparing for the day he'd meet his final college basketball challenge: being not just good but being great.

As Thompson says: "The wanted posters are out on us. Playing Georgetown is instant motivation. We're learning winning's not bestowed just because you have talent."

Those who come to Thompson's door are in for many a surprise. Starting with the door. To look at it, you think it must lead to a stairwell or storage closet. You nudge it open to peek inside.

The shock can make a mouth fall open. Here, in dirty-socks-and-towels McDonough, is an elegant, tastefully underfurnished room—appointed with Oriental lamps, Early American furniture, photomurals of Washington vistas and faint sky-blue walls and rugs.

Mitch Kupchak and Mike O'Koren visited Thompson recently. Both were agape. "They sure didn't think it looked like a coach's office," says Thompson. "Kupchak said, 'Doggone, this looks just like a beautiful Southern home.' "

Thompson's next surprise comes as you cross his threshold. There's no bell outside. And no buzzer goes off when the latch opens. But just as the door is opened wide enough to get through, a tiny noise begins above your head. From the ceiling hangs a set of copper Oriental butterfly chimes. The opening door trips it—the gentlest of alarms. Yet because it hits you a beat later than expected, it makes you feel like an interloper as a gong never could.

"Every player notices it the first time," says Thompson. "They even put one above the door of the training room, so I couldn't sneak up on them.

. . . It's symbolic of letting a person know that they have been properly announced."

The blank door and the gentle alarm system are pure Thompson. Some men are trivially suspicious. They suspect opponents of spying or stealing players. Other men, like Thompson, are profoundly suspicious. He loves and yet distrusts life, in general and in all its particulars. Like the Jesuits, he believes in Original Sin and all the other Division I sins that followed it.

The key to Thompson is this constant two-sidedness, his blend of ivory-tower idealism, animated by a Catholic social conscience, mixed with street-wise cynicism. The books on Thompson's shelf are all chosen for impact on players.

There, pragmatic and belligerent, stand, *Power—How to Get It, How to Use It, Winning Through Intimidation, You Don't Have to Be in Who's Who to Know What's What* and two copies of Machiavelli's *Prince.* The only desk motto reads: "To err is human. To forgive is not my policy." Also, there's tame radicalism from Harry Edwards and Dick Gregory. Next, simply utilitarian, are *Your Mastery of English, Spell It Right* and *The New Etiquette.*

Then the counterpoint starts. Biographies of Harry Truman and former Chicago mayor Richard Daley; they made things work. Finally, the other side appears: Aesop's Fables, James Thurber, *Quotations from Chairman Jesus,* an anthology called *A Controversy of Poets, Ideas and Opinions of Albert Einstein* and, at last, a slim volume of Zen paradox—*If You Meet the Buddha on the Road, Kill Him.*

There's only one basketball text—*How to Break Zone Defenses*—which must be an inside joke, because Thompson's teams have never been able to do it.

And, pointedly, there's only one photo of a player, Derrick Jackson.

"He's the model," says Thompson. "Not just for my players but for me. Derrick taught me more than I ever taught him. You can preach the gospel, but what if you don't live it? Derrick does. He's religious without being intrusive, he's a leader without running his mouth and always philosophizing.

"I talk about having the courage of your convictions, but Derrick's convictions were so strong they terrified me," says Thompson, telling the story of how Jackson, before a big game, told no one that he had bleeding ulcers; instead, he tried to cure the problem with prayer. "I'll never forget going to his room and seeing the Bible half hidden under his bed. That's when I knew how sick he was. If his roommate hadn't told me, he could have died.

"Derrick [second-leading scorer in GU history] thinks I'm much too worldly," says Thompson, relishing the irony of a player worrying about his soul. "When he was drafted by the NBA, he didn't even try out, just sent the general manager, Pete Newell, a thank-you note. Newell still talks about it. Derrick's in the ministry now. He called me after his first sermon."

Thompson recalls the conversation went thus:

"How'd it go?" said Thompson.

"I think it went well," said Jackson.

"More important," needled Thompson, "how'd the collection go?"

"What!!??" screamed Jackson.

"Derrick," said Thompson, "the criterion for coaching is winning. And the criterion for preachin' is collectin'."

So what we have here in Thompson is a cynical idealist who lives elegantly and proudly behind a door with no name in an office with butterfly chimes to warn him of interlopers. Dan Rather is his friend, but Derrick Jackson is his model. He wants to win too much and has been a fool for glory more than once; but he knows it and wishes he could change pieces of the past, like having a recruit—Ralph (Brown) Dalton—play in a summer tournament under an assumed name. Above all, he's committed to protecting his players from a world of sin and disappointment until they have half a chance to battle it on equal terms, armed with etiquette and rhetoric, a sheepskin and a deflated basketball.

The core of Thompson is that he's one of those rare people who are determined to have it all: glory with wisdom, fame with morals, respect with love. Most settle for half the package, or much less. He wants to preach and collect.

So far, in his tenth season, Thompson is on schedule. But since Ewing arrived, the task has gotten harder. In a sense, the pursuit of greatness in sports can seem like one of those addictive video games. Your reward for wiping out one screen of invading enemies is that the next wave comes just a little faster. You're on a rush, but you're cooked.

The subject of Ewing shows the depth of Thompson's worry.

"When I think about Patrick's situation, I am very much afraid . . . especially because Patrick is extremely sensitive. He reminds me of a proud warrior in full dress who stands for what he believes in. That inner dignity may come from Patrick's Jamaican heritage. Unfortunately, not too many American blacks have that [dignity]. Perhaps something in Patrick stayed intact, not broken, because of where he grew up. He's not an apologetic person. . . .

"Patrick is a victim of his own success . . . I worry what he might do to his own image. But I worry more about him losing his competitive edge, becoming too tame. I've told Pat that your public image is not everything, but it is something to someone who plans to live a public life.

"If we have shielded Patrick, it's for a reason. Everybody wants a piece of him and everybody has their sensible rationalization. Well, the intent is always good, but the harm is always real."

Nothing prompts Thompson's righteous indignation more than a chance to stand as Ewing's protector. "I challenge any of these coaches who talk about Patrick's grades to go public with their own players' transcripts. There's at least one player on every team in this area who did worse than Patrick. I dare 'em. I challenge 'em to compare transcripts."

If Thompson's heat seems excessive, it's partly illusion. He's convinced that what's happening this year is, basically, what happens every year.

For nine seasons, Thompson's players could lose a game or two each year they should have won. Remember Drake and Oral Roberts and Boston College and St. Joseph's? A young player could commit a few flagrant fouls, or even blow his cool a couple of times. Remember Big Sky Shelton? A senior could have a shooting slump and GU would be awful for two weeks. Remember Jackson? Thompson could get mad and throw his annual tantrum at someone. Like Lefty Driesell. Or he'd put freshmen off-limits to the press until midseason. Also, a blue-chip player could have a mildly disappointing career. Like Al Dutch.

And nobody cared. Not really. Folks let the little stuff slide and cheered.

Now, in a sense, nothing's changed. Same old stuff. GU loses to Connecticut at home. Maybe the Hoyas shouldn't have. This time, the freshman with the happy elbows is Ewing. Used to be Merlin Wilson. Thompson likes his centers mean. Learned it from Bill Russell. "It's not a position for saints," Thompson says. And so it goes. The slumping shooter is Sleepy Floyd. The Thompson temper has focused on a reporter or three. The classy Dutch-like D.C. forwards who shoot smooth, but don't yet do much heavy-traffic rebounding, are Anthony Jones and Bill Martin.

The inevitable speculation about "can he take the next step up?" shouldn't bother Thompson. After all, he's addressed this point to his players for a decade.

"People ask me, 'Is Patrick happy at Georgetown?' I tell them that I couldn't care less," he says. "The phrase 'pursuit of happiness' misleads people. You don't have to feel happy all the time. But you do have to constantly reestablish yourself. I've told Patrick that you go from 'Who's Who' to 'who's he?' many times in your life."

Now the teacher must reestablish himself, prove that he can take his program from good to great. If John Thompson, with all his calculating self-defenses, well-intentioned wariness and genuine ideals, has not laid his groundwork properly for the task, what coach has?

The Period That Ends All Sentences

April 8, 1984—Late Monday night in Seattle, John Thompson gathered his Georgetown Hoyas around him and told his new NCAA champions where he hoped they would direct some of their thoughts in their hour of joy.

"There were a helluva lot of players who came before you who are not in this locker room tonight but who helped make this possible," Thompson said he told his players, thinking of many a Merlin Wilson and Craig Shelton, Derrick Jackson and Tommy Scates. "Don't forget all the people who got this program where it is now."

On Friday afternoon, after nearly a week of celebration following the Hoyas' 84–75 victory over Houston Monday night, the same notion was at the core of Thompson's emotions as he prepared to attend the team's basketball banquet.

"We didn't win the national championship in 1984," said Thompson. "We started winning it back in 1966 at St. Anthony's [High School]. You don't just hatch into the championship game. We worked like hell for a long time, worked through trial and error. I made fifty million mistakes.

"People in Seattle asked me, 'Did you give any thought to [this or that]?' and I felt like laughing. Over those years, I've given thought to everything about basketball that you can dream up."

But, mostly, he thought about the past and how, in his case, it has defined the present.

To many basketball fans, the Hoyas are a phenomenon of the Patrick Ewing era, a team that only became visible in the last three seasons. To them, Thompson's squad may represent a blend of enormous talent and equally remarkable discipline and team spirit. To some, Georgetown also may represent "Hoya Paranoia" and intimidation bordering on the unsportsmanlike.

However, to those who have watched Thompson's program closely from the beginning—and even before the beginning, when he was at St. Anthony's—the Georgetown story has the sort of inevitability and thematic unity that one expects in fiction, not in life.

"The people who know me and know the program realize almost nothing has changed in twelve years," says Thompson.

Memory and the public record support him. Few men's actions and impact on those around them have been as consistent, as based in a fully formed view of the world and as ruled by principle (critics might say stubbornness) as Thompson's.

"This [win] will do me the most good psychologically," says Thompson. "It will free me in some ways. A national championship was something I was obsessed with. It was something I selfishly and personally wanted to do. I wanted it very badly.

"I told my players all year that I had won every championship possible in basketball except one. I was on championship teams in junior high and high school [Carroll]. We won the NIT when I was at Providence. The Celtics won the NBA title. I coached high school champions. I was an assistant coach for the [gold medal '76 U.S.] Olympic team.

"After the Houston [title] game, one of my players came over and said, 'Coach, you finally got that last one.'

". . . Now I have the period that ends all sentences: 'I won the NCAA.'"

Thompson will also now admit, for the first time, that the presence of Ewing has been a special burden for them both.

"I also did not want it thrown in Patrick's face forever that he never won an NCAA title. I have so many things thrown up in mine, but I'm used to it. They say, 'Ralph [Sampson] never won the championship.' And Akeem [Olajuwon of Houston] may end up hearing that, too. Well, Patrick deserves that title because he exemplifies what an athlete should be. It would have been a tremendous injustice if he hadn't gotten one. And I would have felt very bad because I am the pilot. . . .

"I saw Patrick play as a sophomore in high school when I went to Boston to see a player named Little. I wasn't even sure of Patrick's name, but I told [former assistant] Billy Stein, 'Get me him and I'll win the national championship.' . . . If you recruit a player like Patrick, you definitely feel that, in his four years, you should be able to win a title. And he has a chance to win another one."

Thompson has always felt that troubling pressure to win. Part of it is his personal makeup. There is also a deeply racial reason. From the day that infamous sign ("Thompson the Nigger Flop Must Go") was stuck through the McDonough gym window during a game in 1975, the controversial and outspoken Thompson has been doubly aware of how many enemies would love to see him fail.

"When people congratulate me on being the first black coach to win a national title, I don't know exactly how to feel. This is a sport that's been dominated by blacks. So what does it tell you that I'm the first black coach to win the NCAA? That I'm the first black coach smart enough? Don't try to sell me that. Don't expect me to say, 'Thank you, I'm honored,' when people bring up that 'first black . . .'

"But in another sense, I am very proud to be the first black coach. I was at the barbershop down by the bus terminal, what I call the car barn, in Northeast today and the drivers just emptied out coming over to congratulate me. I'm not an idiot. I know why they were so happy. A lot of it was because I was black.

"I have to guard myself against not enjoying things like that. I have to tell myself to make sure we all enjoy this as much as we should. You know me, always looking for the pessimistic side."

As has always been the case since 1972, when he first put freshmen off-limits to the media and began setting up screening measures to limit and even shape interviews, Thompson's players have been difficult to portray.

In particular, an old question is on the front burner again: Do Georgetown players ever have fun? "When we're alone we talk a lot of foolishness," says Thompson. "We'll laugh and say, 'We did it. We showed 'em.' That's our nonpublic image."

Thompson said that after the Hoyas beat Kentucky, his players poked some private fun at the so-called Twin Towers. "But you don't broadcast that and hurt the feelings of great players like [Sam] Bowie and [Melvin] Turpin. That's just fun behind closed doors."

To the sporting nation at large, the Hoyas seem to have become symbols of one controversy after another this season. To those close to Georgetown, all the issues seem naggingly familiar. For instance, every Hoya power player under Thompson—from Wilson to Scates to Shelton—has played with flying elbows and some intimidation.

Thompson played that way as an All-America; his hero, Bill Russell, broke a couple of jaws in the NBA. The only time Thompson is unhappy is when he doesn't have a center who runs the risk of being called a bruiser.

"We did have an aggressive team this year, maybe too aggressive a few times. . . . Freshmen still have things to learn, especially Michael Graham. He's a lot more aware of certain things than he was at the beginning of the year, and he'll get better in those areas. But I'm not afraid of a young player making mistakes. And I don't want to change an aggressive young player's game too much and take away his competitiveness. . . . I did the same thing with Patrick," says Thompson of Ewing, who had a hair-trigger temper as a freshman but, for the most part, since has joined the mainstream of the college game.

Thompson also is defiantly oblivious to the needs and demands of the national sporting press. As he's always been. "The problem now is that a lot more people can be inconvenienced by the way I am," says Thompson. "This has been given a special significance that it just doesn't have. It isn't only the media that I keep off my players' backs. It's everybody, including myself.

"I've limited myself in contact with my own players. I never see them until after four P.M. They can't come into the basketball office or gym before then. Our players have to have time for a somewhat normal college life."

Georgetown is a private university and Thompson says what he does is entirely his business. Thompson has made his own rules and then lived with the consequences. The shock is that he's applied similar standards to the major-market media and to the school paper.

As for the fairly famous Brent Musburger of CBS, who criticized Thompson's strategy and the play of Michael Graham during the tournament, Thompson calls him "Musburg."

"During the SMU game, Musburg said, 'When I have a team on the run, I don't go into a delay,' " Thompson says. "Well, Musburg never had anybody on the run. He's never coached anywhere. He's never run anything, other than running his mouth.

"I've always tried to be firm in my convictions—maybe being principled and stubborn aren't too far apart—but people become stunned and shocked when you do it on a national level, not just a local level where everybody knows you already. I've bitten my tongue a helluva lot more this year than I ever have before. . . . You can't always be popular and successful, too. . . .

"I think I will take suggestions from people I respect. But it's true that I completely ignore the people I don't respect."

Thompson knows how to carry a grudge and isn't one to forget slights. Out of the blue he volunteers: "I was irritated by what those [local] athletic directors said in that story in the [Washington] Post talking about how we wouldn't play them. Well, they ought to understand that you never have a successful program unless you make money. Why didn't they say, 'Thompson is a good businessman?'

"All those schools had an opportunity to hire me. When I was at St. Anthony's [for six years] the only university that offered me a job was Georgetown [then 3–23] and I took it. I haven't turned down one job in Washington. Heck, I worked at Federal City College and they passed over me twice. . . .

"People say, 'He's changed. He won't play the local schools now.' Well, we worked ourselves into a position where we could play the people we wanted to play. I can remember when schools wouldn't give us games. . . . That's the cold, cold reality of human nature."

Of all the recurrent annoyances that bother Thompson, the one he feels is most unfair, most unfounded and most hurtful is the insinuation that he is anti-white.

"If I talk a lot about race, it's because I'm asked a lot of questions about it," says Thompson, who then tells a story to make his point. "When we were out in Spokane last month on St. Patrick's Day, I went out and I watched the parade. Those Irish people were, as my mother would have said, 'strutting their stuff.' They were proud for one another. There was no hate in them for others and no hate from others toward them.

"I felt good for them. But I knew that blacks haven't reached the point yet where we can go out and celebrate our blackness and not have people feel threatened. When we talk about our black pride, it's often felt as anti-white. That's not it at all. . . . I believe the time will come when we'll see blacks having something like that St. Patrick's Day parade and not have any hate in any direction."

A Little
Night Music

December 22, 1984—

"The wind blows hardest at the top of the mountain." —John Thompson, Georgetown coach.

It's after 1 A.M., the time that John Thompson often returns phone calls. His voice is a deep, husky, confidential rumble—amused, almost chuckling.

Maybe he likes the idea of the phone ringing in darkness, startling the unsuspecting object of his voice; catching people off guard or knocking them off balance on purpose is Thompson's equivalent of the Socratic method.

Or maybe Thompson just likes the ambiance of heightened insight and intimacy that seems to attach itself to the middle of the night. There's little Thompson enjoys more than playing with words, nuzzling ideas to see what new configurations they may fall into against their will.

Or maybe his life is so full it's the only time he's got left. His national

championship Georgetown University basketball team has an 8:30 A.M.
practice in a few hours, then, immediately after, a cross-country flight to a
game tonight at nine at New Mexico. Thompson sounds tired already.

Perhaps no man in sports wants victory more and trusts it less than John
Thompson.

"The real world is the cruelest world I know," he says, and it is a thought
appropriate to a dark hour. "We have to anticipate that real world. What
we're going through now is a false sense, a fantasy. Feels like a setup."

Some will see this as Exhibit 1,001 in the Hoya Paranoia case that has
been made against Thompson's program. Others will simply say that it is an
extension of an out-of-fashion but defensible worldview: that life will get
you if you don't watch out, so you better work hard on the D.

"I know what's happening out there. Every coach of every team we play is
saying, 'Georgetown is the greatest team ever put on the face of the earth.
No way we can beat them.' Then if they win they get twice as much credit
and if they lose they get no blame. That's called 'fattening frogs for snakes.'

"We are beatable."

In basketball, it sometimes seems that anticipation is everything. How
often a half step of speed loses to a full step of intuition. Anticipation also is
part of coaching. The man who best imagines the future can best prepare
for it.

Many coaches would see this Georgetown season as a kind of reward for a
dozen years of hard work. At the moment, the Hoyas seem to be head and
shoulders above any other college team and perhaps a few NBA teams, too.

It's not fanciful to speculate that Georgetown might go undefeated this
season and even reach a point where it is compared favorably with the
greatest college teams ever.

Senior forward Bill Martin seems to have changed from a solid but tenta-
tive player into a truly good one, and point guard Michael Jackson has
accepted the necessity of being a leader. Sophomore Reggie Williams always
has had NBA talent, with David Wingate not too far behind. With Patrick
Ewing at center, they are as swift, acrobatic and exciting a team as college
ball has seen since Bill Walton was at UCLA.

"If we didn't believe the 'experts' last year when they said we wouldn't
win the NCAA, why should we believe them this year when they say we
will? Last year taught us to believe in ourselves among ourselves."

If Thompson has a bedrock passion, it is for exposing what he sees as
false values. His top compliment to Ewing is that "this young man's done
miraculously in this world of distorted values. He's far more personable than
people think, especially when you consider that he's been propositioned by

so many people. He's naturally a little suspect of their motives. When everybody seems to be trying to get a piece of you, rather than just talk to you as a person, it can make you that way."

One liability of adopting a high moral tone (and that's certainly the most familiar string on Thompson's violin) is that you get on the nerves of just plain folks who wonder where you got so smart and, especially, where you got so sure.

If his Hoyas have a disappointing season—you know, something disastrous like losing a game—there will be plenty of folks in the basketball subculture who'll have to suppress a smile.

Yet it is another of the subtleties of Thompson's viewpoint and coaching style that his methods and morals are exactly the kind designed for life on top of the mountain where that wind blows. He has always taught his teams to ignore outside judgment and appraise themselves. He's always insisted that no loss means anything except an NCAA tournament loss.

Even when nobody much wanted to talk to his players, he insulated them from the press as though they were, well, amateurs, or, maybe, teenagers put in his charge, or even college students with schoolwork to do and personal problems to solve.

What was, for a decade, a prickly policy adopted on principle is now a very practical aid. That is, unless you think a twenty-year-old plays better after giving a thousand interviews about how great he is and how important his half-formed opinions are.

For the next three months, Thompson will worry and complain and argue and chastise. Nothing will please him.

"Last year, I was tellin' them how awful they were until the final buzzer of the final game," Thompson said, laughing, deep in the night. "When they looked at the score and saw they'd won the national title, they must have thought: This is over. This guy is crazy."

When the wind blows hard at the top of that mountain, the best advice is to grab something big and solid and hold on tight. Fortunately for the Georgetown Hoyas, John Thompson, who may be even better suited to staying at the peak than getting there, is available.

Resistance, Rebellion and Success

January 16, 1989—When John Thompson walks, everybody listens. Martin Luther King would be proud.

Georgetown's basketball coach taught one of his best lessons this weekend. He showed his players, and many others, that if you lay the proper foundation, if you get your résumé in order, if you analyze your position and articulate it clearly, then you can both protest and get results at the same time.

You can be a rebel but not a martyr.

Isn't that part of what King wanted? A society where blacks could work their way into the mainstream of American life so completely that people like Thompson could become powerful insiders whose words—and even walkouts—would be viewed with wide respect.

If you want to change a system, first master it. Thompson has. Such an approach always matched his temperament. Thompson is a conservative man, a devout Catholic, a devoted capitalist—an establishment figure if there ever was one. His message to every Hoya for seventeen years has been the same: because of men like King, the American system now works better; so make it work for you.

To the world outside the McDonough gym, Thompson may sometimes sound militant because he never minces words, seldom spares feelings and has an acute sense of injustice. At times, he takes "Don't Tread on Me" to extremes. But to those under his wing, his message is so conventional as to seem quaint. Dress for success. Speak for success. Study for success. If pleated pants and ycllow power ties are in fashion, then that's what you'll see Hoya players wear. A Thompson team on the road looks like a cadre of IBM trainees between lectures.

Because Thompson has paid his dues for so long, it's almost impossible to find criticism of his Saturday-night protest when he walked out before his team's game with Boston College. Whether his position on Proposition 42 is right or not, Thompson has demonstrated a larger point. If you spend a dozen years working your way up—from being assistant Olympic coach to a member of the Olympic selection committee to president of the National Association of Basketball Coaches to U.S. Olympic coach—then people take you seriously. It's really respect, not money, that you can only get the old-fashioned way—by earning it. What would be considered hotdogging in most coaches is considered "statesmanlike" when Thompson does it.

Touchingly, several Hoya players offered to join Thompson and, perhaps, sacrifice a game and their place in the national top-twenty rankings. But it was correct for Thompson to explain that it wasn't their place to demonstrate. They hadn't earned it. Besides, Thompson is a pragmatist. He knows that your voice carries farther when you win.

To help us feel, and perhaps share, Thompson's anger at Proposition 42, let's tell two old stories.

Once, I met a D.C. eighth-grader from a slum project who was so shy and inarticulate that some thought he might be mentally retarded. I interviewed him several times in high school and thought the same. Soon after he graduated from Georgetown, he approached me in a Salt Lake City hotel lobby. "Excuse me, sir," he said, and proceeded to introduce himself modestly ("You may not remember me, but . . ."), then ask about my business in Utah and tell me about his plans. All in all, he handled himself like an adult. He played in the NBA. But he didn't have to. Funny how employers often hire polite, bright, confident young people.

Another former Georgetown player, from the meanest D.C. high school district, once phoned me at home. He'd averaged two points a game at GU. I expected a sob story. Instead, he told me he was a broker for E. F. Hutton and asked if I needed an investment counselor. In two minutes, he left his phone number, told me his professional specialties and said if I ever changed my mind, to call.

My guess is that one or both of these young men might, under current rules, fall under Proposition 48's academic guidelines and, therefore, fall prey to Proposition 42 also. That is to say, they might be prevented from getting any scholarship money as freshmen unless a booster paid them under the table.

John Thompson is mad because he knows that success stories like these exist by the hundreds around this country. Some jocks from poor backgrounds come to college as near-illiterates and leave the same way; they never overcome their cultural deprivation as kids. But plenty of such youngsters—the majority in my experience—catch fire if they get a strict, caring coach who handcuffs a book to their hands and convinces them it's the most powerful weapon on earth. These are the teenagers who are worth protecting from Proposition 42, which would, in effect, keep them out of college.

To John Thompson, real equality is something a person creates for himself with his head, heart and hands. Laws should keep a society's economic playing fields from being too tilted; but, finally, social justice for a historically oppressed underclass cannot be legislated. As the Reverend Jesse Jackson always preaches, people must forge their dignity for themselves.

That's why "work" is the word closest to Thompson's heart. If you start out behind in a race, but courageously refuse to quit, there's only one way to catch up: run awful damn hard. It's not fair; it's just the truth.

This week, Thompson has pointed out many times that standardized tests—on which Propositions 48 and 42 are largely based—are meant to measure where a person is, not where he can go. In twenty-three years of coaching in both high school and college, Thompson has seen countless players catch up and get back in the larger race. Sports, where hard labor usually does produce results, seems to teach the lesson well.

Because Thompson has laid the foundations of his professional respect so deeply, he has held the attention of the nation without saying a word. Time probably will prove that the sound of his footsteps walking out of Capital Centre was enough to begin the process of changing a bad NCAA decision.

Georgetown's coach has spent his career telling players that, if they had the guts to play catch-up, they could join society as full members. He was certainly not going to sit still while a rule change barred a generation of such players from that race.

Interlude

The America's Cup: Reductio ad Absurdum

February 10, 1987—The Skipper handed the America's Cup to the Gipper yesterday. Dennis Conner held high the silver trophy he had lost years ago, then presented it to his President. Outside the White House, a 30-knot wind seemed to howl and lament. Could the Fremantle Doctor have followed America's foremost sailor home from Australia?

The man who invented the America's Cup by losing it three and a half years ago, then invented himself by winning it back last week, came to the gold-bedecked East Room to collect one of the first installments of his great tribute of praise.

Seldom has a hero who symbolizes so many ambiguous qualities—a man who is a blend of frightening obsessiveness and indefinable genius—received such unqualified encomiums. For spending years of his own and others' lives (not to mention tens of millions of dollars of other people's money) on what was, until recently, an obscure elitist yacht race, Conner heard himself hailed yesterday by President Reagan as a symbol of all things glorious and American.

True, yet peculiar.

"Today, the Cup that went down under has come back up," said President Reagan before one of the largest and noisiest crowds ever assembled in that vast room where one entire wall is covered by an American flag. "It is only appropriate that we should be greeting the skipper and crew of the *Stars & Stripes* here in front of the Stars and Stripes.

"I just have to believe that it says something about the competitiveness of American technology that, this time around, the United States entered perhaps the best-designed and most technologically advanced twelve-meter yacht ever christened," said the President. "Still, no matter how sleek the yacht, it all comes down to what the skipper and crew do in the open ocean."

The President wasn't quite practicing full disclosure here. In the 1983 Cup races, when Conner had the slower boat, he and his crew actually were vital. Conner extended Australia to a seventh race he probably never should have reached. In 1987, Conner and the corporate dollars behind him simply ground Australia down with better research and development. Is this exactly a surprise? After all, wasn't it America, not Australia, that put a man on the moon? It's said of sailboat racing that "it's the only sport that's over before it's over." In the last five America's Cup finals, there have been only four lead changes—just one after the first leg. We're not talking about NASCAR Dodg'em tactics here. The faster boat usually leads at the start, then widens its margin for three stupefyingly dull hours.

Still, the America's Cup has become a symbol. Is it real hard to figure out of what? Let's see, America loses something on the world stage that it once held unquestioningly. Then the United States wakes up, works hard and gets it back. Could we be talking about economic strength vis-à-vis the Japanese? Or military power compared with Russia? Or the persuasive power of moral authority in the world community? Or maybe "all of the above," plus whatever else you want to throw in the pot?

President Reagan, like any wise politician in the presence of an all-purpose national avatar, gave Conner precisely the sort of welcome the nation would have wanted—unquestioning, unambiguous, like the celebration after the round-the-world flight of *Voyager*. Before a huge media gathering, with the Vice President, the Secretary of Defense and numerous congressmen and governors in tow, President Reagan called Conner "a regular American guy, a smart guy who worked his way up from the bottom and deserves the credit for what he's done."

This also may not be the President at his most candid. Conner is not, by his own or any other description, "regular." He's a complete workaholic who has said, "If a crew member will put this ahead of his religion, his family, his girlfriend, his home, his career, then I'll give him a tryout." For years, the Australians called him "the Cranky Yankee." His type is only justified and sustained by glory. In defeat, they are often pitied or disliked. That's one of the gambles inherent in pursuing greatness through obsession.

However, when a man takes his skills to their limit, and, somehow, holds himself together to the end of the task, then "Going for It" can be powerfully intoxicating. The President, wearing the outback hat he won on a bet from Australia's Prime Minister, touched this truth when he told Conner, "In following these races we were all able to follow something ancient and deep within us—man's fascination with wind and water. . . . Hang gliding, dropping in a parachute, doing barrel rolls in a light airplane—those thrills are easy to understand. But the moment of lift in a sailboat is just as much a leap off the earth—airborne. Gentlemen of the *Stars & Stripes,* for a few days, you made all of us feel airborne."

Conner himself felt pretty airborne, exchanging quips with the Commander in Chief. When the President described how *Stars & Stripes* had blown a jib and how Conner, never panicking, had said, "Hey, that's too bad," the San Diego drapery businessman leaned toward the mike and interjected, "That's not all I said."

When his turn to speak came, Conner harkened back to 1983. "You might remember that I made you a personal promise at that time to do everything I could to bring the Cup back home to America where it belongs," said Conner to the President. "So, here it is."

There may be as much unseen underneath Conner's chubby, charmingly awkward preppie exterior as there is under the waterline of his boat, where that hidden mysterious keel lurked for months, troubling *Kookaburra III*'s sleep.

In a sense, Conner is a useful prototype of high-powered American sport in general. To the dismay of some, he has transformed yachting from a sleepy game for rich gentlemen with idle hours into a 365-day-a-year crusade. He dominates the sport, sets its agenda and has no intention of leaving until somebody beats him—maybe in twenty years. Now, 12-meter racing has gone the way of the pole vault and the 400-meter individual medley, gymnastics and tennis, big-time college football and Indy 500 racing. If you want to compete at the top level, well, that's simple—pay the price, make the sacrifice, become obsessed. It's now the American way in sports.

The dilemma Conner has faced, both in losing the Cup to a technologically superior foe and in deciding to commit himself utterly to winning it back, is hardly a simple one.

Recent studies show that the average Japanese worker spends considerably more than 2,000 hours a year on his job and voluntarily turns down more than half of his vacation days. An American worker spends about 1,800 hours and takes his vacation. Perhaps an America's Cup of sorts is at stake here, too. How much is a faster boat, a better-made car or a higher standard of living really worth? As a nation, perhaps we resemble Dennis Conner just a bit as we try to balance the price against the prize.

Basketball

The Boston Celtics

Keepers of the Flame

BOSTON, December 5, 1979—

Here by the filthy train trestles of North Station stands basketball's sweet Garden of sweat.

This is the home of the Boston Celtics: green-clad keepers of the flame.

Once again, they are turning the sooty, smoke-filled Boston Garden into America's least likely gallery of fine art. Masterpieces-in-motion are once more on display. In this Louvre of the underwear game, the third coming of the Celtics may be on its way.

Just as the arrival of Bill Russell in '56 and Dave Cowens in '70 transformed the Celts into world champs, so the appearance now of Larry Bird has jolted this team and its town like an electric shock to the heart.

It isn't the acrid blend of cigar and pot smoke hanging in the rafters around those thirteen world championship flags that has Boston fans rubbing their eyes. Frankly, this city can't believe what it is seeing.

Last season the Celtics were a disgrace to their heritage—dead and stinking to heaven. Worse than merely bad (29–53 in '79), they were repulsive to those who savored Celtic tradition. What could be more ironic and bitter than a Celtic team rich in talent but abjectly poor in spirit?

For twenty years, from '56 to '76, it always seemed appropriate, if accidental, that in all of American pro sports only one team was nicknamed after a non-Indian race of men: Celtics.

Indeed, Boston basketballers thought of themselves as a separate breed within their own game—men set apart not by talent so much as by an idea of how their game should be played. "I was disgusted by what we had become," says Red Auerbach, president and general manager, thinking back on 103 losses in the last two seasons. "I was ready to get out."

Now, Auerbach may eventually become the first man in pro sports to be the central figure behind the construction of three dynasties with the same franchise.

The Celtics not only have the best record in the NBA (19–5), but their staggering margin of superiority—11 points per game—is more than twice that of any other club.

"We're blowing away good teams now—just destroying them. What will we do later?" says veteran Don Chaney, who played with Russell and has seen all three eras. "We're nowhere near peaking. We barely know each other. I'm afraid to say what might happen by March."

Even Boston brass has to scratch its head and hold its breath at the transformation it has wrought. "I don't have time to relish it. I'm too busy worrying," says Auerbach. "I don't know if we're for real. I know that we're not deep and that injuries could kill us." But then, injuries can kill anyone. Don't be coy, cigar face.

"I have to force myself to see the game as it really is—especially our mistakes—rather than let myself fall in love with the final score," says new Celtic coach Bill Fitch, a rare blackboard-and-film workaholic who is also a wit. "I keep thinking that if we go into a lull, we'll come to a stop like a turtle with air brakes. In my job, you don't get to enjoy. You only get to suffer."

Fortunately, Boston fans show no such reserve. The one consensus about these new Celts is that they have—no one knows how—already excited their fans more than any previous team. After having one sellout in three years, Boston had eight in its first eleven home games (all Celtic wins). Attendance here, traditionally scandalously low, is suddenly second in the NBA.

"Celtics: Greatness in Green," says one of the handmade signs created by Rita, the super-fan, who had stopped her colorful cottage industry in disgust the last two years. "M. L. Carr runs on Green Gas" and "Ford: A Winning

Idea" are her paeans to newly arrived sixth man Carr and unheralded guard Chris Ford.

The apparently mysterious transformation of the Celts from the second-worst team in the NBA to the early-season leader is far simpler than it appears. Boston has been twice blessed: they have gained by addition and they have gained by subtraction.

In the last seven months, the Celtics have gotten a new owner (Harry Mangurian), a new coach (Fitch), a new central star (Bird) and a new catalytic sixth man (Carr). Just as important, Boston lost a meddlesome owner (John Y. Brown) and a half dozen players not cast in the Celtic mold.

All this was made possible when Brown took his fried chicken, his wife, Phyllis George, and his political ambitions to Kentucky. "I feel sorry for Kentucky," said one Celtic after Brown was elected governor. "Can a state finish last?"

The sources of the Celtics' misery now seems obvious. Two owners—first Irv Levin, then Brown—pushed a succession of dumb trades on Auerbach. Presenting the fundamentalist Auerbach with Sidney Wicks, Bob McAdoo, Billy Knight, Curtis Rowe and Marvin Barnes was like tying a teetotaler in a chair, then forcing gin, scotch, rum, brandy and vodka down his throat.

"The higher-ups were making the deals," says Boston guard Tiny Archibald, "and the person who was supposed to make deals [Auerbach] didn't have the authority to veto them."

"It got almost unbearable many times," said Auerbach. "Sonny Werblin held the [New York] Knick [GM] job for me for two years. Then, when Levin left and Brown came in, I decided to give it another shot. But that got so bad that I was ready to leave again."

Auerbach and Mangurian have hit it off perfectly. "Not a single disagreement," says Auerbach.

"That's because Red has gotten his way on everything," says Mangurian.

And that, it now seems, was all the Celtics needed.

The new atmosphere—almost one of athletic resurrection—is evident in everything the Celtics do.

"The losers are gone from this locker room. Now the old feeling is back," says Chaney.

As the Celtics romped through a practice session in the empty Garden one morning last week, they sounded like an enthusiastic high school team, teasing each other with all the playground jive that constitutes a private language.

"Sweet J . . . Give that man a ticket . . . Who laid that brick? . . .

Get outta here, little man . . . That was me-an'-you, and mostly me," goes the banter.

The first man at practice every day—often by hours—is Bird. His acceptance has been total—primarily because his style of play is pure Celtic, a sort of taller, slower, more risky version of John Havlicek.

"I call him Kodak," says Fitch, "because his mind takes an instant picture of the whole court. He sees creative possibilities, especially passes, that have never been done."

To the Celts, Bird is like a 6-foot-9 Christmas toy that blocks shots, works diligently on defense and, above all, tries to make his teammates look better. "And," says one Celtic with a smile, "he's nice an' mean. He'll bank anybody."

When Bird makes one of his marvelously deft passes in practice, the other Celts let out a high-pitched twitter: "Birdie-birdie-birdie."

Perhaps the new Celtics are closest, however, when they are engaged in a Fitch ritual—communal film study. Lounging in their locker room after practice, they make a sort of color commentary on a videotape replay of the previous night's game—the kind fans will never hear. Archibald appoints himself the supreme arbiter, pointing out a constant stream of mistakes, nearly invisible lost opportunities and universal selfishness.

"That's right, Cornbread," needles Archibald. "Don't pass it to Red [Cowens]. He ain't workin' hard enough."

The Celtics snicker.

"That's right, Max," crows Archibald as Maxwell shoots while Cowens waits for the pass in vain. "Make him a rebounder."

Occasionally, the Celtics fall silent, listening to Bob Cousy doing the play-by-play on the TV replay.

"I'd like to say something critical about Bird," says the Cooz, "but basically he's just superb in every area of the game."

The Celtics go dead quiet, biting their lips with suppressed amusement as they wait to see how the painfully shy Bird will react to the sort of broad praise they would never grant to each other.

Bird, dressed just like what he calls himself—"a hick from French Lick [Indiana]"—tugs at the tractor driver's cap on his head, pulling it even lower over his beaklike nose.

"Them guys," mumbles the expressionless Bird, looking down at his shoes, "sure know their basketball."

The Celtics howl. Bird's drollery, so dry and understated that it even causes double takes among the hip pros, has struck again.

As the Celtics start to leave the locker room to go home, the irrepressible

Carr "accidentally" lets a dollar bill drop from his pocket—just to see who will bend for it.

Instead of universal cool (the worst sign for team morale), several Celtics dive for the cash. Carr spins and grabs it himself.

"I always leave a trail behind me," says Carr, delighted with his exit line for the day.

If Bird is Boston's conspicuous infusion of talent—$650,000 per year worth—then the infectiously cheerful Carr is the epitome of what the Celtics have always been about.

"Carr exceeds the sum of his technical parts as much as any player in the league," says Celtic beat man Bob Ryan of *The Boston Globe*. "And it would be worth a hundred thousand a year just to have him sit in your locker room."

"Carr has always been a Celtic at heart," says Auerbach. "After he got out of Guilford [College], we gave him a tryout. I released him. But I helped him get a chance to play ball in Israel."

Carr never forgot the favor. He made his way through Europe to the ABA to Detroit, never losing his humor. On signing with the Pistons, Carr announced to a stunned press conference, "I'm changing my name. From now on, I wish to be known as Abdul Automobile."

Actually, Carr—the most sought-after free agent in the NBA after last season—signed with Boston for less than other clubs offered him.

"We got him," says Auerbach, "because he believes in the chemistry of good people working together, just like we do."

A season ago, Carr not only led the NBA in steals and scored 18.7 points per game but was third in the league in minutes played—a pro's most precious possession.

So, on being made sixth man—with his minutes slashed to 26 a game and his scoring average whittled to 14.3, Carr said, "I'll be happy as sixth man, seventh man or eighth man."

Said, the folks of Boston would agree, like a true Celtic—old or new.

Cigar Face

BOSTON, December 6, 1979—

Red Auerbach hardly knows where to begin. The Boston Celtic president has been so smart recently, after being told for two years how dumb he was, that even he finds it a bit disgusting.

Was his best move the hiring of Bill Fitch as coach after Fitch had been fired by the nondescript Cleveland Cavaliers? Was his coup de grace the sweet-talking of M. L. Carr into green Celtic uniform even though the free-agent forward was offered bigger bucks by other NBA teams? Or was Auerbach's best brainstorm his gamble in drafting Larry Bird as No. 1 pick of the year early in '78—then weathering a yearlong $3.25 million negotiation with Bird's agent? After all, five NBA teams bypassed Bird before Auerbach pounced, puffing philosophically, "A year goes by fast." At the moment, Auerbach's acquisitions look like a glorious dead heat.

A year ago, as Auerbach walked to his midcourt Garden seat, he heard people say, "Auerbach really butchered the team." Now, to his face, they say, "Red, we're sure glad you stayed."

It isn't everyone who gets to go from genius to dunce to genius to dunce, and then back to genius—all in one decade. That's been Auerbach's wild progression from '69 to the present.

Right now, Auerbach praises Fitch most—part of his campaign of insisting that he isn't looking over the new man's shoulder. For the first time since Auerbach retired from coaching in '66, his nonintervention protestations are probably close to being the truth.

Fitch is the first Celtic coach since Auerbach who wasn't a former Celtic. "I just ran out of Celtic coaches," says Auerbach with resignation, having replaced Tommy Heinsohn with Satch Sanders, then Sanders with player-coach Dave Cowens last year.

"We had to go outside the family . . . best decision I ever made," says Auerbach. "A generation in people is twenty years. A generation in basketball is six years. No matter how successful you are, you have to have the flexibility to change approach.

"Nothing in coaching is worse than being monotonous."

So the old Celtic system is gone. No more No. 15 play—the triple pick for John Havlicek. No more No. 6—the setup for Cowens's jump hook. Now it is strictly Fitch's system.

Nonetheless, the old fundamentals and the new are still the same. Fitch, like Auerbach, is an anomaly among pro coaches: a teacher who deals with minutiae first and overviews second.

"The NBA is not a fundamentally sound league," says Auerbach. "College coaches, who come up with most of the new ideas, know it. They respect very few pro coaches.

"In the pros, you hear a lot of talk about overall concepts. But I always thought you either had to build from the pieces to the whole or from the whole back to the pieces. I was always a pieces-to-the-whole man."

So is Fitch. He is a fanatically disciplined and meticulous man who disdains ruminative jabber about the theory of the game and prefers infinite attention to detail.

Fitch, for nine years coach and general manager of the Cleveland Cavaliers, not only takes a film projector everywhere on the road but has a vast network of NBA contacts who give him numbing trivia about games all over the country.

"I saw that Scott Wedman scored thirty-eight points on the West Coast last night," a friend will say to Fitch. "Yeah, he got seventeen of them in the fourth quarter off Walter Davis. They posted him up a lot."

"Good Lord, how do you know that?"

"I called one of my friends who does radio in Phoenix at two A.M.," Fitch will answer.

That is one side of Fitch—the fellow who never leaves the house with a wrinkle in his attire, and who has a passion for shopping in malls on the road in search, he jokes, of the perfect pair of slacks.

The question with Fitch, however, is always "Which Fitch?" There seem to be several of him, at least.

Without doubt he is the funniest NBA coach in memory. "I got ejected early tonight so that I could meet with my gag writers," said Fitch last week. "[Johnny] Carson would be proud of some of the stuff I've dreamed up."

The Celtics never know what he will say next. Spotting a despondent Cedric Maxwell slumped on the Celtic bench at practice the morning after a particularly poor performance, Fitch approached his No. 2 scorer. "Morning, Cornbread," said Fitch. "I see you're practicing your game plan from last night."

"????" said Maxwell's face.

"You're sitting on the bench," explained Fitch.

"A month ago, he would have panicked if I had said that," said Fitch later. "But now the players are learning how to take me. Cornbread wanted a word of encouragement from me, so I told him, 'You were absolutely terrible last night. There's no excuse for you ever having a game that bad.'

"They have to understand that the coach gets paid for being critical, not telling them how wonderful they are.

"I've never known a good player who couldn't take a tongue-lashing—so long as it's about a basketball situation—then turn around and go to dinner with you ten minutes later.

"What the egos in the NBA need most is somebody to tell them the truth. This league is full of guys who look like Lon Chaney who wake up in the morning, look in the mirror and convince themselves that they're Clark Gable."

Fitch and his players have a warm rapport, but as one longtime Celtic observer says, "He's the first coach here since Bill Russell that the players view with a healthy fear."

Above all, Fitch is a chronic, wry pessimist, always foreseeing the worst. "I had a 16–4 start once before," he says. "By March, Blue Cross wouldn't touch us. I had a guy injure himself getting off the bus. We started the playoffs with a team that was on a last-name basis."

On one subject, Fitch has a terrible time working up his famous negativity —Larry Bird.

Is it true that the central cog in the Celtics is the rejuvenated Cowens? "We're still a Cowens-oriented team—he's the hub, no matter how much people talk about Bird," says Fitch. "I know how this car was put together."

But Fitch also knows that Bird is the fountain from which all good surprises spring. Cowens is a known and steady factor. Bird is a kaleidoscope of fresh colors. "Larry, right now, in his coach's eyes, is paying the price of having unlimited potential," says Fitch. "I'm never going to be totally satisfied with him."

Then Fitch grins. "I'm determined to find at least one thing that he does wrong in every game."

Bird eats up the criticism with a spoon. Fitch is one of the few NBA coaches who is such a technical fanatic that he is actually qualified to pick at Bird's feathers. "I'm gettin' to hate videotape," drawls Bird. "Coach can tell you everything you've done wrong."

Overall, Fitch may be the only one who has been a match for Bird, who leads the Celtics in scoring (19.1), rebounding (10.1), steals, and is second in assists (4.5) and blocked shots. Bird tries his best to be modest, praising his mates and all the great opponents he is meeting for the first time. But get down to brass tacks and he can't tell a lie. Has he seen anything, even one trick, that surprises him?"

"Can't say I have," he says almost inaudibly.

"Guys my age [twenty-two] were probably the first ones who got to grow up watching the NBA in slow-motion replay since we were little kids. I don't see how you could keep much of anything a secret."

What does he think of the NBA as a whole?

"It's a pretty good brand of basketball," he says.

Just pretty good—nothin' special. If somebody returning from Tibet discovers a higher league, say the Himalayan Hoop Heaven, Larry Bird is ready to go.

"I'm enjoying myself," says Bird. "I always have fun . . . but I don't like to show it much.

"The Celtics know basketball. They appreciate the little things and pick up what you're tryin' to do.

"We're playing well, so you can try to create more . . . take shots you might not otherwise take. You can't be as loose and free when you're losing."

Boston fans still haven't totally picked up what Bird is "tryin' to do," even though they gasp continually and give him standing ovations—the first one just eight minutes into his first game.

"They're good fans," said Bird, a trace of a smile showing, "but I can't tell yet if they'll be as good as Indiana fans. Back home, by the end of the year, I had 'em ready for anything. They'd know what I was about to do.

"When they're anticipatin' with you, that's the best thing. Folks deserve a good show for their money."

Actually, NBA life may suit Bird better than the world of academics.

"I hate to practice and I love to play," he said, beaming. "It's good when you can get revenge so quick after a bad game. I've lost a few pounds, but I'm ready to challenge the schedule. I think I can, 'cause I love this game so much. I ain't quick and I don't jump that well. But I can play."

Bird has even made the beginnings of a peace with the world at large and its nosy representatives—the press. And he is learning to protect himself.

Around French Lick, a man isn't judged by whether he has holes in his socks, but by the quality of his labor. But that ain't the city way. So when Bird spied a hole as big as a quarter in his black socks this week, he casually reached down—looking the other way as he would while making a blind pass—and folded the sock over so the hole disappeared and the dozen reporters around him didn't have one more quaint little tidbit to josh at.

Bird's wisdom is nonverbal. He knows the secret of waiting just a second or two for 10,000 eyes to move away from him before he makes his little gesture of communication with a teammate. Consequently, he never hotdogs, never plays to the crowd, never alienates anyone. He's a purist.

The person most delighted with Bird's personality is Auerbach. "That's the surprise," he says. "As a person, Bird's more than we expected.

"He's easy to coach, not cocky. Knock him down and he gets up, comes after you and knocks you down.

"And he's got a nice, dry humor . . . beat me out of a buck the other day," said Auerbach. "We were in one of those gyms with six baskets. He says to me, 'Bet I can bank one in from here,' and he nods to the basket forty feet away. I said, 'A buck you can't.'

"So he grins, turns around, and we're standing right under one of the other baskets. He lays it in and says, 'I didn't say which basket. Pay up.' "

Auerbach, who has already shelled out millions, only pulled that ancient trick a hundred times himself.

"I warned him," says Auerbach. "I'll get it back." What the club president really means is that he is following one of his oldest rules: You don't handle people. You get along with people.

The force behind the Celtic flame is still Auerbach, the Jewish leprechaun with the instant intuition. The heart of Auerbach's professional life is his office in the bowels of the Boston Garden. It is as good a symbol of the Celtics' perpetual rebirth as any. "I think this office has actually signed players for us that we might not have gotten otherwise," says Auerbach. The first two that might come to mind are Bird, who was drafted a year early in '78 and might have gotten more money by waiting for the '79 draft with a different team, and Carr, who was a free agent.

Perhaps no words can describe the infinite clutter, the muddled charm and the sense of a total unified personality that emanates from Auerbach's pack-rat den. "It's like home," he says with a smile. "Comfortable and full of junk."

All around him are small signs that say, "Think."

"I love to watch people," he says. "And I love to shop."

"Havlicek and [Don] Nelson—I taught 'em how to shop—a jade chess set in the Far East . . . scrimshaw from New Bedford . . . carved ivory in Burma. I like Royal Danish china better than Royal Copenhagen. The painting on the Royal Copenhagen is very ordinary.

"But the main thing about shopping," concludes Auerbach after covering most of the explored world with his anecdotes, "is that it's only fun when you do it on a limited budget. I don't buy to sell. And I'm never extravagant."

And that, of course, applied to men rather than china or chess sets, is the core of the Celtics' success. Auerbach remains the king of the shoppers, the prince of farsighted bargain hunters.

"I've always had to make do with a little less," says Auerbach. "Even when I coached at Roosevelt High in Washington in the '40s I remember stopping a big kid in the hall and saying, 'I want you out for basketball tomorrow.'

"Unfortunately, the kid wasn't very good. His name was Bowie Kuhn and I cut him two days later. I understand he's done well since.

"Since I've been with the Celtics we haven't had a draft pick higher than the fourth man in twenty-five years—and I never spent a dime for a player. We develop our own people and we stick with 'em."

Once more, Auerbach has taken the reins of the Celtics firmly in his hands—shopping for a free agent that he had befriended years before, signing a flighty Bird with the aid of that cluttered office and some malarkey.

Red Auerbach is a venerable institution now. Instead of going on road trips, he returns home to Washington. Sometimes he misses a practice so he can lecture at Harvard.

He is a man who looks semiretired, relaxed, like an unharried patriarch of his Celtic clan.

So how does he feel, watching his handiwork begin to fall in place once more?

Red Auerbach points his cigar for emphasis, and suddenly looks rather young.

"I tread," he says, "with fear and trepidation."

Bird at the Peak

BOSTON, June 9, 1986—

Legends take root and grow on days like this one in the Boston Garden. Legends of heroism and legends of the opposite sort, too.

With his incineration of the Houston Rockets in the sixth and final game of the NBA finals, Larry Bird added another large page to the résumé that he's amassing as the best all-around player in basketball history.

Simultaneously, Ralph Sampson gave more fuel to those who'd damn him as the most disappointing giant in the clutch since Wilt Chamberlain.

Legends, of course, bear only a shadowy relationship to reality. Sport feeds on the pleasure of exaggeration. Get on the right side of the mythmaking machinery and it fuels your own self-esteem while granting a protective aura that daunts foes. Get on the wrong side for too long, however, and woe be unto you. Even if you don't come to believe in your own invisible flaws, others may. Then self-fulfilling prophecy begins.

Bird, with the most impregnable basketball arrogance since Bill Russell, hardly needed another coat of armor; now the 6-foot-9 Boston Celtic has another NBA playoff most valuable player trophy to put next to the three straight regular-season MVP awards he already owns.

Sampson, more stylist than warrior by nature, hardly needed more burdens. Now, after getting himself ejected after a humiliating, childish brawl with a 6-foot-1 Celtic in Game 5, he has another memory—2 points in the first thirty-two minutes as his team fell a hopeless 22 points behind. Talk about being naked before thine enemies.

Though raw numbers say that Bird is the best of his era, they still do not touch the core of his value—especially on days like this 114–97 Celtics victory. His triple-double—29 points, 12 assists and 11 rebounds—seemed to require a recount. Certainly every column was a half dozen short. Heck, Bird's averages for the eighteen games of the playoffs are almost that good: 25.9 points, 9.3 rebounds and 8.2 assists.

The Rockets' Jim Petersen was closer to the majority opinion when he said: "I've never seen anyone who could demoralize a whole team like he can. It's like he doesn't even need his teammates. It's just him, one on five, and he almost beats you single-handed.

"It's the way he does it. Offensive rebound, go right to the corner, three-point shot, nothing but net. He gets you down and then breaks your back."

Normally, Bird doesn't play against the other team; he plays against the game of basketball. Not this time. Bird took this one personally; he played the Rockets. He wasn't a purist, he was a killer. So incensed was Bird over the Game 5 blowout in Houston, plus the unanswered punches Sampson laid on two Celtics, that, as coach K. C. Jones said, "for the last two days he's been the quietest man I ever saw."

Bird had decreed that penance and sacrifice were in order. Guard Dennis Johnson came forward and said to Jones, "Let me cover Robert Reid." And center Robert Parish, ashamed of his Game 5 sleepwalk, asked for Akeem Olajuwon.

D.J. and the Chief may have volunteered for KP duty, but nobody loves dirty work as much as Bird, the former French Lick garbageman. On a floor littered with 7-footers, Bird was the dominant rebounder—in efficiency and violence. In floor burns, no one came close. Once, buried under Rockets, Bird screamed at his mates, "Why aren't you guys down here with me?" On defense, he picked the Twin Towers' pockets all day.

No matter what Sampson did, Bird had decreed it wouldn't be enough. But Sampson was in double jeopardy. No one knows how much all those signs bothered him. Numerous "Sampson Is a Sissy" placards. Plus "Ralph, why don't you fight Marvin Hagler? He's more your size." And "Ralph, I'm 5-foot-2. You'd probably hit me, too." No one knows how much the sarcastic chants of "Shoot" and "We Want Ralph" bugged him as he withdrew further into his shell.

What indisputably hampered Sampson was the way Johnson got in Reid's jersey and rendered him null and void. "I took myself out of the offense. I don't know why. I'm mad at myself," said Reid. "I did the opposite of what I should have done. D.J. got to me and I couldn't get the ball to Ralph. We just didn't take care of Ralph today."

Ralph didn't take care of Ralph either. Kevin McHale used him all day for

29 in-your-face points. McHale's still the NBA's Mr. Underrated to Sampson's Mr. Overrated.

"The crowd didn't bother me," said Sampson. "You've got to lose before you win this thing. We are on the way to being the best." Many words but no further illumination.

"Some guys have to grow. Ralph's seven-four, so he doesn't have to get any bigger," said Houston coach Bill Fitch. "He has to ripen emotionally. But he's come a long way in the three years."

By the time that McHale and Bill Walton, the Grateful UnDead Celtic, had embraced and high-fived themselves to exhaustion with the Celtics ahead by 30 and the Garden doing its earthquake imitation, there were few questions left to be answered. Only those concerning matters of legend.

Are these Celtics—67–15 in the regular season and 15–3 in the playoffs—the greatest NBA team ever?

And is Bird the best who ever played?

Jones, at the risk of insulting old teammates, said, "This team is the best team I ever saw." And Red Auerbach, the first cause of all things green, offered, "This is one of the greatest, if not the greatest team I have ever been associated with."

Even Fitch offered that "Walton, Bird and McHale are all going to end up in the Hall of Fame."

Bird differed. Or rather, couldn't have cared less. "I got a lot of work to do this summer," he said. "We want to repeat."

If Bird and his teammates become the first team since the '60s to repeat as world champions, that will be time enough to undertake such long thoughts.

For now, let's just say that no living athlete in any sport gives us as much continual pleasure and never-ending surprise as Larry Bird.

Len Bias: Living in the Gray

June 21, 1986—Athletes seem uniquely ill prepared for contemporary life because they have been encouraged, from adolescence, to accept the most simplistic views of a complex and ambiguous world.

They're fed black and white, then have to cope with gray. And we wonder how Len Bias can become a born-again Christian one month, then the next month drop dead of a heart attack with cocaine in his system.

When a world of clichés runs into reality, somebody gets hurt. When we ask people to pretend to be perfect angels in public, we're begging for the backlash in private.

We see this in almost every sport every day. Coaches are the players' gurus. What they preach—and it is preaching—is a code of conduct that has vastly more to do with winning games (for the coach) than it has to do with living a life (for the player).

Too often, athletes are given an adult's body, an adult's desires and a child's morals. Instead of moderation, they learn the binge mentality of abstinence in season, then party-hearty. Just don't get caught or embarrass us.

Athletes not only have to cope with fame, wealth and hero worship; they have to face the possibility that they are frauds. Our image-making apparatus seems to insist that scoring average and virtue be connected. Pity the jock who is proclaimed the best of his generation, held up as a paragon, when, in his heart, he must know he doesn't have a clue about any issue more significant than a pick-and-roll.

Those who exaggerate the importance and the virtue of athletes do them no favor. It only sets them up to make the fall twice as hard when they turn out to be human.

If the 1980s show anything about University of Maryland athletics, it's that the school might be wise to get its athletes down off their pedestals and knock some common sense and humility into them.

Ten years ago, at a sports banquet, Maryland basketball All-America John Lucas spoke. He rambled from platitude to platitude, discussed the possibility that one day he might be President of the United States, then sat down to a standing ovation.

I have never seen such innocent vanity and such pathetic lack of self-knowledge in the same person. For me, Lucas has always summed up the athlete's dilemma. He mistakes his talent for character. He uses charm and presence to fake his way through. His vanity is excused as a great man's natural ambition.

And no matter what he does, he is cheered—which just coaxes him deeper into self-delusion. He's hailed, that is, until he screws up; then he gets it in the neck twice as much, because he blew the gravy-train ride so many wish they had.

With athletes, that dichotomous black-or-white mind-set always lies in wait for us. It's lurking around Len Bias's memory now. There's going to be a terrible temptation to judge Bias permanently on the basis of a coroner's report. If his death was a heart attack, make him a saint. If his death was directly drug-related, turn him into a parable for kids about how drugs can ruin the best of them.

On Thursday, a former member of the Maryland state legislature said he thought Cole Field House should be renamed Bias Field House, as long, he said, as "no drugs are found in the blood."

Does cocaine really change our opinion of Bias by 180 degrees? What if, someday, it is proposed that Memorial Stadium in Baltimore be changed to Earl Weaver Stadium. Should the little manager's two drunk-driving incidents prevent it?

For everybody's sake, can't we learn to live more comfortably in life's gray areas?

Lefty Driesell knows this black-vs.-white syndrome to the core. He's a simple, passionate man who wants hard, old-fashioned answers; and he constantly pays an enormous price for the difficulty he has in dealing with subtlety. That, perhaps, is why he counseled his team Thursday as to what parts of the truth to reveal and what to hide.

In the last two days, thousands of people have tried to figure out how they feel about Bias's death. For me, none has caught the mixture of tragedy and disappointment, annoyance and sympathy, better than a tall Safeway checker whom I overheard Thursday. Someone in line said to him, "Too bad about Bias."

"Really a shock. I played for UDC and I was in a pickup game against him just a couple of weeks ago," said the checker. "He had it all in front of him. . . . I hope there were no drugs involved. But I wouldn't be surprised."

"Cocaine was found in his urine."

"Aw, damn," said the checker. "That's a shame. That's so stupid."

"They don't know yet if that's what killed him."

"It didn't help," the checker said. "He was twenty-two. A man. He's supposed to know better."

The checker picked up the intercom phone and said to whoever answered, "They found cocaine in Lenny." He didn't even bother to say Bias. "Yeah, really sad."

Then he started ringing up the next bag of groceries.

Stupid. Sad. A shame. A personal shock. His own responsibility. A blow to those who believed in him. But not such a surprise if you live in the real world, not the hero world. To the checker, Bias was just a local guy named Lenny who made it big, had it all in front of him, but couldn't finish the breakaway dunk. The kind of thing that makes you sad for everybody.

Lots of people in this town would like to have had Len Bias's life. All but the last day of it. To have had his talent, his joy, his fame, his wealth-to-come. He was a hero to them.

Now they don't know whether to be sad for him, or mad at him, or some much more complicated mixture of both.

And no matter what the cops and the coroner say, they're probably never going to know.

That's called living in the gray. It's hard. It never gets easier. It's a game you never win, but you just keep trying. It builds character. The real kind. Not just the sort that's talked about at halftime but forgotten after midnight.

The Edge of Knight

SAN JUAN, Puerto Rico, July 6, 1979—

Bobby Knight, an Ugly American even at home in Indiana, was at it again Thursday night.

The U.S. basketball coach in the Pan American Games was screaming profanities and insults in the face of the youngest player on his team in a voice so loud that thousands of fans could hear him.

"What the hell's the matter with you? Do you think I'm going to put up with this bull bleep?" bellowed the livid Knight, thirty-eight, his 6-foot-5 frame bent over 6-1 Isiah Thomas, their faces inches apart.

The veins and muscles in Knight's satanically dark face bulged as he bumped and badgered his eighteen-year-old guard—not for a few seconds but for minutes as both stood at midcourt. Thomas, his face stunned and blank, stood and took it, as Knight's epithets escalated to the unprintable.

"Loco, loco," muttered the Latin American fans, accustomed to athletic fanaticism, but hardly prepared for the raw, conscienceless villainy of Knight in high dudgeon.

When the first half ended, seconds later, Knight sprinted onto the court, grabbed Thomas and screamed maniacally in his face all the way to the locker room. He benched him the second half. Knight is the coach at Indiana University, when he is not spreading good in the Caribbean by getting ejected from a Pan Am game with his team ahead by 35 points. Thomas, Chicago's top high school player in 1979, has enrolled at Indiana.

Welcome to four years of *The Edge of Knight*.

To call Knight a Jekyll-and-Hyde personality would be understatement. It took Jekyll several seconds of gasping and fang-growing to become Hyde. Knight can do it in a flash.

Knight's face is his fortune, and his sorrow. Even in repose, his expression combines intelligence, animal magnetism and potential menace. Other men's faces show less than they feel. Knight's commonly conveys more— often to his detriment.

This week Knight's multiple personalities have been on vivid display. He has ranted at his team behind closed doors after they won a scrimmage by 13 points. He has cursed players on the bench publicly and loudly.

Knight not only was thrown out of the gym in a game against the Virgin Islands but was reprimanded by the International Amateur Basketball Federation, lectured for half an hour by Pan Am officials and cornered into a tepid apology. "I didn't really apologize," Knight said today. "I just said I wouldn't want to go through it all again."

One federation official called Knight's ejection—the first for a U.S. coach in Pan Am or Olympic competition—"a very serious violation," adding that another infraction would get the U.S. expelled from basketball competition.

Thursday night, after the 82–78 victory over top contender Brazil had pushed Knight's team a giant step toward a gold medal, he was in fine form —analytical, acid, candid, injudicious and occasionally charming.

Those who enjoy hating Bobby Knight from afar are better off if they don't get to know him.

After his nondescript team, one of the least known that the U.S. has fielded internationally, had in successive games beaten its three toughest opponents (Virgin Islands, Cuba and Brazil), Knight blasted his players. "We're just a very, very immature club that doesn't know what it means to be mentally ready to play," said Knight. "I'm disappointed . . . From a spectator's point of view, the wrong team won. The hustling team, the tough rebounding team was Brazil, not us.

"For two days, since we beat Cuba, they've been listening to how good they are—and they played like it. They have to learn that we're not down here to play Rosemary and the Seven Dwarfs."

Of his 7-foot-4 center, Ralph Sampson, the eighteen-year-old prodigy, he laid this opinion on the line.

"Some of those idiots in the pros are saying he's ready for the NBA. And, of course, all the college coaches who know they can't get him go along with that baloney because it puts more pressure on whatever coach does get him. [He's headed for Virginia.]

"Well, Sampson not only isn't ready for the NBA, he isn't even ready for college ball at this point. He'll need all four years. He looks lost on the court against these guys down here. He's not aggressive, he doesn't go after the ball.

"He's used to saying 'boo' to high school kids and they stay away from him. These Brazilians don't know him from a tall ladder. They attack him, beat him up. And he's no factor in the game."

Of all Knight's eruptions here, he saves his best for the critics back home who have relished his ejection and embarrassment. Knight knows that the show of temper that had caused the fuss was practically nothing, a mere tiff to which a macho ref who speaks no English overreacted—judging Knight by his florid face, not his placid words.

"That makes me sick, that just nauseates me," Knight said when told that Joe Garagiola had criticized him on a radio show, pointing out that U.S. coaches in international competition are supposed to avoid incidents, not cause them.

"Garagiola doesn't know beans. He can stick it in his ear. He can . . ." said Knight, enumerating several impossible acts.

"I don't need all this. I've won everything a college coach can win. I don't have to prove myself. I was asked to take this job and I accepted as a favor," said Knight scathingly. "I had a benefit game in Bloomington and raised fifty thousand dollars for the Pan Am Games.

"I'm not here to have a good time . . . I don't like this hot weather or no air conditioning or sitting outside the gym in a bus for an hour waiting for the preliminary game to end.

"If I'd wanted to have a good time, I'd have gone fishing.

"Instead, starting May 20, we had six days of trials, then we played in Italy for six days. Then after eight days off, we've been going at it steady since June 12. This is no damn vacation.

"I'll tell you what made me feel good. As soon as I got here, a Puerto Rican friend came up and said, 'Bobby, as soon as I saw you were coming down, I knew the U.S. had decided to play to win.' "

So there is the Knight conundrum in a nutshell. He is, in one sense, the final product of an American college sports system that takes high school seniors and drills them with the value of one word—win.

As a player, Knight was a brilliant jump shooter who played lousy defense and rode the bench on the phenomenal Ohio State team that had John Havlicek and Jerry Lucas. As a coach, it is always noted—as though it were a contradiction—Knight stresses things like defense, ball handling, rebounding and toughness, the things that were his flaws as a player.

On the contrary, Knight coaches the same way he played. He was a glory hound then, and remains one.

At every opportunity, Knight takes the game away from his players and tries to control it himself with strategies, pep talks or tirades. It is no mistake that he insists that "this game is five to one mental over physical."

In a college coaching profession full of enormous egos who try to express themselves through their players, Knight is perhaps the most insistent on having obedient robots on court.

Ironically, Knight has been castigated here for all the wrong things. His ejection was a picayune incident. It is his almost daily tirades at his players that deserve censure. These players, average age twenty, are not in any sense Knight's players. They tried out for the U.S. team, not Knight's Indiana squad. They are his captive audience.

"These players are all here for one reason," says Knight. "Because they want to make it to the Olympics in '80."

So they have to put up with Knight's grandstanding abuse, his perpetual spotlight grabbing. Their one break is that the 1980 Olympic coach will not be Knight, but that laid-back guy sitting in the Pepin Cestera bleachers here with his feet up on the chair in front—Dave Gavitt of Providence.

Knight merely is prepping himself for an eventual Olympic spot. That is the reason for his enthusiasm for a dirty job.

There is no question that Knight is fit to be the U.S. Olympic coach. His record proves it—he can win, just as he probably will win the gold medal here with a raggedy team. But there are many types of fit coaches, many ways to win. Knight's drill-instructor methods have no intrinsic advantage over other approaches. They merely suit his personality.

The reason that Knight, as he presently is constituted, should not represent the United States in the future is not because he is not fit.

It is because, in the deepest sense, he is not proper.

SAN JUAN, Puerto Rico, July 14, 1979—

Maybe it's because my chair was one of the bigger ones at the press table Friday night that Bobby Knight's wife sat in it with me during the U.S. team's gold-medal basketball victory in the Pan American Games.

It was a tight squeeze, my leg hooked through the arm of the big blue metal chair and me back to back with Nancy Knight as she looked over her shoulder to watch the game.

When she wasn't rubbing her lucky Snoopy basketball doll, she was closing her eyes and putting her face in her hands during free throws in the 113–94 victory over Puerto Rico.

Actually, no one knows how such a large and inviting-looking chair ended up in my possession. Rumor has it that a miffed scribe, seeing many press-row seats taken by frauds and gate-crashers, visited the Clemente Coliseum administration office and purloined the director's chair. After two weeks here, you learn the local customs.

At any rate, something made me look like a logical choice for a woman in distress—probably the chair.

"I was locked out of the parking lot, kept out of the gym, and then, when I finally got to my seat, somebody was in it and wouldn't move. The guard said, 'Oh well, just pack in anywhere, lady,' " the coach's wife said.

"Thanks for sharing your chair," she said, adding, "Bobby's not going to believe this."

He's not the only one.

Just a week ago, I described Knight as "an Ugly American even at home in Indiana."

The uncomfortable fact about reality is that it won't stand still and play fair. The world keeps bobbing before us, changing its masks, revealing different contradictory corners of itself.

You'd think that sports, or a tiny sliver of it, like a basketball game, might be a tamable animal that would not squirm in your hand, then turn and bite. That's not the case. The heroes and villains, even in games, keep changing places when you're not looking.

The problem, in part, is the huge distance between private selves and public identities. Knight, off the court, in his occasional relaxed moods is charming and dynamic. His wife is touchingly loyal. Nevertheless, private personalities get trampled in the public crush. It is the visible Knight, acting in the midst of conspicuous events, who gets judged, while it is the private Knight family that feels the lingering weight.

"We brought our two children down with us. They're eight and fourteen," Knight's wife said. "I'm not sure it was a good idea."

Those are not good ages to see your father ejected from a game, thrown out of a gym, booed at every turn, arrested, put in a jail cell momentarily and finally brought to trial.

This daily soap opera, has been unavoidable grist for the publicity mill here—tangled, funny, bizarre. But it also has, as Nancy Knight said, "been one long Puerto Rico headache for us."

Nonetheless, Knight set the tone of his own theater. He has taken the initiative at every step, keeping the chip on his shoulder till the last and never recanting with any sincerity.

After all, it's not everybody who can chew out an island inhabited by 3.3 million people as though they'd just double-dribbled, as Knight did after Friday night's game. Anyone can be a sore loser, but Knight set new standards for being a sore winner.

"I'm not a diplomat. I don't know anything about foreign policy," Knight said, warming to a postgame tirade. "I just know we beat . . . everybody down here. . . . My players are the only people on this whole . . . island that I care anything about."

There was more, as usual—insults to an American reporter Knight mistook for Puerto Rican, and his wisecracks about Puerto Rican police and Caribbean justice. Those comments have become, though he does not know it, an embarrassment to Knight himself. The shame of these Games is that his bully-in-a-China-shop escapades have overshadowed America's 263 medals.

Certainly, Knight owes an apology to Puerto Rico. No matter how unintentionally humorous and ragtag these Games have been at times, there is no question that this poor island with a per capita income of $2,500 has tried its best to be a good host. By and large, it has succeeded.

Even in the Big Ten, Knight has a persecution complex and sees crooked refs under the bed. Here, he has been truly paranoid. His own inflexibility and inability to see past the hoop to larger issues has caused every childish incident.

However, Knight's real apology should be to the 600-member U.S. delegation, whose performances have been driven out of the relatively limited media coverage that the Pan Am Games get in most of the United States. The already famous Knight, with his passion for being in the spotlight, whether good or bad, has kept many a swimmer and boxer from their once-in-four-years moment of glory.

Naturally, the press has lapped up the Knight sagas—never turn down an easy, flashy angle. But Knight started the fire and fanned its homely little flames.

The painful edge of this affair is that Knight truly believes he is totally right and that Puerto Rico, en masse, has been out to bamboozle his team since it landed.

Rather sadly, Knight, alone among American coaches here, seems to think he's still back in the States—that this is just another basketball tournament, nothing more.

Others learn their simple lessons here. "Puerto Rican fans are knowledgeable and appreciate good performance, regardless," said Lyle Knudson, U.S. women's track coach. "But they prefer countries who share their culture and size. We're the Big Daddy, and there's naturally some resentment."

The Cubans, with a typical knack for political con, entered Bithorn Stadium on opening day throwing dolls to the crowd and waving Cuban and Puerto Rican flags together.

"It's like the poem about the two wings of the same bird," said Cuban star sprinter Silvio Leonard. "Even our flags are the same, only [colors] reversed. The Puerto Ricans always support the Cubans. There's good feeling between us."

American swimmers picked up on the trick, chanting, "Puerto Rico, Puerto Rico," and waving island flags after their teammate, Jesse Vassallo, a native Puerto Rican, won his races. The local crowds immediately adopted the American swimmers as second favorites behind their own entries. It was so easy.

Knight, however, never had a clue, never understood he was a guest in a foreign culture first and a basketball coach far behind. For him, basketball remained big, life small.

As the U.S.–Puerto Rico game ended Friday night, a fistfight broke out in the stands. In the middle of that tension, Knight decided to let fly with his anti-island remarks. Meanwhile, his players eyed the stands and shuffled about, not looking too anxious to make themselves conspicuous as they stepped forward to receive their medals.

As Knight groused, locked in his private world, forward Mike O'Koren, twenty-one, gathered his mates together and mustered them into a straight line, telling them, "Come on, guys. Get that line straight. Stand up tall. You're representing a lot of people back home. Act right. Don't react to anything and don't let any trouble get started. Shape up."

Are you listening, Bobby? It would take only one dawn of understanding to turn Knight into day.

Children for Sale

The Weakness of Sampson

HARRISONBURG, Virginia, May 31, 1979—

Major college athletics in the United States may have reached a watershed of pathos, bitter ironic humor and ignominy this evening. The guerrilla war of recruiting for 7-foot-4 basketball prodigy Ralph Sampson reached a suitably Kafkaesque pass as the Harrisonburg High senior finally announced his choice of colleges.

Almost.

"I guess I'm probably going to Virginia next year," the shy eighteen-year-old Sampson said softly into a battery of microphones at a mass press conference for a hundred reporters.

"If I have any doubt and change my mind, it will be Kentucky."

Jaws dropped. Harrisonburg coach Roger Bergey held his head in his hands.

Surely this was the perfect, bizarre conclusion to one of the ugliest episodes in the splotched and checkered history of brazenly big-time college sports.

Sampson, pressured for more than two years by universities, gradually narrowed his choices from two hundred schools to sixteen to seven and finally, two months ago, to his personal Final Four. Since then, the young giant with the soft touch and "NCAA championship" written on him has become increasingly unable to make his decision—torn between UVA, UK, North Carolina and Virginia Tech. Plus, it should be noted, Maryland, the one college that has hectored him constantly for the last month, refusing to take a hundred polite nos for an answer.

"This morning I was still undecided. In the last two days I've changed my mind at least fifty times," said Sampson, who called today's press gathering of the tribes to finally rid himself of his albatross. "I sat down and talked with myself . . . I even wrote the names down once or twice to see how they looked."

"Ralph was up all night, walking," his mother, Sarah Sampson, said. "He took out the garbage at two A.M. He walked to his girlfriend's house in the middle of the night.

"When his sister left for Atlanta this morning, she asked him, 'Well, Ralph?' and he said, 'I still don't know.' "

After a day at school during which he peeked through windows and sneaked out back doors to avoid reporters and possible lurking assistant coaches, Sampson fled this afternoon for sanctuary to his mother's personnel office at a factory.

The pressure was building. By midafternoon enough television crews were in the Harrisonburg gym so that the total value of their camera equipment, according to one North Carolina TV reporter, was "well over $600,000."

"I'm beginning to question my country's values," Harrisonburg assistant coach Tim Meyers remarked. "We had a TV crew with a private jet do two round trips up here from Raleigh, North Carolina, in one day—just doing updates on Ralph not making a decision yet.

"Jimmy Carter gets criticized for taking a helicopter trip. That can't touch this kind of waste."

Sampson knew, before he left school this afternoon, that two coaches were poised at exactly 6:30 P.M. to call the four colleges and give them his final word. His personal deadline was set. The formal announcement would come at 7 P.M.

When Sampson left his mother after 5 P.M., "he still hadn't made up his mind," she said. "He spent the afternoon answering my phone. We just talked a little."

Sampson's mother had only one request. "I told him that if it was Virginia, why not wait a day or two to sign to see if anything comes up to change his mind . . . you never can tell."

Just minutes before 7 P.M., coach Bergey called Virginia coach Terry Holland with the momentous decision.

"The big guy's made up his mind. It's UVA," said Bergey.

"Are you joking me?" answered Holland, a shy, soft-spoken intellectual of a coach who pressured Sampson perhaps less than any other competitive recruiter.

"No, I'm not kidding," said Bergey.

"Can I kiss you?" asked Holland, as cheering broke out behind him in the Holland home.

"No, I have to make another call [to a losing coach]," Bergey replied.

Moments later, Sampson ducked his head as he walked through the 7-foot-high gymnasium doorway with "Go Blue Streaks" written above it. Then he passed under the wall placard reading: "Sportsman's Creed: Be a Good Sport."

When he murmured "Virginia" into the microphones, a huge cheer went up outside the gym as a dozen or more UVA students, listening to their radios, hollered.

Sampson's apparently simple decision quickly became complex as the press badgered him, bearing down on his careful use of the words "maybe" and "probably."

Nevertheless, Sampson's indecision plainly showed and his voice sounded weak, as if reflecting vexation and almost depression.

"I was nervous before . . . didn't know what to do . . . okay now," he said in fragments. "I don't want to make anybody unhappy. I haven't signed yet. But it'll probably be Virginia . . . Yeah, hopefully in a couple of days. I'll only be going to college for two years, probably, then the pros. All the schools know that's the deal for me."

"What are your academic interests?" yelled a questioner.

"I don't have any yet," answered Sampson.

A member of the Harrisonburg faculty shook his head.

"You would describe Ralph as a wonderful boy who is a rather weak student. He comes to class and just keeps his mouth shut," he said. "I hate to think of him at Virginia with a future doctor on one side of him and a future lawyer on the other. I hope they promised to take care of him, 'cause he'll certainly need it."

That voracious, roving monster called celebrity has turned one of its thousand piercing eyes on this town of 14,405 and its gigantic child. It has been an experience Harrisonburg never expected or learned how to digest.

"VPI said it spent ten thousand dollars just on recruiting Ralph," said Sampson adviser Bergey. "That's big business. Some people have come clean across this country just to sit down with this young man . . . or with me."

Bergey reportedly has been offered an assistant's job at several schools, most prominently Maryland.

"I tell 'em no package deals," declared Bergey, wearing Hush Puppies and argyle socks with his canary-yellow blazer. "I tell 'em to call me the day after Ralph signs when there's no connection between us anymore."

What does he think were the motives of Maryland coach Lefty Driesell?

"That's a very interesting question," Bergey said. "We better not dwell on that . . .

"I'll be interested to see if my phone is still ringing tomorrow."

Recruiting, and the media carnival that surrounds it, has reached such a threshold of distastefulness that even a conscientious set of rules—like those that Harrisonburg High fought so hard to maintain—cannot keep a 7-foot-4 teenager from spending the wee hours pacing the streets of his small town.

Perhaps the appropriate symbol of this day's shenanigans was a TV blow-dry sportscaster who at 5 P.M. could not wait for the final deadline.

Standing in the gym parking lot, he dramatically read his script: "Ralph Sampson decided today to attend . . ."

He read that script four times—each time with equal drama. And each time he inserted the name of a different college.

"Take all four," he said, "then pick the right one."

There was no time to wait.

The private jet was waiting for the film.

No Food or Drink

CAMBRIDGE, Massachusetts, January 28, 1981—

John Thompson feels like a painter who has almost finished the master-piece of a lifetime but still has one last vital stroke remaining; thus he is both exhilarated and terrified.

For the next twenty-four hours, the Georgetown coach will hold his breath. He, like almost everyone else, assumes that a 7-foot diamond of basketball hope named Patrick Ewing sits squarely in the Hoyas' palm. If only they don't drop him. Or have him snatched away.

Ewing, an eighteen-year-old at Cambridge Rindge and Latin School, al-ready bears the marks of becoming one of the great centers in history. He has told coach Mike Jarvis he will pick his college on Thursday. Jarvis and

Cambridge Latin officials, who have established new standards of stringency for protecting a player from the hype and harassment of both recruiters and media, claim they plan to keep the decision secret until an official announcement Monday.

If Ewing says any name other than Georgetown, he will slam-dunk the whole hoop world into stunned silence. Georgetown has led the Ewing derby for more than a year. However, there is a vast difference between being in front and winning the race. That is why Thompson, as he sat in the bleachers here Tuesday night watching Ewing play, resembled a 300-pound mass of suppressed worry.

By halftime in the tiny, hot bandbox, Thompson was sweating like a refrigerator on the fritz. A generous student, taking pity, went across the street at intermission and bought Thompson a quart bottle of ice-cold soda pop. Thompson grasped the precious gift, then looked above his head and saw a sign: "No Food or Drink Allowed in the Gym." Suddenly, Thompson looked at the innocent soda as though it were arsenic hand-delivered by the devil. Or perhaps by Boston College coach Tom Davis, sitting only ten yards away. Or, for that matter, by one of the representatives of the other four schools in Ewing's Final Six—North Carolina, Boston University, UCLA and Villanova. All were in the bleachers.

"Does anybody have a brown bag?" Thompson asked.

One appeared. Thompson slipped the bottle inside, then stopped. "What if the principal sees me and throws me out of the gym?" he muttered. "Lord, I'd hate to lose this kid over a bottle of soda."

Summoning his courage, Thompson took the bottle out of the bag. "If it's in a brown paper bag, nobody'll believe it's just pop," he said.

Slowly, the tempting bottle began its long assent toward the peak of the 6-foot-10 Mount Thompson. But, again, the mission was aborted.

To the constant question: "Just how good is Pat Ewing?" perhaps this anecdote is the perfect answer. He is good enough to make John Thompson, a man of principles, worry about principals.

"It's great to hear that Patrick is expected to make a decision this week," Thompson said after watching Ewing get 21 points, 20 rebounds, 10 assists and 12 blocked shots while playing less than 20 minutes in a 50-point victory. "That's very good news. The longer he waits, the more gray hair I get."

Whenever Ewing makes his final decision, whenever it is announced, one thing is certain: nothing about Ewing is going to be secret or serene much longer. This is the player whom Jarvis describes as "part Bill Walton, a bit of Abdul-Jabbar, a whole lot of Bill Russell and even more Patrick Ewing."

By that hyperbole, he means that Ewing can become as versatile a scorer, passer and all-round team player as Walton, as fluidly graceful a giant as Abdul-Jabbar and as intensely motivated a rebounder, shot blocker and winner as Russell. In addition, Ewing is a power-game player who loves to sprint baseline to baseline and is a natural transition player. That opens the possibility that he may bring his skills to more parts of the court, more of the time, than such players as Walton and Moses Malone, with whom he is being excitedly compared. "I wouldn't disagree with that assessment," Thompson said.

What part of Ewing's game would Thompson work on first?

"Catching the ball."

Why?

"Because if I get him," Thompson said, "he's going to be doing a lot of it."

Ewing may not be as tall as Ralph Sampson, or as quick and fierce around the basket as Malone, but, all in all, he has the qualities that make coaches drool. Above all, his temperament shows in every gesture on the court. He is intense, self-motivated and obviously driven by vastly higher standards than the modest necessity that he crush high school players.

On defense, he looks like a wide-roaming hockey goalie who wants a shutout. He is that oh so rare player who obviously regards defense, total intimidating control of the defensive backboard and the quick long outlet pass as his primary duties. He considers all five offensive players "his," yet he is so agile that he seldom commits fouls—certainly not the clumsy kind usually associated with youngsters.

"The first thing that opened my eyes," Thompson said, "was when I saw him fire an outlet pass, then get down and stuff in a quick miss at the other end. The other great big men wouldn't have gotten to midcourt by then. He does everything well, but his trademark may be that no big man has so enjoyed running or been able to run so well and so much. The key to beating a Chamberlain or Jabbar is to be where they aren't."

"I hate to see a big man walk," said Jarvis, once an assistant coach at Harvard under Satch Sanders.

On offense, Ewing can do the flashy things—fancy dribble, shoot a soft jumper, spin for finger rolls. He's a natural athlete and would be a fine forward at 6-6. But, unlike so many big men, he knows he's 7 feet and is determined to use every bit of his crushing natural advantage.

His whole offensive game is like a practice session for some higher league. He demonstrates early, to please the crowd, that he can do the cute stuff. Then he heads for the hole and spends the rest of the night polishing the thankless skills—fighting for position, spinning from one post to the other, timing his break for the lob pass, trying to get, or at least keep alive, every offensive rebound. Most surprising of all, Ewing is both greedy and unselfish. He is greedy in the sense that even when his team is far ahead he is bearing down more than any other player, trying to exhaust himself by gobbling every rebound, being a part of every fast break. Yet after the game he said, "I wasn't particularly intense tonight. I just enjoy the game. The coach takes me out and rests me so much [out of pity for the opponent] that I can't wait to get back in. I just hate to miss the fun."

By contrast, Ewing is unselfish in that he practically has a phobia about being singled out as better than his teammates. He always tries to pass before he shoots and takes more satisfaction in the "showtime" of his mates than his own.

This freshness, which Thompson calls "almost an innocence," probably should be credited to Jarvis.

"This has been the most unusual recruiting of any player of this magnitude in history," Thompson said. "For once, the player is recruiting the schools, instead of them recruiting him. Patrick takes the initiative and has the controls.

"For instance—and nobody will believe this—I couldn't find the gym tonight. I've never been here. I've never seen him play a high school game before. And I've never called him on the phone at home.

"If it weren't for the way Jarvis has run this, I wouldn't have had a chance. With Wilt, Moses, Sampson—any of them—to have a shot, I'd have had to spend more time in this gym than in my own. And I'd have had to be on the phone every night.

"For once, a great player has been recruited without anybody feeling they've prostituted themselves. Ewing hasn't solicited flattery. In fact, the whole thing has been done at such a high level that it almost frightens me. It's at the point where you think you must have forgotten something."

That's not to say that Boston hasn't been pleading with Ewing to stay home. On Monday night, Ewing's whole team was at the Boston College–Villanova game and the capacity Boston College crowd began several spontaneous chants of "We Want Ewing."

After the game, Ewing was in the Eagle locker room, where he had what the NCAA calls a "bump" with coach Davis. That means the player and the prospective coach just happen to be in the same place at the same time—bump into each other, don't you know?—and exchange a minimum of pleasantries, before running in opposite directions like a pair of Caesar's wives. Davis, rightfully gun-shy since his program has become tied up in the middle of an alleged point-shaving scandal, didn't say a word to Ewing, merely walking through his sphere of influence, casting a wholesome smile in his direction and nodding imperceptibly.

The style of his recruitment may be part of Ewing's legacy. "He hasn't been wined and dined and super-called," Thompson said. "The reason is entirely Ewing and Jarvis. No matter what anybody says, it's the kid and those around him who set the tone. . . .

"Every year at GU, I've felt that we lost at least one recruit because he thought we weren't really interested in him when, in fact, we were. Every year, I practically plead with the kid, saying, 'Don't judge me by how many telephone calls and visits I make. Judge my intentions, not my attentions. How can I do justice to the twelve players on my team if I'm spending all my time pampering you?' "

Thompson recalls a story about Seton Hall coach Bill Raftery, whose team was trailing by 30 points in a game last year. "He wrote a note on a slip of paper and sent it to the other team's coach via his manager. It said, 'I surrender.'

"I think," Thompson said, "that Cambridge Latin has probably been getting a lot of notes like that."

And, starting very soon, Thompson may begin getting them, too. But that won't be known until Monday, and Ewing, when he talks to the press, isn't giving any hints.

"I've talked to a couple of other guys who've been recruited," said Ewing, "and it's hard to believe what they say—being called on the phone twenty-five times a day. To tell the truth, I've barely noticed it."

The total number of calls from coaches that Ewing has received has been zero. Breaking this rule means expulsion from consideration.

"When I think about college," said Ewing. "I just think about how much fun it will be. Most of all, I want to see if I'm as good as everybody says I am." Whatever Ewing's final place in basketball history, he already has one distinction. No player of mega-talents has ever come through the pernicious American recruiting system with so little damage. "Guys say to me, 'Aren't people always bothering you?' " said Ewing with genuine perplexity. "I just say, 'No.' "

On the issue of the college of his heart's desire, Ewing just says, "I'm not saying nothin' until Monday."

And if that is Georgetown, the Hoyas, who have everyone back next season, surely will be ranked in the preseason top ten, and would have a strong shot at the NCAA championship. But no one of official rank at Georgetown wants to speculate on what the addition of Ewing would do to the program or the effort to build a new on-campus arena, for fear of offending Ewing—or breaking sticky NCAA rules.

It's all part of an absolutely unparalleled situation that has been created where a hermetically sealed star actually exists. "I'm gonna love this weekend," says Jarvis. "The papers have been guessing all along, but now they're getting desperate. I think it's hilarious. One paper that covers Georgetown has already said that Patrick is going there. Today, *The Boston Globe* called up and told me they were prepared to write a story, based on unnamed sources, that Ewing was definitely going to North Carolina. They just wanted my comment.

"That kills me. They've got sources. I'm his damn coach and I don't know where he's going."

Centers of Attention

Kareem

LOS ANGELES, May 6, 1980—

In America's world of hired muscle, Kareem Abdul-Jabbar stands tallest, both in base salary and in stature, 7-2 or more.

Finally, in his seventeenth year in national sports consciousness, Abdul-Jabbar, now thirty-three and balding, is performing with an enthusiasm and intensity that may bring his play up to the level of his reputation.

From Power Memorial High to UCLA to the Milwaukee Bucks to the Los Angeles Lakers, Abdul-Jabbar has proved to be the finest center of his era, mixing finesse with a dispassionate artistry. Abdul-Jabbar played basketball the way he did everything—with an aloof connoisseurship and an intimidatingly cold desire to please himself in a private domain beyond outside judgment.

Whether he was adding to his exotic personal collections—vintage boxing films, Oriental rugs, 3,000 jazz albums, texts on Asian philosophies, manuals on the martial arts—or mastering the finger roll, Abdul-Jabbar was a model only child of the '60s: brilliantly exceptional and self-centered.

Soaring sky hooks, balletic blocks and deft, no-look passes pleased his sense of what was most beautiful in basketball. He perfected the combined skills of shooting, shot blocking and passing as no other giant has ever done.

Rebounding, hustling in the transition game, shouldering the complexity of being a team leader or risking the exposure of his private feelings in the public arena did not appeal to him at all. So he largely ignored them.

Abdul-Jabbar established himself as one of the worst-rebounding 7-footers in history—his board stats barely half those of Wilt Chamberlain or Bill Russell.

His demeanor, especially during his decade in the NBA, was so enigmatic that it was bound to be interpreted as benign indifference at best or surly moodiness at worst.

It is hard for a gigantic black who can dunk on his tiptoes to hide in front of a million eyes, but Abdul-Jabbar, with his shy, nonviolent nature and his reclusive bent, did his best.

He turned thirty with a full beard, goggles that made him look like the Fly, a defiantly implacable exterior and a defiant faith in the Hanafi Muslims.

No wonder he was beset with migraines. Bright lights, noise and pressure could make him feel like "the Alien was trying to get out through my eyes."

Yet his whole basketball life was predicated on constant performance under pressure amid bright lights and noise.

Such a life full of contradictions might never have reached a pleasant place of psychic rest during Abdul-Jabbar's basketball career.

In recent seasons, as it became unavoidably noticeable that his teams had won only one world title in his first ten years, the constant poking at his guarded private life was exacerbated by caustic appraisals of his basketball skills.

Against this background, the most pleasing sight in these NBA finals may not be any particular dribble, pass or shot, but the expression of release and satisfaction on Abdul-Jabbar's face. As though hidden lesions had been broken beneath the skin, he has begun to show the normal range of emotions that are at work behind every human face.

After a lifetime of accentuating his differences, cultivating elitist tastes and refining the giant's natural gift for intimidating those within his sphere, Abdul-Jabbar has finally discovered that it does not diminish him to show that, basically, his heart works the same as those of smaller people.

"A lot of things have fallen into place this year, on and off the court, for Kareem," said his business representative, Tom Collins. "The chemistry is just right. Everything is going his way."

From a certain point of view, not a great deal has ever gone against Abdul-Jabbar. But growing up is never easy, especially when there is so much of you.

Abdul-Jabbar's streak of luck is long this year. The Lakers drafted Magic Johnson, a perfect point guard to complement any center. The Lakers' new coaches—first Jack McKinney, then Paul Westhead—were the most intelligent, the most naturally attuned to Abdul-Jabbar's views, of any that the center had ever had.

"If Kareem came back in another life, he would probably be a poet or artist. He has a great eye for details," said Westhead. "No NBA player has his concentration."

While most players' statistics shrink against the superior competition in the playoffs, Abdul-Jabbar's have always improved—his 30.2 playoff scoring average is the best in history. Then, and perhaps only then, has he deemed the game totally worthy of his attention.

The new Laker brain trust has also been cognizant that even an ecstatically happy Abdul-Jabbar will always need considerable rebounding help. A fleet of battleships has been imported for the purpose—6-foot-11 Jim Chones, Spencer Haywood and Mark Landsberger.

Although it's nobody's business, the best change in Abdul-Jabbar may have come from a saucy new girlfriend, who, he says delightedly, "is the first person who ever called me an 'ass' to my face. She's done a lot to help me take myself less seriously."

It is enormously difficult for a millionaire giant who has been feted since he was a child not to see himself as a sun around which others must revolve. Abdul-Jabbar has, however, always done well at looking out as well as inside.

"I notice everything. I always look into people's eyes," Abdul-Jabbar said this week—a span in which he has never been a more gracious interview. "I guess that, being a New Yorker, I developed what you might call a penchant for sitting back and observing.

"Some things I'm real sharp at. Other things escape me. I'm sharp at seeing things. But reading what you see can be a problem. . . . Maybe it's just naïveté, or just being too idealistic about things, but there's a lot of things about people that I don't understand."

This is a more modest tone of voice than that of the twenty-three-year-old who, when choosing a new name in place of Lew Alcindor, picked one whose translation meant "generous, powerful servant of Allah."

Like so many of the campus stars of a dozen years ago, so seriously and nobly self-absorbed, Abdul-Jabbar has—with age—picked up on a bit of Bob Dylan's self-deflating insight with "I was so much older then . . . I'm younger than that now." Now Abdul-Jabbar can grin on court, jump up and down in childish anger at a ref's bad call, slap hands with Johnson or go roller-discoing.

Abdul-Jabbar still cuts his eyes quickly to see what those around, and behind, him are making of him. His speech, at least outside his basketball inner circle, still has an ingrained cautiousness.

However, he will now attempt little jokes and plays on words. Of Seattle, he said, "They say they like to play with their backs against the wall. Well, they're about to go over the wall." When Philadelphia's Darryl Dawkins complained that the refs were protecting Abdul-Jabbar, he said cryptically, "Tell Darryl that if frogs had wings, they'd be swallows."

Last week, Abdul-Jabbar even made what he calls "my first locker-room speech" when he chewed out his mates at halftime against Seattle. The result: an instant Laker romp.

Laker boss Jerry Buss is so pleased with his obviously altered star that, supposedly without provocation, he tore up Abdul-Jabbar's paltry $650,000-a-year pact for two more seasons and extended it to an easy-to-remember $1 million a season for four more years.

If, amidst this confluence of good fortune, good teammates and universal affection, Abdul-Jabbar were not playing the best in years, that would be the surprise.

Chamberlain had his muscle and vanity, Russell his scowl and mystery—and his manic laugh. Abdul-Jabbar, after years of yoga, self-defense training and meditation, is discovering that a smile and some old-fashioned pep may be what works best for him.

He has the NBA tying itself into knots with mind games.

The 76ers have temporarily given up on letting Dawkins, the fundamentally atrocious Lovetronian, play defense on Abdul-Jabbar, switching him instead, for Wednesday's second game, to the Lakers' humble collection of big forwards.

Caldwell Jones, 7-foot-1, will start on Abdul-Jabbar. And what does Jones think? "I'll try to hold him under thirty-five. If he gets forty, you really got problems."

Sixers assistant coach Chuck Daly holds out similar low hopes for the Philly defense: "Once Kareem gets the ball down low, you couldn't stop him with an airplane."

Abdul-Jabbar, naturally, will not concede that his performance has altered this season. "It's just that time of year," he says, meaning that the playoffs are his meat. Others know differently, and tease Abdul-Jabbar very softly.

"Kareem is gettin' old," says Jamaal Wilkes, loudly enough for him to over-hear. "The man definitely wants another [championship] ring on his finger."

"I am old," Abdul-Jabbar replies with a smile. "And I want this as much as I can want anything."

Throughout his Laker career, when the gold-clads have been in fourth-quarter trouble, they have made no secret of their basic play. It's called fist down, with the sign for it being a fist held down and to the side. What it means is get the ball to Kareem in the low post if you have to drop-kick it in there.

Fist down is still the most devastating and unstoppable single play in basketball—get it to Abdul-Jabbar, then get out of his way.

But a fist is no longer the proper symbol.

"To me," said Abdul-Jabbar's longtime friend Lucius Allen, "he has be-come the Kareem he always wished he could be."

The fist is gradually to show the true hand of the man.

Moses

December 31, 1986—The highest-paid man in Washington earns every penny. Long after his workmates are gone, he sits on a stool and watches the clock. Not to punch out. The ice needs time to do its job. Ice can't be rushed. But it's dependable, like him. He has punished himself to his limit. Now his warrior's body must heal. Ice encases both knees. A tub of ice soothes his foot. One thumb is taped, a finger splinted. He looks like a gigantic old king, exhausted, but with battles still to fight in wars not yet even imagined.

Moses Malone is legal tender. You can take him to the bank. He makes $2 million a year and is a bargain. What he gives a team, and the city that's lucky enough to watch him, is an appreciation of homiletic phrases like "the dignity of labor," "know thyself" and "through mastery of one thing, all things." An honest man is still hard to find, but an honest workman plays center for the Washington Bullets.

Monday at Capital Centre was Hard-Core Night. Only serious NBA types show up for the Warriors. Moses, the avatar of the hard core, showed up, too. For the cognoscenti, he had 35 points, 11 rebounds and 3 blocks and put the whole Golden State team in foul trouble with 21 for 22 free throws. Malone made 16-foot jumpers, drove to the hoop from the circle, filled lanes on the fast break and twice even led fast breaks. Golden State sent three centers against him; they shot 6 for 24. In the final minute of a

20-point romp, Malone was the only starter left on court—still contesting a meaningless offensive rebound. Tip, tip, keep it alive, Bullets' ball. For his exit, a standing ovation.

The Philadelphia 76ers traded Malone last summer thinking he was worn out, ready for the scrap heap. Deal him while somebody's still dumb enough to pay top dollar for a war-horse about ready to drop. "An old thirty-one," they called him, the same words the Cincinnati Reds once pinned on Frank Robinson, the year before he won the American League MVP award.

One-third through the NBA regular season, a preliminary verdict has been reached. The Bullets robbed the 76ers blind.

As long as the ice holds out, Malone seems tolerably productive. He leads the NBA in rebounding, in offensive rebounds and in drawing fouls. He is averaging 25.8 points a game, his best mark in five years. He has never shot free throws so well (.837). He is blocking more shots than he has since he was a rookie. No team has ever asked him to play so far out on the floor so often or run the court so much.

"He has much better outside skills than I thought," says coach Kevin Loughery. "The more minutes he plays, the better he gets. His intensity just wears out the other team, then he starts raisin' it another notch, maybe two or three."

There may be a snap, crackle or pop down the road. But so far Malone has been indestructible, while the other pivot of the trade, Jeff Ruland, played just two 76ers games before going down with a chronic knee injury. Also in the deal, Terry Catledge gives the Bullets as much as Cliff Robinson did, and with more gusto. And the Bullets get a No. 1 pick in '88.

"Soon as you turn thirty, people start saying you can't play no more. My mind is strong enough to have three or four more good years," says Malone. And as far as he's concerned, that makes it so.

How good the Bullets may be when they get Jay Vincent in action is a New Year's puzzle. They're a guard shy and will stay that way. Roles remain in flux. "We haven't jelled yet," they say. But some teams never do. What's certain is that the Bullets now can dream big without evoking scorn. When you have one of the five greatest centers who ever lived, all things are conceivable.

The town knows this. Bullets crowds are up about 3,000 a game, and Malone is the reason. He has marquee value in a city that adores the best but ignores the rest. "My wife and kids love it here," says Malone, basso profundo. "It's cleaner, less snow, less holes in the road. A better living city. And the fans really know the game."

That's vital because Malone would hate to do what he does for people who don't even know what they're seeing. Few exhibits in a city of museums are so worthy of appreciation.

Malone has a pot tummy, swayback, receding hairline, knock knees, skinny legs, swollen ankles, goggles over his eyes and small, almost delicate hands. "Got point guard hands." Yes, he's a piece of work.

The foes who fear him look like carvings from granite that should be set in a town square. Most are bigger than the 6-foot-10, 255-pound Malone, and younger and higher-leaping. What Malone has are the sudden, decisive movements around the basket of a man 5-foot-10, the dexterous hands of a guard, the threshold of pain of a suspension bridge and the heart of a paratroop division.

One second, he's beating on you in the pivot like a cop with a nightstick; the next, he has spun and gone before the pain of his last elbow to the neck has even reached your brain. He has the smartest elbows and hips in basketball.

The perspiration that pours from Malone's goatee, dripping on the floor in the first quarter before any other player has even broken a sweat, is a kind of human poetry. Where others show up for work, Malone, like that other simple man, Larry Bird, shows up to test others and define the best in himself.

"My game's hard work and pride," he says. "On the all-hard-work team, I'd pick myself five times.

"My main thing is concentration. It's a thinking game. Be wise. Study them, what they do best . . . If I get too Hollywood, I might lose it."

Malone is in no danger of being seduced by glamour. It has taken him too long and cost too much to get where he is. His jumper, his free-throw touch, those quick dribbles when he "takes it to the rack" have been thirteen pro years in the making. Even the sentences that rumble out, like coal tumbling down a chute, have been won at hard labor over his great shyness and limited education. Malone is a dignified, even pithy man.

What is it like to have the highest salary in Washington?

"Not me," says Moses Malone. "That's my wife."

Lt. Robinson

ANNAPOLIS, February 22, 1987—

The finished product met the unfinished fantasy. The gym rat who never grew to 6 feet met the brainy computer kid who never cared about basketball until he suddenly grew to be more than 7 feet.

Kevin Houston of Army, one of the most distinctive little-known players in the history of the college game, tried to gun down the Top Gun, David Robinson, in that surefire All-America's tearful last home game for Navy.

The 5-foot-11 shrimp who can't run, can't jump, has few muscles and never gets off a shot that doesn't come within a millimeter of being stuffed showed why he is the nation's leading scorer. Averaging about 32 points a game, in one chill-producing 9:58 chunk of the first half, Houston outscored Robinson 25–0 and left packed Halsey Field House numb with awe.

Inviting defenders to drape him, then firing through cracks like a boy sticking a peashooter through a chain link fence, Houston missed only one shot and one free throw as Army led 28–23. At that point, he had outscored the entire Navy team. Think on that. Navy coach Pete Herrmann did: "He's a definite All-America. He's so good we're proud of him—and he plays for them."

That was the high-water mark for magic. How many lean-in, fall-back, in-your-face, high-arc shots can hit nothing but net? "You get that rhythm, you get that feeling . . . You're carried along with the flow of the crowd. It's perfect surroundings and you just let it hang out," said Houston. "You don't feel like it can be stopped. I wish the first half had lasted a little longer."

In the end, the team with a developing Goliath named David beat the one with a polished David named Kevin. Navy won, 58–52, though Houston prevailed—38–18—in a personal showdown that will endure as the most interesting hoop war in service academy history.

"If anybody sees a better show than that in the NCAAs, call me and tell me which game it was," said Army coach Les Wothke. "I'd like to enter an Army-Navy all-star team in the NCAA tournament, because we have two All-Americas who're a credit to all service academies."

The crowd of 6,485 hardly knew which to focus upon: Robinson, whose basketball odyssey is just beginning, or Houston, whose career is almost over, just as it was starting to be noticed.

Houston played the perfect foil. It requires years of hardwood study to learn how to command the space around you on the court and fill it with an entirely personal style. That's what Robinson wants to learn. Houston already has. If he were a Thoroughbred horse, you'd say he was Kevin Houston by St. John's star Jerry Houston out of coach Joe Lapchick. Rocker steps and ball fakes are in his blood. Scraping you off a pick is his birthright. Leaping into a defender to use quickness to neutralize height is his signature. Others square up their whole bodies to shoot properly; Houston needs to square up his index finger.

Send this day's film to Springfield so all memory of Houston won't be lost.

He's headed to the artillery (of course). "If the NBA happens five years down the road, I'll take a crack at it," said Houston. "If it doesn't, I won't be disappointed."

It won't. For some players, like Houston and Ernie DiGregorio, college ball is the perfect stage, just as for others, like Robinson, it is really a poor and painful place to showcase. Before this game, Robinson and other seniors presented roses to their parents at midcourt and got tearful hugs as the crowd gave a standing ovation. "I'm not that sentimental," said the 7-foot-1 Robinson. "I said, 'Aw, come on, Mom.'"

Robinson needed all the game face he could muster. Houston has faced, in his coach's words, "every defense that can be drawn." Robinson has faced every elbow to the kidney, knuckle to the neck and knee to the thigh that less gifted bruisers can administer. He never had a rougher day than this. Army's not tall, but it's wide. And deep. Four Cadets took turns practicing their martial arts on Robinson at close range, collecting 18 fouls.

"Just trying to get me agitated," Robinson said of the tactics, shrugging. "There'll be a lot of bumping in the NBA, but at least the people will be trying to play basketball. When a shot goes up and two guys face you and block you out with their best football blocks and they never even look back at the ball, that's ridiculous."

Actually, Robinson was underestimating Army's strategy. "We wanted somebody on his left shoulder, somebody on his right shoulder and somebody behind him," said Wothke. "He's 7-foot-94 [sic] and a great player. You can't let him go where he wants to go. Still, eventually he wore us down and took charge of the boards. That was the difference in the game."

All that's best and worst in Robinson's game was on display. Those 18 points and 13 rebounds don't look bad. Nor did the shot that put Navy ahead to stay when Robinson almost had the ball stripped, recaught it airborne and sank an impromptu on-the-way-down jump shot for a 50–48 lead.

On the other hand, if Navy had lost, and it could have, Robinson would have been the goat. Five foul shots he missed in the closing minutes—all leading off one-and-ones. Can't squander 10 points.

With Robinson, the starting point of all discussion is an understanding that, when he came to Navy, he was the sort of sweet-tempered, gawky teenager who gravitated to science fairs, chess tournaments and libraries. Unlike other giants of sport, the first impression that Robinson leaves is of a sparking, not yet fully focused, almost kinetic intelligence. Those Rhodes scholar grinds Tom McMillen and Bill Bradley were impressive for their diligence; Robinson comes across as quicker and more imaginative. His mind makes you forget his body in a blink.

Ending now is the first stage of David Robinson's metamorphosis, the shedding of his chrysalis. Now, like Houston and so many others who have narrowed their world for a few years to the size of a gymnasium, Robinson must go about the long, hard labor of turning himself into the finished product.

The Shooter

January 15, 1980—The sports Americans have created, and still love best, all hinge on the flick of a wrist.

The spiral of a forward pass, the biting snap of a curveball, the soft backspin of a jump shot are the hallmarks of our indigenous team games.

Among our native creations—football, baseball and basketball—perhaps there is no central weapon as democratic, yet undeniably aristocratic, as the jump shot.

Everybody's got one, but they sure aren't equal. Occasionally a shooter can be made. But mostly they're born. The gift of "touch" is a silver spoon, even if it is discovered on the bleakest playgrounds.

The shot—its quality and purity—is the gold standard of the hoop world. The gifted shooter carries with him a sense of princely authority, a kind of regal legerdemain. To any predicament, he has the solution. Possessor of an invisible scepter, he is an heir to adulation.

"When you feel a streak comin' on, you become unconscious; you feel like you could lie on your back, close your eyes, and it would go in," says George Washington University coach Bob Tallent, who has the highest scoring average (28.9) of any major college player in Washington area history (as a Colonial in 1968–69).

"You could feel ten or eleven in a row comin' on," says Tallent. "When you get like that, it doesn't matter what defense they're in, or who's on your team. The rest of the game fades away.

"You get hot and that's it. The game belongs to you until you cool down. You know what you're doing and where you are, but it's like you're in a trance, or surrounded by some kind of aura."

Most of basketball humanity has to blend and flow, fitting into a five-man jazz ensemble where the riffs are shared and the harmony, not the solos, is what matters.

But the shooter always senses a higher possibility, the chance to wire into the collective fantasies of the crowd.

"Every fan is just waiting to get on your wavelength and give you their energy," says Tallent.

"The shot is a total motion, a groove. No two shooters are alike, but they feel the same when they're on," says Kevin Grevey of the Washington Bullets, lifelong bomber and NBA "H-O-R-S-E" semifinalist.

"With a crazy streak shooter like me, one or two baskets will trigger me. I'll start throwing them in from everywhere. It pumps up your whole game. You do everything better and your confidence and concentration are total." Like any gunslinger, the shooter has his nightmares.

"What you do to others, they can do to you," says Grevey. "If Cazzie Russell missed his first few shots, he'd play terrible defense all night. If he made his first one, he was like a man possessed.

"The in-your-face guys can drive you crazy. When Doug Collins [of Philadelphia] got hot against me in the playoffs one year [28 points in one half], I felt like that cartoon character Ricochet Rabbit. I thought I was a ball caught inside a pinball machine.

"When they shoot you down, you just want to hide."

The quarterback and the pitcher—those other protagonists in our most common athletic fantasies—always have forces working in opposition to them. They are always at the mercy of others to some degree, whether teammates or foes.

The shooter is the most nearly solitary of our team heroes. At his instant of truth, after he has dribbled, driven or scraped off a screen, there is nothing in his universe except the ball in his hand, the rim in his eye and the righteousness born of a lifetime's practice in his heart.

"Shooters are oblivious," says Catholic University coach Jack Kvancz. Sometimes it seems like they don't think at all. They don't get the sweaty palm.

"When the game gets tight, they want it. They want it when everybody else is glad to give it up. Shooters, as a group, aren't even the best athletes on the team.

"How do you make people like that?"

Tallent knows where the making of a shooter starts. When he was twelve years old, growing up in the mountains of eastern Kentucky, where every Appalachian peak seemed to produce a Zeke from Cabin Creek, Tallent came under the sway of "King" Kelly Coleman.

"All shooters start by imitation," says Tallent. "I hitchhiked thirteen miles each way so I could rebound for him and throw the ball back to him. I was in the sixth grade and he was averaging 18 points a game for Waylon High.

"Like all shooters, there were lots of tall tales about King Kelly, some of 'em pretty-near true.

"Adolph Rupp said he was better than Frank Ramsey and Cliff Hagan combined. So that's all you need to know," says Tallent. "But Kelly had a wild streak. Oblivious on the court and off it.

"I remember them throwing him in the shower for the whole first half of a high school game. He scored 42 in the second half.

"When he played my school, we double-teamed him from the moment he stepped off the bus. We held him to 75 points," said Tallent.

"He was a big sloppy-looking guy—6 foot 4, 220 pounds," recalls Tallent.

"But he could do anything. One time they booed him for three nights in a row in the state tournament, even though he scored 52, 46, and 29.

"He was crying after the third game and told the reporters, 'By God, I'll show these city people. I'll score 70.'

"He didn't, though," says Tallent. "He only got 68. But it's still the state tournament record."

Every area of America, from Iowa to Far Rockaway to Turkey Thicket playground in Northeast Washington, has its King Kellys. For every long-distance runner, there are hundreds who savor the loneliness of the long-distance shooter, practicing from the moment the sun rises over the mountain or the tenement.

"The only generalization you can make about shooters is that they can all put it in the hole," says Bobby Dandridge of the Bullets. "There are pure shooters, improvisational shooters like me, mechanical shooters like Elvin Hayes and guys like George Gervin with weird releases.

"I never went to any basketball camps," says Dandridge with an appropriate curl of the lip. "I don't know any of that jive about fingertips and watching the rim and making your arm look like a box.

"I'm a playground scorer. I don't have a shot. I have many shots," says the owner of 15,000 NBA points.

"I may change my release two or three times a season. Sometimes I don't know if I release the ball with one hand or two. I go on my emotions. If my emotions say I'm going to make the shot, then I'm going to make it."

The inside of a shooter's mind is the last frontier. Perhaps no aspect of any sport is as inexplicably streaky as shooting. Whole teams go hot and cold, defying probability by being both incredibly good and bad in the same game.

"Practice is different from games, and even various parts of the game are different," says Kvancz. "Some guys can shoot at four P.M., but not eight. And some can shoot at eight, but not in the final minutes.

"I don't coach perfect form because, in the clutch, the elbow sticks out, the feet kick and the kid reverts to all the habits he's had all his life. I tell 'em, 'Drop-kick it in if you have to. Shoot the way it's comfortable, not the way that looks good, because it's mostly in your mind anyway.' "

In fact, the basket is rather wide. It is the mind that is narrow. If the hoop were only four inches wider, two balls could go through it at once.

"It's scary to see a good shooter go bad," says Kvancz. "One year, Glenn Kolonics [a top scorer at CU] was going so rotten that I ordered him to grow a beard. I told him he couldn't shave until he had a good shooting game.

"Well, Kolonics looked like Grizzly Adams before he ever got his touch back."

"I remember the shot when he got it back," says Tallent. "Kolonics came into our gym in January with this full beard. His first shot hit the back rim, bounced about ten feet straight up and swished on the way down.

"That was it. You could see his eyes wake up. He lit us up for about 32 that night."

Most great shooters know they will be roughed up, punched, gouged and elbowed. It comes with the turf. And most react as Jerry West once did.

"Kentucky put in a big old horse named Allen Feldhaus to do some enforcing against West when he was at West Virginia," says Tallent. "In two minutes, Feldhaus had broken West's nose and sent him to the dressing room.

"Jerry came back in the second half with a face mask on and scored 24 points. When you get the good ones angry, it just helps their concentration. When you're mad, sometimes you think you'll never miss again. Pat [Tallent] and I both kinda liked it rough."

Perhaps the most despised shooters are not the streakers or the guys who talk trash or even those who seem to shoot better the more closely they are guarded. The worst are the shooters who add injury to insult.

"I used to hate Zelmo Beaty," says Bullet Wes Unseld. "He couldn't jump much and he couldn't shoot too well if he was closely guarded. So he worked out a shot to keep defenders away from him.

"His release was designed so that his follow-through would clobber you in the face. He slugged me hundreds of times for free."

"The worst at that today is Lloyd Free," says Unseld's teammate Greg Ballard. "He's got his leg kick at the end of his shot perfected so that he kicks you in the groin. Then he's the one who falls down, rolls around and gets the foul called his way."

A whole language has grown up around the jumper: jack it up, stop-and-pop, shoot the J, fire the pill, shoot the rock, run-and-gun, hoist it, fill it up.

The permutations never end.

"They call me the Heist Man," says Barry Frazier, who was a 35-point-a-game jump shooter for the small-college University of the District of Columbia. "Why? Because I can really heist it."

Those occasional dark hours come when the shot disappears.

"Sometimes you think you couldn't throw it in the ocean," says Grevey. Adds Tallent, "I can't believe it but even Brian Magid [of GW] has gone into a slump. He's seven for his last thirty-one, and he's got the longest range I've ever seen."

But for the shooter the dawn always comes.

"You get alone in the gym and say, 'Think soft,'" says Grevey. "You see how many shots you can get off in thirty seconds. That way, you don't have time for flaws. You go back to your old instincts."

Or, like Bill Bradley, you start with lay-ups and never shoot from more than ten feet until you have made twenty-five in a row and thus reinforced your confidence.

Finally, the shooter gets the one break he needs—a sloppy roll, or a bounce that goes straight up, then down and through. Suddenly, the fantasy, the dream of a thousand solitary hours, becomes a temporary reality.

"You're hot," says Tallent, remembering. "You and the crowd have a special relationship. They call you a gunner, and they never give you credit for the other parts of the game that you can play. But when you're hot, they're all with you.

"Was I a gunner?" Tallent laughs, the chuckle of a shooter. "Hell, yes. You're cocky. You can't believe it if you miss. You feel unstoppable.

"I always knew that if I had room, if I could see the basket, it was goin' up. And the hell with what anybody thought."

Does that touch ever leave? Can Rabbit Angstrom, years later, running through the back alleys of John Updike's mind, always pick up the ball from schoolchildren and recapture the sweet loneliness of the long jumper?

Tallent smiles. "It never leaves."

Interlude

How Windy
Is That SkyDome?

April 13, 1990—Baseball is not necessarily an obsessive-compulsive disorder, like washing your hands a hundred times a day, but it's beginning to seem that way. We're reaching the point where you can be a truly dedicated, state-of-the-art fan or you can have a life. Take your pick.

These days, longtime baseball lovers face tough questions. Do you have to be in a Rotisserie league? Is it mandatory to read the *Elias Baseball Analyst* cover to cover with a highlight pen? If you haven't digested Bill James's latest 598-pager, are you still allowed to express an opinion while in the park?

Finally, with saturation baseball on cable, are we allowed to just say no to multiple games on TV almost every day?

The last straw for me was the new baseball box score in *USA Today*.

In more than a third of a century of following baseball, I can honestly say that I've never looked at a box score and thought, "I wonder which way the wind was blowing." Now, I'll always know.

This box score also tells us how many runners each hitter left on base, how many pitches each pitcher threw (and how many strikes), how many inherited runners a reliever allowed to score, and (we are not making this up) the ratio of grounders to flies for each pitcher.

Baseball, often a refuge from the boredom of nit-picking reality, seems to have invented a new kind of homework. Once you could escape *to* baseball. Soon, it may be hard to escape *from* it.

It should be noted that this protest is being written by a lifelong baseball nut. I've been guilty of inventing new statistics and analyzing anything that breathes. My position always has been that baseball was uniquely appealing because it was so open to inspection. "Only dull to dull minds," as Red Smith said. Like any fan, I wanted more data.

Then, in the '80s, I got it. Slowly, at first. Then, by the gross. My wishes were granted with a vengeance. On opening day this week in New York, as Pirates pitcher Doug Drabek (a .132 career hitter) faced the Mets' Dwight Gooden with the bases loaded, I harangued the reporter next to me about The Info Overload Crisis. "When are we going to learn that baseball, despite all the stats, is a hopelessly open system? It's inherently unscientific. You can't really prove anything. Why don't we go back toward the mystery and poetry of the game?"

Drabek cracked a two-run single off Gooden. "See," I said. "Who could have predicted that?"

The victim of my speech got out his *Elias Baseball Analyst* and turned to Gooden's page. "The batter Gooden most hates to face," it said, "is Doug Drabek, 4 for 6 with two doubles."

That, of course, is the problem. Some of the new stuff is just wonderful. I never dreamed anybody would be able to tell me Steve Finley hit .286 on balls hit to the right side, .471 straight away and .154 to the opposite field. Or that, in his career, Bo Jackson bats .298 against groundball pitchers (pitchers who induce more grounders than flies) but only .204 vs. flyballers —the largest such gap of any player in ten years. Everybody in baseball knows that Bo, like Greg Luzinski (the last comparably muscled man), can't hit a fastball above the belt or anything on his hands. But it's nice to know the size of Bo's problem. No wonder he hit .053 in late-inning pressure stops with runners in scoring position. He's helpless against top relievers with the game on the line.

However, even those of us who think that Elias and James have arrived at a similar and enormously useful place, feel the need to draw a line somewhere.

Perhaps the most fanatical of all baseball stat fiends are the half-million folks who've formed their own Rotisserie leagues. They pay money to draft real players onto their imaginary teams. At the end of each season, the team with the best stats (according to arbitrary criteria) wins the most money from the pot. Simple. Apparently addictive. We all make choices. I hate Rotisserie baseball.

So, I asked my friend Steve Wulf of *Sports Illustrated,* who invented the darn thing, how his bloody cottage industry was doing. "I'm completely sated with it," he said. "It has gotten out of hand."

In particular, it bothers Wulf that the stats used to evaluate Rotisserie players have, to some, become synonymous with real excellence. Simplistic fantasy and complex reality become confused. "There's a big difference between a great Rotisserie player and a great baseball player," said Wulf. "Please quote me. . . . It even worries me that two owners, Bill Giles [Philadelphia] and George Bush [Texas], own Rotisserie teams. The next owner of the Padres too."

If you own a real team, why would you own a Rotisserie team? Sorry, I forgot. The Phillies and Rangers. If you owned them, it might be nice to start over.

Our problem in this Info Glut is one of selection. Personally, I'm obsessed with the *Elias Baseball Analyst.* When it was first published, I thought God had read my mind. Since most of the *Analyst* is raw, uninterpreted data, 99 percent of the book is junk. That makes it neater. You get to dig for gold. And there's plenty in a book with hundreds of thousands of entries.

Still, even the best of Elias and James is a little troubling. Many of us originally turned to baseball as a mild rebellion against the Information Age. There was too much to know about too many important subjects. As a result, the world felt less manageable even as it became more knowable. In one corner, we wanted to reverse that trend. Baseball was a smallish, not too important subculture of 650 players where, without enormous effort, it was possible to know most of what was worth knowing. Also, what was not known about baseball had a lovely open-ended mysteriousness about it.

Who was better in the clutch—Babe Ruth or Lou Gehrig? Why couldn't Warren Spahn beat the Dodgers? Was Ted Williams as good a run producer in the late innings of close games as Joe DiMaggio? We have no answers. How nice! Well, that is not the case any more. We've reached the point where there's no end to how much we can dissect the thing we love.

But should we? Man seeks knowledge and, often to his dismay, finds ways to acquire it. Once picked, the apple must be eaten. Once it has been eaten, the garden isn't quite the same.

Ray Leonard

Sugar Ray, Inc.

March 30, 1980—Sugar Ray Leonard is the champ that nobody owns.

Because of it, the parasitical promoters, middlemen and managers of boxing are afraid that he will succeed. Already, some of them, particularly promoter Don King, are laying traps to bushwhack him and take his crown if he won't buckle under and pay tribute.

Leonard wants to prove that a fighter with only a high school education—and a couple of honest friends—can bypass the grifters, own himself, make millions of bucks and handle himself with dignity. This is a new idea in boxing. To many in the predatory sport, Sugar Ray Leonard, Inc., looks more dangerous with a fountain pen in his hand than with a glove on it.

Now that he is welterweight champion, Leonard is finding out just how down-and-dirty his business is. In the four months since he stopped Wilfredo Benitez, Leonard has struggled on several fronts to prove that there are no strings on him.

"People still see me as that kid with the Olympic medal around his neck and his hands full of play money," he said. "They mistake my kindness for weakness. But my kiddie days are over. I have responsibilities. I'm as grown a man as I'm ever going to be. If I could do, say, go like I did when I had nothing, I'd be the happiest man in the world. But I can't."

Sometimes, Leonard and his adviser–best friend Janks Morton will take a car ride at 3 A.M. just to think, talk, feel the road flying under them. Just to be free and simple again. "We just ride," said Morton. "We've been all around the beltway in the middle of the night." But when the car stops, Leonard always reaches the same conclusion. "I've changed. I'm older. I have to advance and find out what's next on the agenda."

Leonard has declared his independence—his new agenda, his metamorphosis into the adult champ—in several ways. First, he assumed the responsibilities of a family in a full legal sense by marrying his childhood sweetheart, Juanita Wilkerson, in a ceremony with their six-year-old son, Ray Jr., as ring bearer. Then Leonard drastically shook up his entourage.

"Basically, it's just Mike Trainer [attorney], Janks and me now," said Leonard. "We make all the decisions."

When he was a child, Leonard was swaddled with advisers. Now, as his own captain, he has trimmed ship. "A couple of people had to learn who was working for whom," said Morton. "They worked for Ray, not he for them." Eased to the background has been Leonard's childhood trainer, Dave Jacobs. "Dave just couldn't stop thinking of Ray as his little-boy son," said Morton.

Another person with lessened sway is Angelo Dundee. "Angelo was pushing him to the front a little too much, or, at least, letting other people give him too much credit for matchmaking and career guidance that he knew he wasn't responsible for," said Trainer. "This show only has one star and that's Ray."

"I'm a lesser character in this play," Dundee said with a smile.

In that eternal boxing game of who-gets-credit-for-creating-the-champ, it is Morton and Leonard himself who now get the accolades. "Without Janks, there wouldn't be any Sugar Ray Leonard," said Leonard.

In the ring, Leonard believes he is just beginning to find his true style.

"Against Benitez, people didn't see me, just a shadow," said Leonard. "In the future, I'll be a better craftsman, and more artistic, too. [Muhammad] Ali called me the night before the Benitez fight and told me not to do anything flashy because the judges would resent me hot-dogging against a world champion. 'None of our stuff,' he said. I was a basic boxer that night, and very cautious. Now I can go back to fighting my way because I'm the champ. You have to take a chance to get a chance. I'm so relaxed now. No worries. I'm thinking clearer.

"That night against Benitez, I was almost psyched out in the ring. I felt hypnotized or lost. I went rounds without hearing what my corner said. I've never been so mentally exhausted. Now, I can go back to doing my thing."

Out of the ring, in his alter-ego life as a twenty-three-year-old black businessman, Leonard has also shifted gears and given new orders to those around him. The Leonard-Morton-Trainer triangle has decided to tone down Sugar Ray's gallivanting, tub-thumping style as the challenger who would promote his fights with any PR gimmick. "To do some of the things he used to do would be embarrassing now," said Trainer. "We've told some people who have helped us a lot in the past not to sell him so hard. I've told Ray that in promotions and advertisements, if you start cheap, you end cheap. Ray may have been caught doing a few demeaning things in the past. That won't happen anymore."

"Janks and Mike have told me, 'Don't sell your face for free. People can get sick of looking at anybody.' We're cautious. We observe. We're willing to wait and go for the big ones because I'm there now."

And, at last, the big ones are coming to Leonard, who wants very much to join O. J. Simpson as one of the few black athletes who have become what Leonard calls "commercial men." Endorsements from Ford, 7-Up and a Boston sporting-goods firm are already signed and a multiyear contract for more than a million dollars with Adidas is close to fruition, according to Trainer. TV commentator work with Home Box Office, as well as a TV special with Shirley MacLaine are lined up.

"Now, the offers that we were never sure would come have come," said Trainer. "I may feel like a genius now, but I could just as easily have felt like an idiot."

Potential for considerable bitterness has been avoided. "The business angle of all this has been crazy and cruel," said Morton. "It's hurt Ray plenty." Sensationalized stories about Juanita filing a paternity suit against Ray when, in fact, she had merely filled out forms to get food stamps long hurt Leonard's endorsement chances.

"It killed every commercial he could have gotten after the Olympics," claimed Morton. "Bruce Jenner puts his face on a cereal box. Mark Spitz, who can't even talk on camera, holds up an after-shave bottle. All he has to do is not drop it. Ray, who's a natural actor, has to work four more years after the Olympics to start getting major offers. It's better not to think about it too hard. Ray doesn't. I've seen him come from a dollar to a million with a smile."

Leonard has asserted his adulthood in many ways—as father and responsible family man, as a fighter determined to define his own style and name his own advisers and as a jock businessman with precious few years to capitalize on his fame. His toughest and most important battle of independence, however, has just begun. Leonard has taken on the whole structure of the boxing establishment.

Nobody owns a percentage piece of Leonard and never has since the day Morton brought in his buddy, Trainer, to make Leonard a one-man corporation who wouldn't be cheated or corrupted. "I've seen athletes gypped and forgotten all my life," said Morton. "I have a high school friend who played thirteen years in the NFL and made all-pro. Now he's in a car wash. For once, I didn't want the world to win."

Instead of selling percentages of himself, Leonard pays a flat fee for services rendered to him. He has been his own matchmaker and his own promoter. His lawyer negotiated his own private TV packages and his arena deals.

Boxing has never heard of any of this before. A legion of sticky-fingered middlemen were getting frozen out. "We work very hard to make money," said Trainer, who is retained on a flat hourly fee basis. "But we are making it for Ray—not the matchmaker, the promoter, the arena owner, the agent, the manager, the trainer. All these do-nothing middlemen, who just make a few phone calls, are being asked, 'What's your cut?' It scares them to death. We offer them a fair profit. They want an under-the-table killing."

"Mike and I want to see the day when Ray only has verbal agreements with people around him," said Morton. "That puts him in total control. He can fire anybody on the spot. After all, prizefighting is a very special sort of profession. When the bell rings, we all grab the buckets and stools and run out. It's Ray who has to take his life in his hands in the ring.

"Nobody should own a fighter. You have a contract or a license on a dog, not a person. It doesn't sound businesslike, I know. But if a man's word isn't good, what else is left?"

This new monster—Sugar Ray Leonard, Inc., which really means Leonard's fists, Morton's heart and Trainer's savvy—unsettles boxing so much because it is uncontrollable. "I never touched boxing before Ray, and the day he's finished, I'm finished," said Trainer. "Nobody else in boxing will speak up because they all feel that they can be taken advantage of somewhere down the road when they're handling some other fighter or when they need a favor.

"I'll grant that Sugar Ray is a special case because of his TV fame from the Olympics. Nevertheless, we're trying to prove the ideal case of how a promising fighter can be handled with his own good at heart. To one degree or another, what we've done can be done with any quality fighter anywhere."

What do boxing's powers say to this? "Ray Leonard is ducking Roberto Duran, the number one welterweight contender," said Don King, who "owns" the rights to promote any Duran fight. "Leonard is turning his back on the American people. He's getting bad advice from Mike Trainer. If Leonard won't fight, we'll see that the WBC strips him of his title."

Of all Leonard's decisions in the last four months, his most far-reaching is to fight the powerful King tooth and nail. He's given Trainer the word to take off the kid gloves. "We've offered Duran a million-dollar guarantee plus a percentage of the entire fight proceeds," said Trainer. "That's double his best fight purse.

"I've also made a fair and profitable offer to King for his services—in a limited capacity. King can handle the foreign TV rights, the undercard contracts and the arena revenue at the second site for the undercard. If he worked it well, that could bring him five to six hundred thousand dollars," said Trainer. "But that's not nearly enough for King. He's seen this payday coming for years. In fact, he's bankrolled on it.

"To control Duran, King's paid him very well over the years—more than he was worth, and maybe even some out of King's own pocket . . . So, King's in a panic. Out of frustration, he's acting ridiculous and irrational about the Leonard fight. He's probably promised Duran two million, and counted on plenty for himself, too. It was a helluva shock for him to come to me and be told we didn't need or want him, but that we'd give him a cut to be friendly. King's position is that if he cannot promote the fight—and at the profit that he deems fit—it simply will not take place. Nothing to do with Leonard. But everything to do with King," said Trainer.

The Leonard camp has no illusion that virtue and Sugar Ray's handsome smile are going to help them through this briar patch of intrigue. "King thought I couldn't buck him," said Trainer. "Or he thought he could mesmerize me like he does boxing people with his ridiculous parables about tigers eating lions. Or he thought we'd buckle when he started slinging mud, like saying last week that I'd offered Duran five hundred thousand under the table to buy his contract away from King.

"We've learned that only one thing works with these people. If you don't have options, you're cooked. If they know they're the only game in town, they've got you. They've made me feel like I'm representing the challenger, not the champ, the way I've been phoning and sending letters for months with no response whatsoever. But we're not going to crack. It's against every sound business principle we've tried to prove can work.

"This sanctioning and paying off is a farce. The day's coming when it will be abolished. Then these guys will be out in the cold. They've picked the wrong time for a test case. Sugar Ray is one of the few fighters who's powerful enough, because of his talent and popularity, to buck them."

Part of Leonard's growing up is his indoctrination in the simple lesson that the sport he once found so pleasant and easy is full of pitfalls. "Everything I've learned and seen, I tell Ray," said Morton. "Athletes are the world's most easily forgotten people. You lose the grip you thought you had. Nobody wants you. My old friend Kenny Norton is in town . . . thought he was an actor. I don't see any more *Mandingo* movies.

"Nobody likes to see you do too good. They secretly want to see you fall. Ray probably has more enemies in [hometown] Palmer Park than anywhere else."

"What I have can get away so easily," said Leonard. "I try never to forget it. Before every fight, I think about the same thing: what I have to lose."

Leonard still has his ebullience, but he also has a dead-sober streak now. He sits in the same suite of rooms on the penthouse level that Muhammad Ali had when he defended his heavyweight title here. On the hotel door there is no number. It's been removed for secrecy. On the littered dining-room table inside, where Leonard is autographing pictures, there is a stack of hundred-dollar bills lying casually beside a half-empty cup of coffee.

"I don't like to do the things I used to do," said Leonard. "If the little things that made you laugh don't make you laugh anymore, that doesn't mean you've 'changed.' It means you're older. I used to litter myself with jewelry. I found that I was losing myself. I was like a baby Sammy Davis. Now I'm more conservative. I feel like I've been placed in a sphere where it's hard to know which direction to go—north, south, east or west—to create the least confusion.

"I just like to sit around and talk with friends. But I'm not like Ali with people always around him. Like parasites," said Leonard. "I'm more interested in a few people. The one thing I hate is when friends start asking me about my fame and money. And they get that look, just like the people in a shopping center when they're all waiting for the first person to ask for an autograph so they can all stampede. When the conversation turns like that, I get discouraged. That person has destroyed every bit of confidence and respect I had in him. He has put out the fire."

Leonard has drawn the protective circle around himself much closer. His wife and child, his parents, his trusted advisers Morton and Trainer, his brothers and sisters. Being a boxing king may not be so different from being one of those uneasy Shakespearean kings.

Once, when Leonard awoke in the night, it was to stand in front of the bathroom mirror and throw combinations. "I stand in front of the mirror firing as fast as I can until each punch is perfect, the way I imagined it," said Leonard in those first post-Olympic months when he turned pro. "I love perfection. I want to be a master."

Leonard doesn't do that anymore. "I know what I can do in the ring. I'm at ease with it." When he wakes in the middle of the night now, it is for other reasons. As Morton says, "We just ride. We've been all around the beltway."

Those aren't sad nights. They are just nights of change. Nights of growing up. Nights to think about what it means to be champion of the world.

Barney Ross, Henry Armstrong, Roberto Duran

June 21, 1980—Roberto Duran scored a fierce triumph for fighting barbarism over boxing art tonight as he blasted the WBC welterweight title away from Sugar Ray Leonard in a fifteen-round unanimous decision tonight. The Panamanian pounded every available inch of the brave Leonard from the first bell to the last in a battle of constant vicious action, toe-to-toe bludgeoning and far more infighting than finesse.

"I win easy and convincing," said Duran, who becomes only the third man in history to have held both the lightweight and welterweight titles. Barney Ross and Henry Armstrong were the others, Armstrong having moved down from welterweight to lightweight. "The difference was here," snarled Duran, placing his hand over his heart, "and then here," he added, tapping his head.

The difference tonight—and it was a tiny one, both in the three judges' eyes and in the eyes of nearly 50,000 spectators—came from deep inside Duran's brawling guts. The man with the "hands of stone" attacked without

surcease for the first five rounds, building a large lead in points and beginning an ugly restructuring of Leonard's handsome face.

For a few fleeting rounds, Leonard rediscovered the middle of the ring
and fought a tactical long-range style that led to many a ringing blow to
Duran's head. But in the eleventh round these 147-pounders had their
moment of truth. For three minutes, they went at each other with a hail of
head-hunting hooks and uppercut body shots. When that firestorm had
ended, both warriors were standing, but only Duran had the stamina left to
carry the fight—and win a crown—in those last four rounds.

Leonard, the twenty-four-year-old from Palmer Park, Maryland, who,
some say, became a champion without ever suffering a bruise, looked like a
pugilist in the most brutal sense after his evening as Duran's heavy bag of
hate. "I proved tonight that I can take a really big punch," said Leonard
ruefully and ironically, his arm protectively around his stunned wife,
Juanita. "I didn't want to take it, but I had no other alternative.

"He threw his best. I threw my best. The best man came out on top," said
Leonard generously. "I can only go along with what the judges say."

The unanimous decision was proper to anyone who saw the two fighters'
swelling faces—both marbled with mounting pain—after the fight. Duran
had a black eye, but Leonard was halfway to a Frankenstein visage, his mug
full of lumps and swellings. "Duran was what I expected," Leonard said.
"Very, very rough."

The mood of this crowd of 46,317 swung with the emotion of the fight.
At the onset, they were ravenous for Duran, the underdog—being paid a
mere $1.5 million to Leonard's probable $8 million—to trip up the wealthy
American showboat. This province of Quebec has a strong Third World
flavor, a distinct anti-American strain. Leonard speaks English and no
French: two strikes against him. Duran has learned to speak one sentence of
French, and defiantly refused to learn even that much English. Here, that
makes him a hero.

Nevertheless, by the middle rounds, Leonard had so palpably shown his
courage—and had reached Duran's head with overhand right-hand leads
and every conceivable angle of hook—that the crowd rooted for him as he
mounted swarms in the sixth and seventh that backed Duran against the
ropes.

But in the final rounds, as Leonard's crown slipped from his brow, despite
Dundee screaming in his face, "You can do it, Ray. You can do it," the crowd
was back with Duran, rooting for the upset, pulling for the small clenched
man with the heart of stone to win his second world championship and put
the final signature on the mural of his greatness.

Leonard's corner will have to answer much second-guessing. Why did Leonard almost totally abandon his advantage in reach and speed by seldom throwing a jab? Why did he immediately accede to Duran's preference for an all-out brawl and a test of manhood? Why, after his midround successes, did he go back into the trenches with Duran, exhaust himself and doom himself to four more final rounds with his shoulder blades pinned against the ropes?

"Was this a great fight?" asked Leonard's chief cornerman, Angelo Dundee, rhetorically. "No, it was a great wrestling match. Ray went into the ring a champion. And he came out looking like a champion."

This fight was beautiful primarily in its barbarous ugliness. Duran showed a sneering, snarling contempt for Leonard before, during and even after the final decision. He took every opportunity to be unsporting, to make it clear that this fight would be the crowning testament to his long, but underpraised career. The glamorous, unmarked Leonard was like a red cape symbol of everything he detests.

At the final bell, Duran leaped three feet in the air, clicked his heels and waved his arms. When Leonard offered a glove for a tap of mutual respect, Duran swatted it away and looked so furious that Leonard for the thousandth time flinched backward, his mouthpiece covered with blood, as though he expected yet another attack from Duran.

"I gave it all I had," said Leonard with a calm, defiant pride. "I stood my ground. I hit Duran some tremendous shots with every kind of punch I have. I felt I left this fight with dignity."

With dignity, yes. With a reputation now for courage equal to his dexterity, yes. But with his gold belt, no.

"He is good fighter. I am better," said Duran, spitting an orange peel at his press conference. "I am slicker. People think I am only a heavy puncher. I'm also a boxer."

Mostly tonight, however, Duran was a primal force of nature, a wild man on the brink of control who was willing to accept any punch Leonard had to offer if only he could answer in kind. This was not a bout of specific blows. There were no knockdowns. Both fighters were forced to cover up numerous times, but neither was ever wobbly or in trouble.

Until the middle of the fifth round, Duran was in such complete intimidating control that Leonard's shoulder blades were raw and bleeding from being bulled and butted into the ropes. Duran's blows were not the crisp knockout kind, but the corrosive body blows and swatting hooks that inflict pain rather than unconsciousness and sap the will.

Only from the fifth through the tenth round did Leonard control the tempo, dictate the ring strategy and appear to worry Duran. Twice, Duran shook cobwebs from his brain and waved to his fans to tell them he was all right, just as Leonard had done in the early going.

The climax of this epic—*le face-à-face historique*—was the eleventh round. Some deep psychic decision was made that both men—their defenses now sluggish and lowered—would trade blows to the brain until someone dropped. To the astonishment of both, neither did.

It was then that both men had to reach to the bottom of the well of will. Perhaps it was Duran the boy—a fatherless street urchin stealing to keep his siblings fed—who came to the rescue of Duran the man. That Panamanian boy swam two or three miles each day to steal mangoes from a rich man's land. That return swim, carrying his harvest of fruit, almost sank him many times. Duran always reached the shore.

In the final rounds tonight, like a swimmer who sees the land, the Duran legend, the Duran of glorious menace, kept coming off his stool fresher and fresher for every round. By the fourteenth the title was probably his. He beckoned Leonard to come and fight, a dark smile on his face.

After that fourteenth, a typically even and indeterminate round, Leonard saluted Duran, in an unmistakable gesture of respect that he assumed was mutual. Duran curled his lip and waved away Leonard with the back of his hand.

This fight, which has now lived up to its billing, may gross $30 million—the most in history. Yet the potential for a rematch, with all the inherent chances for altered strategy, might have a dollar figure that boxing has never even dreamed about.

"Time will tell. Time will tell," said Leonard. "We have to put people back together. My wife is my main concern."

After their work this evening, both Duran and Leonard probably will find themselves more loved and more revered.

Pain

MONTREAL, June 21, 1980—

Boxing at its best is beastly.

If that assumption holds no appeal, then you cannot relish the stirring and horrid spectacle of Roberto Duran's public assault on Sugar Ray Leonard here on Friday.

Boxing is about pain. It is a night out for the carnivore in us, the hidden beast who is hungry. Few men have ever become world champion without facing that dark side of their game; Leonard was one.

Leonard might even have arrived in this cosmopolitan city to defend his WBC welterweight crown still believing, at twenty-four, that his profession was a sport rather than a disturbing, paradoxical arena where vice and virtue sometimes exchange roles once they enter the ring. Duran, who has been the quintessential creature of the ring in his time, acquainted Leonard with the true facts about his business.

After a lifetime of hard work but almost effortless success inside the ropes, Leonard finally came face to face with the core of boxing: suffering. He passed the test of personal courage but, because he was so intent on that examination of character, he neglected the tactics of his art and lost a crown. Someday, if the '80s turn out to be a decade of Leonard evolution, this fight—may prove to be historic because it brought a great young fighter face to face with fear.

Duran, only the third man ever to be both lightweight and welterweight champion, won a unanimous decision over Leonard by a slim and controversial margin. Leonard won a unanimous and incontrovertible decision over fear. This defeat was his letter of credit to a doubting world that thought him a likable boxer but not necessarily a heroic fighter.

Few nights in history, certainly very few in the last twenty years, have met boxing's highest and most dubious standard of greatness: the constant, relentless and mutual inflicting of the maximum tolerable amount of pain. By that measure, the Leonard-Duran conflagration was worth every penny of the $30 million that it probably will gross. No one who is fascinated by watching men under extreme duress was cheated.

Duran, given his choice, would fight fifteen rounds in a telephone booth without any intermissions. Only the Panamanian brawler, among current fighters, can monopolize 399 square feet of a 400-square-foot ring. Duran's victims sometimes wonder if they have room to fall. That was the case for the first five and the last five rounds of Friday night's classic, which was as riveting as boxing can be without knockdowns or copious blood.

Experts will argue interminably over why Leonard fought what appeared to be a brave but hopelessly stupid fight. Why didn't he jab? Why didn't he dance? Why didn't he circle? Why didn't he slide when Duran tried to cut the ring? Why didn't he clinch or push off more to avoid the infighting? Why did he stand toe to toe countless times and exchange hooks to the head and uppercut digs to the gut? Only Leonard had the absolute and unarguable answer. "I had no other alternative," he said.

Early in the fight, when Duran was fresh, and late in the fight, when Leonard was tired, Duran made certain that the fight would be conducted only one way—his way. Wherever Leonard was, there was Duran—less than arm's reach away and throwing leather without surcease. In such circumstances, no man can dance, or jab or slide. Once Duran is within the parameters of an opponent's defense, and both his hands of stone are moving, a fighter has only one choice: exchange punches or call for Mama.

The tone of a brutal and elemental evening was established quickly when prelim lightweight Cleveland Denny was carried out unconscious in convulsive paroxysms so strong that doctors could not get the mouthpiece out of his clenched jaw. Denny is in intensive care. (Note: Denny later died.) For any in the crowd of 46,317—the once-a-year boxing fans like Jack Nicklaus —who might doubt, that twitching body on the stretcher was a declaration of boxing's basic nature.

When Gaetan Hart, the man who knocked out Denny, was told that his last punch hardly seemed powerful enough for such damage, he was offended. His last opponent left the ring in a coma and required eight hours of brain surgery, so Hart, with his matted hair, tattoos and rearranged features, is proud of his punch. In his life, it is what he has. "When I hit Denny with the right hand," explained Hart, "his eyes go around backwards like this."

And Hart twirled his forefingers as though illustrating how the cherries on a slot machine revolve.

That is boxing. And Duran, the man who, in the ring, has the hands and the heart of stone, knows it better than any fighter of his generation.

Other boxing eras would not have found Duran unique. His personality type would have seemed comfortably familiar: a fatherless street urchin who stole to feed his brothers and sisters, dropped out of school in the third grade at the age of thirteen, turned pro at sixteen, became the athletic pet of a Latin military dictator, won a world title at age twenty-one, and now has a fleet of gaudy cars and a 680-pound pet lion which he walks on a leash.

In any period, Duran would have stood out. But in the '60s and '70s, when Muhammad Ali brought footwork, defense, an unmarked face and poetry to fighting, Duran seemed almost an embarrassing anachronism, a stage in boxing's evolution that the game seemed anxious to act as though it had passed. Duran, with his 71–1 record, seldom got his due. Or if he did, it was done with a shudder as though Heathcliff were being introduced in polite society and might smash the china in a rage.

But boxing never changes. One central truth lies at its heart and it never alters: pain is the most powerful and tangible force in life. The threat of torture, for instance, is stronger than the threat of death. Execution can be faced, but pain is corrosive, like an acid eating at the personality. Pain, as anyone with a toothache knows, drives out all other emotions and sensations before it. Pain is priority. It may even be man's strongest and most undeniable reality. And that is why the fight game stirs us, even as it repels us.

For at least ten of their fifteen rounds, Leonard and Duran set as intense a pace as any fan could wish—they looked like Ali and Smokin' Joe Frazier in the first round in Manila, but because they weigh only 147 pounds, their speed and frequency of violence did not dwindle nearly so much as the fight wore on.

"He threw his best. I threw my best," said Leonard. What landed? he was asked. "Everything," said Leonard.

In the early rounds, there was defense, slipping and blocking of the fiercest punches. In the late rounds, when the blows still carried pain but insufficient force for a blessed unconsciousness, every third swing seemed to land flush.

Only in the middle rounds, starting late in the fifth, when Leonard finally landed enough consecutive punches to make Duran back off for the first time, and extending through the tenth, did Leonard achieve a painless modus vivendi. Then, Leonard still had his speed and Duran had his doubts. The Sugar Man struck and escaped, dealt fire for fire, then had breathing time to regroup.

After those early rounds of perplexity bordering on fear, Leonard gradually gained confidence—more's the pity for him—until, by the eleventh, he thought he was Duran's better. He thought he could reach into the furnace and save the crown that he saw melting there.

The eleventh round was meant for the film archives. Everything that gives boxing undeniable dimension and emotional authority was wrought to white heat then. Money, glory or the search for identity may get a man into the ring, but only facing and surmounting pain can keep him there. Only that act of creating a brutal art in the presence of suffering can bring nobility to man's oldest and most visceral competition.

Boxing has the cleanest line, the fewest rules and the most self-evident objective of any endeavor that people gather to watch. When shabbily done, like the third meeting of their careers between Denny and Hart—a pair of lifelong plodders—few things are so worthless and destructive. Life and death on the undercard is as depressing as the sporting life gets.

However, at certain heights of skill and will, fighters like Duran and Leonard begin to carry with them a symbolic nimbus. They seem a distillation of their backgrounds, their time and place and the people out of which they sprang. Only when Duran is seen in this way does that eleventh round, and what he did after it, seem inevitable.

Here in Montreal, this town of boutiques and glass-and-neon malls where an obsession with the latest imported European fashion is everywhere, Duran's fans and followers have looked as alien as Martians. In swanky hotels like the Meridien, the Regency and the Bonaventure, these people who chant "Cholo"—the word for a Panamanian of Indian descent—and talk constantly with animated delight are distinguished by more than their old, clean, one-suit-per-lifetime clothes. Their hands and faces, like Duran's, have been weathered by eternal forces—the erosion of work, age and the rub of stubborn necessities. In Olympic Stadium on a cool Canadian night, with salsa music in the upper deck, Duran's people—his true kin or those here who have adopted him—cheered with raw conviction.

Out of our pestilential sump holes of social unconsciousness rise up a few strong, if lopsided personalities who create much of our public collective mythology. Duran is a sample of that up-from-under caste that seems simple, unified and forceful. In the eleventh, that absence of complexity proved useful.

Leonard had mustered both his confidence and his resolve. "Sugar Ray is like the rain," said Leonard's sparring partner Mike James before the fight. "Once he gets started, you can't make him stop." Leonard had clouded up and was in full thunderclap. Just as Duran had had Leonard deeply worried and near trouble in his second-round blitz, Leonard now was sure he was going for a kill. "I hit Duran some tremendous shots with left hooks, right hooks and overhand rights," said Leonard.

Instead of covering up, Duran met the pain directly, almost welcomed it. The more his head was battered from side to side, the more his fists flew in return. By midround, Leonard was so arm weary from punching that his gloves slipped to his waist. Duran took the initiative in the assault and battery until, by round's end, Leonard was in another desperate retaliatory rage, storming down punches on Duran after the bell sounded.

The net effect of this sustained firestorm was not a new balance of terror, but merely a change in exhaustion levels. Leonard had gambled and lost. The fight reverted to its early-round syndrome with Duran boring inside against a game but stationary Leonard. Had Leonard resisted the impulse to knock out this taunter, had he stayed with his midround style as long as his energy lasted, those ever-so-close judges' cards (146–144, 145–144 and 148–147) might have been reversed.

It is appropriate that in such a morally ambiguous sport, one of boxing's great fights should leave behind it a mood of nagging paradox. A view of the world—usually unspoken—often hangs around the edges of major sports. Certainly it always has with boxing. The notion that life is a fight is inescapable in this subculture of leather and liniment. The search for glory through taking advantage, the constant pursuit of getting the better of someone, are precepts so ingrained that no one would think to preach them.

As a consequence, those who tend to see the world that way are drawn here: politicians, mobsters, business millionaires, junkies of all persuasions, entertainers, athletes and journalists. It is a night for those who have sharp teeth, or think they do; vegetarians and saints need not apply. However, this shark ethic may have been carried further—reduced really to the absurd—

in boxing than in any other corner of our culture. The big eating the little is gospel.

That is why Leonard entered this scene as such a refreshing anomaly. Essentially, he was a world champion who had none of boxing's shabby back-room entanglements. It was no accident that this fight could gross more money ($30 million predicted) and bring more to the fighters themselves (at least $8 to Leonard and $1.5 million to Duran) than any fight in history. Leonard's lawyer, Mike Trainer, set a precedent of squeezing out middlemen and promoters, keeping the financial books aboveboard and making no private deals.

But as soon as this beastly good fight ended, the big sharks of boxing began circling.

Duran, as devoid of *duende*—that indefinable Latin mixture of style and class—out of the ring as he is chocked with it inside the ropes, sat beside his boxing godfather, Don King, the promoter.

As Duran attacked an orange—spitting seeds and rind in any direction as he held a surly, gloating, graceless press conference—King, his hair electrified and his vanity in full bloom, took out a huge roll of big bills. With great pretense, King began slapping the money in Duran's palm of stone as the photographers clicked.

Not only Sugar Ray Leonard had been beaten but Sugar Ray Leonard, Inc., too. That great perennial enemy of boxing—an honest fighter—had been removed from the game's top rung.

And that, on one of boxing's best nights, was a beastly development indeed.

No Más

NEW ORLEANS, November 25, 1980—

Bullies can dish it out, but they just can't take it. This is an ancient boxing rule of thumb: a seeming psychological paradox that really is a straightforward truth. Sugar Ray Leonard proved the verity of this maxim again tonight as he humiliated Roberto Duran with flashing combinations, glorious boxing skills and audacious courage.

For almost eight rounds, Leonard made a fool of Manos de Piedra, taunting him, beating him to the punch, disdaining him, laughing in his face, then smashing him with lightning blows from both hands.

Finally, with sixteen seconds left in the eighth round, Duran could not take it anymore. His face, although a bit puffy, was unmarked. He had not been knocked down or even severely hurt. But, far more important than that, his Panamanian macho had been slain. The man who had been feared more than any other brawler of his era, the man who had been both lightweight and welterweight champion and brought a 72–1 record into this fight, had been treated as though he were a pathetic little boy in a rage who needed to be cuffed about the head.

So, at 2:44 of that eighth round, Duran did what no one in the entire world of prizefighting ever dreamed him capable of doing: he quit. Later, he said he was retiring from the ring. "I had no idea what happened," said referee Octavio Meyran. "I said to Duran, 'What happened? Go in [and fight].' He said, 'No . . . no more.'"

The Louisiana State Athletic Commission, presumably displeased with the manner in which this fight ended, decided to hold up Duran's purse (a reported $10 million) until he could undergo a complete medical examination.

Truly, Duran had enough tonight. "I will never fight again," Duran said, after losing the WBC welterweight championship that he had taken from Leonard just five months and five days ago in Montreal. "I got cramps in the fifth round in my right arm and side. They got worse and worse. I was weakening."

The lion had quit with a thorn in his paw. The man they said could be stopped only with an elephant gun had thrown in the towel because a faster, younger and smarter man was giving him a boxing lesson and mocked him in the process.

Typically, Duran was brutish to the end. "I feel I am a thousand times a better man than Leonard," said Duran after the fight. "Just because he beat me once doesn't mean I have to respect him. . . . I am going home and count money."

Anyone searching for the cause of Duran's cramps can consider this. They may well have come from the bile when a bully's heart burst.

Leonard, who depended on a complete change of tactics to regain his crown—and prove himself to be a fighter for the ages in the process—was ecstatic, but gracious in his greatest moment. "I beat Duran more mentally than physically," said Leonard accurately. "The things I did, especially in the seventh round, demoralized him. But don't knock Duran. He will always be a great champion."

Told that Duran had made light of him, Leonard said quietly, "That's just Duran's nature. He wouldn't say anything else. I still respect the man."

Asked repeatedly about the shocking moment in the eighth when Duran simply backed away, turned his back and waved a glove dismissively at Leonard as he quit, Leonard showed the spark of genuine feeling. "Maybe Duran had heartburn," said Leonard critically. "Don't talk about Duran quitting. Talk about how badly I beat him. Duran's back, Duran's cramps

. . . It's going to take a lot for people to accept that I beat the Macho Man, the Hands of Stone, a legend.

"It's simple. In the first fight [a unanimous fifteen-round decision] I learned Duran. I could change. He couldn't."

None of the roughly 40,000 in the Superdome for this Super Fight could doubt Leonard's word. By thoroughly licking the twenty-nine-year-old Duran while he was still in his prime, Leonard established himself as a great champion in his own right. And, certainly, one of the most versatile champions in history, at the least.

Every trap was laid for Duran here tonight. The American crowd booed his introduction as much as the Canadian crowd had cheered him. Who should sing "America the Beautiful" but Ray Charles, the blues singer for whom Sugar Ray Charles Leonard was named. Even Leonard's costume was a surprise. Both fighters claimed to want to wear white trunks, with Duran, as champ, getting his way. However, instead of wearing red, as he said he would, Leonard entered the ring all in black (with gold trim) right down to his black socks.

Duran's surprises started immediately. In Montreal, Leonard had proved his courage, his ability to take Duran's best punch. So, tonight, he didn't need to. In Montreal, Leonard started fearfully, losing the first four rounds as Duran swarmed him. Tonight, Leonard danced the whole first round, letting Duran stalk and stalk, then, when he finally struck, nailing the Panamanian with a vicious left hook.

Seldom has any fighter done a more splendid job of going to school between one fight and another. Leonard measured Duran from long range and by the fourth round was stinging him several times a round with clean snakelike hooks to the forehead. When Duran bored inside, Leonard snapped his head back time and again with the uppercuts that he neglected until the late rounds in Montreal.

Most impressive of all, Leonard turned all Duran's stalking and bulling tactics against him. Once, Duran used every ring-cutting technique, got Leonard seemingly pinned and leaped in with a left hook. But Leonard, with a shimmy of his hips like a football halfback, ruined Duran's timing, sidestepped him and popped him in the temple with the jab as he danced away laughing.

Once, Duran lunged so desperately that he went through the middle of the ropes and almost fell out of the ring. The only embarrassing moment all night for Leonard was when Duran once tackled him like a linebacker and knocked him on the seat of his pants with a push.

For Duran, the psychological Waterloo came in the seventh round. "I don't know why," said a grinning Leonard. "I just figured it was showtime."

Leonard stuck out his chin, inches from Duran's gloves, as Ali once had done to Liston, and when Duran lunged, Leonard retracted the chin and extended the gloves, smashing Duran in the mouth with a combination. Leonard did this not once but repeatedly, dancing all around Duran, tempting him, then punishing him. Once Leonard faked a straight right, then swatted Duran with a left hook.

The crowd was in an ecstasy of laughter and cheers as Leonard landed significant, if not crushing, blows throughout the round. "Just keep up the pace, and he's dead," yelled Dundee between rounds. The Sugar Man, however, knew even more. "I watched his eyes between rounds," said Leonard, "and they changed. He tried to sneer and leer. But I knew the truth. What punch paralyzed him? All of 'em."

Just as Liston stayed on his stool for an eighth-round TKO, so Duran's worst moment as a fighter will go into the books the same way—TKO in the eighth.

For the record, his cramps, if they existed, did not appear to damage his ability to fight. His face showed no pain. Between rounds, he did not dramatically favor his side. Certainly, he was in nothing like the pain that Ali, for instance, endured when he fought the last thirteen rounds of a fifteen-round defeat with a broken jaw against Kenny Norton.

Boxing has a long history of champions fighting gamely until the end, even if they have injuries far more severe than cramps, which, at worst, can go away after a couple of rounds. Duran, however, was in no mood to go from bad to worse. His stamina was dwindling, while Leonard was as fresh as in the early rounds. On the three judges' cards, Leonard was ahead, 4–2–1, 4–2–1 and 4–3—margins which probably should have been even greater since only in the third round did Duran seem to score better. Duran knew that the first eight rounds were just prologue; worse awaited him and he ducked it.

"I have been fighting a long time," said Duran through his translator. "I have gotten tired of it. I want to retire."

Are you embarrassed? he was asked.

"No, why should I be? This happens to everybody."

For Leonard, just twenty-four, a long reign may be ahead. Certainly, his confidence should take a quantum leap forward after this night. In Montreal, he seemed dazed and almost lost as he entered the ring. Tonight, Leonard was so together, so relaxed, so confident that he was loose and smiling during the introductions. He was so delighted by Ray Charles singing, and the hug and kiss that the blind musician gave him just before the first bell, that he almost seemed euphoric. With each round, Leonard seemed more delighted with himself as those long hours of gym lessons were paying off in trumps.

On Basin Street here, in the St. Louis Cemetery, the names of many Lou'siana men are on the aboveground tombs. The epitaph on many reads: "Killed in a duel."

That is the epitaph for Duran tonight. This evening, Sugar Ray Leonard had the feet of a Bourbon Street tap dancer, the blended combinations of a fine Dixieland jazz band and the punch of Ramos gin fizz.

It only took Roberto Duran eight rounds to see enough of this demoralizing mixture. For the rest of the boxing world, which has years more of the developing saga of the Sugar Man ahead of it, this night was just the delicious first course in the long championship feast of Sugar Ray Leonard's career.

Deliverance

LAS VEGAS, September 16, 1981—

All questions about Ray Leonard were answered in the affirmative tonight.

The now champion of all welterweights entered the ring in Caesars Palace against Thomas Hearns wearing a robe that bore one word: "Deliverance." Deliverance, that is, from doubters, from all those who thought him a smiling, shallow, plastic commodity and not a champion of the terrors of the ring.

In a fashion more brutal, exhausting and testing than any man could wish —even for an $8 million guarantee—Leonard knocked down Hearns in the thirteenth round, then stopped him in the fourteenth.

At 1:45 of that round, referee Davey Pearl decided that, after two full rounds of almost ceaseless beating at the hands of the Sugar Man, Hearns had had enough for one night and awarded Leonard a technical knockout. It was the first loss for Hearns in thirty-three fights. Leonard is 31–1.

United Press International reported that Pearl said Hearns had taken twenty-five consecutive punches to the head without blocking or ducking one. "I'd stop it again one hundred times in the same circumstances," Pearl said.

In one of the best, and cruelest, fights in recent boxing history, Leonard overcame triple hurdles to win in the richest prizefight of them all.

First, he trailed on all three officials' cards entering the fourteenth round, despite the fact that in all three of the fight's most vicious rounds, the sixth, seventh and thirteenth, Leonard had blasted Hearns from corner to corner in search of a knockout that seemed imminent.

Much debate, no doubt, will surround the scoring of judges Duane Ford (124–122, Hearns), Chuck Minker (125–121, Hearns) and Lou Tabat (125–122, Hearns). There was no scarcity of veteran ringsiders who had Leonard ahead on points. Nevertheless, before the thirteenth round, when Leonard began a swarming attack, manager Angelo Dundee was screaming in his fighter's ear, "You're blowin' it, kid. You're blowin' it."

Second, Leonard's left eye began swelling in the middle rounds and, from the tenth onward, was so hideously gorged with swelling blood that Leonard said, "My vision was about a half to a third of normal. I couldn't see his right hand coming anymore."

Finally, in a ring where the temperature from desert heat and klieg lights was over 100 degrees, the easily dehydrated Leonard was so close to collapse that, a minute after the fight's end, he was so wobbly-kneed that he almost collapsed and fell as his entourage celebrated around him.

Frequently, in the wake of his knockouts, Leonard is asked what punch did the damage. Usually, Leonard, who now has Hearns's World Boxing Association crown as well as the World Boxing Council title, will say, "I'll have to wait to see the films. It happened too fast."

That was the case tonight. Leonard hit Hearns with everything, then hit him with everything again and again. Never, not even in the final seconds when he was eating leather by the gross, did the implacable, expressionless Hearns's face change.

In the thirteenth round, Hearns was on the canvas three times. Both Dundee and Leonard thought all three should have been knockdowns. Referee Pearl, almost certainly correctly, ruled the first a combination slip and push. The third, when Hearns was left sitting on the lowest rope by a left hook, then shook his head "no" when Leonard begged him to come to midring, was ruled a mandatory eight-count.

Hearns's second trip to the canvas probably should have been ruled a knockdown as well. Leonard, his forehead in Hearns's chest, fired a dozen punches in one unbelievable nonstop combination that did not end until Hearns was sitting, dazed, in his own corner. That one Pearl also called a push-slip.

Leonard's damage in the fourteenth left little doubt. Hearns was blank-eyed, dizzy and defenseless against Leonard's last half dozen blows.

"In the last two rounds, I brought it up from my guts. I had to do this for Ray Leonard," said Leonard, wearing sunglasses over an eye that will never grace a TV commercial.

Leonard was lucky he made a hero's final stand. If he hadn't knocked out Hearns in the fourteenth or fifteenth, he almost certainly would have lost a decision even if he won both rounds.

"I thought it was a close fight, but I was certain Ray was ahead," said trainer Janks Morton. "I don't know what fight the judges were watching. . . . Part of the problem is that Ray won rounds big while all the ones Hearns won were small, no-action rounds. But they all count the same because the judges score them 10–9. They won't score a round 10–8 or 10–7, even though they should."

"We'll never win a close decision," said Leonard's lawyer, Mike Trainer. "I'm bitterly resigned to that. Tonight was a perfect example. We could have lost a fight we won. "Boxing is a close-knit fraternity, and Ray Leonard, and his way of doing business, aren't part of it. . . . A whole lot of people in boxing want Ray out of the sport and off the front page. They want him retired and on the Carson [Tonight] show so they can do business the old way.

"We'll never get a break, just like Ray lost the first Duran fight. If it's close, we'll lose, 'cause everybody is buddy-buddy."

"This surpasses all my professional accomplishments," said Leonard. "I proved that I am the best welterweight in the world. . . . I apologize to Tommy Hearns for all the things I said about him not having any brains. He is a great fighter. In my book, we are both still champions."

When Hearns, looking far fresher and healthier than Leonard, arrived at the postfight press conference, Leonard graciously grabbed the hand of his 6-foot-2½ erstwhile opponent and held it aloft. Leonard's wife, Juanita, dressed in white, kissed Hearns on the cheek.

"I'll never say anything against Ray Leonard," said Hearns. "I didn't underestimate the man. I fought my best. . . . My body was prepared, but maybe my head wasn't. He hurt me, I won't lie. He hurt me in the sixth and at the end. He hit me some great body shots, but it was the left hooks that did the damage.

"He taught me that you can't make mistakes against a great fighter. What mistake? I'd drop my right hand after I threw it and he'd tag me with that left hook every time," said Hearns, who by the eighth round was afraid to fire his best weapon, the straight right, for fear of the instant retaliation.

This battle, with a gross that could go as high as $50 million, had a fascinating progression. For the first five rounds, Hearns was the brash stalker and Leonard the counterpuncher. In the second and third, Leonard did the greater damage, even threw his right hand aloft after the third round. But Hearns was winning the other rounds on points.

Then, in the sixth, Leonard lowered the first of his countless left-hand bombs and had Hearns sagging against the ropes, in serious trouble.

At the end of the round, Leonard, who had been sneered at, and hit after the bell in earlier rounds by Hearns, asked the vaunted Hit Man, "Are you hurt now?

"He didn't answer me," said Leonard.

In the seventh, Hearns was in trouble again but escaped. After that round, he changed tactics completely, surviving on the defensive for rounds eight through ten. Ironically, while backpedaling and jabbing, he won all rounds as his towering defense was impregnable, frustrating Leonard's stalking attempts at a knockdown.

By the eleventh and twelfth, Hearns was blending his dancing, pedaling defense with more offense, banging at Leonard's horrid eye. "I was definitely going for that eye," said Hearns.

And Leonard's title definitely was slipping. "I had to lay back in some rounds, wait for him to make a mistake, 'cause I knew my eye was swelling more every round," said Leonard. "I was conscious of that eye the whole fight because it was bruised by a sparring partner's elbow in training and it wasn't completely well."

But after the twelfth, the eye was too far gone for Leonard to be cautious any longer. His strength was ebbing, too.

So in the thirteenth, he bore inside, slammed that swollen face into Hearns's chest and wouldn't leave until the Hit Man had been hit.

"Was I ever in trouble?" said Leonard. "I knew I was in trouble the minute I signed the contract. Hearns dropped some bombs on me, but I psyched him, 'cause I wouldn't go down. I've spoken from the heart about how much I think of Hearns. I hope he'll do the same."

And when he arrived, Hearns did.

"Don't ever underestimate this man," he said, sitting next to Leonard. "We both stood our ground. You definitely seen a show tonight."

And they saw Ray Leonard's deliverance from all boxing doubts, now and forever.

The Best of His Generation

LAS VEGAS, 1989—

Sugar Ray Leonard landed a hundred punches Thursday night. Roberto Duran landed one. Both men got what they wanted and, probably, what they deserved. Leonard left town with victory in one pocket and history in the other. Duran left with his lust satisfied. He got to see Leonard's hand raised in victory above a face covered with his own blood.

Leonard proved that he is the greatest fighter of his generation. Only Duran, the man with world titles in four weight clasess, could have contested him for that honor. And for twelve rounds Thursday evening out behind the Mirage, the magical Leonard proved he is the complete master of Duran.

What the Sugar Man did to the Hands of Stone in New Orleans in 1980, he did again Thursday—but more completely, more start-to-finish and with fifteen pounds more power in his blows.

Leonard won the bendiction of boxing history by peppering Duran at will and pounded the Panamanian brutally on several occasions. The margin of Leonard's unanimous decision in this WBC super middleweight championship bout was one of the most overwhelming that fight buffs will ever see: 120–110, 119–109 and 116–111.

In boxing terms, that's a shutout.

But Duran, in his perverse way, got a kind of moral victory. With one right hook in the eleventh round, Duran got the blood which he had sworn to extract for nearly ten years.

After the twelfth round, Leonard looked like a ghoul from a horror movie, blood streaming from above his left eye and down his whole face. As an added sweet taste for Duran, Leonard's mouth bled after Duran headbutted him in a clinch. The cut was cosmetic, but pleasing to the thirty-eight-year-old loser's eye.

As would always be expected of Duran, he took the defeat with a sneer and his usual consummate bad sportsmanship. "Leonard came here to clown around. I came to fight. Leonard didn't beat me," said Duran through a translator. "Fighting against Leonard in the United States is completely impossible. . . . The referee [Richard Steele] didn't let me do nothing. I couldn't fight."

Later, Duran called Steele "Leonard's Siamese twin."

Steele has a break-'em-apart style that certainly suited Leonard, particularly on the rare and inconsequential occasions that Duran actually managed to chase and clinch Leonard. Had no third man been in the ring at all, the scores would probably still have been the same. Duran was so inept at cutting the ring, so incapable of getting inside that Steele was a minor factor.

The crowd failed to love this fight, which seldom held any action in the first half of any round. Leonard burned the clock, then picked his spots to build up as many points as he wanted and far more than he needed. Late in the fight, the crowd chanted an obscenity: a critique on the lack of knockdowns.

"I fight the way that got me this far," said Leonard. "In the eleventh round, I tried to accommodate the crowd. They wanted a Hearns-Hagler brawl. That's not my forte. . . .

"[But] I fought a heck of a fight."

This fight was a shock to anyone who remembers the videotape of 1980. The difference in the two men is almost frightening. Then, both were welterweights (147 pounds) with Duran actually a natural lightweight. Then, Duran's arms were far from ponderous and Leonard looked like a skinny, almost scared little boy. At least compared with the bodybuilding specimen he's become.

After an enormous fireworks display that, for some, may have evoked unsettling memories of another December 7, the fighters came into the ring. Dressed as each other.

Duran came in white, trimmed in pretty gold, then danced around the ring at high speed. Leonard came in black, head to toe, with a menacing black wool stocking cap. Whatever Leonard's real intentions, his symbolic message appeared to be an unexpected one. I'm here to be an executioner, a dangerous man, a knockout man. He almost pulled off the KO trick twice.

If the first round was slightly Leonard's, then the second may have been even. But the third was not. After ninety seconds of walking in the park, Leonard got serious. He caught Duran with a decent short hook to the head, then, a few moments later, a perfect slam of a jab—hard as he could fire it square between Duran's eyes. By the fourth, Duran's mouth was open occasionally as he sucked air—unusual for him, but not for any fighter at age thirty-eight.

Duran finally got a moment to savor in the fifth round when he mauled Leonard into a neutral corner and head-butted him in the mouth, opening a cut. As Leonard has done so often in his career, he responded to his own blood, or his own fear, with fury. He won the sixth by a titanic margin and had everything to show for it but a knockdown. A straight right started Duran's problems. By the bell, Leonard had hit Duran harder and more often, especially with right leads, than in any round in their history except the eleventh in Montreal. The crowd stood, anticipating a possible knockout, but Duran was far too tough, never wobbled, even when nailed, and even managed half a snarl after the round.

By the last minute of the ninth round, Leonard was in heaven, landing a mega-left hook after missing (for one of the few times) with the right-hand lead that had drubbed Duran's left temple much of the night. As usual, Leonard saved his activity for the latter half of the round and it may have cost him a chance to do major damage. Duran was in trouble, trapped in his own corner, covering up, his eyes glazed, as Leonard spent the last twenty seconds of the round searching for a KO combo.

By now, Sugar Ray was as at home in the ring as if he'd been shadowboxing in his own bedroom back home. He rested and danced in the tenth, but still whacked Duran at will in the last ten seconds of the round. The crowd greeted the gentlemen who have given the world so many superb fights with profanities before the eleventh round. Leonard glanced up in disbelief. The high rollers here may have the dollars, but they don't have any judgment when it comes to fighting.

With one punch—a good hard hook, but not a knockout-type blow—

Duran popped open a gash above Leonard's left eye. Had Duran been more active, or younger, and landed such a punch five rounds earlier, he might have had the makings of a KO. As it was, Leonard danced out the fight, prancing into a solitary place in his sport's history and erasing some of the heartburn from his last encounter with Thomas Hearns.

Duran will have a photograph to hang in the bleak hallway of his grudging soul—a portrait of Leonard awash in blood.

Leonard, however, has something more. The rubber match—*Uno Más*—was his so overwhelmingly that no fight fan will ever again ask who was the better of these men. Leonard lost one fight to Duran to prove his courage. One loss in a whole career. Now, after this whitewash, few would doubt that Leonard could—both young and old—have beaten Duran a hundred times in a row.

Interlude

Comrade Kasparov

March 1989—The most famous and respected of all the Soviet Union's masters of sport looks like a cocky, compact, lightweight boxer. From his flattish nose to his ever-drumming fingers to his sleek, expensive European suits, he is a small, dark and handsome testament to energy and ego.

Although his is only twenty-six, nothing in his manner apologizes an iota for his greatness. "That is why I am world champion," he will say casually. As a competitor, famous for his intimidating personal presence and loved for his audacious "attacks from a clear blue sky," he is a giant to his people as well as an outspoken force for Soviet cultural reform. In his country, he is the symbol of the greatest virtues in his game, what he proudly calls "the fighting spirit."

Gary Kasparov has no counterpart in American games. What baseball, or maybe football, is to Americans, chess is to the Soviets. And with all respect to Bobby Fischer, Kasparov may be the greatest chess master who ever lived.

What we're dealing with here is a man who once played ten matches simultaneously against masters and won eight while tying the other two. Not so impressive? Kasparov was blindfolded at the time.

"Never again. I had three times the energy then [in 1985]," said Kasparov. Then he added, more seriously, "It was like a kaleidoscope." His hands move back and forth, fingers spread apart, over and under each other, as he tries to show what the ten boards looked like in his mind, overlapping, dissolving into each other, then coming back into focus. "Playing the games was not the problem. But afterward, I could not get rid of them." The games would not leave his mind. It took him more than a day to recover, get his mind back under his own full possession, as though a sickness had taken over his body.

"It irritated my brain," says Kasparov. "Order is important to me."

Actually, any aspect of chess is important to Kasparov, including using it for social progress. In the Soviet Union, he stood for *glasnost* and *perestroika* before the concepts gained official sanction. His successful battles against former world champion Anatoly Karpov—the chess equivalent of the dronish Soviet apparatchik—were inspirational to Soviet reformers.

Now, during chess's three-year hiatus between marathon title wars, Kasparov is a country-hopping ambassador for the game. "Chess Against Drugs" is his latest campaign—an idea that brought him to Washington recently to talk to government leaders.

If chess for the underprivileged and poorly educated seems anomalous to some, it seems logical to Kasparov. He likens chess to music and sports in that it cuts through the cultural disadvantages to strike directly at a child's core of natural talent, his inherent gift. "If we can save just one," he said, "that is enough." But he expects much more. "It is simple to learn the moves," he says. "Then you are alone. It is your creation. . . .

"Everyone can play a masterpiece at his own level. If you play music without distinction, or play sports that way, it is not very good, really, is it? But in chess, you go to your limit. For you, it feels like a masterpiece. . . .

"Chess helps children to [cultivate] their ability to analyze. It teaches them to be quiet," said Kasparov. "But above all, it teaches them the fighting spirit."

For several years, a New York-based chess club—The Masters of Disaster —helped inner-city children gain self-confidence by thumping their more privileged rivals in city tournaments.

To sense Kasparov's personality, even when he is trying only to sell a noble idea, it helps to imagine the mannerisms and temperament of an athlete. Picture the pawing impatience of the young Jimmy Connors. Even when Kasparov speaks, and his English is excellent, he seems to grab and bend his listener toward his point of view. Domination by raw kinetic energy has long been his trademark. Even when Kasparov is playing a demonstration game, his hands move on the pieces with a sudden, darting contemptuousness, as if he were almost insulted that his hands must show others what his mind sees.

As soon as he finishes a high-speed, ten-seconds-per-move game against a British grandmaster, he and his beaten foe immediately start playing the game backwards as quickly as their fingers can move, showing each other and a dozen kibitzers some of the possibilities that they had envisioned.

To elaborate all that they had thought would probably be impossible. "The game has become so advanced," said Kasparov, with almost as much unhappiness as pleasure. As a child, Kasparov grew up replaying slashing, romantic games of old masters like Paul Morphy, Jose Capablanca and, his favorite, Alexander Alekhine. Those games could be understood and replayed with relish by average players of no special talent.

But in chess, as in science, each generation stands on the shoulders of the previous generation, starting where the other stopped. Now, chess at Kasparov's level is so exotic that the general-interest player can seldom cope. "True," said Kasparov when asked if the game, as he sees it, is almost prohibitively inaccessible. "Much more difficult."

Fortunately, Kasparov, both as vivid personality and as ambassador for chess, reaches out with elegant grace to offer the world his finest gift—a game that can give deep pleasure and pride to each person at his own level.

Boxing

The Ali Issue

September 21, 1984—When I think about Muhammad Ali, I always get angry. Then I always get depressed. But I never know exactly at whom or what to get mad, or exactly why I should be sad. Today, I'm twice as angry, twice as sad, twice as confused.

Like so many other people, I want to know how Ali, the most famous athlete of my generation and one of the quickest-witted and most charming public figures in years, could end up at the age of forty-two bouncing from hospital to hospital trying to find a way to keep from ending up like a typical boxing victim.

The doctors say Ali has something called Parkinson's syndrome. It's not full-fledged Parkinson's disease, it's not fatal, contagious or progressively debilitating. It can be treated to some degree with medication.

But it's bad. Extremely slurred, slow and almost unintelligible speech at times. Loss of facial expression. Shaking of the hands.

I want to know whom to curse, what law to change, what petition to sign. I think I have a lot of company.

Those millions of us who have cared about the Ali saga for almost twenty-five years want to know if this means that boxing should be banned or headgear should become mandatory. Or was Ali the only one to blame because he got old, greedy and glory-hungry and couldn't leave the ring until he was battered out of it.

We want to know whether we should accuse the Muslims of milking his name and encouraging him to fight or if we should blame "the public" for the way we cheered every ridiculous Ali comeback. We want to know whether we should rip the Big Thinkers who loved to use Ali as an ideological mannequin on which to hang their latest pontifications.

Or should we kick sportswriters and other media types for letting Ali's ego distend for twenty years until nobody could put his swollen head on a diet. We in the press liked him, but never enough to tell him the truth—that if he swallowed his own exaggerations and ours, he'd choke on them someday.

Even Ali probably doesn't fathom the depth and genuineness of the public sympathy that is extended to him now by a whole cross section of Americans. In recent months, he's rambled about CIA agents following him on airplanes and the government labeling him "subversive." "They've got a file on me in the Pentagon six feet high."

Ali may have been "subversive" fifteen years ago, but now it would be an all-day job to find somebody who wouldn't sign a "Get well, Ali" card.

Maybe Ali came to believe his hype that he was "the Greatest"; maybe too many sycophants told him, "That's heavy, champ," too many times. Maybe he was always a sucker for the flashiest and most simplistic sort of radical rhetoric; all that "wise" jive sounded so good in his talk-show rap and all the liberal intellectuals just lapped it up like adoring stage-door Johnnys. Maybe Ali had no compunction about telling a thousand fabulous well-intentioned lies about the good works for world peace or hunger that he was just about to bring to fruition. And seldom did.

But, through it all, how many people ever doubted that Ali's heart was in the right place? Who doubted that he believed in his God and his politics and his mission? Who thought there was an ounce of anything but conviction in his stand against the draft? Who doubted that he gave away most of his wealth and that his deepest satisfaction was in thinking that he had used his fame and talent and power to help others?

In the ring, who doubted his talent when young, his gift for psych and strategy in his prime or his courage when old? In a brutal racket, he often was a gentleman by contrast. That's why it's so disturbing to watch what has happened to Ali.

Everybody even remotely close to boxing has known that he's been sliding badly for years. You'd listen to him and say, "Is he always this bad?" And you'd always get the same answer. "Oh, the champ's just tired. You should have seen him at breakfast (or dinner). He was just like old times." Now the faking is over. Ali says, "[After thirty years fighting] there's a great possibility something could be abnormal. . . . Now maybe people will realize that I'm just human." Neurologist Stanley Fahn said yesterday that Ali may have had Parkinsonism in 1980 when he fought Larry Holmes. The doctor also says he can't tell if the condition was caused by boxing blows until "an autopsy is done."

As usual, the order of the day is to sugarcoat Ali's condition. Doctors say Ali can live "a normal life" with medication. His spirits are "terrific" and he's "responding well to treatment." Pardon me if I have two opposite reactions: I hope so and I'll believe it when I see it.

This is a day when, like a lot of Ali fans who haven't wanted to face his condition, I'm fresh out of upbeat morals, at the bottom of the barrel when it comes to silver linings. Maybe, a month or a year from now, Ali's trips to the hospital will be remembered as a happy tale; maybe facing up to his problems and swallowing a few drugs (Sinemet and Symmetrel) will erase what seems to be the effects of years of right crosses and left hooks.

But that's not how a lot of people feel today. We want to blame boxing for giving Ali such a brutal profession. We want to blame anyone and everyone who had a hand in making him a fame junkie who couldn't quit after he beat Frazier or Foreman or even Spinks. We want to blame ourselves for being satisfied with his masks and never demanding that he show who was behind them. We want to blame everyone who led him to believe that we loved him only for his poems and slogans and comebacks and victories and bravado. Now, as Ali goes into the exhausted remnants of his act, he seems incapable of believing that we ask nothing more of him than that he do the best he can, fight the best he still can.

Ali's life has been one of our public novels for a long time. Knowing every chapter of that life as we do, having in a sense lived it along with him, can we really imagine any other ending than the one we see unfolding? And how long can we watch the rest, hoping for some medical deus ex machina that will bring us a happy ending?

The Worst
of Possible Worlds

December 22, 1979—In hell, boxing would be the national pastime.

In the worst of all possible worlds, prizefighting, awful as its basic premises are, would be dignified and almost ennobling compared to what surrounds it.

That is to say, in that world, where the large majority of the people were poor, uneducated, inured to violence and general hopelessness, to be a boxer would be to wear a valid badge of honor.

In a place that offered no realistic hope of escape, where ideals were debased by the overriding amoral realities of the struggle to subsist, a man who raised his fists and proclaimed the four corners of the ring a refuge of rules, a haven of brutal justice, would be a moral prince.

Since, in our midst, in many cities, we tolerate just such pockets of hell, then have we not given sanction to the fight game—a charter that we cannot yet withdraw?

And those deaths in the ring, like Willie Classen's last month, instead of reserving them for closed-circuit telecasts, as New York has done, shouldn't they be shown on the evening news as a symbolic distillation of everything ineradicable in our society from which we wish to turn our eyes?

Boxing, and especially the sport's central logical implication—death—sends a shiver through polite society. If the legal death penalty appalls the populace so much that, after centuries of public hangings, our cyanide tablets are now dropped behind closed doors, then what must our reaction be to the public execution by battering of an innocent man?

That, of course, is what Classen's death—on November 28, five days after he was punched into a coma at the Felt Forum—amounts to when reduced to its starkest terms. Two men agreed, as part of their contractual agreement with the consuming public, to try their best to knock each other unconscious by means of hitting one another with maximum force in the head with their fists. The state approved. Tickets were sold.

Since the line between unconsciousness by bludgeoning and death is never a clear one—certainly not, for instance, in a murder trial—we should be forced to face boxing's logical implications. But we never are.

Twenty-five years ago, only the names were different. Ed Sanders and Ralph Weiser were New York's boxing victims of 1954.

Jimmy Cannon wrote: "The bums who get rum money for selling their blood to banks do it privately with only a nurse to watch them. Even they can regard the tortured act, this deformed philanthropy, with pride. But pugs give their blood publicly and for money alone. Oh, it's a beautiful racket."

Once again, just as when Kid Paret died in 1962, a commission has met and this week released its handful of safety reforms. Now, after "discontinuing" boxing in New York for a month, the fight game will be free to resume its trade in the new year.

The New York State Athletic Commission has reformed boxing, man's second-oldest profession, in a month. That's like throwing a shoe at a family of roaches in a kitchen corner, then turning the lights off and saying, "Well, they won't be back."

No plans have been made on whether to throw the other shoe.

The commission's major reform, in its report to Governor Hugh Carey, is to institute an eight-hour course for ringside doctors and referees on how to recognize the early signs of neurological trauma.

Will there be tests? Will anyone lose a license if they don't master the nuances of neurological trauma? Who's kidding who? Make sure there's somebody to wake these guys up and send them home after the lecture's over.

"You've got to remember, I don't find doctors lined up outside my office wanting to be panel physicians," said the commission chairman, Jack Prenderville.

No, indeed, not for fifty dollars a night to oversee sixty rounds of boxing. Not when the medical director of the State Athletic Commission—the man who okayed Classen to fight—was, at the time, under a year's suspension by another state agency for submission of false bills and allowing unlicensed employees to give treatments.

Not when the two ringside doctors the night of Classen's beating—one a urologist, the other a pediatrician—now say they never saw any of the punches in the ninth round that led to Classen's death.

Only two commission steps are ameliorative: forcing any fighter who has been knocked out to be inactive for ninety days rather than thirty and a study of the possibility of switching from eight-ounce to ten-ounce gloves.

People who have lived the fight game, however, know that rules and commissions and licensing qualifications barely touch the reality of the sport.

"I'm glad to hear they've gone from thirty days to ninety days. That's the way it is here in D.C.," said Sugar Ray Leonard's lifelong trainer, Dave Jacobs. "And I think they should go to the ten-ounce gloves. The ones we use now are like nothin' on your hands at all.

"But these rules and regulations don't change the game or help it. Boxing can't be too strict, or it won't survive. Crack down on qualifications and, hey, who's going to be left, especially at the club level? You'll kill the roots of the sport.

"You can't put responsibility on the doctors and referees. They don't know a fighter's personal history or how much punishment he can stand. They look to the corner—the manager and trainer—to see when it should be stopped. It's always been that way.

"It's all on the shoulders of the fighter's own people, and always will be. If you don't care for your own man, he'll be destroyed anyway.

"It only takes seconds to scramble a man's brains," said Jacobs, one of the most respected manager-trainers in boxing. "The only people who have an idea of when a fighter's still got his right mind and when he's all of a sudden helpless are the people in his corner who've watched him all his life.

"They should know that you always stop it a few seconds too soon, rather than a few seconds too late."

And that, as long as boxing exists, will be the totally unregulatable line of demarcation between sport, maiming and death—a few seconds.

Willie Classen lived in hell and died trying to fight his way up, if not out.

Classen, who would have been twenty-nine last Sunday, spent time in jail, suffered periods of heroin addiction, was convicted of statutory rape of a woman who later became the first of his three wives and had a three-inch scar on his neck from a broken bottle swung by a girlfriend.

He was arrested at various times for robbery and assault. He also had periods of momentary redemption from his life in New York's El Barrio and the South Bronx—months when he kicked the yellow snow, held a job as a security guard, ran in the mean streets before dawn for conditioning and made himself into a tough enough banger that he battled current middle-weight champ Vito Antuofermo to a split decision before losing.

"Good?" said Jacobs. "I saw him on TV once. The kid was dynamite."

Good enough that he once fought in London. But, of course, that fight (for $3,000) was on forty-eight hours' notice as a stand-in. He was out of condition. He was battered unconscious.

After midnight, his manager asked him if he'd rather go to the hospital for a brain scan or get some fried chicken before the last fast-food place closed.

Classen chose the fried chicken. Six weeks later, New York certified him fit to fight. And one week later, he was dead.

By the standards of hell, Willie Classen led a decent life. And boxing, which killed him, was the best part of it.

Leon Spinks:
No Jokes, Please

February 19, 1978—There is no riddle of the Spinks.

The new heavyweight champion's life is as self-evident as the gap where his two front teeth were punched out.

When Leon Spinks needs to reach to the roots of his boxing fury, he thinks of the father who separated from a wife and seven children, leaving for a legacy the burning words "You'll never be nothin'."

Spinks, the oldest of the seven, felt responsible for the brood and routinely came to school unfed. "Leon would say, 'I left home early so the little ones would feel free to eat,'" recalls one of Spinks's teachers, Charles Sleigh. "I've seen Leon many a day have school doughnuts and water from the fountain as breakfast and lunch. I wouldn't mention his father's name to him for anything. I couldn't watch his face."

Spinks, a scrawny child prone to low blood pressure and blackouts, recalls his father bitterly, telling how the old man would hang him from a nail and swat him across the face with a cord, or call him a fool. The father now appears occasionally at the fights of his famous son. "Just shows up some-times," says Spinks's mother.

When Spinks needs that final push on his predawn training runs, he only needs to think of the North St. Louis projects called Pruitt-Igoe and Darst-Webbe where he was raised. The Pruitt-Igoe residence was blown up after the city condemned it.

Of the apartment in Darst-Webbe where Spinks lived for ten years, next-door neighbor Delzora Lenoir says, "When you're raised in a place like this, all you can think of is get out.

"Leon dropped out of school because it was more dangerous to go to Vashon High with the riots and the teachers getting beat up than it was to stay home."

"I think Leon beat Ali because he was just sick and tired of the vermin around here," says another neighbor, Ozell Johnson.

When Spinks asks himself, "Why do I fight?" he only needs to look in the mirror, or listen to his own speech, for an answer.

"You've got to force every word out of Leon," says Sleigh, who was his remedial education teacher. "He's proud, and he hates to make a mistake and have people laugh at him."

All that and much more—his brother awaits trial for assault with intent to kill—make up the mountain of suppressed anger that feeds Spinks the fighter.

On the other hand, sustaining Spinks the man—making him a person described as generous, thoughtful of others, sensitive, disciplined, shy, play-ful—is a remarkable family life built on a rock of a mother, Kay Spinks.

"His mother is one in a thousand," says Vashon principal Cozy Marks, who has seen almost all the Spinks clan. "Strong on goals, and self-pride, and religion.

"That precious woman has had to come into this office so many times. But she never blames the school. She just says, 'I know my boys don't always follow the rules. I try to make a good world for them at home. And you do the same here. But in between we have to turn them over to that other world.'"

When Kay Spinks's boys were beaten and robbed of their food money as small children, she did the job of her long-gone husband, chasing down the young bullies and whupping them herself.

"That story is told now as a funny Mama Spinks anecdote, the perfect one-liner about the little woman at ringside with the Bible in her lap. But it was never funny.

Another story, however—that the Spinks brothers, Leon and Michael, had to fight to survive—is no tall tale.

"The Spinks boys and a friend or two formed their own little protective unit," recalls principal Marks. "They never picked on others, but by the time the Spinkses got to high school, I never heard of anybody bothering them.

"We try to teach our students to resolve conflicts other than through bullets," says Marks. "But I have to admit, our kids have to fight to survive. . . . Anything wrong that's happened in this city, it's happened in Darst-Webbe."

The only enigma about Spinks is how he could rise from this rubble so relatively clean.

"Leon's not a smart person," says Sleigh. "He's a nice person. You could leave him in your office for an hour and he'd never get into anything. I'm afraid he'll get tangled up with characters who aren't as honest as he is."

"People don't really understand Leon. He looks like the worst man in the world," says Spinks's best Marine Corps buddy, Corporal Tony Santana. "He's gentle, thoughtful.

"I got a call the day after the fight. It was Leon. I couldn't believe it. He's on top now and his old pals are still down here [at Camp Lejeune, North Carolina]. But he remembers."

"What's happenin', Bull?" said Santana to Spinks. "Oooops, I forgot. I can't call you Bull no more. I have to call you Champ."

"Aw, cut that out," answered Bull Spinks. "I ain't changed."

"We hope he never changes," says Sleigh. "Where else are you going to find a young man who respects authority, trains on beer and eggs, does push-ups on the top of a moving car, has the endurance of Atlas and the patience of Job?"

The Spinkses are the most close-knit of families, each member resembling a separate and distinct finger which is always ready in a crisis to clench together with the others to make one fist prepared to meet a rough world.

"Each Spinks is completely different from every other," laughs principal Marks. "But they're all for one."

Mother Kay is bubbling, gregarious, full of street-smart quips, good humor and admonitions to pray. "You'd never guess she was quiet Leon's mother," says Sleigh. "When she's talking you can put down the phone, get a drink, come back and she's still going.

"She's told me that she used to be more worldly," says Lenoir, a frequent Spinks babysitter. "But she took to religion real big 'long about after her husband left."

Brother Michael Spinks, the rising light heavy who won an Olympic gold medal as a middleweight, splits the emotional spectrum between Leon and their mother.

"Everybody thinks Leon's quiet and Mike is the talker," laughs Lenoir. "And that's how it is until there's a pretty girl around. Mike is shy, but Leon never had no problems. Leon always have had a big mouth when it's time to party.

"People around here tease Leon that it was his old girlfriend Veda May Calvin who knocked out his teeth. They were always punchin' on each other. Veda May's a big girl. She'd smack Leon pretty good."

Leon is now married, and he and his wife, Nova, have three children, including a nine-year-old stepson.

If Leon was always the first to boogie, Mike was the one in danger of following a good time all the way to jail. "Neither of them was into the drug trafficking," says principal Marks. "But Mike let himself be guided by other things [gambling among them]. He was going deeper and deeper. If it hadn't been for one police sergeant who took an interest in him . . . well, that man saved his life."

It was the Marine Corps that helped give Leon direction. Despite reports that he beat more than one bullying NCO to the punch, during boot camp Spinks eventually took to Marine discipline.

"Leon was proud of his uniform and proud of his status as a Marine boxer," says a former Marine coach. "I don't know where they get this stuff about Leon not training right as a pro. In the Marines you'd see him out at 3 A.M. running on his own."

Marine boxing was a raw and bloody sport. One day at Camp Lejeune an Army fighter, Tommy Johnson, gave Spinks his current unique smile. Much of the rest of Spinks's remaining military career was spent in preparation for three rematches with Johnson.

"Leon made him pay for those teeth," recalls Corporal Santana. "Before Leon whipped him the final time, he had Johnson tame. I talked to Johnson before the fight and he said, 'You know, my idol used to be Muhammad Ali. Now it's Leon Spinks.' "

Despite his mother's teachings, his Marine pride, his Darst-Webbe ferocity, his 185 amateur fights and his Olympic light heavyweight gold, almost nothing in Leon Spinks's past prepared him for his stupendous present.

Of all history's heavyweight champs, Spinks has the least experience, both in the ring (eight pro fights) and in the fight-game jungle. "My greatest fear," mother Kay has repeated, "is that Leon will win the championship too soon, before he's ready."

Already the fight sharpies have spotted this brawny lamb in wolf's disguise. "Every heavyweight that can walk will make a comeback," says match-maker Teddy Brenner. "Spinks is an out-and-out amateur," scoffs Jimmy Young's manager. "The first man who fights him will beat him."

"He's a sucker for a right lead," says Ali.

"You can knock him out with a left hook," says Ali's strategist, Angelo Dundee.

"He eats the jab real good," says butting, gouging mediocrity Scott Le-Doux, who jabbed Spinks to a draw just two fights ago.

Let's see. That's the jab, the hook and the right cross—the three funda-mental punches in the sport. And experts say Spinks can be tagged at will with any of them.

Perhaps the heavyweight crown has never tottered so precariously, nor has its holder seemed so ripe for every sort of plucking.

"Spinks left Las Vegas surrounded by smiling thieves," sighed a veteran sports columnist.

Unfortunately, Spinks's naïveté has been shown too many times already.

"I hear tell Leon thought he'd signed up with the Marines for two years, but they'd got him for four," says Sleigh. Spinks's manager, Mitt Barnes, tells the same tale.

While the other U.S. Olympic winners made cagey money deals, Spinks suffered by comparison. While Sugar Ray Leonard made $42,000 on his first fight and quickly owned 100 percent of himself, Spinks earned around $30,000 for all seven of his 1977 fights.

Manager Barnes, a St. Louis teamster organizer, gets 30 percent of all Spinks's ring earnings through 1979, despite the fact that Spinks has already disavowed him, saying, "I manage myself."

Spinks's adjustment to being the world's most conspicuous athlete will be enormous. The day before the fight he felt his $320,000 purse would ensure that he could reach his eventual dream— "to own a small club and tend bar."

In the wake of perhaps the most totally unexpected upset in boxing his-tory, Spinks was still stunned, saying, "I woke up this morning and I lied in bed and looked at my championship belt. I said, 'I did it. I really did it.' "

Even the kids at Vashon know Spinks is in over his head. "We're using Leon's life as a teaching tool this week," says Marks. "On one hand, we tell them that as soon as you accomplish something, or even try to, people check into your past. Leon proves how a good character is worth as much as money.

"But the kids are embarrassed when they hear Leon talk on TV. They see that education is not like an automobile that can be recalled to get fixed in a hurry. Leon exemplifies the difference between poorness and poverty. Poverty is a state of mind, a kind of despair and giving up. Poorness is temporary, something you never stop fighting against. But Leon also exemplifies the need to stay in school."

Spinks has moved into a fast, head-spinning world. Already gifts are being borne to the new king. A huge gold ring with black onyx dice and seven diamond chips was a token of esteem from a Las Vegas jeweler.

However, even in Vegas, seven is a dangerous, two-edged number to roll. It can clean the table, or it can be craps.

No one yet knows the outcome of the enormous seven that that gap-toothed man-child rolled last week. The question on the table is no longer "Who is Leon Spinks?" but rather "What will happen to him?"

That is the real riddle of this Spinks.

No Dues
Like Boxing Dues

January 8, 1978—"Boxing has been dead in this town for twenty-five years, but us fight people live on. It's in the blood." —Fuzzy Wilson of Finley's Gym.

Blood flowed steadily from his nose and mouth and down his chin, forming a scarlet river from his chest to his boxing trunks.

The vacant-eyed Philadelphia middleweight sat slackly on his stool, his shoulders unnaturally far forward as though he might pitch slowly face first to the canvas. The snaggle-toothed fighter, breathing through his mouth because of his smashed nose, stared blankly across the D.C. Armory ring at Keith (the Sweeper) Broom, the man who had been torturing him for five rounds.

"You all right?! You all right?!" probed the cornerman, searching for any sign of consciousness.

The youngster blinked, his only sign of acknowledgment. Perhaps he was too exhausted for more.

"Then why don't ya do the stuff I been teachin' ya?"

For a moment, the scarlet knight's face lost its expression of wordless suffering. His lower lip quivered with hopeless frustration; he seemed ready to burst into tears.

Instead, he turned and spat a mouthful of blood in the direction of the old handler behind him holding a water bucket.

The red gob missed the bucket and drenched the old man's wrist and shirt cuff.

The fighter answered the bell like a condemned man—one final round of sweepings for the Broom.

"I wish," said Keith Broom of Washington, "that I could have finished him. It would have been a favor to both of us.

"But the man just stood there and took the punishment. On every shot, I was catching nothing but flesh. But he wouldn't fall. I almost feel like I should apologize to him for not hitting him harder.

"It's no fun to take a beating. I know."

For the professional fighter, that vanishing and endangered species, the canvas is the most loathed enemy of all. "I've never been stopped" is the pug's red badge of courage.

"TKOs, I've had 'em. I bleed sometimes," says Broom. "But I've never been knocked out."

That is important, he says.

"When you are badly hurt, you train your subconscious to take over. I've fought almost whole fights when I was unconscious, you might say. The other man was a blur. And some of those fights," he says, "I won."

Once in his amateur days Broom swore to himself that he would quit fighting if he was ever knocked down. Then he was decked twice in one fight and got up to win. He had to change his plan.

Now, before he goes to sleep at night, Broom sometimes feels the knockout punch hit him, feels the sickening gurgle of his own mind flushing down the drain of unconsciousness.

In the darkened room, Broom tells himself, "You're going to get up. Tighten up. Get up. Get up."

Broom says, "Muhammad Ali is great because of his will. He has been out on his feet many times against Frazier and Norton. But no one knew."

Broom knows about reaching to the bottom of the well of will. And coming up dry. In the Olympic trials in 1976, he had to fight a whirlwind named

Michael Spinks three times, including a "box-off" to see who would go and collect the Olympic gold for the U.S.

Now Spinks is known worldwide, while Broom, by a split decision, is starting out at fame's bottom rung again as a pro. Inescapably, Broom thinks about the recesses of the mind.

"They say you can work on your neck muscles so you can absorb a punch better," he says dubiously, "but I think it goes deeper than that. A fighter has unknown resources.

"Sometimes the day afterward, the fight is like a dream you can't quite remember. People tell you the things you did, the beautiful combinations, the knockout, and you say, 'I did?'"

Broom reflects for a minute on this grisly thing to which he has devoted his life, even his subconscious.

"After a fight, the boxers gather around," he says. "It is a fraternity of warmth. Perhaps we are the only ones who understand each other. After the fight, there is nothing but love."

Broom is the exception, a fighter with talent, reputation and even a bit of world travel—from the Soviet Union to Africa to Samarkand—to show for his pugilism.

If he has no job, no immediate plans except his next fight—"I'm floating; I'm not sure"—he has hope. If his first few pro purses have been slim, at least when he says, "I want to be the champ," no one laughs out loud.

Malik Dozier, steamfitter's apprentice and four-round prelim heavyweight, is the rule. He is what the old-timers call a "short heavyweight"—short on everything.

"I'm not looking to be no world champion," says Dozier, of Palmer Park, Maryland. "If I could make enough money out of this game to buy a piece of property of my own, I'd gladly leave boxing the way I came in . . . very quietly.

"I've never had nothing in my life," he says without emotion. "Why should I expect something now?"

But even for a man who expects nothing, boxing has been a disillusionment.

"If you got a name, like Sugar Ray Leonard, boxing's great," says Dozier, "but not if you're at rock bottom like me."

Dozier caught punches from a 6-foot-6, 239-pound behemoth in the preliminary. Leonard's gross: $30,000. Dozier's cut: $150. Before expenses.

"I got four rounds with a beast for a hundred and fifty dollars." Dozier spits out a curse. "Jaw broke, teeth broke. That doesn't cover dental bills for one good punch.

"I'm reaching in my own pocket to fight. I sacrifice, risk my body. Hell, I risk my life. Who's going to care? Nobody."

The primal magnetism of what may well be the world's second-oldest profession often seems inexplicable.

"These fighters take that pain and agony and they put it on their shoulder and they walk it," says George Peterson, a local fight manager. "Sometimes, I think everybody in this game is searching for a ghost."

Fuzzy Wilson has been tracking his specter for fifty years.

"I've always been in hopes of training a champion," says Wilson, sixty-six. "I guess I haven't gotten too close, though sometimes it felt like it."

Finley's is a small, ancient, one-room gym in a loft above a repair garage. No one is certain who Finley is, or was.

Finley's only entrance—a single, unidentified knife-and-graffiti-scarred door at the intersection of three unlighted alleys—makes the cave mouth leading to Dante's Inferno look like a "welcome" mat.

If Beelzebub wanted to take a coffee break from the nether regions, he would look perfect leaning against the door to Finley's Gym, puffing on a sinner.

The stairway to Fuzzy Wilson's lair is narrow and steep. At the top is a hand-lettered sign. Instead of "All hope abandon ye who enter here," it says, "Box at your own risk."

"One in a thousand that come up those stairs is the right one," says Wilson, adding with a chuckle, "Looks hole-in-the-floor, doesn't it?

"I should be old now," he says, "sitting back in a rocking chair with a cane. But it keeps me young sitting here waiting to see who will come up through the floor."

Wilson, quiet, kindly and a light-year from bitterness, knocks an ash on the floor. "I was raised in fight gyms. I couldn't wait to be a man and get this cigar in my mouth," he says, laughing.

"Your fighters are like your children," says the trainer. "There's a psychic wave between you and them in the ring. You're tied to them in spirit. And they worry you so. Gotta call them at all hours. Are you doing your running? Are you eating right? You got a woman there with you, son?"

Fuzzy leans back like a man who has thought seriously about going on the wagon many times. "These damn fighters have cost me one wife, two good women and four automobiles."

But then, Wilson acknowledges, it has been many years since anyone in Washington with good sense got into the fight game for money.

"Used to be that the rotten managers would take your fighters, spin their heads around and rob 'em blind. The managers and promoters were tied into the mob and they'd sit back and live off the fat of the lamb," he said.

"But it's a fool who tries to make money off boxing now. The turnip's given up its last drop of blood.

"I saw there the Cinderella Boy [Leonard] and his manager, Mr. Brains [Angelo Dundee], made forty thousand for his first pro fight. That's great. Maybe it'll revive interest.

"If it's true, that means I can now name on one finger all the Washington fighters in fifty years who have made forty thousand in their entire careers.

"Maybe Holly Mims did, too, even though he couldn't ever get enough work, or a title shot. And Gene Smith made some money."

Wilson looks around the poster-papered walls of his little office as though running the names of a lifetime through his mind. Tiger Flowers, Sonny Boy West, Pop Whitney.

"Tommy Toughy vs. Young Rat Moore," says one placard, yellowed and crisp as parchment, dated November 18, 1821.

"Yes," said Wilson. "Far as I can recall, that's the whole list."

And he held up one gnarled, accusing finger.

Richard Jackson, young yet full of self-reproach, and Roland Pryor, balding and full of regrets, have come out of retirement. That old familiar scent —the revival of boxing—is in the wind again.

Jackson was Leonard's peer coming up through the Washington amateur ranks. "We'd stand toe to toe and bang for three rounds. It was an eyelash between us," recalls Jackson.

But Jackson figured if he wasn't even the best junior welter in Palmer Park, why bother. "I just wanted a place in the street. You know, be a big man . . ."

The night Leonard won Olympic gold, Jackson wept. "I kept thinking: That could have been me," he says.

Now Jackson is a Leonard reclamation project. "Ray takes me everywhere, so I can meet people, stop dreading the world I don't know," says Jackson. "I'm fighting on his cards. This is my only second chance."

Pryor, thirty-four, is what Wilson calls a "gypsy fighter," changing managers, trainers, gyms. Going in and out of retirement.

For several lean years, Pryor was managed by his father, a gospel preacher who saw Satan behind the eyes of every matchmaker and promoter. Perhaps with reason.

Finally, sick of long layoffs and "I was robbed" decisions when he could get fights, Pryor worked Metro construction for four years. But steady money and the civilian life were not enough.

"Man, this isn't me," said Pryor, looking at his waistline one morning. And the crusade began again.

As one of Pryor's acquaintances, Melvin Smith, an ex-Golden Gloves champ, says, "Fighting is the perfect spartan lifestyle. We all know it. You feel like a walking razor, clean and sharp. All your tensions and angers are released into roadwork and sparring.

"Eventually, you know the truth of what you have made out of yourself is going to show within those four corners of the ring," Smith says.

"But out of the ring, you'll do anything to avoid a fight. You know how good you are. You wouldn't dream of hurting your hands on some dummy's head."

Pryor longed to feel like a razor again. "A person can do a whole lot of things," he points out, "but there's one special talent and you can't deny it once you've found it.

"This ring is my school," he says soberly, "and fighting is my life's curriculum."

Pryor talks with manic speed, repeating himself, sometimes brilliant, sometimes dull. His mind works like an old man's, remembering ancient injustices but sometimes forgetting the details of the present.

He worries about the way he stayed awake all night in a state of hyper-excitement before his first comeback victory.

"I've always been a keyed-up person," explains Pryor, handsome, vulnerable, talented, often slighted.

"You wouldn't believe it but I've heard people say I'm getting punch-drunk," he says, giving a chilling forced smile that reveals his deep worry about himself. "I'm not punch-drunk, that's one thing I know."

The only prompting that the Jacksons and Pryors of Washington need to get their gloves on again is the rumor that the fight game will boom again as in the '40s.

In those days, Goldie Ahearn at Turner's Arena in Washington and, later, Eli Hanover at Steelworkers Hall in Baltimore were colorful promoters who found steady work for club fighters as well as contenders.

Ahearn and Hanover are gone, but they are mourned as though the wake were yesterday.

In their era, boxing had a steady pulsebeat of weekly fights. Today, the sport seems to lie dormant for months, given up for dead until some gaudy extravaganza comes along and, like a huge electric shock, makes it flail its limbs in a cruel mock imitation of life.

In the wake of these shock treatments—an Ali title defense at Capital Centre, a Leonard card at the armory, a Don King fiasco in Annapolis—a hundred anxious hands reach to take the pulse of their misunderstood Frankenstein.

Washington's scattered boxing community still becomes giddy in the regal presence of the moribund sweet science's remaining superstars.

The ring announcer working last month's Leonard card became so flustered at having Joe Frazier and Joe DiMaggio at ringside that he intoned, "We will now take a short intermission because there are still lots of people parking their cars in the lobby."

That malapropism perfectly captured the "state of agitated paralysis" that King says grips boxing in Washington and elsewhere.

It is hard to appreciate how desperate Washington's fight folk are for a Moses until one hears King say that Washington is one of his promotional strongholds.

"I have learned how to manipulate human frailty. That is my coin. The truth takes ten years to catch up with the lie," blustered King when he brought the Ali-Evangelista circus to town last spring.

King believes that boxing should advertise its larger-than-life appetites and sufferings. "Me? I'm just your run-of-the-mill egotistical maniac. Just because I'm paranoid doesn't mean they're not out to get me," he crows.

"Don't bring me mortal men to fight. Bring me giants. Don't mince words when you blast me. Lay me out. Make me big."

Washington, however, has not learned the new carnival methods of selling boxing as a seamy sideshow of sports.

At Washington's main pro gyms—Finley's and Oakcrest and Hillcrest Heights in Prince Georges County—the fighters and trainers are still wedded to their razor-sharp vision of the old sweet science, not the new bitter hard sell.

Their world of frayed heavy bags, taped hands, speed bags, jump ropes, weights, mirrors and the small sparring rings stays eternally the same.

If boxing has kept sixty-six-year-old Fuzzy Wilson young, it seems to have made his friend Henry Thomas old.

They sit in the back room of Finley's and don't say much. Wilson is plump, moon-faced, methodical. A boxing Buddha with a short cigar and a reserve as deep as Siddhartha's.

Thomas, only fifty-four, seems the older of the two trainers. He is thin, withdrawn, and counts his words before he spends them. "It's hard to find the old-time smell in the gyms anymore," he says. "I don't know where it went."

Probably with his youth. Boxing always had all his love. "I told my wife if I ever had to choose between her and the fights, she'd lose a close decision," said Thomas without any hint of amusement. "On our wedding night, I went to work in 'KO' Scott's corner. Didn't get home until midnight. She started to leave me that night."

He paused to smile to himself. "But she didn't."

"Nothing's really changed," he continues. "If you want to fight, you've got to work the little towns. The fellows don't talk about it much, but most of the fighters in this town now are driving two hundred, maybe four hundred miles for a seventy-five- or hundred-fifty-dollar fight and sleepin' in cars at night afterward. If they aren't doing it now, they had to do it once. No dues like boxing dues."

Thomas has always been willing to keep his membership paid up. No matter what. When his D.C. job was moved forty miles north of Baltimore, Thomas continued to live in Washington and appeared magically at Finley's every night.

"I caught the five A.M. Capital Transit bus, then transferred to another bus to get home," he says. "Many's the morning I'd hear a car's horn blow and I'd jump out of the bed and think: I've overslept!"

He still winces and smiles ruefully as he tells the old horn story on himself. Yes, he says, the years of travel took a lot out of him. He had a stroke that left his right hand somewhat palsied. Now he is retired.

Every evening, Thomas sits at the top of the stairs at Finley's Gym, smoking cigarettes and watching the men feinting and suffering and punching before him, and he listens to the feet and waits for the footsteps of a champion.

The sign above his head says, "Box at your own risk."

The Man Who Loved Joe Louis

February 8, 1978—My grandfather Joshua was a generous, God-fearing reactionary.

Like many a struggling farmer in Selbyville who endured the Depression, Joshua held fast to two heroes who never let him down: Abraham Lincoln and Joe Louis.

Joshua spoke of both—the rail-splitter and the son of a sharecropper as though they were old friends who had helped him cut ditch banks and slaughter the hogs.

To him, Lincoln meant wisdom, and Louis courage. To a man like Joshua, with little schooling and fourteen hours of work to face each day, those words had a meaning.

Joshua's wife, Sadie, who had two years of college, was ashamed of her husband's friendships with members of the Ku Klux Klan. "Your father thinks it's a social club like the Elks and Kiwanis," Sadie told her daughter Elizabeth. In other times, despite that disclaimer, the children of Joshua and

Sadie might have thought of their father as a man whose views were narrow and who tolerated the Klan. Instead, they remembered him as a man who loved Joe Louis.

That is one way history changes, not only with wars and Presidents but in the stories each generation passes on about what it loves and hates.

Louis's fights were a family occasion in Joshua's home. Everyone gathered around the cloth-covered Philco and listened to the crackling, romantic account of the distant battle.

Joshua was nervous before the fights. As a young man he had run a grocery store, which fared poorly. Whenever a young man of the town would challenge him to a wrestling match, he would shut the store for the afternoon, take off his bow tie, and they would grapple in the dirt of Main Street. Joshua was a good wrestler, a poor businessman.

That night in 1938 when "Joe Louie," as Joshua always called him, fought Max Schmeling, the tension was almost too much to bear. The world listened to Louis and Schmeling that night, but none listened closer than Joshua with his ear just inches from the Philco, his fists moving in pantomime to transfer his farmer's strength to Louis.

When Louis's work of revenge was done, and done quickly in 2:52 of the first round, Joshua had to leave the living room quickly. When he came back he was blowing his nose in a huge red denim handkerchief.

"That was the closest I ever came to seeing my father cry," said Joshua's daughter. "That is, until the day my brother died."

A quarter century later, Joshua still told the story of that fight to his grandson. Joshua and the boy walked down a long dusty road to the farm. "The night Joe Louie knocked out the Nazi," Joshua said, "that was a great day for all of us."

When I met Joe Louis last year before the first round of the now notorious U.S. Boxing Championship on an aircraft carrier off the coast of Florida, his hand was enormous and strong, his handshake soft with the certainty of strength.

"You were my grandfather's hero," I said for the record. "He listened to all your fights and threw every punch with you."

"Yeah, that's good" said Louis, vacant-eyed, not seeming to hear. "Nice to meet you." And he shook the next hand in line.

I had been prepared to meet the wreck of Joe Louis. Many a fighter had said to me, "I just hope I don't end up like poor old Joe Louis, broke and standing in a Las Vegas casino shaking hands."

Louis's bad end has become part of the lore of a bitter sport. Like the myth of his career, the legend of Louis's degradation has become a Bunyanesque tale. His $1.25 million income-tax debt was just the beginning of the Louis decline and fall. By 1960 the Treasury wolf pack gave up trying to collect and closed the Louis case. But the Brown Bomber had become boxing's wooden Indian, wheeled out (for a few bucks) for every title fight to predict an upset. Whenever Muhammad Ali took a radical position, the press flocked to Louis for a counter-quote from the good Negro.

When Louis had a mental breakdown in 1971, his five-month institutionalization became grist for two biographies which painted him as a pathetic paranoid who saw gangland hit men blowing poison gas at his bald head from every ceiling ventilator.

Yet, just as 1930s radio broadcasts encouraged Americans to imagine herculean championship fights, the spotty press reports of the '70s of Louis in old age have encouraged the imagination to create a nightmare of pathos.

The Louis that I have met and talked with three times in the last ten months would have gotten along fine with Joshua. Neither cared a whit for ideology or abstract ideas. Some are insulted that Louis barters his reputation for money. Louis isn't one of them. "There's a buck in it," he explained. "That's the same reason I gave for becoming a fighter forty years ago. What's so hard to understand?"

Louis is only comfortable, certain of acceptance, in the midst of a fight crowd. So he migrates with them whenever possible, not out of some aging despair, but because he is a simple, innocent man who has mastered just one craft.

Joshua would never leave Selbyville for the comforts of the city, not in the face of his last sickness or the loss of old friends. The farm was his sustenance, and he died within sight of the Eastern Shore soil. No one asked why.

Louis, sixty-four, who had major heart surgery in November and was released from a Houston hospital last month, is sure to stay close to boxing until the last possible day, even if young folks shake their heads and say, "Look at the poor old factotum."

One memory of Louis will stay with me—not a glorious film clip from his twelve years as world champ, but a breakfast in Pensacola, Florida, in 1977 when Louis was supposed to be but a shell of himself.

Louis and four young heavyweights had breakfast together, destroying platter after platter of flapjacks. The patriarch of punches listened to their jokes and laughed quietly to himself in the right places. When he told a story, there was silence. When his punch line came, the heavyweight laughs were genuine.

A black derby hat was passed around the table, the property of flashy young contender Jody Ballard. The derby came to rest jauntily on Louis's balding head for the duration of the two-hour meal. It looked at home there.

Joe Louis was in his natural element, and no one at the table could have worn it better.

Interlude

London Calling

June 28, 1981—The proper way to arrive at one's first Wimbledon is to hail a shiny black London cab beside Hyde Park, then sit back in luxury until one has been chauffeured past the long queues of ticket-hungry mortals in Church Road and deposited regally at the main gate of the All-England Lawn Tennis and Croquet Club.

It is not considered proper to leave one's wallet, with all one's money, credit cards and credentials, in the back seat of the taxi.

Nor is it considered absolutely de rigueur to drop all one's parcels in the middle of the street, then chase the cab as it heads back to London, screaming as one goes, "Stop that taxi!"

However, I did it my way.

After all, not everybody can come up to the bobby at the gate in a lather worthy of Bjorn Borg in the fifth set and croak, "Help!" Actually, that's wrong: Borg never has sweated as much as your correspondent was sweating then.

"Left wallet in cab," I panted succinctly.

"You're all right," said the 8-foot-tall officer. "The cabby will return your wallet."

"Huh?"

"London cabbies are notoriously honest."

"I had three hundred fifty dollars in the wallet in cash. Too much, I know."

"The cabby will probably return your wallet," amended the bobby.

It's a peculiarity of human nature that we sometimes see most clearly when our luck is worst; disaster unclouds the vision. Walk down the street on the day you've been fired and you may see suffering humanity with a startling vividness; few tonics surpass the shock of calamity.

So even as small and comic a matter as a man finding himself in a foreign country without his wallet can have a certain focusing effect on the perceptions. Wimbledon, in particular, is a singularly interesting sight to a person who has, momentarily, no credentials, no money, no proof of identity. Of course, in few places in the sporting world is it so imperative to have exactly those things—credentials, money, a sense of identity.

Even after having talked your way inside, left with one pound and a few shillings in loose change in your pocket, you notice that eight bruised, not yet ripe strawberries with a ladle of supermarket cream over them cost more than two dollars. In the sycophantish lore of Wimbledon, this dish is known as strawberries with double Devonshire cream. To a man with no wallet, it's called a shameless rip-off. The poetically named ice lolly for which Wimbledon is famous is a small orange Popsicle which might retail for two cents in an honest world. It costs a dollar.

In short, to a fellow with an empty pocket, Wimbledon looks like an elegant con game, like a down-on-its-luck family of aristocrats who open their house to tourists, giving a glance at the master's bedchamber for a quid. Wimbledon is, in part, a blue-blooded shuck-and-jive, an upper-crust version of Disneyland.

The greatest shock at the championships is the incredible inconveniences to which the public is subjected and the casual indifference with which its aggravations are observed.

First of all, Wimbledon is a zoo. No major American sports event, except perhaps the Indianapolis 500, is so overcrowded; the pathways between outside courts often are completely impassable and the subterranean corridors in the bowels of the Centre Court stadium and the No. 1 Court are so jammed with elbowing throngs that elderly women and children often look frightened and men are shoved and jostled to the edge of real anger.

Quite simply, the All-England Club has decided that it is willing to let 38,000 people a day sardine themselves into quarters that would be filled with 25,000.

"The wife and I went to Wimbledon a few years back, just to say we'd had the experience," said Jack Scagell, a London builder, "but we'd certainly never go again. You can't move, can't see anything. It's much better to watch it on the telly."

It is Wimbledon's central pretense that this is an elegant event, part of the "season" that includes the Royal Ascot races and rowing at Henley-on-Thames. If you arrive by limousine and sit in the royal box with the Duke and Duchess of Kent, maybe it is; for a few hundred people with the correct-color passes, Wimbledon is a chance to sit on the clubhouse balconies and look out over the lawns at the spire of a huge, ancient church on a hill. And, if they choose, look twenty feet down at several thousand people who all seem to be trapped in one great outdoor stuck elevator.

However, it would be closer to the truth to say that Wimbledon is saturated with commercialism. It's true that the one tiny word "Rolex" in neat yellow paint on the main scoreboard is the only brand name that appears inside the large grandstand complex.

But it is also true that a bazaar worthy of Calcutta encircles half of the stadium, offering everything from bonbons to the tackiest Wimbledon souvenirs. Even the members' enclosure—a high-security outdoor café and bar —has been invaded by a legion of sales reps who find it an excellent place to do business over a pint of bitter. And, as always, the players' team room is the site of more deal-closing handshakes than any other venue in tennis. Endorsements, appearances and future tournament commitments are wrapped up there.

It is stunning to those whose basic familiarity with Wimbledon is the American telecast of the semifinals and finals in the gorgeously giant and green Centre Court to realize that the huge preponderance of the tournament exists on outside courts, which are a scandal both for players and for spectators.

By the third day of the championships, most of those grass courts are, to put it mildly, an eyesore. No minor-league baseball infield would show its face if it were half so brown, scarred and patched with makeshift sod. Wimbledon insists that brown grass is hardier and tougher. Then how come the grass around the courts is so pretty while the grass on the courts looks like it has been trampled to stubble?

Wimbledon is the only summer event that is played by people in short pants and watched by people in parkas.

On three of the first five days this week—the days that veterans called typical—the effect of watching Wimbledon tennis was roughly equivalent to sitting through a seven-hour football game on a raw, drizzly fall day. The outside grandstands, exposed to the winds and intermittent rain, are brutal; the inside stands, including Centre Court, are even colder, since the wind seems to swirl once it gets in there, and everything is in shadow.

Curiously, the British seem to regard all these discomforts as the surest proof that they are having a good time. Hardiness, and the conspicuous demonstration thereof, is an English trait. If the sun can be detected behind the steel clouds, that's wryly called "a beach day."

As further instance, on the tube (subway)—which takes an hour and a transfer or two to get from Westminster Abbey to Wimbledon—it is normal for people of all ages and sexes to prefer standing to sitting; vacant seats will go ignored for several stops as passengers stand. That is, until the odd American decides to sit.

That tube lets its passengers off at Southfield Station, which is more than a mile from Wimbledon's gates. The English think nothing of the hike. However, a line of fifty or more taxis stands adjacent to the station, the drivers preying on tourists who either do not know how far away the grounds are or are simply too lazy for a constitutional.

Americans are no slouches at waiting in ridiculous lines to get tickets to a World Series or such, but the British are, far and away, more daft. The daily lines are immense (several hundred yards long and a half dozen abreast), but they cannot touch the unbelievable line that has been building for a week to get the couple of thousand standing-room spots for Saturday's Centre Court final. These zany campers dress in blue jeans, sleep in pup tents and, in some cases, have tuxedos and top hats hung on the iron fences in preparation for the great day. If they get in.

It is fascinating that a nation so obviously hardy constantly goes through such paroxysms of self-flagellation for its supposed lack of national competitiveness. British players, fans and press seem obsessed with the question: "Why are we such good losers?"

"I hate the English attitude of putting up a 'good show' in defeat," said Anne Hobbs, the British woman who upset Virginia Wade and reached the round of sixteen.

"I've gone to America to train with Dennis Ralston because he's helping me get rid of that point of view. It's not enough to be satisfied with playing well. If you don't win, you can't be pleased. If you're good enough to win a set, then how can you be content with not winning the whole match?

"That's the American attitude."

It should be reiterated that a fellow with no wallet is prone to notice the wind and cold; he sees the brown spots in a generally green lawn. And he tastes the sour strawberry, not the sweet one.

In fact, he even has a tendency to anger.

Not everyone can leave his wallet in a cab. But when that same person can destroy public property, vandalize the Wimbledon clubhouse, force a change of championship rules and risk having himself ejected from the grounds—all on his first day—well, that's going some.

You see, Officer, it happened this way. It was after midnight and I was one of the last two reporters to leave the stadium. I had called various police stations, taxi companies and lost and found agencies throughout the day and the notoriously honest English cabby had not returned my wallet.

So when the telephone box next to the pressroom began eating my shillings and giving me nothing but disconnect dial tones in response, I slugged it. Naturally, the entire contraption—perhaps six square feet and thirty pounds in size—came off its plaster moorings, fell four feet to the floor and smashed into countless pieces, coins rolling all over the place.

What you might call the perfect end to the perfect day.

Since I was, by now, one of the last people on the Wimbledon grounds. Except for the gateman, there was nobody to whom to report my damages.

I slept. I awoke. And in every sense, it was a new day.

In a pointless exercise, I reported to the lost-property office in Penton Street to fill out forms.

"My name is Boswell and . . ."

"Oh yes, Mr. Boswell," said the man at the window. "Been expecting you. I suppose you'll be wanting your wallet."

The driver's number was 11824. He didn't even leave a name or address. As is British law, he was entitled to a 10 percent finder's fee for returning a lost wallet, which came to $35 of the $350. I doubled the reward and wondered if that wasn't rather small recompense for someone's saving your life in a hostile land.

On arriving back at Wimbledon, I learned immediately that there was a hot news story brewing. Vandals had broken into the hallowed grounds and smashed a telephone box in the pressroom in search of cash. Apparently the damage had been done with a large bat or, perhaps, an ax.

No one knew as yet what other larceny had been done on the grounds. Police would investigate. All doors to the portion of the clubhouse containing the various pressrooms would now be locked at a far earlier hour, vastly inconveniencing all American journalists.

"I'll tell them I broke it, apologize and pay the damages," I said to the one other reporter, Barry Lorge, who had heard the thing that went crash in the night. "I feel like a fool, but I don't suppose they can shoot me."

"Don't be so sure," said Lorge, president of the Tennis Writers of America. "This is Wimbledon. In a hundred and four years, they've never had a vandal before. They're already making rules. They love to make rules. And enforce them. There are a lot of very stern old men around here."

Lorge ushered me into the presence of the head of press operations, Roy McKelvie, an Irishman with a rubicund face and a reputation for temper. "He'll blow his stack," predicted Lorge.

I told my story.

At the end, he said, "Well, accidents will happen."

He phoned the "telephone boys" to come repair "a rather well-smashed box." And he wouldn't hear of any payment of damages.

If losing wallets produces one form of insight, then being forgiven for our sins produces another. We see others more generously, cut them a little more slack. The strawberries began to taste better. The crowds could be tolerated.

As events conducted in the real world are judged, Wimbledon seemed to be doing rather decently after all. Where could you find so many roses and pink and purple hydrangeas? What stadium in any sport could match the labyrinthine catacombs here, the sense of place and tradition?

Today, as this Wimbledon reached its midpoint, the sun tried to break out from behind the constant quilt of clouds over London. It failed. The skies over Wimbledon remained gray and chilly, not at all the setting one might expect for the world's greatest tennis tournament.

In other words, all things considered, a beach day.

Golf

Mr. Jack Nicklaus

A Finish Worthy of the Start

All in all, it's probably good that Jack Nicklaus never completely lost his love handles, always had a squeaky voice, couldn't tell a joke, was color-blind, couldn't resist raiding the refrigerator for ice cream and had a lousy sand game. (Yes, and he backslid a thousand times on the damn cigarettes, too.)

Otherwise, in the distant future when his career and his legend are discussed, few would be able to believe that such a person—almost embarrassingly close to being an ideal competitor and sportsman—could actually have existed. In fact, as he ages, it might be helpful if Nicklaus would do something wrong—get a parking ticket or make a bad business deal—just so his psychobiographers won't have to throw up their hands in despair.

Few careers, in any walk of life, have started so spectacularly, then continued steadily upward, almost without interruption, for so long. Success, which has ruined many, only refueled Nicklaus. Each piece of good fortune seemed to be reinvested at compound interest. Neither twenty major golf championships, spread over twenty-seven years from 1959 to 1986, nor a personal empire worth hundreds of millions of dollars seemed to disorient this son of a Midwestern drugstore pharmacist. He took himself seriously, but not as seriously as his responsibilities—to his talent, his sport, his family, even his public image.

Yet, just as soon as you started to think you had his diligent dutiful character pinned down and encircled, word would seep back to the PGA Tour that Nicklaus the Practical Joker had struck again, usually in some new installment of his lifelong battle with his friend John McCormack, a tournament director.

Once, after blowing a tournament that McCormack had run, the eternally stoic, always utterly self-controlled Nicklaus walked calmly into Mc-Cormack's office and destroyed everything in the room, right down to the picture frames.

After the sounds of smashing and crashing had stopped, Nicklaus walked out, composed and smiling, leaving McCormack and the rest of the golf world to wonder—and never find out—whether his true feelings had been rage or amusement.

Even Nicklaus recognized the problem of living such a relentlessly mythological life. (Let's see, is that five Masters and six PGAs that I've won or six Masters and five PGAs?) Once, while playing in the '75 Doral Open, he sank a 76-yard wedge shot for an eagle at the 10th, then, two holes later, he holed a 77-yard shot for another eagle to take the lead. No TV cameras were on him. His gallery, on a remote part of the course, was only a hundred people. For once, he was almost unobserved. When the second eagle disappeared, Nicklaus dropped his club and began spinning around in circles like a little boy who makes himself dizzy until he falls down. He finally stopped before he flopped.

After his round, after he had won again, he was asked why he had gotten such an attack of silliness. "When I made the second one, it just all felt so crazy," he said. "I was almost beginning to believe some of the stuff you guys write about me."

For such a down-to-earth man (sometimes even a slightly boring man), to become so genuinely heroic almost seems like a joke on the rest of us. Everybody talks about maturing—getting better, not older. More than any athlete of his era, Nicklaus did it.

In the 1960s, as he surpassed Arnold Palmer and established himself as a Goliath of golf, Nicklaus was a sports hero but nothing more. Call him Fat Jack. Then, the young, tubby and titanically powerful Nicklaus may have been the most awesome golfer who ever lived. Bobby Jones watched Nicklaus as his towering 300-yard drives airmailed the farthest fairway traps and as his iron shots from the rough snapped back with mystical backspin. Jones's pronouncement: "Jack Nicklaus plays a game with which I am not familiar."

In the 1970s, as he lost weight and, to his shock, turned from a frumpy fashion frog into a cover boy, Nicklaus established himself as the greatest and most dignified of all golf champions. Slowly, he became a true national hero: the Golden Bear. He not only carried his sport; to most people he actually *was* his sport.

Finally, in the 1980s, when he re-created himself once more as an aging, flawed and beloved everyman—winning the Masters at the age of forty-six with his adult son as a caddie—he became a world hero: the Olden Bear.

Perhaps someday we will learn that Nicklaus was, in some respect, not entirely what he appeared to be. In an age when athletes often seem to be made entirely of clay, Nicklaus remained almost too good to be true for decades at a time. Not "too good" in the Goody Two-Shoes sense. (Ask McCormack about the morning he woke up to discover that "somebody" had ordered that his entire front lawn be buried under several tons of horse shit.) But "too good" in the sense of too decent, too organized, too creative, too lucky, too smart in business, too good a father to his five hell-raising children, too solid a husband, too wise in his self-analysis, too gracious in defeat, too cheerfully and generously joyful in victory.

How'd this guy get so squared away, so sane, so productive? How come his children didn't hate him? How come the small-print news items always said, "Third-round leader Jack Nicklaus flew home last night in his private jet to watch a Little League game, attend a school play and grill a few steaks in the backyard. He will return in time for Sunday's final round." How could this guy, by age thirty, be on vacation more than half the year so he could raise his family, yet still crush everybody's bones? Chi Chi Rodriquez called him "a legend in his spare time."

Where's the divorce, the scandal? How come, for thirty years and still counting, Jack always looked at Barbara as though she were the real reason for it all. And she looked at him like she was fairly proud, but like she might also have to grab him by the ear and straighten him out at any moment. Once, in the late '70s, I stepped into a hotel elevator and caught the old married Nicklauses doing a little necking between floors.

Why weren't his foes—men that he inevitably diminished—insanely jealous of him? How many victories did he take from Arnold Palmer, Lee Trevino, Tom Watson, Seve Ballesteros and Greg Norman? Yet many of his adversaries became his true friends, all were his admirers and some, like Norman, practically worshipped him and sought his advice—which he always gave. Perhaps only Watson, the Stanford psychology major, kept a prickly distance and successfully resisted Nicklaus's subtle seduction. Almost all Watson's greatest victories, in particular the '82 U.S. Open, the '77 and '81 Masters and the '77 British Open, were snatched directly from Nicklaus in confrontations which, while formally respectful, had a certain amount of tangy spin and edged byplay. Once, the pair even went jaw to jaw in the scorer's tent behind the 72nd green at the Masters because Watson thought that Nicklaus, playing ahead, had been waving derisively at him (Take that, kid) as he pulled the ball from the cup after a birdie.

How could Nicklaus set out to build a fabulous golf course and a great tournament in his hometown—the Memorial in Columbus, Ohio—and have it work right off the bat? Okay, having amassed a fortune estimated at several hundred million dollars doesn't hurt. The proud bear, son of a pharmacist, would have used dollar bills to fertilize Muirfield if that's what it took. But it's also true that Nicklaus the course designer and tournament director was as much an instant success as Nicklaus the teenage superstar.

Perhaps part of the reason is that Nicklaus was, and remains, a man who is inspired by failure, or even the thought of failure. Defeat always prodded his bearish nature into slow, inexorable, productive action. For example, in the spring of 1980, Nicklaus, then forty, had been in a two-year slump. "Is Nicklaus Washed Up?" was the standing headline. "I'm sick of playing lousy," said Nicklaus publicly. "I've just been going through the motions for two years. First, it irritates you, then it really bothers you, until finally you get so damn blasted mad at yourself that you decide to do something about it. I've decided to do something. And I will. Or I'll quit."

Privately, he was even more blunt. At about this time, I casually mentioned to Nicklaus how nice it was that Lee Trevino had made a strong comeback the previous two years. "Yes," said Nicklaus, suddenly grabbing me by both shoulders, "it's almost as nice as this year when Nicklaus made his great comeback."

That year, Nicklaus won the U.S. Open and the PGA. No player since has won two major tournaments in the same season.

Typically, Nicklaus loved periods of struggle even better than those periods when his game was ticking smoothly. "These are interesting times," he said during one of his slumps. "The game is most fun when you are experimenting. One day you're great, the next day scatterload. But you're learning. No, that's not right. I probably have forgotten more about golf than I will ever learn. What you do is remember some of the things you thought you'd never forget."

Because he never feared failure, or experimentation, Nicklaus seemed

especially suited to golf—the game of perpetual humiliation and embarrassment. Nicklaus approached his whole game, perhaps his whole life, the
same way he lined up a putt. Slowly, confidently and from every angle.
When the ball went in the hole, he would give a pleasant perfunctory smile
—mostly to please his gallery, since he'd expected to make it anyway. When
he missed, his look of fierce, sometimes forbidding concentration deepened
as he analyzed the problem. What had he forgotten? The grain of the grass,
the evaporation of the dew? This was a man who once explained casually
that he had chosen an odd-shaped putter because it combined "the largest
possible moment of inertia and the smallest dispersion factor."

"When you lip out several putts in a row, you should never think that
means that you're putting well and that 'your share' are about to start falling," Nicklaus once said in the mid-'70s when he was at the peak of his
powers. "The difference between 'in' and 'almost' is all in here. If you think
the game is just a matter of getting it close and letting the law of averages do
your work for you, you'll find a different way to miss every time. Your frame
of reference must be exactly the width of the cup, not the general vicinity.
When you're putting well, the only question is what part of the hole it's
going to fall in, not if it's going in."

Whether Nicklaus or Jones in his heyday was the greatest golfer of the
twentieth century is a question that they will probably have to decide at
match play over the next few ones in the Elysian Fields. Perhaps Nicklaus
will be allowed a millennium to practice with hickory shafts, while Jones will
be given a few thousand years to decide whether graphite, beryllium or
square grooves suits his taste.

It will not require eternity, however, to decide which man had the greatest golf career of the twentieth century. On that score, Jones, the amateur
who retired at twenty-eight with no worlds to conquer, abdicated the crown.
At a comparable age, Nicklaus also ruled his sport. But he kept competing at
or near the mountaintop until he was past forty-five, accomplishing more
great feats at later ages than any player.

Only Jones was as dominant in his youth as the 215-pound Fat Jack, who
won his first U.S. Amateur at nineteen, his first U.S. Open at twenty-two,
and then quickly added his first Masters and PGA at twenty-three. (In the
first 34 major championships of his pro career, Nicklaus had 7 victories, 18
trips to the top three and 20 majors in the top seven.)

No one, however, was ever as consistently exceptional in his thirties as
the trimmed-down and glamorous Golden Bear. He took a physique and a
game that others thought was the best of all time and radically remodeled
them in the interests of consistency and longevity. And he actually got a

little better. In what we might call the middle third of his career, starting with his 1970 win at the British Open, Nicklaus had 8 wins and 20 finishes in the top three in a span of 33 majors. He also finished fourth 4 times and was in the top ten in the majors 31 times in those 33 events. Feel free to do a double take. That streak is beyond comparison and almost beyond belief. In that period, Nicklaus also won the TPC and the Tournament of Champions—perhaps the next most prestigious events—three times each.

Finally, only Ben Hogan, after his car wreck, was as inspirational at the end of his career as Nicklaus, who was, by then, a ridiculously beloved Olden Bear.

Most golf fans assume that Nicklaus's greatest accomplishment in his own eyes was his record in the majors. In his first twenty-five years as a pro, from 1961 through 1986, Nicklaus played in exactly 100 majors. He had 18 wins, 18 runners-up, 9 third places and 66 visits to the top ten. Yet ask Nicklaus if his play in golf's biggest events is, in fact, his defining accomplishment, and he balks. He knows that what he's done in the majors is bound, hand and foot, with something vague, yet of broader importance.

"Basically, the majors are the only comparisons over time . . . played on the same courses for generations. All the best players are always there. But I'm just as proud of the whole way I've managed my career, the longevity of it. . . . You only have so much juice. You try to keep what you've got left so you can use it when it means the most."

Nicklaus has illustrated—as vividly as any public figure in our national life —how to manage talent over time; how to organize a balanced and productive life; how to continually revitalize our enthusiasm for our work. To many, Nicklaus is a symbol of successful labor. Yet he is also a marvelous symbol of creative laziness. By age twenty-five, he was already cutting back his tournament appearances. By thirty, he barely played twenty times a year.

However, when he worked, he concentrated utterly. No player ever changed his game more radically than Nicklaus after his weight loss, then again after his thirty-fifth birthday when he, essentially, tinkered with every aspect of his swing to create a more aesthetically pleasing whole. No other player ever attacked the short game after his fortieth birthday and improved immeasurably—partly because he had been so bad for so long. And nobody else ever tore apart his putting, and came out with a new, goofy-looking kind of putter, after age forty-five—then win the Masters with it.

As Nicklaus recedes from golf's center stage, his victories in athletic old age now seem to hold us most tightly. Why? Because they prove that—as we suspected and very much prefer to believe—he was a special person, not just a special athlete. By craft and canniness, he discovered a succession of temporary stays against age and self-doubt—almost against mortality itself. And, repeatedly, he prevailed. With dignity. With easy good grace. With many of the qualities that seem to lose their substance unless some special person can live them out, embody them on his own terms.

"If you don't mind, I'm just going to stand here and enjoy this," said Nicklaus at his mass press conference after his shocking Jack Is Back victory in the '80 U.S. Open at Baltusrol.

When he finally spoke, he said, "I have to start with self-doubt. I kept wondering all week when my wheels would come off like they have for the last year and a half. But they never came off. When I needed a crucial putt, or needed to call on myself for a good shot, I did it. And those are the things I have expected from myself for twenty years.

"I've wondered if I should still be playing this silly game. . . . You see guys who have been winners who get to the point where they ought to get out of their game. They are the last to know. They make themselves seem pathetic. It hurts to think that that is you. . . .

"Once a time is past, it's past. I'll never be 215 pounds, hit it so far or have my hair so short again as I did when I was here in 1967 [and won the Open at Baltusrol]. You can never return. I've lost the '60s and '70s. We all have. I'm not the same. I have to look to the future. I have to see what skills I have now. I have to find out what is in store for Jack Nicklaus in the '80s. I can't look backwards, because that man doesn't exist anymore."

Nicklaus tests himself in opposition not to any one man but to everyone in his game simultaneously. He measures himself by only one standard—the attempt to be the best golfer who ever lived and the best who ever will live.

Throughout his career, Nicklaus has confronted his own limits and flaws with less desire to blink or turn away than any golfer, perhaps any athlete, of his time. Only reality interested him, not self-delusion. When thwarted by bad luck or injury, poor performance or better foes, he suffered, accepted his situation, regrouped and then relentlessly returned.

His greatest return—unless, of course, he wins the British Open on the Old Course at the age of seventy-five—came at the 1986 Masters in what, by something approaching consensus, was the Golf Event of the Century.

That moment, as Nicklaus walked up the final fairway at Augusta National, became the frontispiece in a whole generation's book of sports memories. The place of respect that the Louis-Schmeling fight, for example, may have held for our grandfathers, that image of Nicklaus achieved for millions. In the last half century, perhaps only the U.S.-U.S.S.R. Olympic hockey game of 1980 had a comparable transcendent power over the general non-sporting public.

An exemplary man, a full and rounded adult, was doing an almost impossible athletic deed, and doing it with amazing cheerful grace—ignoring every odd, lovin' every minute of it, waving his putter to the crowd like a scepter. Yet Nicklaus later freely admitted what everyone could see—that he had tears in his eyes "four or five times" as he played, so moved was he by the standing ovations that swept him along through every hole of a tumultuous, cascadingly dramatic final nine.

Despite all that emotion, despite the depths of his famous concentration on every swing, Nicklaus also walked between shots at times with a bemused, almost disbelieving expression on his face—as though he were sharing an inside joke with the world, but not with his competitors, who could only see his closing scores being posted. Starting at the 9th: birdie, birdie, birdie, bogey, birdie, par, eagle, birdie, birdie and finally one more par as his last long birdie putt stopped in front of the hole—one inch from a 29 on the homeward nine.

Of all his victories, all his glory days, this was the most accessible. After all, Nicklaus had spent nearly two years reading stories about how he should stop embarrassing himself and retire. All around him, eyes were being turned away. He arrived at the Masters, for the first time in his career, almost an object of pity. Nicklaus actually stuck a "Jack Should Quit" story to his refrigerator door during Masters week.

"I kept saying to myself, 'Done. Washed up. Finished.' I was trying to make myself mad, but it didn't really work too well because I thought it might be true."

As he walked the closing holes, Nicklaus was talking to himself some more, but the words were very different. The crowds had him crying, something that had happened to him at the '78 British Open and '80 U.S. Open —two of his previous premature valedictories. "We have to play golf. This isn't over," he kept telling himself. "What I really don't understand is how I could keep making putts in the state I was in. I was so excited I shouldn't have been able to pull it back at all, much less pull it back like I wanted to. But I did. One perfect stroke after another. When I don't get nervous, I don't make anything. Maybe I've been doing it backwards."

Bobby Jones was certainly golf's best player/writer, but Nicklaus may have been its best extemporaneous player/talker. He wasn't funny or colorful or charismatic. Instead, he seemed to have a rarer gift—simple, unadorned insight. He knew exactly what was on his mind and, whenever politic, he said exactly that. He spoke almost without spin—no double meaning or hidden agenda. His words were a pane of glass that revealed an analytical, well-lit and fairly guileless mind. Of course, maybe it's only decent for a fellow to be candid and sporting when he can spot the world one-a-side by the age of twenty-one.

Nicklaus never gave a better press conference than describing how he agonized while watching Greg Norman's final 15-foot par putt at the 72nd hole which would have forced a playoff. Nicklaus had never before rooted against a foe.

"I was sitting watching TV as Norman kept making birdies. So when he came to the last putt, I said, 'Maybe I'll stand up.' I like to win golf tournaments with my clubs, not on other people's mistakes. But when you're coming to the finish . . . I'm in the December of my career . . . Well, somebody did something to me at Pebble Beach as I remember," said Nicklaus, recalling Tom Watson's 71st-hole chip-in at the '82 U.S. Open.

Perhaps the '86 Masters crystallized three aspects of Nicklaus's character which—independent of his enormous talent—will be remembered and revered as long as golf is played.

First, Nicklaus was appreciated as a man who loved his family as much as, and probably more than, his fame.

"To have your own son with you to share an experience like that is so great for him, so great for me. I have great admiration for him. He's done a wonderful job of handling the burden of my name," said Nicklaus of son Jack Jr., twenty-four. ". . . If it wasn't for my kids, I probably wouldn't be playing now. You've got to have a reason for doing things. Last time I won [at the '84 Memorial], Jackie caddied for me."

Second, his late-career success demonstrated Nicklaus's ability to accept the fact that golf is an unmasterable game. That knowledge was his key to being a master. Instead of searching for the perfect method or clinging to what had worked in the past, Nicklaus constantly reworked and remolded his game, enjoying the very same process of perpetual loss and rediscovery that panicked and infuriated other players. In the two weeks before the '86 Masters, Nicklaus had made key changes in his full swing and his chipping method and was using a new putter.

Finally, Nicklaus's old-age triumphs exhibited to everyone the unmistakably clean core of his competitiveness. A regal sense of joy in combat, which is the heart of great sportsmanship, was evident throughout those victories. Nicklaus was having fun, expressing his best gifts, actually enjoying the same kinds of pressure which crush so many people in so many walks of life. And he was doing it long after he should have been washed up.

By the end, with many of his golfing gifts gone but his character intact, Nicklaus's play seemed to speak for itself: "This is life. Look how hard it is. Look how great it is."

Sr. and Jr.

March 29, 1987—Few great men know when to quit. Few fathers know how to defer to a son.

Has anybody ever done both at once? Well, somebody's trying. Jack Nicklaus is history. Long live Jack Nicklaus II.

In case you missed it, and most have, Jack Nicklaus's career is done. He has retired. His days as a serious competitor are over. From now on, he's just in it for fun. Golf as avocation, not vocation—middle-aged hobby, not self-defining obsession.

That's what the man says, anyway.

He'll still play. But he will not really try, not the way Nicklaus tries. And he refuses to pretend he is trying.

Practice? Preparation? Hassle? Worry? Forget it. All behind him at forty-seven. Oh, he'll play the four majors as long as he enjoys hitching up the wagon. "Being part of the scene," he calls it. And, probably, he'll play one or two tune-up events before each biggie, just so he doesn't embarrass himself.

If, covered with rust and age, he happens to fall into some blessed state of golfing grace, he obviously will try to win. Could he pull off such a victory? "I don't know why I couldn't."

But don't judge him on the future, he says. He's drawn the line: 100 majors as a pro (1962 to 1986), with 18 wins, 18 runner-up finishes, 45 in the top three and 66 trips to the top ten. That's what all the young limber-backs get to shoot at.

"Winning the Masters left me in a position to leave the tour on a high note. I don't consider myself a regular tour player anymore," Nicklaus said at a Miami news conference this month. "It's not something I really want to do, but it's something that makes a lot of sense at this age.

"To be a part-time golfer with a deteriorating game over a period of time —which is inevitable—and erode all the great memories I've had, and that people have had watching me play, doesn't make sense. . . . I have semi-left playing. If I play well, I play well. If I don't, I don't. I'm not going to get myself irritated."

In case you missed it, and most have, Jack Nicklaus, Jr.'s, career has begun. He's picked up the fallen flag. Turned pro. Decided to get serious. Dedicated himself. At twenty-five, he's decided that the fun is behind him and it's time for some serious Nicklaus-style labor.

Two years ago, he rarely broke 80 and had "the worst short game on earth." An all-sport athlete with little time for golf, he'd never even won his hometown Palm Beach Amateur. The name Jack Nicklaus weighed on him throughout his teen years. Any sport but golf was his favorite. Then, a week after graduating from college, he won the 1985 North-South—a top nation-wide amateur event.

Last April, he caddied for his father in the Masters. And his dad showed him, at arm's length, why the winning is worth all the work. Behind the 18th green, they embraced in a picture American sports will not forget. By August, Jack Jr. had decided to turn pro and Jack Sr. had decided it was time to retire with his myth intact. The Masters was the fulcrum around which both decisions were made.

Such psychological symmetry only occurs in reality. As usual, history, not fiction, gets the best plots.

"I'm more interested in his game now than I am in mine," says Jack Sr. "Mine's not very interesting now."

These are hard days for both father and son. One, coming down from 80, the other, going up from 70, seem to have met at 75—a level of play that is pure purgatory for a pro golfer. (Yesterday, with a two-round score of 144, the elder Nicklaus missed the cut at the Tournament Players Championship by one stroke.) Two weeks ago in Fort Lauderdale, one scene capsulized this period in their lives.

Jack Nicklaus was on the final green. Jack Nicklaus, Jr., was on the final tee. Simultaneously. You could see them both, the father studying his last putt, the son loading up his last drive. The old man wanted to make the cut; the kid just wanted to prove he could cut it.

Around the 18th green Nicklaus Sr. trudged, bundled against the raw March wind, trying to read one last putt so he could keep playing in the Honda Classic. The week before, at Doral, both he and Jackie had played in the same pro event for the first time. Both missed the cut. Maybe if one survived this time, the other would, too. Maybe the rookie could earn his first PGA Tour dollar in his own home neighborhood.

Arms clamped around himself for heat, crouched on his haunches like a small panda, the father glared down the line of his final putt as he'd done thousands of times. This kind of willpower eight-footer, when you grind your jaw, focus every mental muscle, then roll that miserably stubborn ball in the heart, had long been his forte.

Naturally, he made it.

"That'll do it," he said grimly, exasperated by five hours of mental and, at this stage of his career, physical effort. "Seven over par. The cut'll be seven, maybe eight."

"The stat man just projected the cut as six over," Nicklaus was told.

"He isn't out here. He hasn't felt this wind," says Nicklaus. "Seven makes it easy. No sense even discussing it."

Nobody discussed it. Nicklaus guesses cut scores, winning scores, you name it, better than anybody. The correct number comes into his head, then he shoots it. Just like he told his family on Sunday at the 1986 Masters: "65 wins it." He shot it. He won it.

Inside the scorer's tent, the father paced, peeking casually around the back flap to watch his son conclude his final hole. Yet Nicklaus never stepped out where the boy could see him watching. "What's Jackie?" he asked.

"Eight over with three to play the last we heard," he was told.

"He's got a chance. It would be great for him to make the cut here. A tremendous boost," said Nicklaus. "He's improving but he's a while away. He's come a long way from the kid who couldn't break 80. . . . He's gonna do all right, gonna do fine. There's nothing I can tell him. I can't play in 'em [for him]. . . . I give him a lot of credit for wanting to try it."

Would he enjoy watching his boy cash his first check?

"He's won money. In Australia. In Europe," snapped the father.

Sorry about that, Jack. Well, then how are you playing?

"I wouldn't have any idea," said Nicklaus. "I haven't played enough to know. Not very well.

"Is that Jackie's ball in the middle?" he said. "That's really bad. Of all the holes where you want to release it and really let it fly."

A friend of the family came to the tent, gave the father the word. His son was ten over. Forget it.

Nicklaus looked off toward the tall, lean young man in the red sweater and yellow hat, the son who looked and acted more like his sweet, easygoing mother than his laser-eyed father. The look that passed over the face of the man who may be the greatest and richest world athlete of his time was hard to decipher. You could watch him for a dozen years on tour and never see it. Pity, maybe, for the burdens his name has put on his child? Or just love? Certainly that.

Nicklaus walked to the gallery ropes and began signing autographs. He told his caddie to go in out of the cold. "I'm going to wait for Jackie."

Nicklaus almost seems to relish the dilapidated state of his game and the diminished heat of his internal fires. Is he coming as close as possible to duplicating his son's state of mind? Does he subconsciously feel that a less fiercely determined and less polished dad can do a better job of empathizing with a less gifted and less driven son?

"I don't want to play practice rounds anymore. I was glad it rained Wednesday," said Nicklaus Sr. "I suppose it's a fact of life that you're not going to be as interested as you get older. And that's a terrible thing for me to say because I've always been very interested in playing golf." He laughs. "But I'll be plenty interested when I get to Augusta.

"I certainly have played enough golf to know how to cope with the situation if I should find myself in contention. Last year, when I got something going, how to play came back very quickly. I just have to play enough so that if I do get going well, I can be able to sustain it.

"I must still be pretty interested or I wouldn't be so aggravated now. I wanted to give myself a good swift kick out there."

When father and son finally met in the scorers' tent, both knew the day's outcome. Jack had made the cut. Jackie missed. No commiseration was necessary, none was offered. The father, who says his fires are banked, seemed more prickly and annoyed than the son, who says his fires are stoked.

Joe DiMaggio once said, with only slight exaggeration, "No boy from a rich family ever made the big leagues."

As the sun went down, the wind grew even colder. A young pro in a mood for humor walked past the Eagle Trace clubhouse carrying an umbrella with all the cloth torn away and the spokes twisted in every direction. Barbara Nicklaus, mother of five, keeper of the Bear and, by acclamation on tour, the Best Thing That Ever Happened to Jack, laughed at the umbrella joke as she shivered.

No, she didn't want to go inside. It wasn't that cold. She'd just hug her sweater closer and chat with everybody who passed. She was waiting for her pair of Jacks to finish a network interview.

"When Jackie was born, Jack was only twenty-two," she said, trying to remember a time when her husband was three years younger than her son is now. "He made a silent pact that when his son went to college, he didn't want the boy to say, 'I wish I'd known my dad.' He vowed he'd never be apart from us more than two weeks and, in twenty-five years, he never has.

"Between them, there's no problem. His dad's a good friend because he's always made the time to be there with him. If the relationship is right, then the rest usually turns out all right."

For Barbara Nicklaus, life is only as complicated as you decide to make it. She has a knack for finding the smooth handle. "You don't worry about things like 'How will he cope with being Jack Nicklaus, Jr.?' It never crosses your mind," she said. "When he was little, somebody asked him, 'How does it feel to be who you are?' Jackie said, 'I don't know. I've never been anybody else.'

"Jackie had a few tough years. But the pluses of being Jack Jr. certainly outweigh the minuses and he knows it."

To counterbalance the weight of the family name, the Nicklauses gave their children extra time to reach decisions and extra elbowroom to make choices.

"We never cared if he picked up a golf club," the mother said. "But it is kind of a vicious circle. You don't care what he does as long as he enjoys it and tries his best. But you're thrilled if it's golf."

The Nicklaus children tend to be rambunctious, prone to the mild scrape; the parents, for their part, seem extremely confident of their children's judgment. Barbara in particular couldn't care less about maintaining any public family image.

"Jackie really enjoyed college. I don't think he knew the day he graduated what he'd do next," she said, apparently quite charmed about that indecision. "But he won the North-South the next week. . . . Now he's learning. He'll get it. And he's growing up. He had a great month in Australia. Then he played in Europe, including Paris. That's the first time he's traveled to a foreign country by himself."

If the Nicklauses care that Jackie did not get on the PGA Tour through the Qualifying School last year, you can't tell. This year he'll play five tour events on sponsors' exemption, then see a lot of events like the Madrid Open. "He just needs competition and time," said the father.

Finally, the Nicklauses escape their interviews and son sidles up behind mom.

"Do you have any money?" he asks.

"Like a lot?" she says.

"Uh-huh."

"No, but your dad does."

You could call this ironic. But it seems more like homey. It's hard to be first-generation millionaires yet manage to be old-money unpretentious, but the Nicklauses don't do too badly. Their apparent comfort level with their fame is one of the tour's frequently noted marvels. Jackie says it wasn't always as easy as he's made it seem in recent years.

"[Being Jack Nicklaus, Jr.] was toughest from about thirteen through seventeen. I think I was most bothered by it then," he said. "When I got away to college, that's when I adjusted. I'm proud to be his son, but I want to be recognized for what I accomplish, not what he's done.

"Being Jack Nicklaus's son doesn't hit one shot for me. That's the good part. What I do is mine. But I have to remember that you have to crawl before you walk. I can't be in a hurry to make my own name. It's no use me comparing myself to the superstars in the sport.

"If I accept that improving is a slow process, I'll be all right. I can see the improvement. Two years ago, it was only fifty-fifty that I'd hit the green from twenty yards out. Honest. That part of my game has improved a hundred and ten percent."

It is far too soon to offer even the most preliminary guess on the golf future of Jack Nicklaus, Jr. He's an athlete, a Nicklaus, and he hits it a mile. But he's not really a golfer yet. He waited a long time to get started. Of course, Ray Floyd never became properly serious until he was past thirty and got married. He was inclined to have a great deal of fun first. Now he's forty-four and the reigning U.S. Open champion.

"Tell Jackie that," says Barbara Nicklaus. "He'd like it."

She and Jack have to get home to Lauderhill, Florida, about fifty miles away. They'll hop in the family helicopter, and give their neighbor Greg Norman a lift in the bargain.

There's room in the chopper for Jack Nicklaus, Jr., just as there was on the trip down in the morning. But again he says thanks, Dad, but no, thanks. For now, he'd rather drive back. Maybe someday. When he's earned his own helicopter.

Our Dear Watson

The Chip

PEBBLE BEACH, California, June 20, 1982—

Fifteen years ago, when he was just a teenager and Jack Nicklaus was already established as the king of golf, Tom Watson would find a way, on Sunday mornings, to be the first dew-sweeping player on the Pebble Beach Golf Links.

"I'd drive down here from Stanford [University] and tee it up at seven A.M., when I'd have the whole course to myself," said Watson this evening. "Honestly, I did fantasize about coming down the stretch head to head with Jack Nicklaus in the U.S. Open.

"Then I'd get to the last couple of holes and say, 'You've gotta play these one under par to win the Open.' Of course, I'd always play 'em two over. And I'd say, 'You have a long way to go, kid.' "

Tom Watson has had to come a long, slow, arduous way. But today, all his fantasies, plus one piece of magic so outlandish that even a boy playing at sunrise would never dream it, became reality. And history.

With one shot that will live in the retelling as long as golf is played, Watson wiped away—like a Pacific fog along the cliffs evaporating with the morning sun—the last blemish on his great and growing record.

Years from now, it will probably be forgotten that Watson won this 82nd U.S. Open by two shots over Nicklaus in a breath-stopping back-nine duel. In time, the details of this misty Monterey evening may fade—even the trenchant fact that, with Nicklaus and his 69 (284 total) already in the clubhouse, Watson finished birdie-birdie on the 71st and 72nd holes to slash his way out of a tie with the fabled Golden Bear.

In 19th-hole lore, only a few will recall that Watson's pilgrimage to his first Open title was carved out with a week of creditable work (72-72-68-70) for a six-under-par total of 282. To be sure, no one will recall that Bill Rogers (74), Bobby Clampett (70) and Dan Pohl (70) tied for third at 286.

In the end, only one moment—one shot that epitomizes both Watson and his game—will last. Already Watson calls it "the shot . . . the greatest shot of my life, the most meaningful."

It's that one swing, and no other, that prompted Nicklaus to grab Watson in a fraternal bear hug as he stepped off the final green and tell him, "You son of a . . . you're something else. I'm really proud of you."

Naturally, Watson remembers the embrace a bit differently: "Jack said, 'I'm gonna beat you, you little SOB, if it takes me the rest of my life.' "

So, for the moment, we will forget how Watson began the day tied for the lead with Rogers. We will pass over the jubilation that swept this seaside links as the dormant Nicklaus birdied five straight holes on the front nine—the 3rd through the 7th—to forge, momentarily, into a one-shot lead.

We will negligently dash past the details of how two bogeys by Nicklaus—one perhaps abetted by a former U.S. President—plus a cross-country birdie by Watson, pushed the thirty-two-year-old redhead back into the lead by two shots. And, finally, we will gloss over Nicklaus's classy birdie at the 15th and Watson's wild drive and bogey at the 16th that deadlocked the pair for the lead one final time.

The scene thus set, we must return to the one moment from this Open that will outlast and, unfortunately, diminish all others. Outlined against the blue-gray sky of Carmel Bay, Watson stands locked in ankle-deep rough beside the 17th green. In trying for a daring birdie—hitting a two-iron into the breeze at the 209-yard par-3, Watson has, instead, put himself in just the predicament for which Jack Neville built this course in 1919.

No shot in golf is a better test of nerves, experience and touch than the "grass explosion" from high, unforgiving U.S. Open rough to a pin on a glass-slick green that is only 18 feet away.

Watching on TV, Nicklaus, who was going for a record fifth Open title and twentieth major, says he thought, "There's no way in the world he can get up-and-down from there [for par]. Even if he has a good lie, you couldn't drop the ball straight down out of your hand on that green and keep it from going less than ten feet past the pin. I figured: Now he's going to have to birdie the last hole just to tie me and get into a playoff [on Monday]."

Watson's opinion was different. "I'm not trying to get this close," he recalled telling his caddie. "I'm going to make it."

Why shouldn't he have thought so? Perhaps no man since Arnold Palmer in his prime has so consistently willed the ball into the hole from ludicrously improper places. On the 10th, Watson was on a cliffside amidst wildflowers; he hacked to the fringe 24 feet away and sank his Texas-wedge shot to save par. On the 11th, he sank a 22-footer from the fringe for a birdie. And at the 14th, he was in the frog hair again, and holed out from 35 feet. As Nicklaus put it: "Yes, yes, I heard about all those shots. Just another tap-in for Tom."

With this preternatural confidence, which is his trademark, Watson stepped into the weeds by the 17th quickly and, opening the face of his sand wedge, "sliced across the ball and slid the edge of the club under it. It was a good lie, with the ball hanging in the middle of the grass. If it had been down, I'd have had no shot. . . .

"As soon as it landed on the green, I knew it was in," said Watson, whose whole face was alive with hunger as the ball trickled and broke—a full foot and a half from left to right.

"When it went in the hole, I about jumped in the Pacific Ocean," said Watson with a laugh. He ran at least twenty yards around the edge of the green, his putter over his head in victory and his feet carrying him he knew not where. Then, commanding himself, Watson spun and pointed at his caddie and yelled, "Told ya!"

"He was chokin', chokin' bad," Watson said with a grin. "He couldn't utter anything."

Neither could Nicklaus. "When he makes that, the golf tournament's history. . . . I've had it happen before, but I didn't think it was going to happen again. But it did. . . . How would I evaluate that shot? One of the worst that ever happened to me. Right up there with [Lee] Trevino's [chip-in] at Muirfield [on the 71st hole of the '72 British Open]."

An almost certain bogey that probably would have lost his Open and branded Watson a gagger had been turned, in a twinkling, into one of the most gloriously improbable Open-winning birdies in history.

Had Watson merely parred the 17th, he would have had to birdie the 18th to win. And nobody has ever birdied the 72nd hole of the Open to win. As it was, Watson's downhill 18-foot birdie on the last hole was a wonderful crescendo for a day full of tremulously roiling drums. But had Watson needed to make it to win, it might have been a tougher proposition.

Watson's playing partner, Rogers, said of that soft shot into history, "He couldn't have hit a better shot if he'd dropped down a hundred balls."

"Try about a thousand," said Nicklaus drolly.

Told of Nicklaus's oddsmaking, Watson—as superb a green-side magician as Nicklaus has always been bear-pawed—said, "Let's go out and do it. I might make some money."

Watson faced up to every sort of Open pressure today. "I was on pins and needles all day."

Watson woke up nervous, then calmed himself by reading two newspapers "front to back. Ask me anything about the earthquake in El Salvador or the budget problems." His swing was loosey-goosey all day—he missed only one fairway, but his putting was nervous and cold on the front nine, especially when he missed a two-foot birdie putt at the 7th.

Perhaps Watson was unhinged by all those bear tracks he had to walk through. As he trudged through the 3rd through the 7th, all he heard was buzzing talk about how Nicklaus, after a shoddy bogey-par start, had been knocking down flags for five consecutive holes. By the time Nicklaus had made two-foot tap-ins for birdie at the 5th and 6th, he was tied for the lead. And when he sank a 12-foot curler at the gorgeous 7th to take the lead, his caddie—son Jack Jr.—jumped nearly two feet in the air and began applauding.

Nicklaus misclubbed himself at the over-a-gorge 8th and was lucky to make bogey from a hanging lie on the edge of a precipice. That, however, won't be the bogey that haunts him. At the 11th, tied for the lead, he had a flat, slightly downhill 18-foot birdie putt that he slid four feet past and missed coming back. What could have accounted for his only mental lapse of the day?

No one will ever know for sure, but lovers of anecdote might enjoy the fact that former President Gerald Ford, a notorious three-putter, walked down from a course-side house and stood conspicuously by the 11th green as Nicklaus three-putted. Ford then came forward to shake Nicklaus's hand and exchange pleasantries at the 12th tee—an intrusion into serious work that no normal citizen would, presumably, have dared to attempt. Call it the Presidential Bogey or Jerry's Whammy.

In the gathering dusk around America's most lustrously atmospheric links, Watson was aglow with pride and vindication. Asked, teasingly, "Why can't you win the PGA?" he said, "Up till now, it's been: Why couldn't Sam Snead and I win the Open? Now it'll be: Why can't Arnold Palmer and I win the PGA? Well, I'll stay here all night and talk about it."

Time and again, Watson had to return, as he will have the pleasure of returning for the rest of his life, to the Impossible Shot.

"I had no alternative," Watson said finally, with his best freckled, gap-toothed smile. "For you, it's impossible."

But not for this country's overdue and deserving U.S. Open champion.

Young Tom Meets the Road Hole

July 23, 1984—Seve Ballesteros, the Road Hole and, perhaps, the ghost of Harry Vardon all conspired to deny Tom Watson his sixth British Open title today at the St. Andrews Old Course.

This was the day when golf's most historic stage seemed set for Watson to complete a Scottish Slam and take his place beside the legendary Vardon as the greatest Open champion since the days of old Tom Morris. Instead, Watson putted as though Vardon's spirit had an overlapping grip around his throat. Yes, you could also say Vardon kept his grip on the record.

While Watson declined to win, striking 73 blows on a beach day when birdies abounded, Ballesteros was most adamant about accepting the invitation.

Ballesteros, who lost confidence early this season while struggling on the U.S. PGA Tour, shot a closing 69 for a twelve-under-par 276 total that broke the Open record at the Old Course by two shots. That 276 broke Watson's heart by two shots, too, after Australia's young Ian Baker-Finch, co-leader with Watson after three rounds, stumbled out of contention early and finished tied for ninth at 79—284. Germany's Bernhard Langer (71—278) finished in a tie with Watson for second.

"It's really nice to win the best tournament in the world at the home of golf—St. Andrews," said Ballesteros, who, after parring the notorious Road Hole (the 17th), took the lead with a 15-foot birdie at the 18th moments before Watson bogeyed the 17th.

"Tom, I know you were looking for a sixth to tie Harry Vardon, but you're still young enough to win," added Ballesteros, who also won the '79 British Open at Royal Lytham as well as the '80 and '83 Masters.

Watson had himself to blame as much as Ballesteros. Only 16 of the 63 players in the field had worse rounds than Watson, the 1982 and 1983 champion, who missed four putts in the four- to eight-foot range.

"Seve played very well as far as putting pressure on me, but a balky putter was the single most important reason I couldn't perform today," said a tight-lipped, fiercely disappointed Watson, who had chances to open a lead on the front nine. "I couldn't put any distance between myself and the field."

One dramatic passage at the Road Hole this evening will, no doubt, be the segment of this day that finds itself frozen for the ages in Old Course lore.

In time, we will forget how Watson and Baker-Finch began this day two shots ahead of Ballesteros and Langer. Memory will lose the details of how Watson, the greatest putter of his time, rolled the ball so miserably that, frequently, he was walking toward the hole in disgust before the ball was a third of the way toward its target.

Few will remember how two front-nine three-putt bogeys took Watson out in 37 and allowed Ballesteros to hold a one-shot lead for a few fleeting minutes in the Loop. And only antiquarians will recall how the pair—probably the two best golfers in the 1980s—jockeyed for the lead as they headed home, first Watson, then Ballesteros taking a one-stroke lead before slipping back into a tie.

What will be remembered, and told a thousand times from Edinburgh to Santander to Kansas City, will be the way these two men came to the notorious 17th—the Road Hole—tied at eleven under par and how their fates diverged at that juncture.

On the hardest hole on earth, on the oldest course in creation, Ballesteros made par from the rough on the wrong side of the fairway and Watson made bogey from perfect fairway position.

All week Ballesteros, twenty-seven, laughed and promised, "Tomorrow I will par the Road Hole." On Saturday, after his third straight bogey there, Ballesteros amended his vow, saying, "If I don't par it Sunday, I will come back and play it Monday until I par it."

This evening a beaming Ballesteros, who had rounds of 69-68-70-69, said, "I keep my promise. I won't have to come back tomorrow."

But it was a near thing. Ballesteros hooked his drive and faced a 200-yard shot to the pin. "I told my caddie, 'This is the most important shot,'" said Ballesteros a minute after walking off the last green. "And it was."

His six-iron shot landed short of the green and bounced safely onto the right side, 35 feet from the pin and far from the cavernous Road Bunker. "We got this hole this time," Ballesteros said before barely missing his birdie attempt by two inches. "That was the same six-iron shot [from the left rough] I had twice before this week. This time I hit it right."

Brandishing his putter like a sword and inciting the crowd with his dark smiles, Ballesteros marched to the 18th and came home like a great champion. "Watson is Watson," he told his caddie. "He will par seventeen somehow. We must still make birdie."

Ballesteros was wrong, but it was a quality thought and elegant execution. "Ah, the last putt—very exciting. A lot of break. Just in the side. I nearly miss it. I almost killed my caddie with my hand [in celebrating]."

While Ballesteros was gnawing on the 354-yard 18th, Watson was grieving at the 17th. Where Ballesteros, with a flier lie in the rough, could negotiate his 200 yards with a six iron, Watson needed to nail a two iron to fly his 200-yard shot to the green. Power is nice.

"I pushed it right," said Watson of his second shot on the 461-yard into-the-breeze beast. The ball bounced over the road and off the low stone out-of-bounds wall, leaving Watson with a severely restricted backswing. An awkward chip 30 feet past the pin was the best he could do.

As Watson lined up what he assumed would be a last-ditch putt, a roar came from the 18th, where Ballesteros had struck for his fourth birdie of the day. Watson's chances for victories at all five Open courses in Scotland and his hopes for a sixth Open title would have to wait.

This victory was a great vindication to the proud Ballesteros. He insists that "I didn't play bad this year [in America]. I just didn't win." It's also true, as Jack Nicklaus said two days ago, that "Seve has put a lot of pressure on himself by waiting so long to play in the U.S. I don't envy his position. He's expected to win. He should have come over a couple of years ago."

"Probably he is right," said Ballesteros this evening about Nicklaus. "I don't know what percent, but probably right."

Just a week ago, Ballesteros was in the doldrums. "My confidence has been very low this year." But in a practice round Jaime Gonzalez and Emilio Rodriguez told Ballesteros that his weight shift was completely backward. He was swaying forward on the backswing, then falling back on the attack; in a day, he got the weight shift, from right back to left side, straightened out.

"I will buy them a couple of beers," he said.

Olympic Tradition

SAN FRANCISCO, June 21, 1987—

Tom Watson joined Ben Hogan and Arnold Palmer today. Much to his dismay. Equals in glory, they're now equals in anguish as well, all heartbreak victims of the Olympic Club and perverse quirks of final-day U.S. Open fortune.

Scott Simpson joined Jack Fleck, Lou Graham and Orville Moody this chilly, thrilling afternoon. "I never thought I was good enough to win the U.S. Open," said Simpson, who calls himself a short-hitting plodder. But Simpson did it—shooting 68 in the final round and birdieing the 14th, 15th and 16th holes to sweep past Watson with shocking suddenness. Most of all, Simpson did it with a nervy sand shot and 8-foot par putt to hold his lead at the awful 17th, the hillside horror some call golf's worst hole.

After bearing the burden of the lead for three days, the great and resurgent Watson lost this Open by one slim shot in the last hour—277 to 278. When his 35-foot birdie putt from the front fringe on the last hole rolled to the lip, an inch or two from glory, Watson knew the same depths of dejection as his predecessors in Opens played on this shadowy course of sighs.

"It happened to Ben Hogan. Jack Fleck birdied two of the last four holes on him [then beat him in a playoff in '55]," said Watson, who shot 70. "I have no reason to feel ashamed. But I sure am disappointed. . . . [This proves] there's a lot of golf left in Tom Watson. This renews my resolve about my career. The afterburners are turned on."

Far from feeling ashamed, Watson should have swelled his chest. He flirted with collapse, bogeying three of the first five holes. Even his wife, Linda, was in tears as she watched. Then Watson played the final eleven holes with three birdies (at Nos. 8, 9 and 14) and no bogeys. Only one other man in the field played that stretch without a bogey—yes, Simpson, who birdied four of the last twelve holes.

"If I ever played a round this good, I sure can't remember it now," said Simpson, thirty-one, who has won only three tournaments in nine years on the PGA Tour. "I just kept making all those key putts. It was probably the best putting round of my life."

All day, Watson, in the last group, watched Simpson, just up front in that bright pink sweater, as he walked round and round brutal putts, then drained them. Five times Simpson saved par with putts of 10, 8, 3, 4 and 10 feet. His birdies were no slouches as he found the cup from 30 and 10 feet at Nos. 1 and 7, then sank killers of 4, 20 and 15 feet during his winning birdie streak.

Open pressure was on display all day. At one front-nine juncture Watson, Simpson, Larry Mize and Ben Crenshaw were all tied at even par with Bernhard Langer and Seve Ballesteros. All but the two protagonists faded badly. Ballesteros (71) was third at 282, a distant five shots behind Simpson, but one shot ahead of Crenshaw, Langer, Curtis Strange and Bobby Wadkins.

How on earth did Simpson, known through much of his career as a poor stretch player, survive the back-nine roller-coaster ride? He survived by remaining ignorant.

"I never looked at a scoreboard until after sixteen," Simpson said. "I thought I might have a good lead [by then]. But I saw Tom was still right there [one shot behind]. I knew it would be a fight then. . . .

"I resisted [looking] because, in the past, I've looked and invariably it's hurt me more than it's helped me. I got caught up in it and lost sight of what I had to do."

In a curious way, this Open turned into a duel between Watson's self-reliance ("I looked at every scoreboard because I wanted to know where I stood") and Simpson's fatalistic faith.

"I made a commitment to the Lord that I wasn't going to get angry this week," said Simpson, a born-again Christian who, though expressionless even in victory, has often had lapses into temper on the golf course. "I was real determined to stay cool and do my best."

This Open, which will rank with the best for drama, reached its crucial juncture at the 14th hole. Watson, on the tee, was one under par. Simpson, on the green, was one behind. By the time Watson reached the green, Simpson had made his little 4-foot birdie and matters were tied. Nobody else was in sight.

As Watson lined up a 24-foot downhill birdie putt, Simpson struck again. Watson could hear the birdie roar from the 149-yard 15th and knew he was behind. Watson answered like the 31-time champion that he is, trickling his putt into the hole.

Now it was match play, Simpson steaming briskly ahead, concentration locked in place. As Watson stood 100 yards behind him in the 16th fairway, watching, Simpson faced a 15-foot birdie putt. "You never hope a guy misses a shot," said Watson afterward. Then paused mischievously.

Simpson was in a zone of self-assurance. All his plans, going back more than six months, were working. After three years of trying to become a long hitter like Watson, Simpson finally gave up the struggle as a Christmas present to himself. "It took a while to forget all the stuff that three or four teachers had told me," he said. "I went back to Hogan's fundamentals. I decided to get back to my game whether I hit it short or not."

After making what proved to be his Open-winning putt, Simpson raised one hand a few inches to the crowd, then looked back down the fairway toward Watson and gave a barely perceptible nod, as though saying, "Matched me once. Now match me twice."

Watson couldn't. All he had left was pars. Still, the horrific 17th awaited Simpson. Like so many others this week, he hit an excellent drive only to see it kicked right by the slick fairway into nasty side-hill rough. Simpson's four-iron shot found the left front bunker and his explosion curved six feet past the hole. After dozens of practice putts as partner Lennie Clements finished the hole, Simpson ran yet another cold-blooded putt into the center of the cup.

And this one was made when he knew the score.

Simpson's play at the 18th hole epitomized why he won this Open. Two-iron shot in the middle of the fairway. Eight-iron shot in the middle of the green. Commercial putt one foot below the hole. Tap in. Collect $150,000. Go from No. 9 on the money list to No. 1 with $465,896—high rolling for a man who's never finished higher than twenty-second.

On Tuesday, Jack Nicklaus (77) said that Olympic would "reward the golfer who's very straight, very simple, does not try to be a hero, uses his head and plods along . . . like Hogan."

"That's me," said Simpson cheerfully afterward.

Because of his complete self-effacement on the course and his ultra-cautious playing style, Simpson has always been Exhibit A for critics of colorless pro golfers. That has bothered him little, if at all. He freely acknowledges that fans confuse him with Tim Simpson, who looks nothing like him. "I've gotten a lot of 'Go Tim's' in the past," said Simpson. "He'll probably get a lot of 'Go Scott's' now."

Long after Watson's last-gasp putt died left of the 18th hole— "Yeah, I had a good idea it was going in the hole"—Simpson was still trying to grasp capturing an event that, as a child, he says he was never bold enough to think about winning, even in fantasy. "It's going to take a long time for this to sink in," said Simpson.

When Hogan and Palmer had their hearts hurt here, they never recovered. Neither won a major title afterward. For Watson, the addendum to this day may be happier. He never lost this Open. Someone took it from him.

For many of the 26,800 here, that will only be partial compensation. It is Simpson's bad luck that, marvelously as he played, he will be part of Olympic's continuing tradition of unwritten heroic headlines. 1955: "Hogan Wins Record Fifth Open." 1966: "Palmer Breaks Hogan's Open Scoring Record." 1987: "Watson Completes Comeback with Open Triumph." Chuck 'em all in the circular file. Right next to "Dewey Wins."

Shark Attacked

Acing the Fours

TOLEDO, August 12, 1986—

In defeat, they hide. Sometimes even the best of them. After the very worst defeats of a career—those that combine somebody else's miracle and their own ignominy—it takes a gun to get great athletes in front of the mikes and notepads to relive how they've suffered and failed.

Nobody in any sport ever lost worse than Greg Norman did today. Or took it better.

Norman was beaten in the sixty-eighth PGA by the most spectacular last-hole shot in the history of major tournament golf. One instant, Norman seemed to have a playoff in hand, maybe a win. The next, his fate was out of his hands.

One moment, Norman was a few paces from the 18th hole in the fringe —his par and his share of the PGA lead fairly safe. The next moment, Bob Tway, nearly out of sight in a bunker, had holed his explosion for a birdie and was jumping up and down like a man with a cattle prod in his knickers.

Norman didn't just lose to a once-per-century optical illusion. The Aussie —who seems to be the only Shark that gets attacked—had to cope with the fact that he had collapsed, his game disassembling under pressure.

He drove wildly—seven times into the rough, five of them on dufferish rolling hooks. He shanked a short iron and made double bogey 6 after an ideal drive had left him 100 yards from home; that is an exquisite torture usually reserved for bogey golfers.

And he putted with hands of stone. One 20-footer rolled off a green and back down the fairway. He didn't hole a thing all day. If the gritty Aussie had not scrambled his fins off for five saves, he would have shot a smooth 80 instead of that brutal 36-40—76 on a day when 73 would have been enough.

For the fourth time in four months, Norman entered the last day of a major tournament with a lead and, for the third time, he didn't win.

Think he doesn't remember his shank into the crowd at the 72nd to hand the Masters to Jack Nicklaus? Think he doesn't remember the huge second- and third-round leads he squandered at the U.S. Open and the Sunday 75 that sent him from first to twelfth? For that matter, think he doesn't remember the playoff 75 against Fuzzy Zoeller at Winged Foot?

If anybody should have been a cad today, Norman nearly had the right.

In the scorer's tent behind the 18th green, Peter Jacobsen grabbed him behind the knee and squeezed hard twice, as if to tell him, "Hang in there, Sharkie. We all die a little out here."

Nobody from the PGA came to invite Norman to the trophy presentation ceremony or to ask him to the pressroom. "Guess they don't need me," said Norman. "I'll just go to the locker room, change my shoes and leave, I guess."

Norman started to leave Inverness, but one man mentioned that the press would probably like to hear him. So, for five minutes, Norman waded through the crowd, a prisoner in search of his own executioners. Along the way, he met his wife and children, who looked as though they wanted to hug him and cry for a few hours. But they were in public. So Norman set the brave chin-up tone and they followed. Fans spoke and he smiled, waved and answered them.

Arriving unexpected and unescorted in the pressroom, Norman wasn't noticed. So he simply waited for the inevitable Shark sighting. A PGA official felt so bad for Norman that he couldn't even spit out the first question. "Don't choke on me now," laughed Norman.

"The whole deal changed right there," Norman said of the 11th hole, where he caught two tough breaks during his double bogey—a lie in a divot in the fairway and a buried bunker shot.

"You have to expect the unexpected. . . . The better man won today. You have to swallow your pill every now and then. . . . I had a chance to win and I didn't. If I play halfway decent, I win."

Instead of branding Tway's shot lucky—which to a degree it was—he simply pointed out how Tway had made almost equally marvelous trouble shots by the 15th and 17th greens to save par. "When it went in, I said, 'Oh, hell,' " said Norman, characteristically blunt. "Well, it was all over and done with then, wasn't it? I had to try to gamble and hole my pitch shot. Go in or go home. But I couldn't."

Norman had almost made it. Just as he almost made it through this PGA. In a moment, he could go back to his hotel and do a remodeling job that Mr. Ramada would remember forever. Though he'd thrown a ball at his bag and slashed a couple of clubs at the ground in anger, the fuse hadn't reached the dynamite.

One more question, please.

"Is the choke monkey on your back again?"

Norman blew half a fuse. "I did a helluva job and got beat. That's all," he said. " 'Is the monkey back on your back?' That's some question. No. It's not. I'll probably go win next week and the week after. Thanks for ruining a good press conference."

Norman, definitely mortal, definitely hot of collar, left quickly.

Jacobsen, who finished third, saw the incident and said, "Greg is one of the classiest ever to play this game. That's why he's so popular with all the other players, even when he beats us."

Whatever you do, please don't ever say "Holy Toledo" to Norman.

He deserves more.

If courage is grace under pressure, then class is grace in defeat. Pressure may still get the better of Norman at times, as it certainly did today, but he's got defeat's number.

Before this day began, Norman fans could claim their man was the greatest player in the game at this moment. Now Tway supporters can say that player-of-the-year honors are in doubt.

If Tway, the new kid, is already trying to challenge Norman, the new king, that doesn't detract from Norman's conduct this afternoon. Everybody gets eaten alive by the pressures of the devil's game, even a certain Bear. What happened to Norman today befalls every player. Sometimes the game wins.

They say—and it's a cruel saying, mean as golf—that until you've won under the heat in a major championship, you've never really played pro golf.

By that strictest of all standards, the Almost-Great White Shark still has not mastered his sport. He won the British Open last month in a walk when gents named Tommy Nakajima, Ian Woosnam and Gordon J. Brand were his closest foes. But it's folk like Jack Nicklaus, Raymond Floyd and Tway who are the desperadoes in this game. And, three times this year, they've torn golf's greatest trophies out of Norman's gifted grasping hands.

Tway, like Nicklaus and Floyd, won the pay and the play from Norman. But, in a sense, Norman still won the day. Anybody can lose. It happens to the best of 'em. Like Greg Norman, who, when he loses, is indeed the best of 'em.

Hero Worship

AUGUSTA, Georgia, April 12, 1988—

Jack Nicklaus's shadow is long and many have withered in it. Now, for a couple of years, the Bear has had his arm around a Shark—Greg Norman— trying to coax and coach that greatly gifted and enormously appealing Australian to the golf throne. Once more, despite all the goodwill in the world, Nicklaus's attempts at choosing a successor have not seemed to help his protégé.

Tom Weiskopf followed Nicklaus to Ohio State, then to the PGA Tour. Some feel that Weiskopf never played with full enthusiasm because Nicklaus had drained the golf world of possibility. Next, Nicklaus befriended Hal Sutton after the "Bear Apparent" beat him head to head down the stretch at Riviera in the 1983 PGA. Nicklaus loves those who can test and best him. Where Weiskopf had been mercurial, Sutton was a workaholic. Still, in his own way, Sutton was unsteady at the top.

Now comes Norman.

He learned golf from two Nicklaus books given to him by his mother. It was Nicklaus who first told Norman that he should come to the U.S. tour a dozen years ago. And it was Nicklaus who kept encouraging him, almost needling him to put glory ahead of easy wealth in the Far East, until he finally came to play the PGA Tour in '83.

Over the years, Nicklaus took to playing practice rounds with Norman, as he once had with Weiskopf and later with Sutton. Next, Nicklaus offered advice. Norman credits his fine play in the final round of the 1986 British Open—his only major title—to a tip the night before when Nicklaus sought him out in a restaurant.

Not long ago, the Normans moved to North Palm Beach, long the Nicklauses' address, and put their oldest child in the same school the Nicklaus brood had attended. Barbara Nicklaus helped the Normans find a home and, according to *Golf Digest,* Nicklaus even gives Norman advice on the new home he's building now.

The link is real, strong and much talked about in golf. Nicklaus loves Norman's power, his almost Palmeresque charisma and, perhaps above all, his exemplary sportsmanship in defeat. You can't teach the generosity that Norman has shown toward Fuzzy Zoeller, Bob Tway and Larry Mize when they have torn major titles from his hands.

Also, Nicklaus sees Norman as the most Americanized of the great world players; Norman's wife, Laura, is even from the Washington area. And Norman has been a trouper, supporting U.S. tour stops, like the Kemper Open, and positioning himself perfectly to continue the Palmer-Nicklaus-Watson progression in golf supremacy.

But is it going to work that way? Norman is thirty-three and has only three wins in the United States. Where Scotland's Sandy Lyle, thirty, has won two majors, a TPC and three European Order of Merits, Norman has no victory of historic significance on American soil and only one Order of Merit on the Continent.

Sometimes it seems that Norman, who arrived as a force in '84 just as Watson faded, has every gift of golf greatness except timing. Only two men have ever sunk shots from off the green to win major titles on the last hole and both did it to rob Norman. Put the '86 PGA and the '87 Masters in his pocket and this story would read much differently.

Also, Norman frequently plays just superbly enough not to win. Sunday at the Masters, trailing by eleven shots, he tied the course record on the front nine (30), had a shot at the Masters mark of 63, but managed "only" a 64—just enough not to pressure the leaders.

"I knew if I got it to five under I could win the golf tournament. . . . The boys would be wondering, 'How the hell can he shoot 62?' and they'd be worrying about my score instead of their score."

Asked if he creates enormous burdens by expecting to win every event, he answered, "No, because I think you can do it. That's the way I feel every time I go into a golf tournament, that I have the ability to win every time I tee it up. If you don't have that attitude, you might as well not be out there. You just become a pawn on the shelf. It doesn't work [for me]. It's just my nature to be that way, I guess."

No player in postwar history has set such a standard for himself and survived the pressure, except Nicklaus.

When Norman falls behind in a major, he becomes desperate and, as yet, has never rallied until it was too late. At the '87 U.S. Open, British Open and PGA, his pattern was identical—play decently for a round or two, then start gambling and, finally, blow apart. He finished the Opens 74-77 and 74-75, while the PGA was his worst—78-79-79.

Many cite Norman as being in a slump this season when, in fact, he has been spectacular in a weird way. In Australia, playing against kangaroos and koala bears, he won three of four warm-up events. On the PGA Tour, he has been exceptional, finishing third, eleventh, eleventh and fifth at Pebble Beach, Bay Hill, the Players and the Masters. That's an average of $32,000 per start. On those brutal courses, he's had a 64, two 66s, a 67 and two 68s. It's those seven-over-par rounds—a very high ratio—that have undone him. Worldwide, Norman already has won $313,000 in '88, a million-dollar pace.

"I'm going to crack this egg," Norman vows of the Masters. And you can almost see his teeth gritted. Such aggression is Norman's strength, but also his Achilles' heel. His strategy tends toward the reckless, just as his self-expectations are off the graph. His first putts are often too bold and his flirtations with woods and doglegs seem akin to his off-the-course fascination with all forms of speed and flight. Risk attracts him.

Sunday at the 10th hole—his 485-yard, par-4 Augusta nemesis—Norman used a three-wood, not a driver, and was amazed that the hole's contours deposited the ball exactly where his best drives always ended. "I told my caddy, 'Maybe I'm getting older and smarter.' I know what club I'll be hitting there every year."

Can Norman ever throttle back and find a creative, productive cruising speed? In a car, on a golf course or in his demands on himself, he never has.

Listen to Norman on Sunday. What other golfer could make his sport sound like the Indy 500?

"You've got no idea what the pressure is like, the adrenaline flowing through your body, the anticipation on every shot, the hope that the ball lands in the right place. . . . Nobody in the world has any idea what goes through your mind and your system when you play the back eight holes at Augusta National. We try to play the game that's most suited to how we feel. Yes, I was aggressive out there today."

Greg Norman, an athlete who may always be ruled by his emotions, has, perhaps, added a new term to our sports lexicon.

The thrill of defeat.

The Choke Factor

The Year of the Gag

November 1989—One thing elevates golf from the realm of games to the world of sports.

The choke factor.

Of all our American sports, golf is the most consistently humiliating for its stars. As Tom Watson once said: "We all choke. You just try to choke last."

What happened to Scott Hoch at the Masters, Tom Kite at the U.S. Open, Greg Norman at the British Open and Mike Reid at the PGA Championship—suffering a totally humiliating, self-inflicted collapse under pressure—is what makes golf a legitimate big-time, big-money sport, rather than a tofu-and-quiche pastime for yuppies.

Baseball, football, basketball, boxing, tennis, hockey, track and the rest can claim skill, grace, strength, speed, stamina, strategy and a dozen other virtues as their core source of attraction for us. Basically, golf offers us the spectacle of people under enormous strain unraveling before our, and their own, disbelieving eyes.

It's man against himself, with man usually losing quite badly.

A fellow proves, for several days in a row, that he can play a certain course in a dozen or more strokes under par. On most holes, he makes a birdie or finishes with a tap-in par. Then, when he only needs a final decent round on Sunday or perhaps one or two pars to get to the house and claim his prize, he suddenly turns into the rankest of amateurs.

"The pressure of golf can change you so you hardly know yourself," Joe Inman, a journeyman pro, once told me. "You have more electrical connections in your head than a whole city. You'll do anything to keep 'em from going blooey on you in the crunch. I have only one goal in golf—to leave it with my sanity."

No year in memory has left as many images of despair in defeat as 1989. At the Masters, Ben Crenshaw watched in horror as Hoch backed away from a 20-inch putt to win a playoff against Nick Faldo.

"It's a good thing I don't carry a gun," said Hoch after he missed, then eventually lost to Faldo.

That April day, Reid also collapsed when it seemed he'd won. "Things happened so fast," he said. "One minute I was in control, then, faster than a blinking eye, bogey, double bogey. That's baseball."

On the 71st hole of the PGA, Reid got a second chance. He led again. That is, until he took four strokes to get down from the fringe, 30 feet from the hole, for a double bogey. His final blown putt was inches longer than Hoch's at Augusta.

Ironically, Reid sped up his normal ritual as much as Hoch had slowed his down. That didn't work either. As Reid's ball lipped out, who was standing behind him—a few feet away, his head turned so he could not watch the deed—but Scott Hoch.

At the post-tournament press conference, Reid said, "Somebody tell me this is only a game," then added, "Does anybody know where you can go around here for a good cry?" Pretty soon he was crying as he talked.

Between the Masters and the PGA came the most brutal unraveling of the year, all the worse because it took most of a round to complete and because it happened to such a superb player—Kite.

"A lot of people who entered this tournament don't have the opportunity to be scared to death tomorrow," said Kite, after taking the third-round lead in a major for only the second time in his long career. "I anticipate it. I welcome it. I want to be nervous. Do I have total control? Nah. Neither does anybody else. . . . It's you against yourself and you hope you can stand up to it."

Not even eighteen years of pro experience and millions of dollars in prize

money could immunize Kite from playing himself on Sunday with a triple
bogey and two double bogeys—one of which included a wood from the
rough that traveled less than 50 yards.

"I'll come back. And I will contend in more majors. I promise you. I'll
survive," said the grim little Kite, who, like Hoch and Reid, has never won a
major. "But it's a bitter pill to swallow, to have a chance to win and perform
the way I did. That's by far my worst round this year and probably the worst
I've had in five years."

The longer you watch tournament golf, the more inclined you are to
believe it's the most mentally torturous of all sports. Only in golf is a player
given as much time as he needs to tie his own noose.

"You're completely alone, with every conceivable opportunity to defeat
yourself," Hale Irwin once said. "What really matters is resiliency. There's
going to come at least one point when you want to throw yourself in the
nearest trash can and disappear. . . . It's like you're walking down the
fairway naked. The gallery knows what you've done, every other player
knows and, worst of all, you know. That's when you find out if you're a
competitor.

"The longer you play, the more certain you are that a man's performance
is the outward manifestation of who, in his heart, he really thinks he is."

Courage is grace under pressure. What a raw deal. How come it couldn't
be something easier? In golf, at least, cruel demands for mental and emotional courage can be justified because the game demands no physical courage. The only bones that break are those in the skeleton of the personality.
The only blood that flows is from an internal hemorrhaging of self-esteem.

Peter Jacobsen, another of those fine millionaire players who has never
won a Big One, once explained how he felt about the prospect of someday
playing a major-winning shot: "Am I going to have the guts to stand in there
and hit the best shot I can and accept the consequences? All those practice
shots don't mean a thing. You have to be able to stand on the last hole and
say, 'It's due right now.' And then perform."

As if golf weren't cruel enough, you can actually perform too well. Norman shot a 64 in the fourth round of the British Open, then birdied two
holes in the four-hole playoff. However, on that fourth and last playoff hole,
Norman was so spectacularly pumped up that he hit his drive under the lip
of a bunker that no one—not even he—ever dreamed could be reached. He
ended with an "X."

Still, Norman should not forgive himself too quickly. With the exception
of a couple of famous 18th-hole failures at the Masters, Norman's problems
with pressure have come in the early rounds. He's like Johnny Miller, who

once admitted, "The first round of the Masters has killed me for fifteen straight years."

Let's be honest. Everybody, in every sport, plays loosest and best when they're behind and have little to lose. Norman's closing rushes have something homely mixed with their handsomeness. If he's this good, then where was he for three days?

This has been a painful year for those close to the pro tour. Almost every cheer for Nick Faldo, Curtis Strange, Mark Calcavecchia and Payne Stewart has been balanced by a genuine note of sympathy for the victim of the day. Norman is as well liked as Kite is respected. No one could dislike Reid, and some who did not care for Hoch before the Masters found that he grew on them in defeat.

As Crenshaw once said: "The game embarrasses you until you feel inadequate and pathetic. You want to cry like a child." In the gentlemanly world of golf, so excessive a punishment for such small crimes is frowned upon as somehow unsporting.

Deep down, however, the pro's pain is secretly his badge of pride as well. He may not look like a Greek statue, but he has, in a sense, been forged in fire. Golf is serious sport because, of all our games, it is constructed in such a manner as to extract the greatest mental and psychological price. Four consecutive days of play. Deliberate pace of play. Constant scoreboard watching. No foe but yourself and, consequently, no excuses.

Still, following golf up close takes almost as good a stomach as watching Lawrence Taylor tackle Joe Theismann.

After he lost the Masters, Hoch carried his small son Cameron in his arms to the clubhouse as reporters followed. "C'mon over here. Daddy needs a hug," said Hoch.

When he got inside, Hoch—who once missed a playoff in the PGA because of a 72nd-hole three putt from 8 feet—slammed his visor against a wall.

"Why did you do that?" asked Cameron.

"Because I goofed up," said Hoch.

"Daddy, did you goof up again?" asked the child.

"Boy," said Hoch with a pained smile, "you really know how to hurt a guy."

Don't Carry a Gun

AUGUSTA, Georgia, April 10, 1989—

Ben Crenshaw watched Scott Hoch back away from his tap-in putt to win the Masters in a playoff. Two harmless feet. Probably less. Nick Faldo would be beaten. And Hoch, a dependable ten-year journeyman, would be a lovely sliver of golf history. "Jesus, hit it," implored Crenshaw, putting his hand to his mouth as he watched the TV screen.

As Hoch continued to circle and pace, working himself into putting paralysis, Crenshaw put both hands to his face in empathic fear and said, "Oh my God."

In the history of golf, no one had missed a putt so short to throw away—simply rip up and burn—a major championship. Although Hoch three-putted from 6 feet on the 72nd hole to miss a playoff in the '87 PGA.

Hubert Green held the previous record for Major Squandering with a 4-footer here on the 18th green in 1978. But that at least was a real putt. Not a slam-dunk, inside-the-leather, collect-the-green-jacket gimme. By comparison, Doug Sanders's one-pace putt to reach a British Open playoff was lengthy.

When Hoch finally did the horrifying deed, knocking the ball entirely outside the hole and four feet past, Crenshaw's face fell forward in his hands. As a golfer—that is to say, a continual victim of inescapable humiliation—he couldn't watch such disproportionate crime and punishment.

Any child who watched the fifty-third Masters this sullen and soggy afternoon will, one assumes, never be tempted to become a professional golfer. Who'd choose such a thing? Finish second, win $120,000 and use it to buy cyanide.

At least Hoch could joke about it. "It's a good thing I don't carry a gun," he said after Faldo put him out of his sopping-wet misery with a 20-foot birdie putt in the gloaming at the second playoff hole. "It's gonna hurt, knowing all I had to do was two-putt for all the immortality and all that other stuff that comes with these majors. I'da been sharin' that."

He hasn't figured out the worst of it yet. Although Hoch's won more than $2 million on tour and a Vardon Trophy, not too many people know how to pronounce his name because he's only won three events.

It rhymes with choke. And after playing twenty-three holes in five under par this day, he deserves a far better memorial. After all, he simply fell on his sword last. What he did on the 10th green, the greatest men in golf had been doing all day.

Seve Ballesteros? His hopes and all his gallantry on a marvelous day splashed into the water at the 16th hole when he was just a shot off the lead. "I was thinking [birdie] two and got five," said the Spaniard, who, on his thirty-second birthday, led for a short time after making seven birdies in the span of ten holes. "When I saw my ball flying right at the flag . . . I could not believe what happened. It was only a matter of a couple of yards. Then, it spun back in the water and my tournament was over. . . . I guess my destiny was not to win."

Greg Norman? After thrilling the throng with three straight birdies to tie for the lead, he made a lame bogey at the 72nd hole with a weak approach and a weaker pitch. All he needed was a par to get in the playoff. His thoughts? Don't ask. For the first time in all his major disappointments, he bolted for the parking lot. Perhaps the memories of 1986 here and 1984 at the U.S. Open, when he also bogeyed 72nd holes and ended up a loser, were too strong even for his sharkish courage.

Crenshaw? He began the day at 9 A.M. with a four-shot lead with five holes remaining in the rain-interrupted third round. On a wet but windless day with the easiest possible scoring conditions, Crenshaw made nothing happen all day until he birdied the 70th and 71st holes to tie for the lead. What'd he do? He collapsed instantly with a bogey.

"My glove was wet and slipped and I pulled it into the trap. And that was that," said Crenshaw, who, hard as it is to believe, had run out of towels. For want of a nail the shoe was lost, and so the horse, and so forth. "We thought we had one more," said Crenshaw in disbelief. "But we didn't."

Mike (Radar) Reid, the world's most accurate golfer in recent years? He had this Masters in his hands more securely than anybody except Hoch. But he three-putted the subtle 14th, then dunked a simple wedge shot into the water at the easy 15th for a double bogey.

Unfortunately for those who play it for a living, that's golf. Especially the Masters. "This is probably the hardest tournament in the world to win from the front. Probably ninety percent win from behind. . . . There's so much pressure here. This course asks for perfection," said Faldo.

In fact, Faldo never carried the burden of the lead for a second all weekend until he found himself in the playoff. Like so many others before him, like Gary Player (64) in '77 and Nicklaus (65) in '86, he freewheeled it from the rear. Then, as soon as he had no one in front of him, Faldo lost this Masters with a bunkered bogey on the playoff's first hole.

Hoch just unlost it for him.

"You just stand there and watch," said Faldo of the awful feeling as Hoch prepared for his winning tap.

In golf, the wheel of karma never stops turning—so long as you keep plugging and let it work its will. For a decade, Crenshaw suffered. But he got a Masters. Tom Kite's long, stoic battle continues. Last year, Faldo lost a U.S. Open to Curtis Strange that he thought he should have won. "That slipped by," Faldo said. "But this makes up for it. Sure, certainly does. . . . What does this mean? Gosh, the world."

A world lifted, at any rate, from your shoulders. For strong losers like Faldo, the hour of vindication usually rolls 'round. Strange, for example, can joke about Rae's Creek. Now it's Hoch who'll have to relive his putt a million times. "I wasn't even that nervous," he said. "I didn't want to miss an angle. I said, 'This is for all the marbles. Just firm it. Then I didn't line up the putter and I pulled it on top of that. . . . At that speed, I needed to keep it inside [the] left [edge]. But I pulled it. It was a terrible putt.

"There was a split second of indecision. I adjusted as I was over the ball. Between my brain and my hands, the message got crisscrossed."

Golf's most vicious illusion is that he who gags last gags worst. Actually, the penultimate victim has played better than anyone, except the champion. Some reward. "I feel good about myself," said Hoch, defiantly, almost convincingly.

Crenshaw, who has now finished second or been just a shot behind in six major championships, had the dank evening's wisest words—for himself and so many other brave failures here.

"I'm laughing now, but when the time comes [alone], it'll be painful, believe me. . . . [But] you're never cursed in this game. You just do your best and go on," said Crenshaw, adding with a rueful little chuckle, "Any way you can."

Father's Day

BROOKLINE, Massachusetts, June 20, 1988—

Everyone in golf who knows Curtis Strange knew where his thoughts would turn as he walked up the 18th hole of the Country Club with the U.S. Open championship safely in his hands today.

He would think of his father, Tom, and their years together in his boyhood when golf was their bond and passion and almost a blood vow between them. He would think of the man who died when he was fourteen, nearly twenty years ago, leaving a paternal memory of superhuman size and demands, deep-carved demands, that would drive and lash Strange all his life.

Everybody knew, almost to the word, what Strange would say as soon as he had finished the work of beating British Open champion Nick Faldo, 71–75, in this 18-hole playoff. Strange would not talk yet about putts and sand shots, about "sheer guts," about how he ignored ten visits to the rough and five trips into sand traps. He would not talk about how he kicked the ball all over wind-whipped eastern Massachusetts, but willed his way to a dozen one-putt greens.

"I think you wait for a moment like this in your life to thank the people who've given you the advice, enthusiasm and knowledge to continue on," said Strange, picking every word, pausing as much as ten seconds between phrases as he cried quietly. "I have to thank my dad. This is for my dad." Then he waited.

"And that's all I can say. I've been waitin' to say that a long time," said Strange. "I just wish he could have been here. . . . I screwed up the '85 Masters. But let's not be bringing that up. Let's be havin' fun. . . . This is the greatest thing I have ever done . . . the greatest feeling I have ever had. My two kids don't even know [yet] what the hell this means to me."

This U.S. Open meant everything to Curtis Strange. More, perhaps, than it ought to mean to anybody. Even he has admitted that countless times, talked about the coiled spring of ambition inside him that drives and torments him, even as it pushed him to Arnold Palmer scholarships at Wake Forest and seasons as the No. 1 money winner on the PGA Tour. "I'm too hard on myself," he says. Yet this week he has barely slept. His eyes are bloodshot. And Sunday night, after coming so close to throwing away this Open, he couldn't even eat. For nearly twenty-four hours, he was a taut bow, "Waiting to go." Waiting to atone.

Faldo should have finished Strange when he had the chance, when he had all those cozy birdie putts on the back nine Sunday. He shouldn't have waited until this nasty, windy afternoon when both he and Strange would, inevitably, be blown off the short grass into the high heather and have a war of hearts, not swings. Eleven times Faldo missed the green and six times he ended up with bogey—five times in the last six holes as the long battle just wore him out.

Strange, the grinder's grinder, the bad boy with a bit of a sneer, just kept holing those heartbreakers: 3 feet, 6 feet. Sorry, Nick. No lip-outs today. Strange hit only seven greens all afternoon, but three times he set the huge crowds roaring with birdie putts of 10, 22 and, finally, 29 feet at the 5th, 7th and 13th holes.

Strange never trailed, not for a second. When he birdied the 13th, it was the day's kill shot. Faldo three-putted for bogey a moment later to put Strange ahead by three shots. "The turning point," said Strange, who never led by fewer than two shots thereafter.

The door opened only once after that, for a second at the 15th hole, when Strange was trapped and had to bogey. But Faldo slapped that door on his own foot. He fragged an easy chip shot all the way across the green into the fringe and bogeyed himself.

"I don't know what happened on that one," Faldo said.

Now Strange could come home on cruise control. When Faldo, gambling for birdie, bogeyed the 17th, Strange thought: It's over.

More than a golf tournament was over for the thirty-three-year-old who has won $3.6 million but, until today, never a major championship. Always money. Never glory. Never what his father, the romantic, valued most—stature in the game.

"We all have our egos and we want to be respected, not just as a person but as a golfer," said Strange. "This [Open] means Curtis Strange might be looked at a little differently. . . . It means I got to that next level, damnit."

The earnings at the next level aren't bad either. Strange pocketed $180,000 for the victory; as runner-up, Faldo received $90,000.

Strange is the player that fellow pros on the tour always have worried about. Tears and fury ran just beneath his skin. His mask always was full of cracks, the rage or hunger waiting to erupt. Friends worried when he got publicly scalded by Palmer for his bad temper at the Bay Hill Classic a few years ago. They worried when he blew that Masters after being four up on the back nine. Think what that would do to any player. Imagine what it does to Strange.

The final round of the U.S. Open always falls on Father's Day—another bad break for Strange, who tries too hard, berates himself too much, on the best of days. Once, on an Open Sunday, a fan approached Strange between nines and said, "Win it for your dad."

"That did it," recalled Strange. "I was in tears on the tenth tee."

Now, the friends of Curtis Strange—a group that has grown enormously in the last three years after he met the indignities of Rae's Creek with fresh dignity of his own—don't have to worry anymore. He's come into the clearing.

Because he faced the worst when he lost the Masters, because he discovered that people forgave him, empathized with him and even liked him in failure, Strange was able to cope with his near-collapse here on Sunday. But it was far from easy. A night to regroup helped.

"After my [three-putt] mistake at the seventeenth on Sunday, I didn't want to lose today. . . . I just didn't want to face you guys if I lost. I hate to admit that, but it's true," said Strange at the postmatch news conference. "[A loss] would have been something I would have had to get over. But it would have been tough. Those things affect us."

Faldo seemed unfazed by his defeat. In fact, he seemed so proud that his nerve had held on his long shots—"I had it going in the right direction all day"—that his ineffectual putting hardly seemed to enter his mind.

"I just never put enough pressure on Curtis. . . . It felt like a helluva long day," he said, after roasting in the mid-90s heat. "[And] I think my five spectators did a helluva job."

For Strange, the path to this Open title has been a long one. Along the way, he learned—although he'll be the first to concede not completely—how to relax, how to enjoy others, how to forgive himself, how to fail and how to carry himself like a champion of the game. "That Masters wasn't going to intimidate me or ruin my career," said Strange. "It even motivated me, to a point. What I've done since says, 'This was not going to devastate Curtis Strange.' "

As he came down the 18th fairway this hot, breezy evening, the throngs straining against the ropes to praise him, Strange raised both hands above his pepper-gray head in salute. In the gallery, his twin brother, Alan, almost a golf pro, hugged Curtis's wife, Sarah. Then, after the final putt, after he had joined Francis Ouimet and Julius Boros as Open playoff winners at the Country Club, it was Curtis's turn to hold his wife tight and saying nothing for a long time. Finally, Strange's lips moved. He seemed to whisper, "I made it."

And if he didn't, he might as well have.

Interlude

Responsible
for Himself

January 20, 1974—Gene Williams cannot remember just when he decided to live.

From the moment on Thanksgiving Eve 1966 when he was thrown to the mat during wrestling practice at St. Albans School in Washington, D.C., and heard his neck snap, he knew what had happened. "My body from the neck down was floating in space. Only my head was on the ground.

"The doctors," said Williams's mother calmly, "told him right away, 'Gene, we can't establish a close personal relationship with you. Ninety-seven percent of our spinal-cord patients die.'"

While in traction for six weeks in the intensive-care unit of a local hospital, Williams heard patients in adjoining beds enter, conscious or unconscious, and die.

One death was more important than others. Williams says it, in part, "inspired me."

A construction worker who had fallen five stories was brought in unconscious. "I heard about the accident on the radio," recalled Williams. "He never regained consciousness and I never saw him, but for five days I listened to his breathing in the next bed.

"People who heard the radio spot didn't know he was still struggling. But it doesn't matter how many other people know—if you know."

So the first of Gene Williams's seemingly endless hurdles passed; at some deep level, he feels he decided not to quit and die.

And then he almost did die. Not once, but several times.

With holes drilled in his skull for traction, he developed bursitis of the jaw, couldn't eat and lost 75 of his 180 pounds. In October, Williams had been an All-Metropolitan tackle for the league-champion football team. By January he had wasted away to a near-skeleton.

Like all long-term bed patients, he was prey to infection. In February a bladder infection sent his fever above 104 degrees.

"The doctors told me, 'See, Mrs. Williams? We told you not to get your hopes up,'" said the mother.

Desperate and furious, the mother cursed the specialists "who had almost killed Gene," and followed the advice of "a great male practical nurse."

The two packed the emaciated boy in ice and gave him alcohol baths for eight hours until the fever abated.

In June 1967 Mrs. Williams, looking almost as haggard as her son, wheeled the patient out of the hospital against doctors orders and off to the Rusk Institute in New York City.

Williams entered Rusk "just skin and bones," according to Dr. Donald Covalt, associate director of the institute at New York University.

His injury, a cervical fracture of a fairly high nature (between the fifth and sixth vertebrae), left Williams a "high-level quadriplegic"—that is, paralyzed in all four extremities.

The long rehabilitation in which Williams learned to use what arm, wrist and chest muscles he had left was, according to both Williams and his father, "one long athletic event. The simplest movement was a wrestling match."

Williams entered Rusk a near-invalid but left driving a Chevelle.

With limited use of arms and wrists, but none of the hands, Williams could wheel himself to his car, hoist himself into the front seat, haul his wheelchair in and drive. "The car was a lifesaver for him" said his father.

The story of Gene Williams, who is now twenty-four, is "a mile or two beyond anything I've ever seen here before," according to Dr. Covalt.

The patient does not see it that way.

"Once I decided not to die, a clear choice never presented itself," he said. "You go with what you've got."

For Williams, the true rehabilitation, of the spirit and soul, began only after the physical rehabilitation—the months "that were like hell"—was behind. The required skills of driving a car, being able to get out of bed and dress himself, hold eating utensils and turn the pages of a book were only the beginning.

He went back to St. Albans to finish his senior year in 1968 and to help coach the football team. "He was a damn good coach," said St. Albans athletic director Gary Gardiner, who remembers Williams's chair being carried down the Cathedral steps at graduation by teammates. "That was the last time I broke down and cried like a baby," Gardiner said.

Gradually, perhaps Williams's most revealing quality emerged. "People felt at ease with Gene," said track coach Brooks Johnson. "They came to him with their problems."

Refusing to give up the pleasures he could retain, Williams began going anywhere he pleased, becoming fiercely independent. "Most 'wheelies' call ahead everywhere to find out if there are accommodations for them. How high the curbs are. I show up at restaurants, movies, anywhere, and then cope with what's there.

"Some people choke. You ask them for help and they freak out. They stutter that they have a bad back. But some people will choke at anything," said Williams.

For Williams's mother the resurrection was complete in 1969. "He looked healthy again. I remember I said, 'Gene, all of a sudden I can look at you as a person again.' "

In 1970 Mrs. Williams ran for Congress on the Democratic ticket in the 5th District of Indiana. Her son was media director.

He drove more than 35,000 miles, throwing himself into confrontations with Hoosiers opposed to his mother's liberal views.

"I couldn't believe him," she said. "He went to the Lions Club fish fry in Kokomo, where they still have three different chapters of the Ku Klux Klan. He started rapping with the hard hats. Before long they gave him a hard hat and he was serving fish."

The campaign failed, but the young man had learned his mode of operation. "I try not to be governed by situations. By mere luck, I saw beyond what society says you can't do. No matter what, you are ultimately responsible for yourself."

In 1970, with a huge supply of cranberry juice to fight the bladder and kidney stones and infections that plague—and often kill—paraplegics, Williams went to Harvard.

There his appetite—for musicology (his major), political science, psychosomatic medicine and neuroanatomy—ranged far beyond what might have been expected of the bright, crew-cut St. Albans football star who had had trouble in class.

Williams saw Harvard with something of the detachment of an earlier graduate, Henry David Thoreau, who wryly dedicated his *Walden* to the "poor students." By his senior year (1973) Williams thought the ancient academy almost "a comical place," like "a giant department store with canned goods in row 3C."

The academic grind, the rush to classes, hit Williams in "a different perspective. Making it to an early class on time seems much different if you don't know if you'll get dressed."

During his Harvard years he took two trips to Mexico, alone. "I was tossing myself up for grabs," said Williams, who slept in his car. The independence of the Mexico trips, picking up hitchhikers, caring for himself, is to Dr. Covalt the most remarkable performance by a quadriplegic in his experience, illustrating why "this man will be a success in whatever he attempts."

Praise for his fortitude is one of Williams's principal irritations. "This idea of me attacking life is really stupid," he said. Every attempt he makes to live normally is seen as another example of his abnormality.

"I would like to think I would have developed the same way I have, without the injury," said Williams. He is not certain, and never can be.

"I'm moving a little slower now. I see people are not aware of their capabilities. These stereotypes of proper socialization work on you so much. People are out of touch with their own bodies. They stress materialism over feeling good.

"I can see a lot more things than people who spend all day going up and down stairs. In a way the injury opens up a whole lot."

Would the original Gene Williams have become passionately interested in music and the healing arts? Would he have been in the march on the Pentagon in a wheelchair? Would he now be a jazz percussionist with his own progressive group in Cambridge? "I like to think so. But really, I can't say whether I'm better off or worse off than if I hadn't been hurt."

Doctors predict a near-normal life expectancy for him.

During the first months after the friend flipped him on his neck in a routine wrestling warm-up, Williams decided to pass up a chance for a major lawsuit against St. Albans or his wrestling coach.

"A lot of people think I was stupid not to do that. The courts are big in favor of settlement for people who have been deprived of the ability to do manual work. That's a big thing in our society.

"But who was I going to sue, really? The only people I could think of were Vince Lombardi and *Sports Illustrated*. They were responsible as much as anyone.

"When I went to practice that day my neck hurt. I should have had it X-rayed long before. Several doctors told me the wrestling fall was just the last straw, that the damage came from football. But I believed in Lombardi and that ethic of playing with pain, proving how tough you are. Your ankle is one thing, but I ignored a fundamental warning signal."

Because of his remarkable achievements and warm manner, many people think Gene Williams is making it, that the injury does not haunt him anymore.

"I think about it every day," he said in a quiet flat tone. "The question is what you do with it."

The Olympics

The Price of Gold

January 24, 1980—Under the gathering clouds of an Olympic boycott, America's athletes and coaches are being forced to ask themselves a fundamental, but frighteningly unfamiliar, question. "Why?"

The price of excellence in athletics, especially in Olympic sports, has inflated dramatically in recent years.

The 1970s brought into focus a world of international child athletes and prepubescent gold medalists in a host of sports. Those champions who were not children often won their fame in games marred by steroids, amphetamines, blood doping and a whole pharmacopoeia of chemicals used to produce hybrid ideological warriors.

What is the human cost of becoming a famed Olympic-class swimmer, gymnast or track star—the next Mark Spitz, Nadia Comaneci or Bruce Jenner?

What is the lasting psychological or physical price that must be paid, even in obscure and profitless sports, to be the best speed skater or volleyball player in the world?

In this new decade, what is the tariff that a great athlete's body and soul must bear? And is that tax becoming more than the human psyche and body can sensibly bear?

Finally, has the whole issue of the Olympics—whether it can, or even should, continue to exist—come at an appropriate time? Could the demise of the Games even be a blessing, a cleansing of our national view of sports?

Normally, such questions would be unwelcome among coaches and athletes just months before an Olympiad.

However, in these days of Olympic limbo, it is impossible to avoid such queries. They pop to mind of their own accord in every part of the United States.

In New Haven, Connecticut, Frank Keefe, the Yale swimming coach and head of the U.S. Pan American Games teams, said, "My swimmers ask themselves why they have been getting up at five A.M. and jumping in the water by five-thirty almost every day for most of their lives.

"They ask why they have trained outdoors when it was so cold that their footprints froze on the pool deck.

"Even with the Olympics as a goal, kids told me, 'Drop dead, Coach. I'm not doing it anymore. I can't do it anymore. I can't think.' And they disappear.

"That's always been the natural weeding-out process. Our young club teams wear T-shirts that say, 'Take It to the Limit.' You take it to the limit as many times a day as many days a year as you can," said Keefe, also founder of the elite Fox Catcher Farms swim club in Philadelphia.

"Our kids are in the water five hours a day, and lifting weights another hour, seven days a week, for twelve months a year. And that doesn't count going to school," said Keefe, a mere middle-of-the-road workaholic by swimming standards.

"We're in a sport where there's no money to be had above the table or even underneath it. But the Olympics pull you on. We tell each other, 'No guts, no glory,' " said Keefe. "But now, where's the glory? The gem has been taken away."

In Palo Alto, California, Robin Campbell, a world-class middle-distance runner, asks herself why she has followed her coach, Brooks Johnson, from St. Albans School in her native Washington to the University of Florida, to Santa Fe (Florida) Community College and now to Stanford University.

"I have lived so many places and traveled so much since I was thirteen," said the twenty-year-old Campbell, "that my aunt gave me an address book for Christmas. She told me it wasn't for other people's addresses. It was for all of mine, so I'd know where I was.

"I was only home [in Washington] for one month of 1979," said Campbell, who has had constant injuries for the past four years, including a broken kneecap suffered in midstride that slowed her for eighteen months.

"I always try to be nice to all of my relatives in D.C. because you can't tell. By the next time I get home, someone might have died.

"I never show any emotion at home. I'm always hard-faced. But as soon as I get on the airplane, I start to cry.

"I used to love to travel and never come home. I think I've run on every continent. But now I almost hate it. I wish it were like *Star Trek* and you could just zip through space," said Campbell.

"Since 1973, it's gotten worse every year. Sometimes I joke that I'm going to have a nervous breakdown. But I do wonder what's going on in the back of my mind.

"I had a race that would have qualified me for the Pan Am Games in Puerto Rico and the World Cup in Montreal last summer," said Campbell. "I'd worked all year for it. But when my race came, my mind went blank, I finished sixth and barely broke a sweat. I didn't even try.

"I wonder if I really didn't want to go to Puerto Rico and Montreal."

In Colorado Springs, Flora Hyman has been a star of the U.S. women's volleyball team—a co-favorite for the Olympic gold with Cuba—a squad that has been secluded for five years of Marine Corps-style boot-camp training fifty weeks a year.

"I've only given up seven years of my life and my whole future," said the twenty-five-year-old Hyman bitterly. "If there are no Olympics, what have I done with my life?"

Perhaps no other American athletes approach the fanaticism of the fourteen U.S. women volleyballers, who unashamedly accept the training tactics of the Cubans, Soviets and Japanese as gospel.

"Hypnosis, togetherness through common suffering and, ultimately, mind control are my coaching techniques," says coach Arie Selinger, who has taken the U.S. team from nineteenth in the world to number two with a five-year plan that includes reveille-to-taps training six days a week in isolated compounds for years at a time with no vacations.

"More than any sport, volleyball demands team unity," said Selinger. "You must be one body with many heads and one heart. Overcoming the ideas of individuality, profit motive and democracy are among our problems. It takes eight years, I believe, to train a volleyball player to think only of the team in all situations."

The women volleyballers live a spartan, year-round existence at the U.S. Olympic Training Center in Colorado Springs—rising at 7 A.M., practicing from eight until twelve and from two until six, with lunch and sleep between. After dinner come hypnosis and "mind control" sessions, motivational talks or strategy sessions. "You're so tired you can't wait to get to bed," said Rita Crockett.

"The girls, in addition to their room and board, get a hundred twenty dollars a week in expense money," said Selinger, whose U.S. team has played and won all over the world. "It's taken us five years to raise that expense money from twenty dollars a week."

"We've all had school, friends and family taken away," said Crockett, a team member for only eighteen months.

"I gave up getting married. When I came to Colorado Springs from San Antonio, my boyfriend and I were discussing getting married. Now we just discuss getting to be friends again. My phone bill to him is a hundred fifty dollars a week, but I only get to see him four times a year.

"You can put up with everything if you know you're doing it for a purpose and for your country," said Crockett. "But now it looks like I'll never be known as an Olympian.

"I'm twenty-two, and if we boycott this one, I just don't know if I could do this for four more years. I guess maybe I could. One of our girls is twenty-nine and she's been training for six years."

In Silver Spring, Maryland, Margie Weiss sees her whole way of life endangered. She and her husband, Greg, have been training a hundred gymnasts, such as current fourteen-year-old Olympic hopefuls Sheri Mann and Jackie Cassello, for six hours a day, six days a week, for the last four years in their hand-built wooded complex.

The Weiss family life is built around what Margie Weiss calls "the new athletes"—the children who start their careers as soon as they can walk, and, if possible, even before.

Her own infant daughter Geremi took her first steps before the age of one year on a balance beam. Now, at six, Geremi can already do gymnastics tricks that no woman could do at the '72 Olympics, according to her mother.

The Weisses also have more good news about Geremi—she isn't growing. "Early tests indicated that she would grow up to be five foot four," said Margie Weiss. "But I believe that the more gymnastics you do at a young age, the smaller you will be.

"Growth spurts come in two-week bursts. If you're pounding your body, the growth sections of the bones are going to be pounded down," said the mother. "Geremi is really tiny for her age now, which is all right with me."

The Weisses' other daughter, Genna, seven, is already a high diver, with a platform in the backyard. She can do an inward one-and-a-half—a harrowingly difficult and dangerous dive for adults—and has won diving meets for ten-and-unders "up and down the East Coast," in her mother's words.

The Weisses have helped their children have the compact, fatless bodies of perfect gymnasts by a simple method: they stopped feeding their children at the age of eighteen months.

"We rarely have time to stop training to prepare meals," said Margie Weiss. "So the kids feed themselves as soon as they can open the refrigerator. We always have apples, oranges, yogurt and health foods in there, so it doesn't matter what they grab. They can't go wrong."

The Weisses are certain that their children and their pupils are the athletic wave of the future. "The Russians find ninety percent of their athletes. We find ten percent of ours," said Margie, "because they test their children."

"The first of the new athletes was Stephanie Willim," she said, speaking of a Weiss protégé who could have been the Comaneci of '80. "She was a shoo-in. She was doing tricks three years ago that no one else had tried yet."

But Willim suffered disk disintegration problems that led doctors to order her to abandon her career permanently or face being crippled for life.

"The Communist countries are far ahead of us," said Weiss, a candidate for the coaching job of the U.S. women's gymnastics team now that Linda Metheney-Mulvahill has been deposed. "It's lucky that they only give out three medals at the Olympics, not a top forty, or they'd crush us in almost every sport.

"But we're learning. We're starting younger and younger in many sports— swimming, gymnastics, track, alpine skiing, diving, speed skating, figure skating and a lot of others.

"Once, kids went to college to start becoming serious athletes. Now, college is already over the hill.

"You go to college to retire on a scholarship."

What will happen to her children, her pupils, her livelihood, if the Olympics are boycotted? "It's so unjust," she said, "that I refuse to think about it. You can't train like we do with that on your mind."

Margie Weiss offers an example of the ambiguous questions that surround the price of excellence. She is, by any standard, fanatical. Yet the Weisses' gymnastics school is not some six-acre pocket of Romania transported to Silver Spring.

"We understand that the higher you go, the harder you can fall. We understand that it has to change a young person to hear the national anthem played and see the flag raised in a foreign competition for them," she said. "You have to put a cushion under these children. We do it with intermediate goals. Each accomplishment on the ladder has its own worth. You don't have to win a gold medal to know that you're worth something."

Margie Weiss knows why her sub-ten-year-olds can do terrifying stunts. "They're gullible. You can tell 'em anything. They don't shy from danger because they don't know the consequences. As long as what you tell them is what comes true, they believe you."

Yet she also knows the visceral fear of watching a seven-year-old do a flipping dive with her head inches from a high board. She knows because it is her own daughter.

"The scariest moment of my life was taking Genna to the edge of the high board for the first inward one-and-a-half. I could 'spot' for her because she only weighed forty-five pounds. She had completed one somersault before my hands were off her. If I'd waited till she was older, I wouldn't have been strong enough to be sure it was safe," she said.

Above all, Weiss is determined that her and her husband's family school will be just that—a place where all one hundred children have something of a sense of family, even though Mann and Cassello are the only two who live full-time with them.

"I'm adopted," she said. "I know that the mother isn't the one who bore you, but the one who loved you."

It should not be forgotten that perhaps the most fundamental lure of athletics is its harsh, elite and unrelenting difficulty. The very notion of being a champion has always been tied to the idea of discipline, pain and self-denial. The Athenian distance runner who ran back from the battle of Marathon dropped dead after delivering his message.

Maybe the most grueling of Olympic sports is outdoor speed skating, where windchill factors are often far below zero and frostbite, black toes and frozen lungs are commonplace. No one pays a greater price in pain than speed skaters, those hunched-over masochists who often cannot straighten up after a race.

"This year, my motivation suddenly reached a new level," said Nancy Swider, a U.S. national team standout who in '76 set a world record in the 3,000 meters. Others thought Swider was in peak condition. But the twenty-three-year-old decided to lose eighteen pounds off an already hard body.

"I went off preservatives, additives, canned or processed foods, any kind of junk. If I put something wrong in my mouth, I spit it out.

"I've known for years how I wanted to feel. I've seen it in other people.

"It's a look of total purpose and purity. But it's never been me.

"I don't like the word 'religious,' but I think we each have a God-given ability. Just once in my life, if just for a few months for the Olympics, I want to live at the absolute edge of my potential."

That, at the most idealistic level, is the gist of the Olympics.

In fact, the passion for the Olympics, the cultivated psychological need for it, is so great that, for instance, the U.S. women's volleyball team was profoundly divided and shaken two months ago when, after five years, it was given its first vacation.

"I promised them for years that the day they qualified for the Olympics, they could have a vacation," said Selinger. "A promise is a promise, so I had to give them six weeks off. I just got weak."

"The six weeks was history," said Hyman. "Every other team in the world thought we were nuts. Theory says you can't do it."

Some team members didn't even want their promised vacation. "It was voted on," said Hyman disapprovingly. "So they took one."

"The sacrifices that an athlete makes are always woefully overemphasized," said Brooks Johnson, track coach at Stanford. "An athlete is like the workaholic who says, 'I'm doing all this for my wife and family.' Of course, he's doing it for himself.

"Some sort of psychosis is necessary as a driving force for a great athlete.

"The premise of being world champion is that you are not normal. Perhaps you even have to be a little sick," averred Johnson.

"That monomania is necessary. If you don't have it, you can't go the whole way to the top."

Pearls
of the Antilles

HAVANA, April 8, 1978—

Alberto Juantorena and Teofilo Stevenson, Cuba's two pearls of the Antilles, are burnished to full luster here every day like twin crown jewels.

Juantorena, the bright pearl of speed, and Stevenson, the dark pearl of violence, hold Homeric rank on this island because of their gifts.

The world's most renowned runner and its most powerful amateur fighter hold a special place in Cuban legend. Both Olympians, the trackman and the boxer are programmed for Moscow gold in 1980. In this classless society, at least these two men are princes.

A national treasure lies face down in the dust on the track.

From every corner of Pedro Morrero Stadium, feet begin their slow walk toward the fallen "Horse."

A moment before, Juantorena, world track athlete of the year in 1977, had run freely, slapping the palm of a distance runner, teasing a girl and smiling as he jogged past.

In the backstretch, the Horse sat in the sun, cross-legged, meditating in midworkout, his back against the stadium wall. He felt marvelous. This was a day to push his body, sense it, converse with it.

"Some days in training you say, 'This is it.' You feel you can surpass anything you have ever done. At that time, you are afraid, because you think you won't make it. That you will hurt yourself," says Juantorena.

"But you must try or you will never make progress. You feel like an intruder into another world. Sometimes you can reach into that new world where no man has been. Many times you must pull back."

Juantorena, the creature with a conformation like few trackmen before him, barrels into a turn, gobbling meters. Suddenly he pulls up, limping, holding his hamstring. He walks, stretches, sits, folds his leg under him and finally lies face down in the middle of the Tartan track.

The morning sun is already warm. Latin music, sad and slow, drifts across the stadium from the public-address system. A hundred people see Juantorena lying motionless. No one rushes or cries out. If this scene is not routine, neither is it unparalleled.

"Juantorena knows his body like no other athlete I have seen," says Cuban sports photographer Jesus Rocamora. "Others have too much courage, too much adrenaline and too little judgment.

"They will push themselves until they are badly injured. Then it takes weeks or months simply to get back to where they were. Juantorena talks to his muscles, and they talk back."

Nevertheless, out of respect, every athlete, trainer and custodian in the stadium makes the pilgrimage to Juantorena, surrounding him silently as his personal coach probes the long leg.

The Horse gets up and limps off the track.

"You are my personal devil," says Juantorena, glaring at his friend Julio Quintana, who is jabbing a long hypodermic of painkiller into his flank.

"You are the torturer," says Juantorena as Quintana straps an electric-shock machine around the slightly injured hamstring. "As soon as I felt the muscle pull, I began thinking about this damn apparatus," says Juantorena, switching easily from Spanish to English.

"It doesn't really hurt," he says, his eyes bugging out in mock pain, his teeth chattering. "It just itches like hell."

For Juantorena, the needles and shocks and nagging injuries and drudgery of running twenty-five kilometers a day is an inexpensive visa if he can reach the world of sustained speed into which he is always pushing.

"It was said that 400 meters was the last sprint, but we," he says, meaning himself, "proved in the Olympics that the 800 meters could be run as a sprint.

"Now there is a new challenge. Can the 1,500 meters be run as a dash? That is a new idea which we are caressing. It's a possibility."

Juantorena defies classification and delights in his uniqueness. His goal is simple: to own every world record from 400 meters to 1,500 meters, thereby encompassing the world of powerful, explosive dash men and scrawny, masochistic distance runners in the same stunning body.

"You must be loco," he says, "to run twenty-five kilometers a day.

"And you must be crazy to love a sport where you wait a year, perhaps even four years, for one special day of competition. You become so tense on that day that you must disconnect yourself by listening to music or going to a good movie.

"Is that sensible?" Juantorena asks. "And training," he adds wearily. "I must change scenery. The ocean, the forest, the mountains. They are my sedative."

Fortunately for Juantorena, Christopher Columbus, sick and tired of the Atlantic, called Cuba "the most beautiful island I have ever seen" when he landed in 1494. From the bluffs of Matanzas Bay to the mountains of Oriente, Juantorena has taken his mind away from the monotony of Tartan ovals.

"It is bothersome, this aging, this response to biological law," he says. "It makes the task of studying your own body that much more difficult."

At present, Juantorena's mind is split. He sees perhaps his last good chance to crack Lee Evans's world record in the 400 (43.86), which was set in the high altitude of Mexico City, when he competes in Colombia in July. "Everybody is waiting for a world record," he says, smiling.

On the other hand, at twenty-six he wonders if his speed will deteriorate by 1980. He is determined to win two gold medals again, and the 1,500 seems a far easier companion for the 800—in terms of training technique and schedules—than the 400.

"Those little milers," says the 6-foot-3 Juantorena, who looks like an NFL tight end, "they bump each other all the time. I do not think they will bump me."

Stevenson and Juantorena, because they are countrymen and because they both look like huge Rodin sculptures, in both physique and profile, are assumed to be similar.

The two men are as dissimilar as could be imagined. Juantorena is expansive, informal, poetic, trusting, easily amused and absorbed by politics and history. Stevenson is withdrawn, suspicious, imperial and often sullen.

"The world knows that Stevenson looks like a sculpture," says veteran photographer Rocamora, "but they do not know that he also speaks like one.

"Teofilo has great dignity, like Joe Louis, but words are his enemy. He speaks with his lips so tight that I must punch him in the ribs to get a picture that looks like he is smiling."

"Juantorena is the most spontaneous athlete Cuba has ever had, and we are a gregarious people," says Cuban sportswriter Jose Luis Salmeron. "Stevenson may be the least spontaneous."

Stevenson views all but his oldest acquaintances the same way he stalks a ring opponent—with his jab always protecting him, taking a cautious offensive position that can always collapse back into a safe shell of defense.

"Stevenson does not like to be hit, either literally in the ring or figuratively outside it," says an official of the Cuban sports institute, INDER.

"I have worked entire Stevenson fights when I did not snap a single picture," confesses Rocamora. "Either his back is to you or he is covering up or he is exploring with the jab," Rocamora admits. "And suddenly the fight is over and you have missed another Stevenson knockout."

The lifestyles of the two world heavyweight boxing champions—Leon Spinks the professional and Stevenson the amateur—are as different as their dental work.

Spinks's life is turmoil, controversy and potential riches.

Stevenson wakes up early in the Cuban boxing-team barracks on a farm twenty miles outside Havana near El Caño. Guinea hens, pigs, cows and crops give off a pungent smell in the lush Caribbean air. Royal palms, grapevines and almond trees cast their shade and their restful mood over the retreat. The boxers, now preparing for the next world championships in Belgrade, run their wind sprints in heavy boots on paths beaten bare under a grove of mango trees.

The pace is as syrupy as Stevenson's saunter. A battery of trainers, psychologists and scientists infests the camp, testing strength and reflexes, the results of the latest hush-hush boxing techniques that Cuba is adamant about developing.

The meals, served in tin plates and cups and eaten with fingers or an occasional fork, are enormous. The dining-table conversation is a shock. A fight trainer and a visiting national chess master agree that the poems of both Walt Whitman and Pablo Neruda lose their muscular musicality in translation from English to Spanish or vice versa.

Through this disconcerting amalgam of state pugs, shrinks, jock scientists, poetry-spouting trainers, chess geniuses and farm laborers, Stevenson walks like a truculent and totally contented deity.

Like one of the tall palms that surround him, Stevenson stands motionless for minutes in his brilliantly colored tropical shirt, saying nothing, seemingly looking inward.

"I like it here," Stevenson says. "It is a very calm and tranquil place. I am in the phase of physical training now. Most of the technical and psychic things are finished."

He does not wish to elaborate. He walks away when a photographer approaches. His smiles and signs of animation are for a pretty woman.

"Teofilo wisely saves his charm for those situations when it can bring him tangible results," says Salmeron wolfishly. "He enjoys his bachelorhood."

In international competition, Stevenson frequently wins all but one or two of his bouts by forfeit. Nobody wants to get emulsified. How many U.S. amateurs would face George Foreman for three rounds for a long cup and no bucks?

"When I am training and sweating," Stevenson says with a frown, "I do not like to think about the forfeits. I must be prepared to fight every bout, because if I am not ready, they will see it and suddenly everyone will be anxious to fight."

Perhaps not anxious, but it is a useful rationalization so that Stevenson can force himself into the training that he reputedly does not relish.

Stevenson makes it apparent that he considers himself, without doubt, the top heavyweight in the world.

"I have seen little of Clay," he says. "He is old and does not interest me at all. I saw the young one [Spinks] in Mexico and Montreal. He needs much more training."

Only one American fighter draws a Stevenson smile and brings his spontaneous praise. "I have studied the old films of Joe Louis," he says. "He did beautiful things in the ring."

As for the rest of the pro boxing world, Stevenson dismisses it, falling back on his well-coached statement that multimillion-dollar purses do not interest him. "What is a million dollars to me," he says, "compared to the love of my people?"

Couldn't he have both and give the million to the people?

No answer.

Isn't he interested in extending himself to the fifteen-round pro distance? "Even the professionals do not always fight fifteen rounds," he says slyly, looking at his right fist. "Sometimes, I am told, they get knocked out."

The people of America have heard that he has lost twice to a Russian, Igor Volski. They think that Stevenson beats stiffs and is seldom challenged. Is that possible?

"Either my opponents are very bad or perhaps I am not so bad," he says, showing more pleasure at being needled than by dull questions.

Rocamora, the paunchy old photographer, punches Stevenson in the chest and says, "Come on, you big bum. Just give me two rounds."

Stevenson scowls, but is pleased. Rocamora drags the giant around by his shirttail, posing him for pictures against his will, slapping and mocking him. The more he is abused, the closer he comes to a smile.

"He is just a big, docile boy," says Rocamora, mopping sweat off his forehead. "He enjoys a game. He is just as glad to have someone else tell him what to do. He is a good, simple boy with natural dignity. Like Joe Louis."

Half a century ago, Cuba's great dash man, Jose Barrientos, called the "Lightning Blow of the Caribbean," flashed across the sports scene, then disappeared. He was back, and Cuba had no place for him once he could no longer run 100 meters in 10.1 seconds.

Today, there are two "Lightning Blows of the Caribbean": Juantorena's feet and Stevenson's knuckles. Neither is ever likely to disappear from this island's stage.

"Those bad times are gone," says Juantorena. "We prepare our athletes in a way so they can function in society when they are not athletes. Teofilo and I still go to the university and will continue to. I study economics to be an accountant. He is an electrical engineer.

"When I grow older, it will be harder for the little children to accept than for me," he says, smiling. "They come to me and say, 'Why do you always win?' and I cannot answer, because that is such a good and difficult question.

"They are very worried about that. The children will never understand if I lose," Juantorena says, and laughs.

"But at least when I get older, then the mothers will stop punching me. They scold me and say, 'My little boy broke his arm trying to run like you.' And all the fat people here in Cuba ask me how to lose weight.

"I say, 'Come. Tie a rope to our two waists so that when I run, you cannot stop. Then you will get thin very fast.' "

Juantorena takes the diabolical electric-shock machine off his enormous leg. "I am abnormal," he says, and pokes a finger in his side to indicate the top of his pelvis. "Sometimes I think my legs are climbing up to my shoulders."

The only disadvantage in those high pockets comes when Juantorena must leave Morrero Stadium in his tiny old Fiat. "I must fold myself double," he says.

Does the Horse ever wonder about the land to the north where no legend, no Olympic prince, would have to fold himself double, when, with a single Spitz- or Jenner-type commercial, he could buy a limousine?

"America amazes me," he says. "You have the money to solve all your economy. Yet you talk instead of producing a neutron bomb.

"We in Cuba feel very close to the people of America, so generous and gifted. But the policy of the government . . ." He shakes his head.

"Americans live in a country," says Juantorena, folding himself into his Fiat. "We Cubans are building a country. We are small, and still rather poor," he says, tapping his chest, "but very big with sentiments of liberty."

Daredevils

LAKE PLACID, New York, February 11, 1980—

"The luge run gives me such an adrenaline rush that my eyes are flicking like a tape recorder on fast forward. It's often terrorizing, always exhilarating." —John Fee, U.S. Olympic luge team.

The emotional thread that runs through the Winter Olympics is a sense of danger as penetrating, yet as invigorating, as frozen mountain air.

The real chill factor here—especially for lugers, downhill racers, ski jumpers and bobsledders—is the cold breath on the neck of palpably close death.

At the Summer Olympics, the human body must achieve its speed and perform its twists without aids. The potential for havoc is limited. Here, skis and skates are everywhere. The chance for wreckage increases as the tools for speed improve.

The most frightening sound at the Winter Olympics is the squawking voice on a walkie-talkie crying in code, "We got an 81 here."

"An 81" means "disaster."

A ski jumper leaves his ramp for the open sky at 60 miles per hour. The luger on his tiny sled hits 70 mph. The downhiller plummets 2,500 feet in 2 minutes, reaching 80 mph. And the 500-pound bobsled goes more than 90 mph.

Other sports have a history of injury. These four, which form much of the heart of the Olympics, have a history of death. In these danger games, the thrill seekers sometimes call a broken leg or a fractured skull "an escape." To calibrate the degree of daredeviltry, or tabulate the per capita pain, for these sports is impossible.

For instance, the United States' two best downhill skiers—Andy Mill and Cindy Nelson—have had, between them, six knee operations, two broken legs, two broken arms, a dislocated hip, a fractured wrist and a broken shoulder.

The coach of the U.S. bobsled team, Gary Sheffield, calls his sport "the champagne of thrills." Yet Sheffield once fractured his skull in seven places, and inside a month, had two friends killed in crashes.

Ski jumpers insist that they have little fear of flying because their sport, which looks like the divinest madness, is, in fact, the safest of the four. After all, jumpers did not even have to wear headgear for years until five deaths made it mandatory.

Nevertheless, it is probably the luge that is the most dangerous Olympic sport as well as the most terrifying—either to participate in or simply to watch.

The fifty-pound Olympic luge is little more than the toy sled that a child might find under a Christmas tree. It has no brake, no protection.

"We prove that any kid can ride his Flexible Flyer [sled] to the Olympics," said Jeff Tucker of the U.S. team.

The luge entered the Olympics in 1964, but, before a regulation run had been made, one luger had been killed in practice and two Americans barely had missed death.

"Lugers are usually hurt by trees," said an Olympic course official here. "They fly off the track at seventy miles per hour and disappear into the woods. You listen, then start looking."

What is most interesting is not the difference between these various forms of courting fear and seeking thrills, but the striking similarities of personality and temperament among the participants.

Socrates called courage the principal virtue because without it none of the other virtues could express themselves. One man who expresses himself with courage is John Fee, twenty-eight, senior member of the U.S. luge team.

Fee has three passions, none of which he fully understands, and none of which seem to be linked with the others. He is an artist who has spent years making stained-glass windows for churches. He is a fisherman who battles the thirty-five-foot waves and gale-force winds of the Bering Sea to fish for king crab off the Alaskan coast. And he is the United States' best hope for a top-ten luger here.

This combination of qualities—artist, explorer, sportsman—somehow seems to illuminate the confusing character of the daredevils in the Olympics.

"When you see the luge run at night, it is awesome and terrifying," said Fee. "I feel drawn toward it—the brilliant lights, the sense that you are aiming a rifle down the mountain but that you are the bullet.

"At the beginning of the season, the first twenty runs, you seem to be going incredibly fast. But after two hundred runs, it doesn't seem so bad.

"Instead of blinding speed, you get a sense of quietness and controlled speed. You're just there by yourself, feeling every bump in the ice, getting this exhilaration of feeling totally alive. It's an extreme joy.

"I tend to lift my head too high because I want to see around me. It's a blur, but you want to experience it."

Nonetheless, Fee never forgets the ever real danger of his event. Lugers seldom venture into the spectators' area just an arm's length from the chute where the sledders fly past. But Fee did this week. When the first mad luger screamed by, Fee said, stunned, "My God, are we going that fast?

"You feel many things as you stand at the top," said Fee. "Especially at night the eeriness gets to you and you feel apprehensive. You know that in the luge when you make a mistake, there is seldom time to make a correction.

"By the time you realize that you have a problem, it's too late to do anything about it. You don't even realize if you're hurt or not until you stop flipping and sliding and you do an inventory of your body."

Fee is far more candid about his fears than most Olympian jumpers, fliers and sliders because the luge run is actually the safest part of his life—his vacation.

After reading Jack London's *Sea Wolf* five years ago, Fee, an art major in college, forsook the unprofitable profession of stained-glass-window making and headed for Dutch Island, Alaska.

There, he lives on the beach, sleeping in abandoned Quonset huts, until he can get work as a deckhand on the five- to six-man Norwegian boats that set out for king crab.

"It's as close to the life of a whaling ship of a hundred fifty years ago as you could get," Fee said. "You leave port for one to three weeks, working at least twenty hours a day when you're 'on the crab' until the boat is full.

"It's part of the Norwegians' ethic that you don't stop fishing unless the boat is upside down. I've worked the edge of the boat—six feet above the water—when the seas were forty feet and the winds ninety miles per hour.

"I've seen men on other boats go overboard and die. I've fallen in once. The water is thirty-five degrees. It doesn't numb you; it attacks you.

"The Bering Sea is cold, gray, windy and lonesome—something like the mountains that I luge on. But I love something about them both," said Fee, who was on the 1976 Olympic luge team and finished twenty-third.

Fee says, "Perhaps I'm schizophrenic, but I want the maximum intensity in whatever I do."

The 6-foot-2, 180-pound Fee rhapsodizes about how he can feel every bump in the ice, how he has a special sense of floating when he is making an ideal run.

Ski jumpers call that sensation "a feel for the air" and say they seem to be "floating on a bed of air."

Speed skaters, those masochists who might prevent frostbite if they wore sensible socks, instead wear the thinnest hose, or even go barefoot inside their skates, so they can "feel the ice" as it cracks and crushes under them.

As for downhill skiers, the mystique surrounds the ability to "glide," to skim over the snow so that the illusion is created that the skis barely ever touch the ground.

Fee associates his moments of greatest risk, greatest speed and highest adrenaline levels with a profound quiet and sense of control. That mixture is his source of joy.

"Ski jumping's just like . . . when you go off, everything's so quiet; you don't hear anything. It's like everyone's dream of flying. It's addicting," said U.S. jumper Jeff Davis.

And, said downhiller Andy Mill, "I've left fear behind to find solitude. . . . When I leave the start, I leave my mind behind. Conscious thought is too slow. . . . Everything is coming so fast that it's just a torrent of impressions. My whole being is exploding, but my main feeling is contentment."

Wrapped in this thrall, many of these solitary speed freaks of the mountains are shocked back to a proper appreciation of their danger only by a brush with death.

Of the worst day in downhill history, in January 1959 on the Kreuzeck in

West Germany, Curtis Casewit wrote that the first three racers to finish the course said, "Madness," "Oh God, oh God" and "I'm alive."

Yet 89 skiers went down the mountain that day. In all, 39 crashed, producing "one death, six broken legs, two broken ribs and one ripped-off nose —cleanly sheared to the upper lip, bone and all."

The customary response to such disasters—to those calls of "81, 81"—is to pretend they never happened.

"Oh yeah, I get scared once in a while," said Bob Hickey, driver of the U.S. team's No. 1 four-man bobsled. "If I flip over, I don't want to sit there. I try to go right back up to the top and have a good trip down.

"If you go home and think about it, you'll be really frightened by the next day."

It is commonplace for these Olympic daredevils to flatly deny the danger of their sports, pointing fingers at others and saying, "No, no. It's those guys who are crazy."

"I get sick of hearing the luge called the Olympics' most dangerous sport," said U.S. luger Jeff Tucker. "It's not nearly as dangerous as the bobsled."

"Ski jumping is certainly safer than Alpine skiing," said the U.S. coach, Glenn Kotlarek. "There's a bunch of dingdongs out Alpine skiing."

It is a harsh simplification to call these men and women "adrenaline junkies," although they themselves sometimes use the term. Nor is it fair to see them as half-formed personalities in search of cheap thrills.

If any athletes are forced to ask "why," it is these, who must face a mortal choice each time they look down from the top of the mountain.

"The attraction of all this confuses other people. They ask if we're crazy," said luger Tucker. "The attraction is the simplest thing possible. It's the joy of riding down the hill."

Perhaps we must leave the twentieth century, go back to earlier times, to empathize with these souls who find, in our time, no outlet for an excess of courage.

Robert Burton, a contemporary of Shakespeare, chastised those who "do not live, but linger," and gave the valedictory for all those who feel the need to fly down mountains.

"Heaven itself has no power upon the past," Burton argued. "What has been, has been, and I have had my hour."

For those with an ancient and perhaps out-of-fashion sort of bravery, these next two weeks will provide the hours that no power can rescind.

The Heidens

February 10, 1980—On arctic evenings in Wisconsin, the West Allis Ice Rink glimmers in the middle distance beside Interstate 94, chimerical and almost transparent, like a winter mirage that flickers momentarily in a cloud of windswept breath.

Each day thousands of people flash past on the eight-lane highway near Milwaukee looming just a hundred yards away.

There, in twilight, brightly dressed children skate rhythmic, hypnotic laps around a dowdy, dilapidated oval which stands abjectly amid neon signs and smokestacks.

This bleak Benthamite version of a Currier and Ives print is the home of the U.S. speed-skating team, the best winter Olympic squad in American history.

Here Eric and Beth Heiden, brother and sister, twenty-one and twenty, have wrought themselves into great, if anonymous, world champions. Clean, hard, cold and pure as ice, they are as sharp and uncompromising as the blade of a racing skate.

For thirteen years, they have driven themselves, in seclusion, pursuing an ascetic ideal in an orphaned sport.

Yet the Heidens also have know for a long time that during February 1980 they would probably become the most suddenly celebrated pair of people in America.

Even those who hadn't heard of them before the Lake Placid games will soon know them as intimately as the megaton flashbulb of fame will allow.

Speed skating has nine gold medals—five for men, four for women. If the form of the 1979 world championships holds, the Heidens will win all nine.

The world will bear gifts to the Heidens' door in Madison, Wisconsin. And they, if form holds again, will politely but firmly turn the world away. No post-Olympic symphony of dollars is being orchestrated here.

Because their parents are educated, affluent and adamantly strident in running interference, the young Heidens have grown up bright, unaffected and so fresh that they seem radically innocent beside jaded celebrity athletes.

Nonetheless, the minions of mammon will have a hard time leaving the Heidens alone. They are eye-catching, mass-market showstoppers: sibling champions as opposite as fire and ice.

Eric is an all-American 6-foot-1, 190-pound mesomorph who is handsome, tousle-haired, utterly relaxed, with a devilish, almost bohemian, touch to his prankishness.

"I guess I'm a regular person," Eric says. "I don't need Ex-Lax or anything." He is pared down to a volatile essence of muscle. If he flexed too fast, he might explode.

"A Thoroughbred horse on the outside with a stubborn mule inside," Beth Heiden describes her brother.

Beneath the almost freezing calm that has taken him to three consecutive world championships, there simmers a hidden quality: daredeviltry.

"Eric would do anything in this world if it caught his fancy," says a family friend, "even if it killed him."

While climbing in the Alps last November, Heiden heard rocks falling. Instead of feeling fear, he was curious.

"I looked up"—he grimaces—"and a rock as big as a grapefruit hit me right between the eyes and broke my nose."

Undaunted, Heiden tried the bobsled run in an Italian town, but neglected to learn that the course spit the sled out into the city's main street at 50 mph.

On race days the street is roped off. When Heiden and a buddy made the run, they exited at a mile a minute into rush-hour traffic. "It was exciting for a few seconds," says Heiden.

Heiden has only one celebration planned after the Olympics. Then, when a broken leg or fractured skull can no longer steal his Olympic gold, Heiden says, "I want to skate down a luge run."

Has anyone ever gone down a luge run on skates?

"No," he says.

Is it possible?

"No one knows."

Could you kill yourself?

"It's conceivable."

How fast would you be going?

"That," he says, "is what interests me."

If Eric is a swashbuckler, then Beth is an animated, bubbing, 5-foot-1, 105-pound ectomorph who seems like a hank of nerves, skin, bone, brain and long blowing hair.

Nothing about Eric is a mystery. He is proudly self-evident. Everything about Beth is hidden and inexplicable. She seems like a puff of winter smoke blowing around the rink, a pale blue wisp that might easily disappear.

"She is a sparrow," says Eric, "with a tiger hidden inside her."

The sparrow is easy to see. The tiger is well concealed.

In a sport where huge legs, like Eric's 29-inch thighs of stone, have been a common denominator of champions for fifty years, Beth Heiden is more than an anomaly. She almost defies the speed-skating laws of physics.

With the stroking pace of a hummingbird and the precision of an engineer (which is her major at the University of Wisconsin), she has perfected a style her sport never knew existed.

From the beginning, when she was seven and followed Eric onto the frozen lakes of Madison to "skate all over for all day," Beth Heiden has always had a fascinating rivalry with this huge creature a foot taller and nearly a hundred pounds heavier than she.

"I can outrun him. Anything longer than nine miles, I can beat him," she says, grinning. "He has to carry a lot of extra muscle."

Others will always think they see a darker, unconscious side to Beth, the small flame burning so determinedly in the large shadow.

"She's very jealous of her brother," says Leah Poulos Mueller, twenty-eight, two-time world sprint champion and Beth's prime competition in the two shortest Olympic distances. "She can be world champion, but he's the greatest ever. He'll probably be untouchable at the Olympics. She'll risk being called a disappointment.

"She's in the difficult position of defining her identity in terms of an older brother who keeps setting unreachable standards just a year or two before she gets there."

To get a feeling for the Heidens, to sense the weight of their achievements and their cost, it is necessary to go to the one place where the reluctant, almost reclusive, champions can relax among equals and be most nearly themselves: West Allis.

This rugged and bereft old rink, maintained on a volunteer shoestring and always in danger of terminal disrepair, is the mecca of U.S. speed skating.

It has to be. Norway, a country the size of Wisconsin, has eleven refrigerated rinks of Olympic size. America, until Lake Placid's was completed, had one: West Allis.

Many American Olympians must take vows of poverty. Yet few are as proud of their threadbare hardihood as the forty or so skaters who congregate here, many year-round.

"These are the worst conditions of any training site in the world," says Eric Heiden with the undisguised hair-shirt pride and contempt for luxury that runs, like a catechetical precept, throughout the speed-skating subculture.

"We breathe fumes from factories and cars that are close enough to hit with a snowball. The wind's so bad it knocks you off your feet in the turns, because our [windbreak] fences are pathetic.

"And, oh yeah," adds Heiden with a sarcastic grin, "our ice is rather slow. You see, it has cement in it. Wind blows particles from the cement plant next door."

On this rink, the greatest national team in history has been born and reared. The current U.S. squad, led by the Heidens, won 27 of the 30 gold medals at 1979's major international meets.

No other country, since international championships began in 1889, has ever approached such dominance. At European meets, Russian and East German skaters tease the U.S. team and pry at them to discover their classified training sites and secret techniques.

When the Americans tell their tales of a windy rink full of cement and carbon monoxide, where the scenery includes signs that say "Car Wash" and "Hot Wax" and the most conspicuous landmark is not an alp but the Wauwatosa water tower, the Russians laugh nervously and refuse to believe.

"The Russians ask us, 'Where are your personal coaches? Where are your trainers and team doctors? Where is your training equipment?' " says Peter Mueller, a '76 gold medalist at Innsbruck. "They come from a world of ultimate regimentation. To them we look like free spirits and hippies and vagabonds."

Russia claims 500,000 competitive speed skaters, thousands of them kept as state athletes. America has, at most, 4,000 speed skaters.

"We tell the Russians," said Mueller, "that we have no doctors and trainers and individual coaches. At every meet, we smile and tell them the same thing. 'We're just here . . . to beat you.'

"And we always do."

The American secret is not in technique, but in temperament.

On a frigid winter morning with a windchill factor below zero, Eric Heiden rubs Vaseline on his face. Inside his skintight uniform he puts a layer of newspaper to delay frostbite.

Heiden looks a bit drained, his eyes glazed. He and his teammates have returned from six weeks of European competition. Jet lag and strep throat have run through the team. Heiden's temperature is higher than 101.

"In Europe or Russia the skaters are pampered heroes. They would not dream of training on a day like this. They would have a massage and a sauna and go to bed," says Mueller.

"We train through everything. Our only rule is go until you can't go anymore. Then go some more.'

This is the day for the 10,000-meter workouts for the men, the longest and most grueling race in skating.

Heiden ignores the cold, the wind, the lousy rink conditions, the jet lag, the fever. Bent over like a dash man in track lunging for the tape, Heiden strokes endlessly around the 400-meter rink, hands behind his back in the straightaways, then digging with one arm on the turns.

Lap after lap, Heiden cranks out times that are just a fraction off the world record.

This is skating's fundamental and perniciously will-sapping war—the battle against the stopwatch. Because racing is done in pairs, not in a pack, foes seldom duel each other skate to skate. Time is all.

In extremis, when fatigue and freeze attack, that unseen clock takes on the features of a human face and the skater suddenly recognizes his enemy. And it is always himself.

So the worst days are best for training. If the soul has muscles, they must be strengthened, too. Once, Heiden won although his left arm was frozen behind him. When the time came to pump for the finish with both arms, one was numb, unmovable and hammerlocked. But he had never noticed.

By the time he realized, it was too late to lose.

"You couldn't do this for anyone but yourself," says a nineteen-year-old skater named Klaus Reichman, who has left his New York home and taken a leave from college to come here, to be the next Eric Heiden.

"A professional athlete—someone like Pete Rose—feeds off the pressure and the crowds and the energy and expectation that's around him," Reichman says. "It stokes him. It's the absolute opposite here. This must be the purest of all sports.

"When an animal is scared, its face changes," says Reichman. "In an athlete, it's the same. In competition, I've seen Eric's and Beth's faces change. For a moment they're transformed. They go beyond themselves.

"That's what we're reaching for—the moment when we're pure animal."

A few sports, where conditioning reaches an almost hallucinatory level, have what amounts to a private mystical theology.

Prizefighters, in their sweaty, claustrophobic and corrupt underworld, talk a kind of battered, mystical jive. Marathon runners, so seemingly emaciated that they could pass for those early Christian ascetics who tried to tame the body through mortification, have a private language that delineates all the changed states of consciousness caused by their regimen.

American speed skaters rhapsodize in the same disconcerting way, trying to explain experiences that they can't touch.

"You get a special whistling feeling in your ears," Mueller says. "Everything inside you and outside you seems perfect. When it's there, you wish you could keep it forever."

Even the Heidens' mother feels it. "The Europeans and Russians are the children of the Army or miners. They skate their way to a better life. Their thought is: God, get me out of my plight.

"As long as skating keeps them prosperous, they're satisfied," she says, then pauses. "That's the difference between their skaters and ours. Their motivating force is not the aesthetic."

It is necessary to sense the power of skating's thrall to appreciate the aura of almost defiant innocence about the Heidens. After what the ice has given them, the earth can sometimes seem poor. No wonder the gifts of fame seem tarnished to them, and easy to refuse.

Anyone with a feeling for athletic portraits must sense that one giant and central piece has been left out of the Heiden mosaic. Even mystics must have a master.

Where is that driven, supremely organized, borderline-neurotic force that we find at the back of many champions?

Her name is Dianne Holum. An Olympic gold medalist in 1972, she not only coaches the U.S. speed-skating team but, in a sense, has created it out of her dogged, patient and nurturing will.

"Old skaters never die, they just lose their edge," goes the pun in speed skating. For the Heidens, Holum is their whetstone, their constant source of a fresh edge.

In Europe, where he is legendary—mobbed like a rock star on the streets of Norway—Eric Heiden knows one of his first incredulous interrogations will always be: "Is it true that your coach is a woman?"

"To them," says Heiden, "it's the equivalent of the Pittsburgh Steelers being coached by a cheerleader."

"I get bombarded in Europe," says Holum. "I'm the only woman in a man's world. It stuns them. They just stare at me."

Holum could care less if she was accepted, loved or hated. Her obliviousness is sublime, her single-mindedness chilling. Holum's narrow, concentrated face, with her hair hanging like blinders beside her eyes, is forceful and charming in a severe, idiosyncratic way.

"I coached for seven years for no pay," says the twenty-eight-year-old Holum, who discovered the Heidens in Madison youth skating programs when Eric was thirteen. "It was a work of love. I realized that coaching requires an eye—and years."

Holum's theories on spending the majority of a year's training away from the ice are radical, but simple. "We have made our disadvantages [in lack of rink facilities] into advantages. A skater's enemy is boredom. The Europeans are tired before the world championships arrive."

Other countries get on the ice in early August. America greets West Allis, which is a public campground in summer, in late October. "Sometimes I can hardly remember what ice is like," jokes Beth Heiden.

During most of the year, Holum's skaters can be found off the ice—cycling, running, playing soccer, swimming and enduring a universe of calisthenics invented by Holum.

The Heidens have concocted a mini-gym below and to the rear of the kitchen in their parents' big suburban Madison home, complete with slideboards, gymnastic rings, medicine balls and weight belts.

When Heiden finishes his indoor workout, he goes to a nearby park where he has made his own 200-yard dirt oval, a track where he can exactly duplicate the steps—the pushes in the straights, the digging in the corners —of a 400-meter rink.

In the duck-walk position, Heiden races around this oval at full running speed, firing his legs behind him like some enraged turtle gone mad. Heiden does twenty-five laps without stopping.

"Any sport helps a skater," says Holum. "Contrast that with swimmers.

They're burned out young. In the water, they can't even talk. When they're out of the water, the coach is usually yelling at them."

Holum's training is the absolute opposite. Her skaters always talk, always joke, always tease, always have fun. In temperament, they seem like surfers on ice. Just as surfers prize their ancient autos called "woodies," so these skaters compete to see whose "beater" car can be closest to a total wreck on wheels.

On a blistering summer day, Holum's troop will end a five-mile run by flopping in an apple orchard while Holum, a bandanna around her head, collects flowers or wild mushrooms.

Holum would never scream at a skater. Yelling would be a trivial emotional lever compared to the deep and subtle gears that Holum must move to have her way. She uses many of the mother's tools—years of affection, encouragement and psychological nursing, rather than the conventional coach's techniques.

She does so because, in the face of the profound windchill cold of 50 degrees below zero, nothing less would work. Holum is a stroker, an ego builder, a high priestess who knows that for all her guiding and goading she can never absolutely protect against the loss of will—almost a loss of faith— that haunts them all at times.

Who, every day of the winter, spends hours outside in a skintight, paper-thin nylon suit? "Taking off your warm-ups," says '76 Olympic gold medalist Sheila Young, "is like jumping in a frozen lake naked."

Profound cold is the dark devil that saps a skater's faith. Frostbite, black toes, white nose, frozen lungs and the danger of gangrene are the grist of a speed skater's war stories.

"We've all walked around with black toes," says Eric Heiden. "It's just part of the job. But the worst problem is in another place." And he pulls out a pair of woolen Danish briefs with a nylon jockey cup.

"The metal plates on the bottom of the skates just suck the heat out of your body," says John Lovell, America's only world-class marathon skater. "I've raced 1,500 meters when the windchill factor was 70 below zero. When they got me back inside, I was in the fetal position shaking for half an hour."

If all good skates must have an edge, so must they also have the proper rock.

Every skate blade is flatter or rounder than another in heel-to-toe curvature. That degree of curvature, which can be changed according to the nature of the race, is called the rock—the very subtle degree to which a skater can rock back and forth as he stands on his skates.

If Holum is the Heidens' source of competitive edge, their grinding stone, then the young champions need only look to their parents to identify their rock—their fundamental setting.

All speed skaters must "change their rock" depending on the distance of the race. But, in a sense, the Heidens never do.

"Eric and Beth have had the perfect pedigree," says Mueller.

Nancy Heiden, daughter of the University of Wisconsin's former hockey coach, is still a ranked tennis player in the state. Her husband, a surgeon, remains one of the leading age-group cyclists in the country—state senior champion in '79 and second nationally in his class.

"My memories of growing up won't be so much of talking together, but that we were always doing something together," Beth says. "Skiing, backpacking or taking canoe trips with our grandparents."

"We've always felt that if you're going to have children, you're no longer the center of things anymore," Nancy says. "Why have a family if you're not going to do things together?

"The outdoors has always been our love. Perhaps Madison develops that kind of attitude. People here are conscious that they are part of an aerobic community, sort of a neighborhood biodynamics lab. Our whole local society is pitched that way."

The step from outdoors folk to Olympians, however, has been gigantic, one which all the Heidens view with an ambivalence bordering on revulsion.

Eric, Beth and their parents will talk publicly, but not often. The Heidens plan to make some bucks off their notoriety, but hardly a fraction of what they could.

"Others may be open; our family is closed," says Nancy.

"I don't enjoy having a public identity," Eric says. "What Mark Spitz and Bruce Jenner did turns me off. It kind of ruins what they did. The Olympics are not just some career step you take so that you can be exploited."

"Maybe we don't thrive on attention as much as we should," Beth says, "but I feel sorry for athletes who are national heroes."

The slow blossoming of Eric and Beth as skaters was a process that was initially enjoyed for its own sake. Their emergence as champions was a surprise, not the culmination of some inexorable family-plotted progression.

"It galls us all that people assume we've raised our children with the sole thought of winning gold medals," Nancy Heiden says.

"A child isn't born into the crib with an Olympic dream, the way ABC-TV would have you believe. It makes me sick to see how the Olympic athletes are presented to the public: 'He's been dreaming of this every day for years.'

"That's bizarre. And it's pathetic," she says. "Do we really want to idolize people that one-dimensional?

"Our children have grown up on the same street with a Nobel Prize winner and the heads of departments at the university. They're not impressed by the word 'Olympics' or by themselves.

"All this flag waving about winning for the U.S.A. is a little strange to us after the total lack of support America gives its athletes," Nancy says.

Yet the saddest quality in many Olympic athletes is the pervasive sense that, as they receive their medals, they have come to the end of a childish, joyous and futureless passion, one which may derail the rest of their lives.

"I think that's one of the best things about this," Nancy says. "It should be futureless, absolutely futureless. There better be more to life than being an ex-champion cutting ceremonial ribbons."

So even as the Heidens prepared to capture the world, they prepared to escape from their sport.

"Fame's okay for a while," says Eric. "But right now, I think it's nice the way skating is in America"—that is, unknown.

"Short-range, I guess I'll probably be a famous face for a year or so. But long-range, I assume I'll be forgotten pretty quickly, except maybe around Madison.

"That's the way I'd prefer it."

The Heidens have quick and anchored answers to questions about their futures. Both will retire from skating. Both plan on graduate school—Eric is premed; Beth wants to be a civil engineer and build bridges. Beth is mastering her fourth foreign language, while Eric is attacking Norwegian, "so I can talk to my girlfriend Cecilia in Oslo."

"We're already thinking beyond the Olympics," Nancy Heiden says. "I expect we'll just dive into something else. That's always been our way."

"We're all mapping out our family canoe trip through Canada after the Olympics," whispers Beth. "We're not telling anybody where we're going."

No longer will Eric and Beth be in the supreme state of sustained athletic perfection, when they are both superhuman and subhuman—part mystic, part animal. Canoe trips will replace frostbite as they explore a new and larger map—one on which speed skating can hardly be found, a tiny dot called West Allis.

Their rock is set. As it has always been.

□ □ □ □ □ □ □

LAKE PLACID, New York, February 15, 1980—

"Eric Heiden is the biggest, greatest skater there has ever been. The rest of us are waiting for the next Olympics. Now, the medals are delivered before the race begins." —Frode Roenning, Norway, bronze medalist.

The skates of Eric Heiden have a special sound.

As he passes, others on the ice listen, then turn their heads, as though Heiden's arrival were heralded by a signal as clear and familiar as the first notes of Beethoven's Fifth Symphony.

The atonal Heiden symphony is a high-pitched screech made by the ice crushing beneath his push, followed by a sharp click as the toe of his right skate flicks the ice in an unnecessary but distinctive personal signature.

"Squeak, crush, click," said U.S. coach Dianne Holum, her back to the Olympic rink. "That must be Eric."

This twenty-one-year-old 190-pound demiurge of an athlete, who was almost unknown in his own land until this month, won his third gold medal of the Winter Olympics today, breezing at 1,000 meters. No man has won more gold in these Winter Games.

Soon Heiden's name will be as familiar to Americans as the sound of his skates has become to the competitors whom he has crushed in every significant international race of the last four years.

Heiden does not win; he destroys and demoralizes. His foes here are prostrate before him and his skate blades seem to have slit the jugular of their racing will.

Before Heiden sprang full-grown from Holum's head at the tiny U.S. speed-skating colony in West Allis, Wisconsin, the world had known skating sprinters and distance racers and even all-rounders.

But Heiden is everything—the champion of every distance from the shortest (500 meters) to the longest (10,000 meters).

This Olympics is Heiden's one-man stand against the world, a tour de force of training, courage and grace under pressure. The best skaters in the world are specializing at one or two distances, hoping to ambush Heiden.

With no success so far. Heiden has set Olympic records in all three of his races. If he wins twice more, he will be the first person in the history of the Olympics, Summer or Winter, to win five individual gold medals.

A trackman who dominated every distance from 400 meters to 5,000 meters might be roughly comparable. And no such creature has ever appeared.

Nevertheless, it is doubtful, no matter how great Heiden's fame now, that the U.S. public will have sufficient time to appraise, savor and truly understand his work.

Heiden, nearly anonymous outside his hometown of Madison, Wisconsin, has been an athlete of world stature since 1977 because he is the king of a sport that epitomizes power, pain and poise.

Heiden's 6-foot-1 body, a volatile essence of muscle, seems to strain at his skintight gold suit like a power plant in which his 29-inch thighs are the principal pistons. Those rippling pins, almost grotesquely defined, are the key to his success.

"I don't have a lot of leg speed," Heiden said today. "I don't run the turns like a sprinter. But I get the most out of every stroke."

Watch Heiden, muffled in a greatcoat, as he warms up, hands behind his back, body moving like a metronome. Each stroke is a separate isometric exercise, a distillation of applied force and extreme patience.

"I take twelve strokes in the straightaways and, usually, ten in the turns. I keep track," Heiden said. "Others take more."

But no one explodes in the turns like Heiden. He is so strong that, he says, "I have trouble turning in the inside lane." He means that his power is too great for such a narrow space.

Many athletes have muscles. Few have Heiden's strength of mind, his mulish will inside a Thoroughbred's physique.

"You plan the perfect race in your mind," he said. "You figure your strategy. But the last thing you do is think about the pain. You anticipate it, so you can ignore it."

Each race has different pains.

"After the 1,000 or 1,500," he said, "your throat may burn for half an hour. Then you stuff up for a couple of days, which is kind of a drag."

In the 5,000 and 10,000 meters, "you're so hunched over that you can't get a real breath. Your left thigh, which takes the force of every turn, really kills you. The last couple of laps, you just struggle."

The final ingredient is Heiden's profound composure, his almost languid, leonine bearing. His spirit, like his stroke, is deliberate, yet fluid.

Others here must fight to relax, a contradiction. Even Heiden's sister, Beth, the women's world speed-skating champion in 1979, has been knotted by anxiety, finishing seventh, seventh and fifth in an embarrassingly poor Olympics.

Yet Heiden must prod himself to wake up in time to collect his next gold medal. This young man is one of those sleepy-eyed killers.

Heiden is a premed major at the University of Wisconsin, where he hopes to study to be an orthopedic surgeon like his father. He is part of the "no big deal" generation. A little pressure, some excitement: it just perks him.

All around him are high-wired folks: the protective Holum; the arrogant young agent-lawyer Art Kaminski; the cracklingly smart and ambitious mother, Nancy Heiden, with her raccoon coat and fashionable sunglasses. They would claw out the world's eyes to guard Eric.

In their midst, Heiden shrugs and grins, yawns and makes a friendly joke. But at intervals, perhaps to keep a ring of distance around himself, Heiden pulls daredevil stunts, climbs the Alps, rides a bobsled, talks of celebrating his Olympic triumph by riding down the luge run here on his skates.

Slowly, precisely, powerfully Heiden strokes his way around the Olympic rink as he meditates and prepares himself.

Only days ago, it seems, he arrived—the hero that a harried nation badly wanted.

Now, this young man whose name will go down with the greats of Olympic history is a national relic.

Dan Jansen,
Dan Jansen

CALGARY, February 15, 1988—

"After the first death, there is no other," wrote Dylan Thomas. However, sometimes we wonder. Fresh deaths, even watching the death of hopes or the death of some long labor, arrive with a power that shocks us.

When speed skater Dan Jansen fell Sunday night in the Olympic Oval, millions of people all over America, perhaps hundreds of millions around the world, felt a pain of unaccountable sharpness.

For a young man they barely knew, and for his dead sister, whom they knew not at all, they felt a pity so personal that it seemed to require explanation.

A week ago, Jansen became world champion at 500 meters. Sunday evening, he was the favorite for the gold medal in that event. For a year, his sister Jane, the mother of three young children, had fought leukemia, hanging on. Earlier this month, she told him to race in the Olympics no matter what. Sunday morning before sunrise, he spoke to her on the phone, although she could not speak back. Dan told his brother Mike, an Olympian in '84, to give Jane a kiss for him. Three hours later, she died. Ten hours later, Dan false-started, then fell, barely ten seconds into his dash.

Seconds after Jansen crashed into the rink pads, all chance lost, he raised his arms over his head for a moment. Who would know what words to put on that gesture to the heavens? Then he ripped back his cowl and buried his face and dark hair in both hands.

"As soon as I got to the turn, the next thing I knew I was in the pads," said Jansen, two hours after his fall in an interview with pool reporters. ". . . It just felt like it slipped out from under me. . . .

"Not only do I never fall, but I rarely jump [false-start] either. I was sort of confused after I did that. It was strange. . . . Why today, I don't know. I felt the best I've ever felt coming into this race. . . . Maybe it just wasn't meant to be."

Every family faces deaths. Nothing is more commonplace or profound. Every individual has failures; countless people come up short on projects that cost years of effort. All that is universal. However, what befell Jansen on this Valentine's Day combined so many forms of sadness that many minds were truly troubled.

"As soon as he fell, my heart sank," said U.S. team captain Erik Hendriksen. "I'm not used to seeing so many things go so bad so fast and see a time that's supposed to be so wonderful as the Olympics go so sour."

Such a tangle of emotions can seem almost beyond endurance—too complex and contradictory to resolve. For instance, if Jansen had won a gold medal Sunday evening, would that really have been so much better? Would perfect self-command at such a time be an unmixed tribute? If he had won, how could his family (in which all nine children have been competitive speed skaters) have truly celebrated? Or truly mourned?

The Olympics, in its best moments, symbolizes a worldwide desire for a community of man in which peaceful competition and a spirit of fellowship are paramount. In that way, the Olympic movement aspires to be a celebration of human accomplishment through labor, willpower and courage.

At first blow, what happened to the Jansen family Sunday seems like a denial of the striving and idealism the Olympics wishes to embody. Work your hardest, do your best to love, and a disease or a misstep can still undo you.

But as we digest the sorrow, is that really the day's true kernel?

"I had always planned on staying and skating because I know that is what Jane would have wanted," said Jansen. Now he must decide whether or not to race in the 1,000 meters on Thursday—an event in which he is one of the serious contenders, but not the favorite. Though his mother and father are back home in West Allis, Wisconsin, Jansen says he will.

"It's very important," said Jansen. "Once again my family wants me to just go on now. . . . I know Jane would have wanted that. . . . I'm just going to go out there and try to put this behind me. . . . There's nothing I can do about today. . . . We'll see what happens Thursday."

That he failed in the Olympics on this Sunday evening means nothing— except that he is human, except that his grief overpowered his craft. He false-started. He clicked his skates in a turn. Can't a fine man's emotional wires be crossed by the death of someone he loves?

In a sense, everything we do, all that we build or discover or accomplish, is an act of will performed in the face of our mortality. Even for those of the deepest faith, some of that defiant courage is a necessity for living.

That Jansen tried, and that he says he will try again on Thursday, even if he falls again, means everything.

The refrain for this Sunday evening might be: "And death shall have no dominion."

□ □ □ □ □ □ □

CALGARY, February 19, 1988—

Just thirty-six minutes after the fall, Dan Jansen looked ashen, but composed, a bit confused, but almost relieved. He spoke slowly and sensibly, answering every question on a worried world's mind. Perhaps Jansen, in one of the saddest hours any athlete will ever know, was one of the few people here with a mature perspective on what he'd endured.

At twenty-two, this son of a policeman and a nurse, all of whose nine children have been cops or nurses or Olympic speed skaters, seemed to have reality pegged in a way that the millions who now pity him might envy.

Above all, Jansen said, he couldn't believe two things: how bad his own luck could be and how warm the heart of the world could feel. If Jansen leaves these Winter Olympics feeling worse about the fairness of his sport, he says he will always feel better about other people.

At a moment when many might have felt bitterness or self-pity, Jansen said, "I'd like to thank everybody who helped me. . . . What's happened in the last week has put everything in an absolutely different perspective and I don't feel as bad as I would have. . . .

"I've had so much support all week from my friends, my family and people that I don't even know, people from all over the world. It's just really helped. A lot of people told me how proud they were of me to go out there and do my best. It's really lifted my spirits."

Some, older but perhaps less wise than Jansen, may never feel quite so sanguine about what they saw this evening in the Olympic Oval. In a sight that many have never seen at this elite level of speed skating, Jansen caught an edge and fell untouched in a straight less than 200 meters from the finish.

Catching an edge in a straight. "It happens to everybody sometime," said Jansen. Joe DiMaggio probably tripped rounding third base sometime. But not to lose the last game of a World Series. Jansen himself could never remember falling in any race, much less twice in a week. Even in practice, he said, he hadn't fallen in six months.

"I trained so many years," he said, "and I didn't even finish a race."

The very instant that Jansen seemed to have a gold medal and an Olympic record in the 1,000 meters in his hands, the very moment in fact that his brother Mike turned to his sister in the stands and said, "He's gone through the three toughest turns . . . he's fine now," Jansen toppled as though poleaxed.

Just a blink before that, the scoreboard had flashed his 600-meter split time—.31 second ahead of eventual winner Nikolai Guliaev of the Soviet Union at the same juncture.

"Dan went by me just before he fell; he was flying," said team captain Erik Hendriksen. "He wasn't dying. He didn't look like somebody whose legs were full of lactic acid. If he'd brought it in [to the finish], we're looking at 1:12.9 [and a gold medal]. . . .

"I just can't believe it. It looked like he was going to make it right for himself, for the team and for his family."

Few have much doubt that Jansen's false start and, later, his fall in the first turn of the 500 on Sunday were, in some unspecifiable way, connected to the death ten hours before of his sister Jane. As too many know too well by now, he talked to her before dawn, just three hours before she died.

Since then, however, he seemed to have gathered himself. His first 600 meters tonight merely reflected a week full of powerful practice runs by a man who won a world title at 500 meters eleven days ago.

"I felt very, very strong . . . just before I fell, I felt like I was still accelerating," he said. "Then I was down. . . . I really don't know what I thought. I just could not believe it. . . .

"For some reason, I don't feel as shocked as I did after the 500. I think part of that was because of the whole day [Sunday] and my sister passing away that morning. Today, maybe there is a slight sense of relief that I can go home tonight and spend the weekend with my family. They're not going to be disappointed at all. They know I came and did what I could."

The Jansen family has been shocked in many ways this week. Condolences and encouragement have swamped the Jansens from all over the world. Small kindnesses have inundated them in West Allis, Wisconsin. As a tiny example, telephone operators have been giving the family a free long-distance phone call each day to Dan. "This restores your faith in humanity," Dan's father, Harry, has said.

Just this afternoon, the U.S. speed-skating team gave Dan Jansen a card, and cash, to start a trust fund for Jane's three young children. Those who've been to the West Allis rink, a place of chilly old showers and high raw winds, know that extra nickels in the speed-skating community are rare.

This week has brought a family death and two world-watched defeats to Dan Jansen. Yet, as he caught a midnight plane back home, he actually seemed to leave Calgary not only intact but, somehow, a larger man.

Interlude

Me-itis

December 1989—Whatever happened to humble heroes? If Lou Gehrig were alive, would he wear a Mohawk haircut? Or write a tell-all biography at age twenty-two about his former college team? Course not.

If Joe Louis were champ, would he deck himself in a dozen gold chains, then name himself "Prime Time"? No way.

If Jim Thorpe were in his heyday, would he do a TV commercial pretending to "know" all about sports in which he'd never accomplished anything?

If Walter Johnson won the final game of the World Series, would he kneel to say a public prayer? Then yell into a camera, "I'm going to Disney World"?

Would Bronko Nagurski sell himself as "the Refrigerator"? Would Sammy Baugh wear a headband in the Super Bowl criticizing the commissioner of his sport? Would Babe Ruth—yes, even the Babe, who'd do most anything—have a 900 number to make a buck off his fans by telling them what he ate for breakfast?

If Joe DiMaggio had somehow gotten himself banned from baseball, would he decline comment, saying he was saving his story to sweeten the book deal?

These days if a college football team isn't trying to run up a 100-point score, then a college basketball team is trying to full-court-press its way to 100 points in a half against a pathetic foe.

All together now, everybody paint your face or chest in your team's colors, wear a Hog or a Dawg mask, chant an obscenity and hold up your bedsheet sign that says, "We're No. 1." Then unscrew your head and spike it in the nearest end zone.

Some of us who aren't old enough to remember the good old days are becoming nostalgic for them anyway.

What would Bobby Jones and Sugar Ray Robinson think of today's braggarts and blowhards? They loved celebrity and hobnobbed with the highest. The real Sugar Ray—now even nicknames get purloined in the interests of hype—drove a pink Cadillac. And Jones created a tournament to his own memory. But they didn't make fools of themselves. They combined personal style with class.

Once modesty was the norm. For every Dizzy Dean, there were countless Babe Didriksons and Bill Tildens. Now we cling to athletes who have a sense of propriety as though they were the last examples of some noble endangered species. People such as Chris Evert or Michael Jordan or Cal Ripken Jr., who have an innate sense of reserve, seem like treasures. You can do a zillion ads like Evert, or wear fur coats and invent new dunks like Jordan, or sell milk like Ripken and still remain essentially unpretentious. Granted, the difference between self-expression and self-glorification is a knack, a gift.

But once upon a time it was far from a rare ability. The current vogue of *Home Run Derby* (a '50s TV show now being replayed on ESPN) is not primarily due to curiosity about the batting stances of Hank Aaron or Mickey Mantle or Willie Mays. Rather it's the corny interviews we love. Why? Because those players were unfailingly modest—even a little bashful. Their answers were not rehearsed or self-promoting. Common decency and a common touch were expected of them. And they demanded it of themselves. If in private some of them were louts, at least they'd been trained to hide it.

As recently as twenty-five years ago, no one gave a high-five after a homer, much less a low-five or elbow bash. A curtain call was reserved for a 500th home run—maybe. A tip of the cap was a big deal. Self-congratulation was viewed, as it should be, as beneath a person of real talent or character. The act was self-evident, self-explanatory, to those capable of grasping it.

In sports, humility was enforced rather than encouraged. An athlete's dignity, not his salary, was his calling card. If you "showed up" your foe, you got a fastball in the ear or a blind-side block.

Wilt Chamberlain never smashed a backboard, because nobody doubted that he could. Bill Russell didn't have to talk trash at his foes. He just stared at them. He didn't *try* to scare them; he *did* scare them. Jackie Robinson never wore a Day-Glo lime-green batting glove. He concentrated on stealing home, not headlines. Bob Cousy never dribbled between his legs as he came up court unguarded, although he might dribble between your legs once you tried to cover him. One is showboating, the other is art.

To what do we owe our current glut of athletic hubris?

The easy obvious answers might be TV and money. Lots of exposure and lots of wealth can swell your head.

But how much more famous can you be than Rocky Marciano or Jesse Owens? Athletes were joking about making more money than the President of the United States in the 1920s.

Instead of blaming TV or million-dollar deals, perhaps we should also give sarcastic thanks to the radical '60s and the conservative '80s.

The first begat an unreflective worship of freedom. Truly gifted athletes such as Muhammad Ali and Joe Namath mirrored the times with their poetry and predictions, hairstyles and hip fashions, tasseled shoes or white spats. Thanks largely to them, a pernicious cliché took root: "It's not bragging if you back it up." Oh? Who says? Bragging is bragging—period.

Gradually the message of the athletic Age of Aquarius became clear: if you're good and also gauche, you'll be even richer, even more famous.

Unfortunately unfettered expression is a curse when you have nothing to say. Now, a million imitation Broadway Joes later, we have a generation of jocks who think that greatness isn't certified until there's a candy bar named Reggie or a chocolate soda called Pete. The end result is someone like Deion Sanders, who actually believes he's speaking an undeniable truth when he says, "They don't pay nobody to be humble."

The '80s have given us an equally unreflective worship of personal wealth. When we respect what a person has, rather than how he got it, it's no wonder many athletes consider it a crime not to capitalize on every "opportunity."

In sports, as in much of a modern consumer society, the real thing begets the knockoff. The genuine article degenerates into the copy. Ali was a unique self-creation. But what can we say about "the Boz," "the Fridge" and

"Neon Deion"? Imitation may be the sincerest form of flattery, but it's a poor substitute for identity.

Luckily tastes and trends tend to go in cycles. Maybe the farewell tours of Kareem Abdul-Jabbar and Julius Erving were a good sign. Perhaps the children who've grown up in the '80s have had keen eyes. Somehow between *Wrestlemania VII* and *Halftime at the Super Bowl,* perhaps they've noticed the real athletic iconoclasts of the last decade: Wayne Gretzky, Larry Bird, Joe Montana, Walter Payton, Nancy Lopez, James Worthy, Don Mattingly and Dave Stewart.

Here's hoping.

Tennis

Bjorn I
Dethroned

LONDON, July 4, 1981—

On this Fourth of July, America's tempestuous tennis fighter, John McEnroe, declared his independence from the King of Sweden, Bjorn Borg.

In what may in time be regarded as the most famous single match in the sport's history, McEnroe shattered Borg's incredible 41-match Wimbledon win streak in today's championship final.

Controlling his thundering first serves, his lightning volleys and his electric temper, McEnroe scored a clean 4–6, 7–6, 7–6, 6–4 four-set triumph over the man who had won five consecutive Wimbledon titles.

The victory took on a bittersweet taste afterwards when the tournament committee recommended a $10,000 fine for McEnroe's behavior in his semifinal match Thursday against Rod Frawley.

The end today came so suddenly that even McEnroe could not, for a second, believe it.

The twenty-two-year-old New Yorker stared blankly at the linesman, whose hands were palms down, indicating that McEnroe's crisp forehand volley had, indeed, kicked up chalk deep in the corner. For the first time since 1975, Borg could not get to a shot on Centre Court when he absolutely had to reach it.

Then reality hit McEnroe in the face, physically spun him around, as he fell to his knees facing his parents in the guest box and allowed his face to explode into an open-eyed, open-mouthed expression of joy, disbelief and relief.

For 200 minutes, McEnroe and Borg played on terms as even as they were superb. At that moment, McEnroe had won 156 points, Borg 155.

And at that 200-minute mark, Borg had just added the greatest chapter of his life to his reputation as the ultimate escape artist.

Borg, the implacable twenty-five-year-old who always seems to be cornered but never slain, had just dodged a match point.

Throughout all Borg's six years of adventure here, no man had ever before taken him to the extremity of match point. Not Jimmy Connors, who led him two sets to love here on Thursday, nor the seven other men who forced Borg to five sets only to lose.

McEnroe had reached that instant when, with one more well-placed shot, victory was his.

And what had he done? He'd butchered a simple backhand a yard wide, hacking like a tense weekender.

That Houdini trick by Borg topped a day when the title holder had saved himself from disaster repeatedly. Fourteen times, McEnroe had blasted and attacked until Borg faced a break point on his serve. And thirteen of those times, Borg had won the point.

How many times could McEnroe mount his attacks with the best offense in tennis against Borg, the epitome of defense? When would McEnroe's will, patience and ability to throttle his hot temper finally crack as those of so many others had before him?

Surely, Borg would persevere and endure stoically and, yet again, find a way to win when his foe snapped. But this balmy afternoon, with a princess, a former king and a future queen in the royal box, Borg's luck and skill ran out. The last two points, and absolute vindication, would belong to McEnroe.

First came a crushing overhead smash into the cheap seats to create a second match point. Then, as befit his style all day, McEnroe charged the net, coming in behind a deep return of a weak Borg second serve. Borg tried one last forehand topspin passing shot. But McEnroe, the quickest and best net man of his era, leaped to his left and punched that volley into Borg's vacant forehand corner.

Within minutes, McEnroe, proudly wearing his U.S. Davis Cup jacket, was on national TV back to the States, saying in his most boyish and beamish way: "Happy Birthday, America . . . Hello, Stacy [to his girlfriend, Stacy Margolin]. Everything's okay . . . America, I didn't get a speeding ticket, I'm not a terrible person . . . All you people in New York, go out and party for me . . ."

McEnroe's words to America were from the heart, but earlier he had helped his play with some words from his savvy head.

" 'Close the door on him, close the door,' I kept telling myself," said McEnroe, who lost, 8–6, in the fifth set in last year's 55-game final against Borg—a match that frequently has been called the most dramatic in history. "You can't let him back in the match."

McEnroe closed the door from start to finish this day. Never has this 5-foot-11 left-handed blend of power and finesse given so fine a demonstration of proper grass court techniques. "I really don't see why John ever loses to Borg on grass," said semifinalist Rod Frawley before the match. "He has every tool to beat him there."

This was the day he used them all. Nine times McEnroe served untouchable aces. On 37 occasions, he blasted service winners that Borg could not even put back in play. And 30 times, McEnroe blasted a serve, followed it to the net and put away a crunching volley. Finally, on 15 other points, McEnroe came to the net out of a rally and volleyed a winner.

That's 91 points for McEnroe on pure power tennis where he attacked and left the best counterpuncher in tennis helpless to retort.

For two weeks, McEnroe has complained about many things—linesmen, umpires, referees, scheduling, the weather, the courts, the fans, the British press. He has called many people many things, some of them printable: "the pits of the world . . . incompetent fool . . . idiot . . . disgrace to mankind." With today's recommended fine, McEnroe's penalty list at Wimbledon finished with two warnings, three penalty points, $2,250 in fines and $12,500 in recommended fines that will be decided upon by the International Tennis Council.

It is even conceivable that the ITC will decide on a suspension (of undetermined length) for McEnroe at some future date for his shenanigans here.

Nevertheless, of all McEnroe's complaints here, the one that has been closest to his heart has been his groaning about his own misplaced first serve—the central weapon in his arsenal. "Can't beat Borg unless I serve better," he has said repeatedly.

"I picked a helluva match to serve well," said McEnroe with his crooked grin afterward.

That is understatement in the extreme. One hundred times McEnroe cracked his first serve into play—100 to 164. And those were the 100 nails in the coffin of Borg's winning streak. By contrast, Borg, who served supernaturally in the fifth set last year when he lost only three points in seven service games, was mortal this day, putting only 86 of 151 first balls in play.

Never was the contrast more telling than in the two tiebreakers, in the second and third sets, which probably decided this match. McEnroe put nine of ten first serves in play and won eight points, while Borg managed only four of nine.

As a direct consequence, McEnroe dominated both tiebreakers, winning easily, 7–1 and 7–4.

"When he needed to win an important point, he hit his first serve in. His game depends absolutely on his first serve," said Borg, who heretofore was considered to have a monopoly on capturing big points. "He missed one serve in two tiebreakers," said Borg with a shrug.

That eloquent shrug said, "That's what I'm supposed to do."

In bizarre fact, it was McEnroe who was Borg-like and Borg who was a touch like McEnroe.

This match, watched by Lady Diana Spencer, former King Constantine of Greece and Princess Grace of Monaco, had only one semiserious dispute in which the young, thirty-eight-year-old umpire had to look down sternly from his high chair and intone, "I saw it out." The man grousing was Borg.

On two other occasions, Borg recorded mild disapproval. "One complaint exceeds Borg's average, and three constitutes the record," commented the man from *The Times* of London.

McEnroe, by stunning contrast, was not only a model of deportment but so unflappable that the crowd ended up cheering his manly, if somewhat showy, self-restraint.

In the second set, a rude fan in the standing-room-only crowd, some of whom paid as much as $1,200 per ticket to scalpers, shouted, "Call for the referee, John," just before McEnroe served.

McEnroe, upset, served one of his ten double faults, then said to the fan, "Thank you, very much."

Later in that set, a very dubious line call cost McEnroe a break of Borg's serve—particularly galling since McEnroe failed to convert the first ten break-point chances he had. Normally, McTantrum might rage. This time, he put his hands on either side of his head and squeezed, as though trying to keep his brains from exploding. Then, subdued, he raised his arms in a mock victory pose—triumph over oneself perhaps—and received a cheer.

The real, genuine test of McEnroe's self-possession, and the act of will which may have saved his day, came in the tenth game of the pivotal third set, Borg leading, 5–4, and trying to break McEnroe to grab the set.

At 15–30, McEnroe hit a volley an inch past the baseline. The linesman called it good, the point continued and McEnroe won it for 30–30. After play stopped, the umpire overruled the linesman, saying over the loud-speaker, "The ball was out."

McEnroe, preparing for his next serve, spun around as though bashed in the back of the head with a sap. Suddenly, instead of being 30–30 and no big deal, he was down 15–40 and facing a double set point.

In short, that one call could, without exaggeration, transform the entire match.

One shot hence, McEnroe could be behind two sets to one. "With Borg, two sets to one up is a lot different than two to one down," said McEnroe. "You have to stay ahead of Borg to beat him, that's all there is to it."

McEnroe went into a froglike crouch, leaning on his racket, as though straining with all that was in him not to unleash all the rage he has felt here at what he considers a cast of Wimbledon officials who are out to intimidate him with their authority.

McEnroe paced. He walked in circles. This was no joke. This was the match.

He composed himself. How he composed himself, Borg never will forget.

Crash: a booming first serve and a put-away overhead. Boom: a service winner down the middle to Borg's forehand.

Twice more in that game, Borg reached set point. And twice more McEnroe's serve-and-volley game rebutted. First, it was another identical service winner down the middle of the chalk, then a gutsy deep second serve and a volley.

Only against Borg has McEnroe ever totally constrained himself. He did it last year in the final. Let him say why. "I know I need every ounce of me to beat him. I can't waste anything. On those set points, I not only didn't complain, I didn't even yell 'Come on!' to myself."

"It was very important to win the third [set] when I had those four set points," said Borg.

"Maybe if I win just one of those points . . ." His voice trailed off.

The suddenly gracious McEnroe, the tennis genius who has an allergic reaction to smiling, actually managed to smile.

Slowly, he said, "I won Wimbledon."

All the details were washed out. How Borg broke in the fifth game of the first set to get an early lead.

How no one could break in the second set. How McEnroe sent a shudder through the crowd by double-faulting to break himself early in the third set. And how, finally, McEnroe, down, 4–1, in that crisis of a third set, finally broke back after Borg had held his serve his first fourteen times.

"In a couple of hours, I'll start getting very relaxed," said the second American male to win Wimbledon on the Fourth of July in 104 years, Jack Kramer in 1947 being the other.

Finally, after all the abuse he has given and taken here, what flashed through McEnroe's mind as he knelt on Centre Court in his victory moment, when he accidentally dropped into that prayerful posture that Borg seemingly invented and patented?

"I thought," he said with a grin, "I gotta get up again, because Borg always does."

And, of course, after 3 hours 22 minutes of battle, at precisely 5:30 P.M. on an English summer evening, McEnroe still had enough spring left in his legs to pop up to the standing position, just as Borg always has.

That was appropriate. McEnroe has stolen the Wimbledon spotlight from Borg for this entire fortnight, with either his tennis, his tantrums or his talk. Now he has commandeered both his crown and his gesture of triumph. In the pleasant evening, the crowd, including a pro-McEnroe harlequin in full red-and-green regalia and bells, gave McEnroe unstinting applause. However, they held back just a bit. They were waiting. Bjorn Borg walked out last for his second-place medal. And that, quite rightly, was when the cheering stopped and ovation began.

The Iceman Goeth

NEW YORK, September 13, 1981—

The ice age of tennis ended today.

And an era of fire began.

It wasn't the warmth of an autumn evening that melted the ice in Bjorn Borg's competitive heart in the final of the centennial U.S. championship. Rather, it was the blast-furnace heat from John McEnroe's diabolically diversified arsenal that left Borg's game a damp puddle at the bottom of Louis Armstrong Stadium, 4–6, 6–2, 6–4, 6–3.

This was the day McEnroe not only defeated Borg but owned him, controlled him, demoralized him and, with an indisputable swagger, defied him.

Perhaps Borg—rich, married and now a ten-year international veteran—will find some way to return to Sweden and freeze his will to its former hardness.

That is an issue for the future. At this hour, the incendiary McEnroe, twenty-two and still rising, has completed a power shift at the top of tennis.

McEnroe has beaten Borg before with huge stakes on the table: in the final of the '80 U.S. Open and this past Fourth of July, when he demolished Borg's 41-match Wimbledon winning streak. However, this final was the first time that Borg truly lost to McEnroe.

On those other occasions, even when McEnroe threw his arms skyward in triumph, there was a sense that the victory was for one day, and one place, only. Borg played nobly until the very end and was defeated only on the scoreboard, not in the depths of his stomach of ice.

This victory—McEnroe's third straight Open title—was a different, more encompassing tale. He knew it, but had the grace not to insist upon it.

Asked if he had now mastered the master, McEnroe said honestly, "That's too complicated to answer simply. I don't think I could beat him on clay. But I'm comfortable against him on all other surfaces."

That was the word for McEnroe today: comfortable on the same court with Borg. No one has truly looked that way for five years. By contrast, it was Borg who looked uncomfortable, tactically confused and at sea.

"He's put so much pressure on himself, especially to win the Open. That's not necessarily the right thing to do. Everybody knows his record here [now 0–10] and how important it is for him to win it. I don't think he needs to keep saying it himself. . . . Maybe it doesn't help him," said McEnroe, who added, "Of course, I mean, I'm glad he did play that way [that is, poorly]."

In the two greatest showcases of tennis, McEnroe has, within nine weeks, beaten Borg twice in four sets—both times after spotting Borg the first set. Today, Borg had few excuses. In fact, he got most of the breaks.

McEnroe had to struggle through five sets the day before. In contrast, Borg escaped Jimmy Connors in three razor-sharp, shockingly easy sets. That, one might assume, would help Borg; however, McEnroe turned it to his advantage. "I watched how Connors kept blasting every shot, giving Borg pace, letting him get in a groove," said McEnroe. "I swore I'd change speeds."

Next, Borg, so often a miserable starter, got "into" the match early. After McEnroe rebutted by winning the second set easily, Borg retaliated by going up a break in the third set, only to see that advantage grabbed back from him, too. Even in the fourth set, Borg managed the beginnings of a typical comeback—the kind that unravels nervous foes—when he negated a dramatic McEnroe service break with one of his own.

That juncture, with McEnroe leading the fourth set, 3–2, was the crisis moment when, for the past five years, Borg would probably have held service to draw even, and then finally pull away.

Instead, Borg, in effect, broke himself; he went down, 4–2, by committing four errors in one game. With his fans imploring him to "dig deep," Borg suddenly found that his margin of error for beating McEnroe on a fast surface had finally become too minuscule to endure. The demand for splendid passing shots, acrobatic service returns and continually flawless, deep ground strokes was too great.

In the end, with the crowd pleading for him to act like the old Teen Angel of the mid-'70s, or the Iceman of the late '70s, or the King of Sweden of recent history, Borg gave a listless final bow.

Borg barely held his own serve, after surviving two match points, then managed only one meager point as McEnroe served out the match with authority.

At the finish, the clock showed that McEnroe had dispatched Borg in less time, and with less strain, than Tracy Austin had needed to beat Martina Navratilova the day before.

Borg, normally moderately patient in defeat, made a quick no-comment exit after what may be his most hard-to-swallow defeat. Being dethroned has never been fun.

Anyone who wants to sugarcoat Borg's dash for the parking lot can say it was caused by anxiety in the wake of a threatening phone call. However, the best available information after the match was that Borg made his let's-get-outta-here decision even before being told about the crank call in midmatch.

Borg arrived here talking about how he had to win this U.S. Open to fill out the total portrait of his tennis greatness. This evening, it was McEnroe, the new boss of his sport, who was making similar noises of his own.

"I keep hearing how, to be considered one of the real greats, you have to win the French Open [on clay]," said McEnroe. "That's never been one of my real priorities, but I think that sometime in the future it will be. I can certainly improve a great deal on clay."

That was McEnroe's backhanded way of saying that on every other surface he is now, and intends to continue being, the ruler of his sport.

As far as McEnroe is concerned, it's all part of the same great thaw that he has brought to what was, until recently, a cold, cold sport.

Raiders of the
Lost Art: Fun

NEW YORK, September 10, 1981—

Even from the topmost rim of Louis Armstrong Stadium, you could hear the last sweet note of the horn sounding for John Newcombe and Fred Stolle.

The sun was going down, sinking, like the careers of the two old Australian tennis legends. Darkness crept into the deep bowl of the stadium, turning the afternoon warmth to cool.

At this hour made for inspiration, not perspiration, no one was leaving the centennial U.S. Open. Drama is rare, even at vast events concocted solely to produce it. And here, at the bottom of the tennis bowl, was something real.

On display was tormented, alienated youth against cheerful, graceful age. Or, to put it differently, a vanished tennis era of devil-may-care characters pitted, with a nothin'-to-lose grin, against a new age of callow cash and bad manners.

In short, those funny old champions, Newcombe and Stolle, were in a war with those grim, humorless children, John McEnroe and Peter Fleming, the best doubles team in the world.

The combined age on one side of the net: eighty. On the other: twelve.

No, nobody walks out on that. Especially not in the fifth and final set. Especially not in one last tiebreaker.

"I'm beat . . . fatigue, I guess," said Newcombe, thirty-seven, winner of seven major titles, including three Wimbledons and two U.S. championships.

"Is that what you call it?" gibed Stolle, forty-three, winner in his bygone time of both the French and U.S. titles. "Some call it age."

They laughed. As they had laughed throughout the afternoon and into the evening. As they had made the large crowd laugh—when Newcombe accidentally conked his partner on the head with a volley, or when Stolle ended up on the wrong side of the net and pretended to be ready to play, three men against one.

But the laughter was mostly on the outside. Inside of all four men was fire.

The match, which had begun as a curiosity, had turned serious long before.

The kids—the defending champions—had won the first two sets, 6–2, 6–2. But they couldn't resist rubbing it in.

Before the match, all four had dressed in the same locker room. "We were joking about what we were going to do to them," recalled Fleming. "But they were, too."

Newcombe and Stolle weren't sure it was all joking. "Fred warned me that if they got a loose ball, they'd gun for us," said Newcombe.

Early in the third set, McEnroe hit Stolle on the neck with a point-blank volley.

"I got really mad at Fred being hit," said Newcombe. "A shot like that could put out his eye. There were two balls hit at me like that, one at my head and one at my crotch. But then, I just forgot about them. I feel sorry for them both. In our day, we never forgot it was a sport. I think they take it over the fringe . . . kill the opponent, like it's a jungle. That's all crap. They're missing out on all the pleasure."

"The game used to be a lot more bloody fun," said Stolle. "That's why you see us old guys out here playing whilst we can still enjoy it a bit. I'll wager there's not many of the top-ten players today who will be playing when they're forty-three."

The oldsters won the next two sets, 7–5, 7–6.

McEnroe and Fleming held their heads at breaks, sitting apart, while Newcombe and Stolle chatted, then took the court first.

In fiction, the old-timers win the tiebreaker at dusk. In reality, youth wins easily, 7–3.

Afterward, McEnroe and Fleming were clench-jawed. Even in victory, men can be humiliated.

Being told Newcombe's remarks didn't help.

"When you're hitting a ball a hundred miles an hour, it's ridiculous to say that you're deliberately trying to hit someone," said Fleming. "It's just not valid. As for us not enjoying the sport, okay, those guys played in the [pre-open tennis] days when all you got was expense money, trophies and some good parties. But why can't they understand that it's a different world now?"

"Newcombe doesn't have to feel sorry for us," said an upset McEnroe. "John Newcombe is the perfect example of somebody who will take advantage of everything and use it for himself—whether it's playing to the public or the press.

"I can't win either way," McEnroe said. "If I talk, I'm wrong, and if I don't, people will think I'm wrong."

While McEnroe and Fleming suffered in victory, Newcombe and Stolle basked in defeat, recalling the time, fifteen years ago, when Stolle beat Newcombe in the final of Forest Hills here.

"Different days, different kind of people," said Newcombe. "I won a runner-up plate. We had a party and served food on it. When the blokes got to the bottom and saw 'runner-up,' they gave me a hard time about what sort of fellow is proud of finishing second."

"Didn't you finally throw that plate in a gorge?" asked Stolle.

"Yes," said Newcombe, "when I realized who I'd lost to. . . .

"When I came here in '67, all I got for two weeks' expenses in New York for my wife and I was five hundred dollars. We ate takeout food every night. And I had just won Wimbledon," continued Newcombe.

"You had to play for the game itself and the good times and the friends. It seems like now, with so much more money, there ought to be more fun.

"But there isn't."

As McEnroe and Fleming left tonight, the silent crowd gathered before them to get autographs.

These men are rich celebrities. Their signatures have a value.

As Newcombe and Stolle left, the fans asked for no autographs from the has-beens. Instead, they applauded.

These men, you see, are heroes. And the smiles on their roguish faces are their signatures.

Jimbo, the EKG

LONDON, July 6, 1984—

Jimmy Connors is the electrocardiograph of tennis.

He checks out your heart.

Today, Ivan Lendl failed another physical.

Some players look at your forehand or your serve for a weakness.

Connors looks into your eyes.

Few athletes in any sport truly epitomize one specific virtue. Connors does. He's the grist of grit and grunt. He's the King of Hearts.

Connors may not be too brilliant, though he's savvy enough. His tactical tennis flaws have been known for a decade, but he's too cussedly stubborn to change them. He'd rather lose his way, hitting a thousand forehand approaches into the top inch of the net cord, than win with a style that isn't his.

Also, his manners and vocabulary have at times been the crudest of almost any athlete in sport. Today, he held his nose and told the umpire, "You stink."

Nobody ducks out the back door faster after a defeat than Connors. He's always been a sore loser who doesn't like to listen to the music. And with his large, economy-size ego and his waspish tongue, Connors has never been the circuit's most popular player. As though he cared.

But he'll fight you. He'll test you. He'll give you his best and see what you've got for an answer. And that's a lot.

Sometimes, when he meets a courageous foe, Connors creates fabulous defeats. That's happened in historic matches with Guillermo Vilas and Manuel Orantes at the U.S. Open and with Arthur Ashe, Bjorn Borg and John McEnroe here.

In a sense, because he never changes, never quits, never hits a slump and almost never gets injured, Connors is a sort of benchmark for measuring the greatness of others.

When Borg decided that he couldn't be the boss of bosses, he retired; the Iceman had what it took to win, but not what it took to endure periodic defeats.

When Connors, who was ranked No. 1 in the world for his first five pro years, learned that he couldn't be the obvious top dog, he decided to stick around like a bad dream and give everybody hell until the day they had to drag his body off the service line.

And that's what he's doing to this day. Jimmy Connors gives full value.

McEnroe, who will meet Connors in Sunday's final, put his foe in clean perspective today when he said, "You could beat Connors a hundred times in a row and he wouldn't acknowledge it. . . .

"He's thirty-one but he's still in good shape. I've never seen him visibly tired in any match," said McEnroe, who, at twenty-five, probably isn't as fit as Connors. "Today, Lendl looked stronger in the second set. He was hitting the ball harder, looked like he was in control. But by the middle of the fourth set, Connors looked a helluva lot stronger than Lendl.

"Jimmy's good at seeing when you're tiring . . . when you're vulnerable."

McEnroe mused for a second, then said, "He'll have to retire someday but it'll probably be after I do."

This afternoon on Centre Court, Connors looked across the net at Lendl and saw a sight he's been familiar with through 103 tournament victories and $5 million in purses, both records. Connors saw a man with wobbly legs and that glazed look of athletic death in his eyes.

"I jumped on him," said Connors.

What Connors does to weak-souled foes is tantamount to a mugging. His favorite target is Lendl, who seems to have been created as his foil.

Entering today's semifinal, Lendl had won twenty consecutive games against Connors. Yes, 20–0.

Whenever this pair met for modest stakes over the past three years, Lendl was almost always a winner, five times in straight sets. But on the three occasions when they have locked rackets for huge stakes, Connors has won four-set wars every time. Lendl will spend many an old man's winter night wondering how he lost those U.S. Open finals to Connors in 1982 and 1983.

"I've had good success against him in major events," said Connors, letting sleeping dogs lie.

To be fair, Lendl showed definite improvement today over his Mandlikova-like fades against Connors in the past. This time, he didn't roll over until the final set. Even that's something Connors would rather die than do.

It took a lot to crack Lendl this time. But a lot is what Connors deals out when the big cash is on the line.

When, in the first set, Lendl won a tough-to-swallow tiebreaker that had been on serve through nine points, Connors's reaction was to get mad. Instead of whimpering about bad breaks—and he'd gotten some—Connors stomped on Lendl in the second set, breaking him in the very first game and serving out.

The pivotal third set was pure Connors. The greater the pressure, the better he liked it and the more he milked it. Before big points, he would get a towel to rub his racket handle as Lendl was forced to feel the moment.

When Connors wasn't blowing on his hot little hand, he was pawing or kicking the grass with his toes. Above all, Connors was doing what he does best—putting pressure on a great server's serve. The harder Lendl thundered his cannonball serves at Connors, the harder he sent them back.

Ten times in one set, Connors got a break point. That's a month's worth for Lendl. Eight times Lendl saved the point. But twice he failed. When a feeble backhand by Lendl barely reached the bottom of the net at 4:30 P.M., Connors finally had the break he had sought for two and a half hours.

A broken heart.

After that, Lendl was useless, losing eight of the final nine games. Deep in the fourth set, Connors even indulged in what can only be called a piece of rather crass taunting, calling to Lendl in a girlish voice, then pointing to his ear to indicate that Lendl was starting to hear things.

Lendl blanched, but was too far gone to retaliate.

Many here take it for granted that McEnroe, with his 54–1 record this year and five straight victories over Connors, will have a strawberries-and-cream cakewalk Sunday.

Connors fed that impression by doing stretching exercises (to prevent cramping) throughout a postmatch press conference in which he did everything but enter with a cane and ask for a shawl.

"Maybe I was tired and just didn't show it," he purred.

McEnroe knows better. "He fakes it pretty well," said McEnroe of the man with five U.S. Open and two Wimbledon titles. "Connors loves it when you write him off. He likes to be counted out. He loves this position. He knows I'm expected to win, but he also knows he has a good chance if he plays particularly well."

Did the human EKG machine, with his cramps and creaks, think he could beat the torrid McEnroe Sunday?

"That's what you gotta buy a ticket to find out," Connors snapped back.

At least you know you'll get your money's worth.

Queens
of the Centenary

LONDON, July 7, 1984—

Martina Navratilova and Chris Evert Lloyd brought two kinds of tennis, two kinds of athleticism and two kinds of personality to Centre Court today in the final of the 100th Wimbledon singles championship for women.

Because both brought courage, intelligence and sensitivity as well, both won on all counts.

This centenary, in a sport that has long been a contemporary metaphor for sexual politics, may have proved that what you choose to be isn't as important as how well you do it.

As a tennis player, Navratilova, who won her third straight Wimbledon title (7–6, 6–2), is all serve and volley, power and speed. Evert, who played superbly in defeat, is patient precision and errorless execution.

Their match today did not prove which has the better approach to the sport. Navratilova, twenty-seven, is at her career peak these days and was on her best surface this time. Turn back the clock five years, put this pair on clay, and Evert, twenty-nine, would (and did) look just as great.

Just because Navratilova is the hot item of the moment is no reason to forget how comparable these two careers will probably look in retrospect. Evert: six U.S. Opens, five French, three Wimbledons, one Australian (fifteen majors). Navratilova: five Wimbledons, two French, two Australians, one U.S. Open (ten).

Navratilova had it right when she said today, "Can you imagine, thirty to thirty [in career matches]? Nobody's ever played that many times, have they? I wish we could quit right now and never have to play each other again. I wish we could end up even. We've played so many times on so many surfaces that it's not right for one of us to say we're better."

"So," said a grinning Evert when told of this bouquet, "is she going to retire now, or what?"

As an athlete, Navratilova is state-of-the-art dec-athlete. She lifts weights, plays full-court one-on-one basketball an hour at a time, practices three to four hours a day and follows a diet that includes no red meats, no animal fats, high carbohydrates and limited sugar.

"It's time for the rest of them to get to work and raise their game [to my level]," said Navratilova in a challenge to her sport. "My chromosomes are the same as theirs. I just work at it."

As an athlete, Evert really isn't an athlete. She is more a demiurge, 114 pounds of will and concentration.

"I'm not as great an athlete as a lot of girls out here," said Evert. "My game is eighty percent mental. I have to feel very intense to play well."

As a personality, Navratilova is an emotional, outgoing, easily hurt and extremely smart extrovert. She's at ease in the midst of controversy; she's been there since she defected from Czechoslovakia as a teenager. Having been uprooted so young and thus forced to find her friends and causes in a new world, Navratilova has had a kaleidoscopic array of attachments and experiences in the past decade; she's often made up in bravery and resiliency for what she has sometimes lacked in judgment.

"You have to grow up as a human being before you can grow up as a player. You don't do your growing up on the court or your conditioning on the court," said Navratilova, who admitted freely that, in her early years, she had broken both those rules.

By contrast, Evert is composed, self-secure, aloof at times and thick-skinned. Evert's root system is as entrenched as Navratilova's is shallow but tenacious. For example, Evert's father still is one of her coaches.

When Navratilova is attacked or denigrated, her instinct is to cringe; Evert's nature is to strike back confidently. Three players here this week—Pam Shriver, Hana Mandlikova and Kathy Jordan—popped off at Evert's expense, saying the former Ice Queen is now just one of the pack chasing Navratilova. Gee, they're sorry now.

"There's been a lack of respect, I think," said Evert after proving once again this week that there is as dramatic a gap between herself and Everybody Else as there is between Navratilova and herself. "It's amusing to me and also ridiculous. I question the intelligence behind it. . . . The players themselves should know better. They should know how tough I've been over the years.

"But that's all right. They can keep criticizing and getting me fired up."

Evert has always said she feels at home with a conventional demure femininity, although the little old ladies who cheer her here might not recognize their lacy Chrissie if they saw her at the Hard Rock Cafe. Navratilova seems gifted at getting her private life splashed in the tabloids. Navratilova is a standing challenge to the social conventions of her time and place.

The best news from this day's championship is that neither of these women is leaving us soon. Navratilova reported that she was headed for a dinner of "roast duckling, dumplings and sauerkraut," but that she'd be back on her regimen come Monday.

As for Evert, this may have been the tournament that convinced her that all the best tennis experiences are not behind her. "I feel great about this match," she said. "I still feel I can get better. Martina can only stay the same or go down.

"The last couple of times I played her, I just wanted to win some games. I just wanted to give her a good match. Today, I thought I could win. This is the form I've been looking for all year.

"It's been a long time since I had the desire to play great tennis," said Evert, who, in her quiet, off-camera way, has been through as many changes and trials as Navratilova. "I've tried, but it just hasn't been there. It came back this week."

For Evert and Navratilova, so equal and so opposite, the only proper wish is a long and continuing rivalry.

And one that ends, some far-distant day, in a tie.

So Long, Chris

NEW YORK, September 5, 1989—

For nineteen years of big-time tennis, Chris Evert won the heart of the world with her will.

For her, the temperature could never be too hot at Stade Roland Garros in the French Open. The bounces could never be too bad on Centre Court at Wimbledon. The jets above the Stadium Court at the U.S. Open couldn't rattle her reserves.

For her, the stature of her foe did not matter. Not the majesty of Margaret Court, nor the spunk of Billie Jean King, nor the grace of Evonne Goolagong, nor the athleticism of Martina Navratilova, nor the power of Steffi Graff ever stole her courage from her. She could be beaten, but not broken.

That was then. But this is now. Today at the U.S. Open, in what she says will be the last championship match of her career, Evert played poorly. Whenever she needed to play her best, she played worst, losing to determined Zina Garrison, 7–6, 6–2, in the quarterfinals.

Even the New York crowd, ready to roar and inspire her, barely mustered any cheers. Seldom did the people call her name. Under leaden and threatening skies, everyone seemed to know the show was over. In its own perverse way, such a disappointing act may have been the perfect ending for her fabulous career.

Evert's incredible willpower was her fastball, her finishing kick, her knockout punch. As long as she had it, how could she retire to the life of family and children she has said she wanted so badly? And without that true grit, how could she continue to play and still keep her dignity intact?

After this match, it was not only easy to say, "Thanks," but also to think: Thank goodness.

For nearly two decades, Evert was seldom at a loss to produce the kind of intensity she so painfully lacked this afternoon. No matter how great her deficit or how poor her chances, no matter how many balls she had to chase down and swat back or how many midmatch switches of strategy she had to employ, Evert could, in the end, turn almost any tennis match into a test of willpower. Her lips would tighten, her eyes would narrow, her feet would pitty-pat a little faster, her ground strokes would pick up pace and, invariably, her shots would bite closer and closer to the lines until you knew you were in big trouble.

That's why Evert won 157 tournaments, more than any other player in history.

That's why she won eighteen Grand Slam singles crowns—six U.S. Opens, seven French Opens, three Wimbledons and two Australian Opens.

Evert began to cry as she left the court this afternoon. But by the time she met the media, she was a picture of public poise.

"Well, that's one of the reasons I'm retiring," said Evert, recapitulating how she'd squandered a 5–2 lead in the first set. "I played a great match two days ago [against Monica Seles]. Today I was flat. It's been like that all year. That's why it's time. . . .

"I was fine. I was calm out there. It's just so many matches over my career. . . . It's caught up with me. Mentally, I can't sustain it," said this athlete who, for the first time in her career, did not win a tournament this season.

"This sport is full of people who can play a great match one day, then come back and lose to No. 100 in the world in their next match," added Evert, almost proudly. "What makes a champion, like Steffi, or myself in the past, or Martina, is that we never had a letdown.

"This year, I've had them. That puts me right in there with the average player."

For Evert, whose raw athletic ability—by the standards of pro sport—may have been only a little more than average, the thought of degenerating into an average player was intolerable. She has stood for too much that is best in sports for too long a time to have the slightest smudge left on her public's memory of her. Now she can retire with no regrets and no doubts that she was leaving some great deed undone.

"I was thinking that I'd be relieved when it was over. But I'm not relieved," she said. "Because of what happened two days ago. . . . I thought I could challenge anybody. . . . Win the tournament? No, I didn't think that. But compete with anybody? Yes."

To the end, Evert could compete evenly with anyone in the world—except perhaps Graf. But she couldn't do it day after day. What better definition of the perfect time to retire?

True to form, Evert was a picture of perfect manners in defeat—trying to make the twenty-five-year-old, up-and-coming Garrison feel better about beating her.

The victor actually left the court with doubts about what she'd done. "Chris has been so good for the game, she's been such a lady. . . . To be the villain [who ended her career], it's good for me, but it wasn't good for me," said Garrison. "It might not be the way I want people to remember me."

"Noooo, she's no villain," laughed Evert, who then went on to say how well Garrison had played and how much she deserved to win.

Evert arrived at the U.S. Open at age fifteen dressed in lace and wearing pigtails. Then she was shy and prim—the Ice Maiden, they called her. In the two decades since, she has lived a life in which she has had to grow up entirely in public. Her every romance, almost every date, from Jimmy Connors to Burt Reynolds, has been news—not to mention her divorce from British tennis pro John Lloyd and second marriage to skier Andy Mill.

Part of the price has been a sort of split personality between the public Evert, always onstage, always ultra-nice, and the private Evert, who tends to be spicy and even cynical. One reason Evert and Navratilova have been good friends for so long is that they don't see the world as differently as some tennis fans think. Evert is a bit more the rebel; Navratilova more conventional.

In a recent *Sports Illustrated* farewell, Evert wrote: "It doesn't bother me that the world doesn't know the real me. It's never been a calculated move that I would be two different people. I just am."

If Evert has managed her image as much as her game, then the final results have been exactly what she wanted. She leaves the top level of competitive tennis as an enormously respected world figure—a person who is the embodiment in many minds of a gifted, aggressive woman who also found a way to retain an old-fashioned femininity.

Perhaps more than any other athlete of the last twenty-five years, she has legitimized women's sports for the American public. At one time, that was a hard sell. Now, thanks largely to Evert, it isn't. Others, such as Billie Jean King, were more conspicuous pioneers. But in her demure yet determined way, Evert did wonders to advance the same cause.

Interlude

Pine Valley

November 1988—Golf is the sport of masochists. Haven't we all played seventeen holes of humiliation, then hit one perfect shot on the 18th and heard our foursome echo, like a Greek chorus. "That'll bring you back!" Who else but a masochist would allow four seconds of watching a ball in flight to justify four hours of future embarrassment?

Golf, however, is also the game of heroes. Your correspondent, a garden-variety bogey master, learned this by playing the round of his life—and shooting 110. Come with me now to where masochism and heroism meet, to an innocent patch of forest in the pine barrens of New Jersey, to Pine Valley, where the ultimate pains and pleasures of golf reside in the closest proximity.

Calling Pine Valley a golf course is like calling the Grand Canyon a broad-jump pit. Imagine a barely penetrable jungle of sand, woods and hellacious bramble as seen from a spacecraft. Now imagine a laser carving out eighteen tees, fairways and greens of middling to smallish size. Nothing else. No transition. Just velvet and jungle.

At Pine Valley, only a few holes are ridiculously difficult. But no hole is less than hard. As long as you hit a succession of quality shots—for a pro that might mean no better than his "B" game—Pine Valley is a fairly normal course: little fearsome length, fairly sane greens and almost no water. The Valley starts when you leave the course and enter the barrens. That's how you shoot 67—on one hole. Or 42 on a par three. It's been done. By top players. Babe Ruth once found his ball but lost the course. He had to be guided back to safety.

It's almost impossible to know what it feels like to play Augusta National, Pebble Beach or St. Andrews (the last two open to the public) without actually doing so. But anybody, for no charge, can experience Pine Valley. Go to your local club. Find the densest woods. Tee your ball and drive it as hard as you can into the forest. Find it and hit it deeper. Now, without taking a penalty stroke or lost ball—never allowed at Pine Valley—get back to the fairway. Chip it. Kick it. Putt to an opening in the trees, then wedge through the limbs toward a slightly less dense clump of undergrowth.

Isn't this great? Aren't we learning something? Isn't it amazing how many new shots and unique challenges we've encountered? Are we having fun yet?

Or else, when driving along a gorgeous interstate highway past a marvelous piece of forest, you could stop the car, get your clubs out of the trunk and just tee off. Then tell your friends you played Pine Valley.

Actually, you may yet play it. Anybody might. I can prove it. One day this summer, a friend of a friend of a friend of my wife—a member who'd never met or heard of me—invited me to play Pine Valley. Out of the blue. To fill out a foursome. After trying (and failing) for ten years to play the course. I thought I'd hit the golf lottery. It was like the tumblers of a vault at Fort Knox falling by accident into the proper combination. I was so excited that I almost practiced.

On the 1st hole, I took 9. My caddie, Elmer, a gentleman with thirty years' experience, shook my hand with great dignity and said, "Welcome to Pine Valley, sir." After I sank a long putt for my 10 at the 7th (or was it my 9 at the 10th?), Elmer apologized for not helping with the putt, but, he explained, "I don't line 'em up for double digits," which must cut down on the job considerably.

That is why you come to Pine Valley. To be insulted, mocked. To take 9s. I had six of them, give or take a stroke. That's how you shoot 110 without a lost ball or penalty stroke on a day when you hit twelve of the prettiest dead-straight tee shots in the history of mankind. It was probably the best ball-striking round—a ludicrous expression when applied to my game—of my life.

Pine Valley, you see, completely reverses the normal experience of playing golf, especially for a duffer. Usually, we play to avoid disaster, to limit the damage, to save strokes, to be smart even if we aren't talented. Over the years, the humbling game does indeed humble us. When we come to the hardest hole—the one that demands a heroic shot simply to survive—we take out an old ball and pray.

At Pine Valley, there are only heroic shots. You could play a hundred normal courses and never face one hole as fraught with possibilities as the easiest at Pine Valley. Like the man said, at Pine Valley you're always one swing from a 10. So, out of necessity, you discover your courage. After a couple of holes, you realize that caution is senseless. Nobody gets out alive. So you might as well have fun.

Step up, nice and composed, and play the shot Ben Hogan would love. Not the longest ball you own, but the purest, the most properly struck. Better than your best. Because nothing else will play.

In one afternoon, I hit a summer's worth of memorable shots. When you have back-to-back 10-foot birdie putts at Pine Valley, you don't forget it. In fact, I can't remember a single mistake. But I can recall almost every shot on the dozen holes where I made par or bogey. Because Pine Valley can make a bogey feel like a birdie.

For perhaps the first time in twenty-five years of golf, I stopped thinking about the ball, stopped worrying about where it would land, stopped considering my score. After a while, I just imagined the target, thought about the feeling of the swing itself and didn't even bother to look at the shot until it was long gone. Yes, just like those millions of perfect practice swings we all take.

No, Pine Valley is probably not really a golf course; and it's just as well that, with little space for spectators or cars, no major tournament ever has or ever will be played there. Medal play would be meaningless anyway—probably immoral.

However, there's no denying that Pine Valley is a magnificent test—of something. Perhaps it's a place for us golf masochists to meet a smidgen of the golf hero hidden deep inside. We always knew we were one of the two. At Pine Valley, it's nice to discover that you're a bit of both.

Baseball

My Hero

March 1990—A baseball hero is a toy of childhood. Electric trains, cowboy guns and plastic soldiers are the same kind. But with a baseball hero a youngster reaches out, for one of the first times, into the world outside the family. That connection with a big, mysterious environment gives a certain sense of power; a child discovers that it can invest its affections and actually get something special back in return. However, hero worship also brings with it the first morsels of the sort of pain and fear that we come to associate with the word "reality." We begin to learn about adult disappointments and the profound uncontrollableness of nature.

I was fortunate. I got a wonderful hero. When I was eight years old in the spring of 1956, somebody gave me my first pack of baseball cards. Pathetic as it sounds, I can still remember where I was standing when I opened them —beside a coffee table in the living room. In that pack was only one player from my hometown team, the Washington Senators. I'm convinced that, by the luck of the draw, the player on that card was destined to be my first (and, as it turned out, only) hero. It could have been Herb Plews, who made four errors in one inning, or Chuck Stobbs, who lost thirteen games in a row.

But it was Roy Sievers.

At that time, he wasn't the best player on those bad Nat teams. Mickey Vernon was. Sievers, however, was about to blossom into the best home run hitter in the American League. And I had "spotted" him—that is, stumbled on him—a year before it happened. Maybe that's why, to this day, I'm still childishly certain that I have a special lucky relationship with baseball.

At the ages of nine and ten, I felt intimately connected with the most mythic public performer in my town—a man who hit 42 home runs in 1957 and then 39 in 1958. That doesn't sound like so many, but, for that sliver of time (so symbolic to me), it was more than anybody in baseball except Ernie Banks. Yes, more than Mickey Mantle or Ted Williams, Hank Aaron or Willie Mays.

Sievers never failed me. In the pulp magazines and sports pages of the time, he was portrayed as modest to the point of shyness, as well as unselfish and charitable. On his home runs, he always trotted the bases with his head down as though embarrassed and anxious to get back into the dugout. Every story discussed the wide respect he'd earned by making "a dramatic comeback" after a shoulder injury nearly ended a promising career that had begun with a Rookie of the Year award in 1949.

When I finally met him, he surpassed all expectations. One night in 1958, when he was at the height of his fame and I was ten years old, my mother took me to Hecht's department store, where Sievers was giving autographs. Not selling them. Not hawking an autobiography. For all I know, maybe not even getting a fee from the store. Just giving autographs.

I got lost. Thought I knew better than my mother where he would be. So I took off on my own. As the store closed down and I knew he had to leave, I cried with a frustration perhaps only children know.

Finally, my mother found me. Sievers should have left a half hour before. But he was waiting. Alone. For the mother and the lost little boy to come back.

My only memory is that he was big. But the picture, "To Tommy from Roy Sievers," in big, handsome looping script, can still be unearthed, in mint condition, in a pinch. There was another picture, too, a standard-issue "Roy Sievers" that my mother had taken in case she couldn't find me in time. That one went on the bedroom wall and had darts and insults thrown at it after many an exasperating strikeout or pop fly came over the radio.

I watched Sievers play many times in Griffith Stadium and on TV. But what I remember much more clearly is reading about him, keeping scrapbooks of box scores and statistics and, above all, listening to absolutely every game on the radio. Or should I say praying on the radio? The incredible power of that daily connection is the unique hold that baseball has on its fans.

Listening to that radio under the covers long after bedtime, I learned that heroes fail, even my hero, that they fall from public favor while they are still in yours, that ultimately there is a world that does not care that you are listening in.

In his prime, before injuries and Harmon Killebrew pushed him out of the headlines, Sievers was given a "night." Not the kind that Ted Williams and Stan Musial got, with fancy cars, but a night with plenty of speeches and a station wagon. Vice President Richard Nixon did the talking, and Sievers hung his head and cried when Nixon shook his hand. That required a breakfast-table explanation.

In 1959, Sievers's play went downhill; there was trade talk. I wrote in a protest to Calvin Griffith—an eleven-year-old's letter. Griffith wrote back— a club owner's letter. With fans like me, Sievers would never be traded. There was nothing to worry about. And would my family and I be interested in season tickets?

Before the next season, Sievers was traded. By that time I was too old to cry . . . much. After that, his name was no longer a constant part of my thoughts. When I was seventeen, Sievers was traded back to the expansion Senators from the Phillies in midseason of 1964. I barely noticed. At the time, it never crossed my mind that he escaped the Fold. (Or, perhaps, missed his chance to prevent it.) I had my own high school games to play, and besides, I wore Ted Williams's number.

Still, for years, when the name would sneak up on me on a TV sportscast, it would give a little private shock, like certain girls' names when you don't expect to hear them.

A couple of years after college, when I was working as a copy aide in the sports department of *The Washington Post*—fetching coffee, covering high school sports and trying to find a way to get a story longer than six paragraphs in the paper under my byline—I decided to search for Sievers.

There he was, in his hometown St. Louis phone book, living in a place called Spanish Lake. And there he was, again, picking up the phone and chatting with me for an hour like it was nothing. Answering personal questions about how the A's had fired him as a minor-league manager ("too nice") and how his son Robin was getting scant encouragement from the Cardinals in the minors.

He sounded relaxed and fairly happy, like a man who didn't require much to be content, certainly nothing as grand as hitting 318 home runs in the major leagues. Working as a salesman for the Yellow Freight Company and raising three kids was okay by him. "I'm set up fine here," he said, although he couldn't keep a certain gentle bewilderment out of his voice when he talked about how Eddie Yost was still in the major leagues, as a coach with the Mets. How do you do that?

The night I called him, Watergate was near its height. Not too far away, Woodward and Bernstein were probably digging. I asked my childhood hero what his fondest memory had been. Roy Sievers said it was the night Richard Nixon shook his hand at home plate. "I'm sentimental. That was really touching . . . in Washington I got to meet four Presidents and have lunch with two. That's wonderful for a kid from St. Louis."

From the day I got his baseball card to the day I interviewed him (and got my first decent story in the *Post* sports pages) was sixteen years. Then I didn't hear of Sievers again for sixteen more years. His name vanished from baseball so completely that, even to a writer on the baseball beat, like me, he was nonexistent.

Finally, one day in 1988, a friend asked if I'd seen that TV commercial for the Maryland lottery. The funny one with the two old Senators ballplayers talking about how small salaries were in the '50s and how much money you could win now in the lottery.

I watched with trepidation. Sievers would be sixty-two years old.

In the commercial, Sievers looked young, handsome and happy, with a great smile. At least that's how he looked on my TV.

Billy the Kid

Alfred Manuel Pesano

NEW YORK, May 23, 1977—

The idea is taking shape here—as it did in Minnesota, Detroit and Texas before—that victory may not be worth the price, if the price is Billy Martin.

The New York manager is on the ropes in his beloved Yankee Stadium as surely as if his name was Billy Conn and Joe Louis was closing the ring, muttering, "You can run, but you can't hide."

For all his forty-nine years Martin has loved nothing better than a brawl, but now he is trying to run, trying to hide, trying to rabbit-punch his way out of the clinches. His pinched, fever-blistered lips clench tighter, his Durante nose juts defiantly, his eyes dart suspiciously.

With one breath he says, "Everything will be all right when the pitching comes around." With the next he snaps, "If we were fifty games ahead they wouldn't get off my back."

"They" are all the enemies Martin has made in thirty pro years, plus the enemies he just thinks he has.

Martin's baseball life—which is to say his life—is an open wound, festering fast.

His team is in third place, not first. Attendance is down more than 150,000. The earned run averages of four of his best pitchers, Catfish Hunter, Mike Torrez, Don Gullett and Ken Holtzman, are disasters—4.18, 4.47, 4.94 and 5.35.

At all his managerial stops, Martin has been in a constant race to see whether he would wear out his welcome first with the front office, the press or a few key players. This time it may be a dead heat.

Martin has never made it to Year IV in any job and this is his third season with the Yanks. The Martin Express is on schedule.

Billy the Kid's personality runs on iron rails. Once the track is chosen, there is no way to swerve or go back. A disciplinarian, a baseball absolutist, Martin treats his players, his bosses, his interviewers and his public just the way he treats a pitcher who must be relieved.

"When I go to the mound," he says with relish, "we don't have a discussion. I tell 'em."

For the last week Martin has been "tellin' 'em" even if it costs him the one job he has coveted above all others and which he swears he would like to hold until he dies.

When his front office activated rookie Del Alston, rather than veteran catcher Elrod Hendricks as he wanted, Martin sounded off so loudly that his owner fined him $2,500 and his general manager gave him a public lecture about who was who's boss. But Martin wouldn't stop. Three times in the last week he has benched Reggie Jackson, the $3 million free agent apple of owner George Steinbrenner's eye.

When word reached Martin that *Sport* magazine was hyping a ten-week-old interview in which Jackson had criticized teammate Thurman Munson ("He's being so damn insecure about the whole [leadership] thing . . ."), Martin took the hard way out. Instead of blasting *Sport* for billing an ancient, out-of-date interview as fresh news, Martin took a veiled rip at Jackson, saying, "Leadership is done by example, not by mouth."

A day later, when Munson was injured, the issue of "Alston vs. Hendricks" reappeared. Out of a tangle of strategic possibilities, Martin picked the tactless one again. Instead of pointing out that Alston had started a ninth-inning rally with a pinch double, he chose to observe that he could not subsequently pinch-hit for Fran Healy because he did not have Hendricks available.

"The last time I talked about this, it cost me money," fumed Martin, choosing to second-guess GM Gabe Paul again, rather than praise Alston for his hit.

"There is a way to simplify most situations and a way to make them more complicated," said Baltimore Oriole Brooks Robinson about the incident. "Martin seems to be able to make things more complicated every time."

Just hours later Martin was back again, making a rat's nest out of a simple May defeat. Instead of explaining to the press why he had benched Jackson or why he had yanked Mickey Rivers in midgame after he failed to hustle, Martin hid in the off-limits trainer's room.

Martin has always treated the press with only slightly less contempt than he has umpires. But even for Martin, last Saturday was a first. Out of a roomful of reporters, Martin managed to curse, push and spill coffee on Dick Young, who not only has white hair but also happens to write a syndicated sports column for the newspaper with the largest circulation in the civilized world, the *New York Daily News*. Martin could have broken a bat over the head of the chap from the *Newark Star-Ledger* and made fewer headlines than he did with a teaspoon of coffee on Young's lapel.

But it was a perfect example of Martin challenging those two things that make him see irrational red: authority and criticism.

Martin has a sign in his office that reads: "Company Rules. Rule 1: The Boss is always right. Rule 2: If the Boss is wrong, see Rule 1."

Martin's difficulty has always been that he wants to be the only boss where baseball decisions are concerned. "Billy understands baseball, but he doesn't understand life," said Baltimore manager Earl Weaver, not in his usual needling tone, but with concern. "You got to do what the owner says. That's not baseball; that's life. That's always Billy's undoing.

"I think the Yankees get along with each other. The only problem I see on that club is Billy and Steinbrenner. Billy told the owner in Texas, 'You sell pipes and I'll run the ball club.' Well, you don't tell the owner and the general manager what to do. You make suggestions."

Weaver also points out that Martin seldom wonders why millionaires would buy baseball teams and nurture them, often for little profit compared with their other businesses. "They want to hear people say how smart they are for the moves the team makes. They want to be in the papers. Above all, they want to be loved in their city," said Weaver.

And that's currently Martin's most serious problem in New York.

The Yankees—as they are now hiding from the press, sulking, barely speaking to each other, playing as individuals and not as a team—are becoming an embarrassment to Steinbrenner.

New York's conscience has been ruffled for some years over that blue-

and-alabaster bauble—Yankee Stadium—gleaming in the midst of the crushing squalor of the South Bronx. The juxtaposition was hard enough to swallow when the Yankees were swift and happy in '76. But now, as the team makes an almost daily mockery of itself, even the diehard fan is tempted to stay away. The front office notices.

For Billy Martin baseball has never been a game, but "a field of honor," a place for earnest, no-holds-barred warfare. At all his way stations Martin has brought victories, but at the expense of innocent pleasure.

Just a year ago New York's fickle fans, whose mood changes as often as the special of Sardi's, called Martin a genius, a man who had won a pennant that no other skipper could have masterminded.

This year those same fans are saying that the only manager who might find a way to keep the Yankees from winning the world's title is that same Martin. The Yanks have bought a team with so much talent that they hardly need a brilliant, hell-bent strategist. Wouldn't a nice-guy Sparky Anderson type—who could Xerox the opening-day lineup 162 times and keep everybody happy—be better?

In his mood of caustic melancholy Martin waits impatiently for Hunter's sore arm to mend, for Gullett to rediscover his pitching motion, even for Jackson to blast seven of his homers in a week. Victory is all that Billy Martin promises, and he knows he is in danger of breaking his word.

A box of expensive Havana cigars sits on Martin's desk. They are a peace offering from Steinbrenner. But a soothing cigar seems unlikely to temper Martin's fierce and contradictory ways. If his past repeats itself, he might well explain his plight as one of Turgenev's tragic characters did: "I could not simplify myself."

Billyball

OAKLAND, May 13, 1980—

Billy Martin is alive in Oakland, but he thinks he's in heaven.

The manager of the Oakland A's, who will be fifty-two on Friday, is back where he was born to be—leading a young, scorned team into first place and clawing his way into the brawl, trying to find somebody to kick or gouge.

The final proof that Martin's life is back on its accustomed track came here Saturday when the scrawny Martin disabled the American League's leading home run hitter, Otto Velez, in a bench-clearing fight. "Is Otto all right? I didn't mean to hurt him," said the solicitous Billy the Kid, over and over, like a gunfighter trying not to appear anxious to find out whether his victim is dead, whether he can add another notch to his gun.

Saturday was a big day for Martin, who, since he turned fifty, could claim only two conquests in combat: a smallish sportswriter and a marshmallow salesman.

But since returning to his home here, where he grew up as a poor, fatherless Berkeley High bad boy, everything has gone right.

After being fired for the fifth time in his career, Martin finally latched on to the lowest rung of the managerial totem pole on the last day before the start of spring training this year.

At that time the marriage between Martin and owner Charles O. Finley seemed one of inconvenience, with Martin desperate for any job and Finley cynically ready for a self-aggrandizing stunt. Las Vegas laid odds they wouldn't last a season together.

Now, the A's, losers of 108 in 1979, have the AL's best record (18–11). Martin, proudly unregenerate, is the reason. Once again, he has begun his perverse managerial metamorphosis from butterfly to worm.

These are the days when Martin is most brilliant, most charming, least self-destructive. Those who have seen him in pinstripes in recent years— gaunt and haggard from tension, drink and fury—would not recognize him now in bifocals studiously on the tip of his nose.

"Billy Martin is the best manager and the most unhappy person in baseball," says San Diego manager Jerry Coleman, Martin's teammate on the 1950s Yankees. "Baseball has been his whole life, and she has been a rough mistress. When I saw him a couple of years ago, he looked seventy years old, like a small rodent who had been backed into a corner.

"Now he's starting fresh again. That's when he's at his best."

An hour after Saturday's battle with the Toronto Blue Jays, all the A's were still in their clubhouse, waiting like delighted little boys to see the replay of their donnybrook.

"What I want to see in this [replay of the] fight is which Blue Jay kicked my guy [Dave Revering] in the head when he was down. We think we know who it was—one of their bullpen guys. We'll get him. Next time there's a fight, if he's smart, he'll stay in the bullpen, 'cause we'll be looking for him," said Martin.

"Let me say again that I wasn't trying to hurt Otto. I like Otto. It wasn't me that didn't like him in New York and wanted him traded, it was Steinbrenner.

"I just grabbed Otto from behind by the arms so he wouldn't get hurt, 'cause I like him. But we both got knocked to the ground and he hurt his shoulder."

The A's laugh nervously. Who is going to be the team hero of this film? And who is going to look like a chump or a coward? Reputations are going to be made, or lost, in the next minute.

Third baseman Wayne Gross tells Martin that one of the Blue Jays has sworn to get Martin for ordering that Woods be drilled. "But," vows Gross, "he's going to have to go through a whole lot of people before he gets to you, Billy." Several A's nod agreement.

The pitch hits Woods. He charges the mound. Just as he gets to Lansford, Gross comes flying out of nowhere and blasts him with an NFL-style shoulder tackle. Four A's clobber Woods from four directions.

Then it happens. For two seconds, the camera pans across Billy Martin wrestling with Velez.

Time and again, the replay slows down to isolate. The A's can't believe what they see.

Martin has Velez around the head, then throws the other arm under the 210-pounder's crotch, and suddenly Martin has Velez over his shoulder like a sack of flour and is ready to body-slam him to the earth like a pro wrestler.

"Look at Billy kicking Otto's ass," yells Gross.

"The biggest guy on their team," says another.

Then, just before the moment of truth, the camera pans away. A delighted smile crosses Martin's face: there's no proof one way or the other.

This is the Martin Method in all its glory: baseball as guerrilla warfare— the surprise attack, give no quarter, ask none.

Already, the so recently pathetic A's have pulled off a double steal and a triple steal. They are four for four on suicide squeeze bunts and three for four on steals of home (two of them in one game).

"I was here for the Last Hurrah," says Gross, "and after nobody was left, I was left.

"I never thought times could get that hard. When I first heard Billy was coming, I was like everybody else—excited, but very doubtful. Like everything else around here that might be good news, I figured it was just smoke.

"Billy's coming has changed everything. We were looking for somebody to teach us. He's so intense.

"The first day he told us, 'If you don't want to win, get your stuff and get out. If you don't give your best effort, you're gone. But if you bust your hump for me, I'll bust mine for you.' "

To the A's, objects of derision, Martin has been a leader in the wilderness of self-doubt about their own abilities.

"He told us, 'Anybody can steal home plate,' even though it's supposed to be the hardest thing in the game," recalls Gross. "And in the first game of spring training, Jim Essian, the slowest man on the team, stole home.

"We've been like a bunch of kids with new toys ever since," says Gross. "He's teaching every minute. He's moving guys half a step, he's calling pitches or putting on plays. He can predict whole sequences of pitches and plays.

"We're sayin', 'Yeah, all right, Billy. Do it.' All he asks is two and a half hours of concentration every day. That's not much. But you better give it to him. He goes nuts over mental errors. He'll look you right in the face and yell, 'Get your head in the game. This is a job.' "

Where others have seen dispirited bush leaguers with destroyed confidence, Martin has seen a nucleus of hope. That's all he needs.

"Because Martin is so unpopular outside his own players, and because he's had so many feuds and fights and grudges over the years," says Coleman, "not many people are willing to admit what a great manager he is.

"In my opinion, he's ahead of the league. No one can touch him."

Almost everywhere he has gone, Martin has looked for the same ingredients—defense up the middle to support his pitchers, speed, contact hitters who can execute the hit-and-run and players who can be prodded or terrified into playing fundamentally solid baseball.

He thinks he's found them all, in raw form, in Oakland. By moving Rob Picciolo to second base and putting disgruntled Mario Guerrero at short, Martin has two natural shortstops on defense and two slap-hitting speedsters on offense.

By putting Tony Armas in right field and Dwayne Murphy in left, flanking fleet Rickey Henderson in center, Martin has three natural center fielders in his excellent outfield.

Martin has, of course, brought in his cantankerous old reprobate of a one-eyed, hard-drinking pitching coach, Art Fowler, to teach the whole pitching staff how to doctor the ball illegally.

"Charlie Finley has treated us just super," says Fowler. "He hasn't come around yet."

Everything Martin has touched has turned to gold, so far. He had five decent starters—potentially the club's strength—and all have stayed healthy. One, perennial air-headed phenom Mike Norris (career record 12–25), has responded to Martin's shape-up-or-ship-out with a 5–3 record and an ERA of 0.36.

"It's easier to manage men who want to be managed," says Martin. "A manager is like a good cook in a kitchen mixing the ingredients in a salad, or a teacher who wants to see his class make A's.

"I taught in New York, but not too many listened. The players have bigger ears here," says Martin, who holds meetings before every game.

Oakland has welcomed Martin back with attendance that is up by 80,000 —more than double '79. "If you were a WPA baby and you had to fight for everything, you'd be cocky, too," Martin tells the adoring East Bay fans. "Growing up here, I was so poor I remember my mother standing in food lines. I vowed that would never happen again.

"I had one suit as a kid, and when my uncle died, they buried him in it. My biggest thrill in baseball was the suit and the suitcase they gave me when I signed."

That feisty urchin persona plays well here. Oakland has known the true Martin ever since, as a Yankee, he would come back here in winter and get thrown out of industrial basketball leagues for sucker-punching opponents.

"Billy will never change," says an old friend here. "He'll still be 'horning' [sucker-punching] people when he's eighty."

"You have to remember," says Coleman, "that most of Billy's boyhood friends are in San Quentin."

Martin, to be sure, is far from the place he wants to be—the manager's office in Yankee Stadium. There, he had a sumptuous office with a bathroom bigger than his entire bare office here. There, if he wanted a postgame drink, he had it in a mahogany-paneled lounge with murals of Babe Ruth and photos of Joe DiMaggio, Mickey Mantle and even a couple of himself. Here, the lounge looks like an elementary school cafeteria with cinder-block walls and folding chairs and folding tables.

At least in a baseball sense, this is the first tank-town stop on the way back to the big show from which he has been exiled.

On Martin's office wall is a poster that says, "There can be no rainbow without a cloud and a storm."

This is the edge of the continent, the Shangri-La-like paradise of bridges and sunsets where lost souls congregate, looking for one last chance. Two months ago Martin was among them. Now, Martin has a team in first place, a mother and two sisters in town, two biographies of him on the stands and a third one on the way. Even his new commercial gives him the last word.

"I take the Pepto-Bismol for my upset stomach, see," grins Martin. "Then I say, 'That's good, by George.' Then I realize what I've said and say, 'By George . . . ugghhh.'

"Then I hold my stomach like I'm really going to get sick.

"Kinda cute."

Martin is happy. His team has just won in the bottom of the ninth, helped by two bunts he has called. His team also has won the fight, and he has KO'd the cleanup man of the foes.

"Bobby Mattick [Toronto manager] says, 'Don't be so sure Martin wasn't trying to hurt Velez,' " Martin is told.

Suddenly, Billy the Kid flares up. "Ask that SOB how many fights he's ever been in.

"Bobby Mattick . . . Bobby Mattick," says Martin, thinking back over the years. "In 1945, Mattick came to see Berkeley play baseball. He signed a kid named Bill Van Hewitt.

"But he didn't sign me. He said, 'Kid, you'll never make the majors. You're too small.'

"So," says Martin, a grudge settled, another slight taken care of, "you see how smart Mattick is."

Billy Martin heads for the door.

He puts on his tinted sunglasses.

"I didn't really mean to hurt Otto," Martin says as he gets on the elevator, though no one asked.

"Now," he says, "I've gotta go fight a plate of spaghetti."

Into the Maelstrom

June 8, 1988—Is the depressing saga of Billy Martin getting more silly or more serious? The incidents that surround baseball's oldest juvenile delinquent become increasingly ludicrous with each of his incarnations as the Yankees' manager. But does the farce of Martin's movable fiasco allow us the freedom to laugh?

Or does the sorrow and rage deep inside this man stop us with its darkness?

The Cross Keys Contretemps of 1986, when Martin followed Ed Whitson from bar to hotel room to parking lot in Baltimore, screaming for a rematch, until the huge pitcher broke Martin's arm, was somber enough.

Now that Martin has given new meaning to the phrase "thrown out of a bar on his ear," we can only hold our breath awaiting his next disaster. Will he get heaved out the side door of a topless bar in the A.M. by bouncers after he's started a fight by punching a patron in a men's room? Will he walk into the lobby of the team hotel at 3 A.M. looking like Banquo's ghost, covered with forty stitches' worth of his own blood?

Oh, you say that's already happened? Even now, it's hard to believe.

Just as it is hard to believe that, a couple of weeks later, Martin picked up two handfuls of dirt and threw them on a young umpire. So soon, Billy? As you go down in the maelstrom, they say the spin gets tighter and tighter.

At every hour we await dispatches on the next installment of this cheap soap. Richie Phillips, lawyer for the umpires union, has already closed out the June balloting for yahoo of the month by bragging that his American League umps will dispense with due process, probable cause, freedom of speech and, who knows, perhaps search and seizure, too, by ejecting Martin instantly on any pretext to retaliate for his sandbox stunt a week ago.

"For Martin to stay in the game, he's going to have to behave like an altar boy," said Phillips after a conference call with all seven AL crew chiefs. "He's going to have to fold his hands, shut his mouth and that's it. Otherwise, he's going to be ejected, ejected, ejected. Every time for the next couple of weeks that he comes out of the dugout, he'll be ejected. Then we'll review the situation."

When all Martin had to do to gain universal sympathy was clam up, naturally he decided to pop off. Pundits were lined up around the block to say that Phillips's hot air was arrogant and asinine. But Billy had to go them one better. After a full day of "no comment," Martin said he'd sue the umps for something or other and that he'd be his normal obnoxious self on the field whenever it suited him.

To what depths can Martin drag this latest best-out-of-ninety-nine-falls bout with adult authority? In retrospect, punching a marshmallow salesman or trying to loosen Reggie Jackson's dentures in the dugout seems like the stuff of Martin's innocent youth. We long for the days when Martin would sucker-punch one of his own pitchers in a bar or deck an elderly club official. Then, he was Billy the Kid, wild and mean, devious and smart, but possessed of tough street strength.

Now, the venues for his disgraces get seedier, his opponents seem even less worthy and, these days, it is usually Martin who visits the hospital. The cowards who once feared him now line up to take a shot at a scrawny sixty-year-old who goes everywhere with a steamship trunk full of troubles strapped to his back. Even Martin's old bodyguard-coaches look exhausted.

All the enmity that Martin has fairly earned—and no man in baseball since Leo Durocher can match him for soul-deep enemies—is now returning on the waters to swamp him when he can least defend himself. Even the umps, baseball's least enfranchised entity, think they can gang up on him.

Someday, somewhere, something's going to happen to Martin, or he's going to do something to somebody that's not funny. Bet on Billy as victim.

It's his pattern. The worst he ever seems to dish out is a schoolyard punch in the mouth. In return, he receives a kind of public pain and humiliation that etches itself in his face with each new shame. Like Yankees owner George Steinbrenner, Martin seems headed somewhere and we want to be far away when he arrives.

Martin has reached a point where even his managing skills—and he's very good, in a narrow short-term sense—can't protect him. His current Yankees couldn't play better in their dreams, and may play worse in reality as the summer wears on and the pitching wears out. Yet Martin is bunkered, even in his own dugout.

Commissioner Peter Ueberroth, like a third-grade teacher at recess, yesterday ordered both Martin and the umpires to "stop it and stop it now." Or he will make them all write on the blackboard. In the past, grade school discipline and lectures from Principal George haven't altered Martin's behavior a whit. He acts cherubic until he figures out how to put his next cherry bomb in a mailbox.

Nothing wears worse than a bad-boy act with age. For years, when Billy the Kid punched a pitcher or took on a guy in a strip joint, his foe went down in a heap. Now, he's Billy the Old Coot and they laugh at him and let the bouncers do their job. Once, when Martin kicked dirt on an ump, that was the end of that. Now, he's told to sit in his own dugout, like the brat in class, with his lips buttoned.

It would all be funny and fitting, and extremely easy to ignore, if we could just be sure that the remaining chapters of Martin's story would be equally insignificant and amusing.

Christmas Night

December 31, 1989—Let's go back seven years to a time when Billy Martin was reigning manager of the year. Flying high in Oakland. Bad boy returns home to glory. Come see Billyball. One day Billy got angry about something —a defeat, a contract. Who knows, who remembers? With Billy, it was always a blur.

Anyway, this particular time he locked the door behind him and went ten rounds with his office. Walls. Furniture. Pictures. Billy hit 'em with both hands.

The office won.

Oh, sure, Billy smashed everything to flinders. He showed that office. But when he came out, his hands were bleeding. Fingers were broken.

The next day, his hands were bandaged and several fingers splinted. Sheepishly, he explained the incident to reporters. As usual, he made up the story as he went along. Some truth, some not. Some of the stuff, he probably couldn't tell the difference. If he'd known why he did it, then he wouldn't have been Billy Martin, would he?

Then a journeyman player named Dave McKay stuck his head into Martin's office.

"Excuse me, skip," said McKay seriously. "Want to go bowling tonight?"

Martin laughed until he almost cried.

That was Billy Martin. One day, he would punch the walls. Or spit into the wind. Or jump on Superman's cape. Or kick dirt on an umpire. Or punch a marshmallow salesman. Or call his owner a convicted liar. Or try to strangle Reggie Jackson in the dugout on national TV. Or get his arm broken by one of his pitchers. Or get thrown out of a strip joint on his ear. Or invent some self-justifying tale so improbable he could barely tell it with a straight face.

Then, the next day—or, sometimes, when the pain was too great, the next year—he would tell some bitter joke about the episode. He might even make a national TV commercial in which he looked into the camera with disbelief and said, "I didn't punch that dogie." Sometimes even he couldn't believe the crazy, self-destructive things he did.

We're not talking here about the full range of Martin's misbehaviors. He actually was proud of many of his "vices." To do anything to win was within his code of honor. So cheating or lying or bench jockeying were next to godliness in his book. Having too much to drink, womanizing, getting in fights and backstabbing his enemies were also part and parcel of being a little tough-guy ballplayer in his era. Real Yankees, like Joe DiMaggio, Mickey Mantle or Whitey Ford, never would hold that against a regular guy from the wrong side of the tracks. Billy knew he had the morals of an alley cat.

What spooked him was fighting furniture, getting himself fired, ruining the thing he loved to do and did extremely well: manage a baseball team.

There's a scene in *The Hustler*—a Billy kind of movie—in which Fast Eddie Felson, the tough kid from Oakland, tries to drown his sorrows and work out his self-loathing by hustling the worst low-life pool sharks in a skid-row dive. After he wins their money, and mocks them by showing just how great he is, they break his thumbs.

"Why'd I do it, Sarah?" pleads Fast Eddie, holding up his damaged hands. "I could have beat 'em and they'd never have known it. But I just had to show 'em."

In the parlance of *The Hustler,* Fast Eddie was a "loser" as long as he gave himself excuses for never reaching his goals either in pool or in life. In *The Hustler,* Fast Eddie is played by Paul Newman. So, of course, he gets wise to himself and becomes some kind of "winner." Billy the Kid never did. He just kept going back to Ames to lose to Minnesota Fats time after time. Except Billy kept going back to Yankee Stadium to lose to New York Fats.

Eventually, Martin's notorious mean streak got worse. His charm and managerial intelligence showed through less often. And his plunges into the demimonde became more exotic.

On Christmas night, he and his accident-waiting-to-happen had their rendezvous. He lived recklessly, excessively, so it's not surprising that he died in the passenger seat of a pickup truck driven by a friend who was charged with driving while intoxicated. For some, sixty-one is young. For Martin it was very old.

For many years, until he hooked up with George Steinbrenner, Martin could fairly have been described as fiery, combative and self-destructive. With the years, with the firings, with the humiliations, that changed. He was no longer fiery. He was a man on fire. He was not combative. Rather, he was a man searching for a fight. He wasn't self-destructive. He was almost universally destructive. It's just that, sooner or later, he got his, too.

By the end, Martin the man—the walking psychodrama—riveted our attention, much as we tried to turn our eyes away. With time, however, perhaps we will be able to take a slightly longer view and also remember Martin the player, the manager, the teacher. If he'd only known himself half as well as he knew his game, he might have been the best.

Hard Time in Chino

CHINO, California, January 15, 1979—

Bennie Daniels, who did five years on the mound for the Washington Senators, is serving a far tougher stretch—three years in prison for misappropriating $100,000 in public funds.

Daniels's story is far more complicated than that, and more sympathetic to him. Some might call him an articulate combination of ghetto Robin Hood and charming, if sticky-fingered, Fagin.

Few things are harder to find in prison, it is said, than a guilty man. Daniels is rarer: an inmate who says, "I did it. I was wrong. But I'm not ashamed."

At worst, he was a man trusted with authority—as a training program coordinator for a Los Angeles hospital—who was tempted by an open till.

At best, he was an inexperienced welfare bureaucrat who could not resist giving job opportunities to the neediest youngsters, even if it meant breaking rules.

"Bennie Daniels is proof that a real nice guy can steal a whole lot of money," said Elvira Mitchell, the deputy district attorney who prosecuted him.

"People in L.A. . . . politicians, athletes, poor people he helped . . . they praise him like the next messiah.

"Even I respect him. Bennie worked out one of the best swindles I've ever seen. If I could just show you the beauty of the scam . . . we still don't know where a cent of the money is."

Daniels always had style beyond his modest ability. In a career swamped with defeat (45–76), he saved his best performances for life's few spotlight hours.

Symbolically, his first game (for Pittsburgh) was the last game in Brooklyn's Ebbets Field. He started the last game in Griffith Stadium and the first in D.C. (now RFK) Stadium.

On John Kennedy's only opening day, Daniels was the complete-game winner. He caught Lyndon Johnson's first pitch one year, then tossed his only near-no-hitter in another LBJ inaugural.

Anyone fascinated by the blend of qualities in this curious man has an easy research project. As the warden says: "Come any day. Bennie isn't going anywhere."

The California Institute for Men lies on ground as flat, gray and drab as any Kansas prairie. Somebody found the one spot in Southern California suitable for a jail.

The long, straight road to the prison gate might be the entrance to some dilapidated, gone-to-seed estate, except that the mood of hueless depression comes from antiseptic cleanliness, not decay.

"No inmates beyond this point," says the sign.

Almost anyone passing through the gates of Chino is assumed to be a prisoner, a prisoner's wife or child or a prisoner's lawyer. In any of those cases, you get no smiles.

"Bennie Daniels?" says the prison guard. "Yeah, he's the guy that don't say nothin'. Big-league ballplayer, huh? Never said so.

"He's been here six months in the same dorm with 'bout a hundred stone nuts. But he's different . . . keeps away from the low riders. The day after he's gone, it'll be like he was never here."

That's how No. B95778 wants it. Daniels stays camouflaged, his character and identity under wraps.

The 6-foot-1, 200-pound prisoner with the shaved head, ever-present sunglasses, the pulled-down wool stocking cap and the Army fatigue jacket could be a mass murderer or a college professor. Mystique plus silence equal safety.

"In one sense, you're probably safer in here than out on the streets," says the forty-six-year-old Daniels. "That's because the unwritten rules among the prisoners are absolute.

"On the other hand, I've never felt pressure like there is in here. It's in the air. You could get killed . . . I mean killed dead . . . for picking up the wrong man's pack of cigarettes."

When Daniels smiles and talks the King's English, he is the man that former Senator roommate Chuck Hinton remembers as "the kindest, most helpful, best-liked, most down-to-earth guy on those teams."

But when Daniels glares, that bald dome makes him look exactly like movie villain Baron Samedi who tried to bury James Bond in a coffin full of rattlesnakes.

In a joint where the dorm radio blares, "I got a tombstone head and a graveyard mind . . . just twenty-two and I don't mind dyin'," it is a useful range of personas.

Daniels had been inside Chino's fences many times before they were closed behind him. Prisons were part of Daniels's job as a counselor with CETA, the Comprehensive Employment and Training Act.

"I'd come here to see young guys and tell them about job programs after they were released," says Daniels. "Now I see some of them in here. And some visit me.

"You have to experience prison life to really appreciate everything you had. Even in minimum security, where you're not locked down, except at night, you just feel so wasted. There's nothing to accomplish. Time slows down.

"About all prison's good for is thinking. You lay there in the night and hear everything. All the feelings come out . . . who hates who.

"Being in jail puts everybody on the same level, and everybody's under that invisible, internal pressure. You hear the braggers, the liars, the ones who are proud of what they did . . . and you hear a lot about what they're gonna do when they get out, too."

Inevitably, Daniels's mind drifts back to the past as he recalls, almost without prodding, the up-and-down progression that led him from the majors to the embarrassment of explaining how he ended up in prison.

"My days with the Senators were my highlight," says Daniels, who pitched for the Pittsburgh Pirates for four seasons. "I've still got all my baseball cards, the photos, the old record books.

"I think I was the first black to pitch an opening-day game—in 1962 for

John Kennedy. I beat Detroit, 5–2. You bet I have the game ball. I could probably remember every out.

"But, you know, I lost my next nine games. Every time I turned around, I was pitching against Whitey Ford. And those Washington teams. We didn't lack much—only an offense and a defense."

Daniels's fifteen pro seasons seem one long, hard rise to that opening-day triumph, followed by an equally arduous decline through four years of bone-chip elbow misery.

In 1961, his first year in Washington, Daniels proved for one clean 212-inning season that he was a bona fide pro—going 12–11 with the fifteenth-best ERA in the league (3.44). "That got me on all the year-end lists of the leaders."

Otherwise, the majors were a 33–65 struggle for Daniels. "He was a big, gutty guy, always pitching in pain, getting no support and losing," says Hinton. "He was an inspiration to me, a big brother. He made no bones, no excuses when he lost. Just took his lumps. He refused to knock a hitter down—too gentle.

"There wasn't a guy in the league that didn't like him. A real athlete. He hit a homer in Yankee Stadium to deep right-center field. He even pinch-hit for us and played the outfield once.

"He looked real good in clothes . . . never extravagant, just stylish. But once he got those bone chips in a freak auto accident, they just took him down. Nobody ever thought of operating on a pitcher's elbow back then."

Soon, Daniels's hair was falling out from worry. "I was worried about getting my five years in for the pension," says Daniels. Finally, in a club-house ceremony in '65, the Senators gave him his first shaved head.

Opening days became Daniels's perverse high point of the season. In 1963 he caught one of the two "first balls" thrown out by Lyndon Johnson.

"Man, he was knockin' people over to get it," laughed Hinton. "He was a nut when it came to souvenirs. I told him, 'Why go to spring training for six weeks, then get spiked fighting for a ball? The Man'll sign a ball for you if you want it that bad.'

"Bennie may be the only guy who has the game ball from every one of his victories, and some in the minors, too."

Victories became harder to get, and the Nats cut his $26,000 salary by the maximum 20 percent every season. Daniels won again on opening day in '65, keeping a no-hitter into the eighth inning. But by the end of the year, the Senators told Daniels that his '66 contract would be assigned to Hawaii in the minors at $9,000 a year.

Daniels was one of that wave of multisport black athletes who signed

baseball contracts in the early '50s, following Jackie Robinson's example.
And he was one of that second black baseball generation that found the
Game had no job openings when their careers ended in the '60s. The visible
pioneers—Robinson, Monte Irvin—were looked after. But the rank and file
that followed, fighting its way through the quota system, retired into a world
of sink-or-swim.

Daniels did a bit of anything to "keep the wife and two kids going . . .
gotta eat, man." Department of Motor Vehicles, aircraft tool estimator, insurance salesman. Daniels was at sea, "trying to catch on to something while
my game was still warm."

"What could a black man do then without a college degree?" asks Daniels.
"I don't mean sweep that broom. I mean start over at a decent job. Man,
they take that candy away from you all at once."

Daniels came home to L.A. and got lucky—the kind of luck that comes
from hard work. Two state jobs kept him happy—one as a baseball instruc-
tor traveling the state giving clinics to youth group coaches.

"That was fantastic," says Daniels. "I was a good teacher." He was . . .
until the state funding ran out.

Daniels also worked his way up at Martin Luther King Jr. Hospital, starting as traffic hazard inspector, then community liaison man and finally
CETA coordinator for the hospital.

That brings us to the edge of felony and the end of certainty.

"I went to baseball meetings in L.A. three years ago and spent two days
with Bennie," says Hinton, now Howard University baseball coach. "I told
him, 'Man, don't you know you can go to jail behind some of the things
you're doing? Are you aware of the severity of what you're into?'

"But Bennie'd just say, 'Aw, Chas, you don't know anything about it.'"

The Internal Revenue Service, the California district attorney's office and
a grand jury were, however, going to learn a great deal about it.

The beauty of Daniels's gimmick was in its outward simplicity, which
covered a Gordian knot of motivation, the core of which probably will never
be untied.

When Daniels had a CETA trainee move on to another job, Daniels never
took his name off his employment rolls. Daniels then continued to fill out
the trainee's time card and forged his signature.

"That is what we charged him with and he pleaded nolo contendere," said
deputy district attorney Mitchell. "We have handwriting experts to prove it."

Daniels claims that when he had a needy, but unqualified, youngster
whom he wanted to give a job, he would pay the youth with the previous

trainee's ongoing paychecks. The prosecutors begged Daniels to give them the names of all those to whom he was benefactor.

"We never got a single name that we could check out," said Mitchell.

"I didn't want to drag other people down with me," Daniels maintains. "I figured I was going to jail anyway. Why mess up the kids, too?"

Daniels paints his troubles with a firm but rather vague brush. When larceny and charity are mixed—as Daniels claims—it makes for difficult distinctions.

"If you do something that's wrong, like I did, you pay for it. You don't fight the system," says Daniels.

"I've been under pressure for several years. I'd think: When are these [police] people going to knock on my door? It was like an ax over my head . . . the agony of sitting and waiting . . . most guys would have jumped the country.

"Anything over two hundred dollars is a felony, so once you get started, you couldn't stop.

"I did too much, I know. Records weren't up to date. I saw Alvin Jackson [onetime Pirate teammate, now Boston pitching coach] a year ago and told him, 'I won't see you next year. I'll probably be in jail.'

"I brought kids into the program illegally, under false pretenses, but you'd see some of them benefit themselves, and so you'd want to help another."

Is Daniels the inner-city nobleman his lawyer paints him to be? "That isn't quite right," says Daniels. "I did things that were wrong."

California, after months of investigation, claimed Daniels did a great deal wrong and richly deserved his present three-year, absolutely-no-cut contract at Chino. "Bennie may be the all-time shucker-and-jiver," said prosecutor Mitchell. "If he hadn't run a good thing into the ground and caught the attention of IRS, we'd never have stopped him."

The IRS tip-off came when the trainees in Daniels's program, the ones who had moved on out of CETA, suddenly noticed they were being taxed for income they hadn't received.

"Daniels's lawyer says he was taking from the rich and giving to the poor," Mitchell noted. "Well, he was taking a lot from the government, and some from the poor, too—in the form of taxes on paychecks they never saw.

"We have no proof, no indication whatever, of what Daniels did with the money. If he kept it, he sure did it with style. His outward standard of living [modest] has changed little in ten years.

"We don't even know how long this has been going on, because the statute of limitations prevents us from going back more than three years. Daniels was over $100,000 in just that time.

"Bennie has either helped a lot of kids—all of whom are keeping quiet now—or there is an extremely big mason jar buried somewhere in California."

Ironically, those same overtaxed individuals were among those who "had us knee deep in testimonials saying that Daniels had helped them enormously," Mitchell allowed. We did an in-depth study of Mr. Daniels and, frankly, we couldn't figure out what to do with him.

"Most people in this sort of situation are desperate to make restitution once they're caught. One woman embezzler sold her house to make good. Not Bennie.

"I told him, 'Pay it back or go to jail.'

"What money?" answered Daniels. "I'm just thankful my baseball pension kicked in when I was forty-five. I decided to start taking it now, because I need it."

California authorities felt intense outside pressure not to jail Daniels. "You wouldn't believe the letters," said Mitchell.

"Don't send him to jail," pleaded Daniels's lawyer, Alex Goldberg. "Let him work with kids."

"Kids?" answered Mitchell indignantly. "I think they've already got a rough idea of what he can do.

"One of our biggest problems in criminal justice is that kids grow up thinking crooks are clever and cops are dumb for being honest. The sting operations in Washington were among the few exceptions.

"Well, I just said, 'Not this year, folks. Bennie either comes up with the cash or he goes to jail.'

"If he'd gone free, we'd have been the laughingstock of the state. The tragedy of this, even now, is that Daniels is probably a hero in his own community. He's doing his time, beating the system and coming out ahead."

There are definitely limits to Daniels's remorse. "There are plenty of people doing this," he said. "I could have been an example. I just happened to get caught. The low man always gets the beef.

"Maybe everything that you've gotten away with in life catches up with you. Anyway, I thought I was right at the time, even though I also knew I was wrong."

Daniels grows tired of all the complexity, the modification of every motive. "Look, I haven't done anything that I'm ashamed of," he says. "Nobody I know is going to hold it against me. Who hasn't been in jail? Half the community where I live has been up here [at Chino] at one time or another. And most of the rest have some skeleton in their closet that could put them here.

"I've done plenty of good, and I haven't done anything that keeps me from looking in the mirror."

As far as Daniels is concerned, the outside world can just forget that pious, elegiac "wasted life" tone of voice. He's lived on the street too long to see himself as tragic; he just sees himself as caught.

Daniels thinks he can do three years—only twenty months if he is paroled in April '80—standing on his bald head. When he gets out, he is convinced he'll rebound without great difficulty.

His wife of twenty-three years, Sue, and his two grown children have stood by him, visiting him each weekend. "That's what really keeps your head together." He has a mailing list of friends to correspond with that is longer than his pitching arm. And he recently won the prison tennis tournament.

When sports events come on the west dorm TV, Daniels never says, "I pitched a shutout in that park."

"I don't even let 'em know," Daniels says. "We got a lot of Howard Cosells in here. Guys who never played anything, and think they know everything about sports."

The thought of the future does not scare him. "After what my wife and I have been through in the minors, then after I quit baseball, we're used to starting over fresh," he says. "This time won't be the worst.

"I know a lot of guys my age—John Roseboro, Tommy Davis, Leon Wagner . . . I won't name names—who are biting dust these days. The crybaby ballplayers now are getting all the phenomenal salaries. Well, let 'em. I guess my generation proved that just being a ballplayer didn't necessarily set you up for much."

A guard wanders past and teases Daniels, calling him "our white-collar offender . . . you must be from Orange County."

"No, no, I'm blue-collar . . . strictly a blue-collar crook," laughs Daniels, pointing to his blue work shirt with his prison number on the front.

"They seem to like me here," says Daniels. "You know, they had me working here as an accountant. I hadn't been in a month when they had me back pushing around pieces of paper with sums of money written on 'em."

Daniels smiles wearily, whimsically. "Do you think they knew who I was?"

Satchel Paige:
Clean Getaway

June 9, 1982—Satchel Paige finally looked back yesterday and death overtook him.

But not in time.

For once, death, and the death-in-life of prejudice, could claim nothing but the skeleton of an old man. Satchel Paige got away free. Thus ended one of baseball's most heroic and tragic lives.

Heroic, because Paige, by endurance and skill, outlasted injustice. Although the majors didn't find room for him until 1948, when he was at least forty-two, Paige left a legend so large that no page of statistics could significantly alter his mark.

"I did not see Walter Johnson, but Leroy was the best I ever saw," said Bill Veeck yesterday. "If his career had run its full course in the major leagues, Paige would have held every record there was.

"He had the best fastball, the best control and the most knowledge of pitching of anyone. Even in his late forties, he warmed up by putting a package of cigarettes on the outside corner of the plate. That was his target," said Veeck, Paige's boss during his five big-league seasons.

"Paige threw overhand, sidearm, underarm and crossfire. All his pitches moved and tailed. He had a great change-up as well as his hesitation pitch and eephus [blooper] pitch. He had a presence on the field that was comparable to no one but Babe Ruth.

"In five years, I believe Ted Williams had one hit off him and Joe DiMaggio two," recalled Veeck. ". . . You could tell that those were the only two hitters he looked on as his equals."

The sadness of Paige's baseball life has little to do with him directly. After all, by living an ill-charted, almost mythical life full of anecdote and folk wisdom, Paige actually may have increased the durability and weight of his chapter in the sport's tome.

The Paige tragedy is that, by his excellence, he proved that fifty years' worth of black-league players had been wronged more severely than white America ever suspected.

On the other hand, Paige's life, seen only as an indefatigable, wise and funny personal odyssey, is a cheerful tale.

"Leroy had tremendous self-confidence, but he was not a braggart. He took enormous pride in performance. But he had his own priorities. Like fishing. Once, in St. Louis with the Browns, he arrived at the park in the seventh inning carrying a huge channel catfish, about eighty pounds," Veeck recalled. "He said, 'Burrhead, isn't this more important than the first six innings of a game?' "

Veeck, known for his broad view, agreed. "Leroy missed a few planes, but he got to the game by the time you really needed him. Once, in Washington at Griffith Stadium, he came in late, got in to pitch in the seventh inning, then finally won the game with a hit in the seventeenth," said Veeck. "My wife and I waited and waited for him afterward because we were supposed to go out for clams. Finally, I found him up in the clubhouse with everybody around him enthralled. He was giving a dissertation on hitting. . . .

"Paige was a natural showman, like the way he ambled into a ball game from the bullpen—this old gentleman, not one to rush into difficulties. But that showmanship was not without malice aforethought. Leroy was unlettered, but not unlearned. He could call on a great fund of general knowledge.

"All those wise sayings he's credited with, like 'the social rumble ain't restful' and 'if your stomach disputes you, lie down and pacify it with cool thoughts,' well, I'd say most of them are actually true," said Veeck.

"Satchel never liked to have anybody beat him at anything," recalled Cool

Papa Bell yesterday. "I was the one who taught him how to control his curveball and throw a knuckleball. A week after I'd showed him the knuckler, he called me over and said, 'Now you throw it.' People watchin' us saw he was throwin' it better than I was, so they said, 'See how Satchel's teaching Cool Papa the knuckleball.' "

Paige met considerable resistance in 1948. The publisher of *The Sporting News* "was always deriding us for signing Paige, saying it made a farce of the game," said Veeck. "Every time he won, I'd send [the publisher] a wire: 'Winning pitcher, Paige.'

"Also, the umpires weren't going to give this old black legend any of the best of it. He threw to a plate that was shorter and narrower than anybody else's. But he still fooled 'em."

In the end, Paige disarmed those who thought they hated him. "He never forced himself on anyone," said Veeck. "He'd sit alone at one end of the Pullman car. But in ten minutes the whole [Indians] team would be gathered around him."

As a St. Louis Brown, Paige had one intractable enemy—Louisiana-born catcher Clint Courtney, who wouldn't even warm up Paige, much less catch him in a game. "Then one day," Veeck related, "I noticed Clint was warming him up. The next week, in Detroit, I walked into a bar called the Flame. There were Leroy and Clint having dinner together.

"Courtney told me, 'My pap's comin' up tomorrow from Lou'siana and he's gonna be mighty mad when he hears about us being friends. But Satch and me figure we can whup him together.' "

Earthquake
at the World Series

5:04 P.M. PDT

SAN FRANCISCO, October 18, 1989—

For perhaps fifteen seconds an entire stadium full of baseball fans awaiting Game 3 of the World Series looked at each other and gazed in stunned amazement at the swaying stadium around them. They felt the concrete stands under them shaking, rumbling, rocking with a nauseating sideways movement, and they waited—holding their breath to see if Candlestick Park would collapse.

The lucky ones didn't know exactly what was happening. The unlucky ones who had felt large earthquakes before not only knew what was happening but knew that this was a big one.

You didn't have to ask yourself, "Am I moving?" You knew you were. In the upper deck, suddenly very high above the ground, your seat—and the entire park—swayed several inches, perhaps a foot, back and forth. Your feet shook with the rumbling.

It was not like a crowd of 62,000 screaming or doing the wave. It was not like the craziest crowd you ever felt. It was much, much more than that.

The shake started small, then built, taking its time, letting you see its work.

High above Candlestick Park, where the San Francisco Giants and Oakland Athletics were waiting to play, stood nine enormous orange light towers. No wind ever made them bend the way they bent on Tuesday at 5:04 P.M.

This was either Pacific Daylight Time or eternity time, depending on how you felt during those seconds. Judging by the thousands of blank, frightened faces, eternity was on a lot of minds.

Some ushers threw up their arms, pleading by their gestures for people not to panic, not to run for the down ramps. Almost nobody moved.

Then, suddenly, more quickly than the shake had come, it disappeared. In a heartbeat—or, by now, perhaps two heartbeats, since most chests were working double-time—Candlestick Park was its benign orange-and-black self.

Instantly, as quickly as any crowd can react to a home run, the packed park cheered. It was more than the nervous applause that people give throughout the world when a pilot lands a commercial airliner in rough weather. It was an expression of profound relief. In the very instant that the full possibility of tragedy dawned on this throng, the reality of safety arrived.

Relative safety, at least. For ten minutes, the crowd talked at such volume you'd have thought the Giants had the bases loaded, Will Clark at the plate and Tony LaRussa striding to the mound to talk.

Anybody who thinks pro athletes are dumb should have seen how fast the A's and Giants got out of their clubhouses and dugouts—where they had been less than a half hour before game time—and onto the solid earth of the stadium's infield. Within minutes, as police ringed the field to keep the crowd from pouring out of the stands, the players were waving their relatives and friends out on the grass to join them. Amazingly, the crowd did not dispute this double standard.

Because most of the power in Candlestick Park was knocked out, and because there was no visible damage to the stadium, the mood of the crowd quickly became excited, a bit giddy and, in some cases, almost festive.

"We just hope it shakes up the A's a little bit," said Wendy Lefferts, wife of Giants pitcher Craig Lefferts. "The Giants can handle it."

"We get earthquakes about every six months in San Diego," said Lefferts's uncle, George. "But my fanny came right out of the chair with this one, and I weigh 285 pounds.

"Can you believe San Francisco, where 50,000 people cheer for an earthquake? I love this town. Nobody panicked."

Nobody believes the worst of earthquakes here until one becomes incontrovertible fact. Three years ago, a tsunami—a kind of tidal wave with crests twenty feet high—was expected to hit here. More than 3,000 people showed up on a cliff overlooking the ocean to see it.

As word of the quake's severity reached the night's crowd by portable radio, the collective mood darkened. Two more minor, barely perceptible aftershocks sent shivers through those in the stadium. News of the partial collapse of the San Francisco–Oakland Bay Bridge, of power failures, of fires, reached the crowd gradually. Not everybody living on the San Andreas fault line here had been as lucky as the fans at what would have been the third game of the eighty-sixth World Series.

Still, when the game was postponed—thirty-seven minutes after the big shake—no one cheered and some booed.

The hero at the World Series this night was much-maligned Candlestick Park, which was deemed structurally unsound five years ago and earthquake-proofed since then.

The old park, built to sway and swing, with rollers embedded deep in its structure, passed its most severe test on a night when hospitals collapsed, houses crumbled, freeways fell and so did part of the Bay Bridge.

With more than 60,000 people in its arms, the 'Stick took a standing 7.0 count, almost, and wouldn't fall.

The Hour of Lead

October 22, 1989—

> This is the Hour of Lead—
> Remembered, if outlived,
> As Freezing persons, recollect the Snow—
> First—Chill—then Stupor—then the letting go—

Emily Dickinson is the poet for hours like this. On a bright summer day, she can seem morbid. On a gray, drizzling October afternoon, with a fresh memory of disaster in the air, she seems to speak directly to us.

"After great pain, a formal feeling comes," she wrote.

Perhaps it is also true that after great pain, we need to find a formal, healing place to reorder our feelings.

Right now baseball looks trivial, inappropriate and, potentially, even insulting to the families of the victims of the Loma Prieta earthquake.

In a couple of days, maybe it won't. After the emotional torment of facing great suffering and huge, often unanswerable questions, we often feel a need for ritual and for manageable meanings.

Maybe by this coming week the World Series, even if it doesn't feel like the World Series, can provide some of that.

Lots of people like baseball because, while it may be lifelike at times, it is definitely not life. When the sport works best, maybe it's life ameliorated, life made less unfair, less capricious, less dangerous, less frightening. If nothing else, all sports (and especially baseball) are concerned with coherence, symmetry, a sense of completeness. We surround baseball with statistics for just this reason—not to understand it so much as to allow ourselves to imagine we understand it. That's comforting.

An earthquake is life at its most out-of-control, unmanageable, terrifying. Baseball is structure, skill, reward and innocent pleasure. An earthquake is chaos. Baseball is one of those places in our lives where we create order, even if it is artificial, childlike order.

One of the reasons that an earthquake at the World Series is so symbolically disturbing is that it illustrates again how, even when we create a place for pleasure and modest meaning—a house, a garden, a family, a school, a park—it can be destroyed suddenly. We are also, perhaps, insulted that things that give us such enjoyment and peace can be made to seem so pathetically trivial.

Saving lives, burying the dead, grieving for the lost, restoring the basic functions of a community are far more urgent and, in that sense, more important right now, than resuming the World Series. But playing baseball again, and going to the symphony or the theater, are not unimportant in their place and time. Even if it requires a stiff jaw to begin those activities again in an atmosphere that feels suddenly alien.

"Doom is the House without the Door," wrote Dickinson. Baseball is one of our many doors out of the house of grief. For San Francisco and Oakland, using that door may be especially important. In a few days those communities may be glad to have a way to shake their fists at nature. Our lives may not be as dramatic as our deaths, but we can still try to live well as the best, and only available, revenge.

People in baseball, like most people everywhere, are showing their best sides in the worst times. Commissioner Fay Vincent, a gentle man severely injured in his college days, is acutely familiar with pain and has a sense of baseball's limited but valuable place in a time of tragedy. He knows that the Bay Area deserves and wants what remains of the World Series—in due time—even if it only feels like a wounded semi-Series.

We grow accustomed to the Dark
When Light is put away . . .

A Moment—We uncertain step
For newness of the night—
Then—fit our Vision to the Dark—
And meet the Road—erect . . .

The Bravest—grope a little—
And sometimes hit a Tree
Directly in the Forehead—
But as they learn to see—

Either the Darkness alters—
Or something in the sight
Adjusts itself to Midnight—
And Life steps almost straight.

This has been baseball's saddest season since 1919. To varying degrees, we have had to adjust to different kinds of darkness throughout this year.

After the lifetime suspension of Pete Rose, we had to think about the damage caused by enormous self-deception and self-indulgence.

After the death of Commissioner A. Bartlett Giamatti, we had to sort out —and some of us haven't done it yet—how we felt about everything from the cigarettes he smoked to the scoundrel who caused him so much aggravation.

When Donnie Moore committed suicide, we questioned the huge importance that we place on the results of our games, rather than the playing of them. At the end of *Bang the Drum Slowly,* Henry Wiggins says, "From here in, I rag nobody." Some of us hope we can show similar restraint in discussing what we mean in sports by the word "choke."

When Dave Dravecky broke his arm while making a comeback from cancer, then broke it again during the Giants' pennant celebration—well, that one's still got baseball people spinning.

In a way, this year has been so grim for baseball that it is difficult to believe that next spring perhaps will bring a labor strike. So much exposure to pain has to teach something, doesn't it?

The work of Jim Abbott, Commissioner Vincent and the Baltimore Orioles, among others, has made 1989 less impossible to digest. Yet a dignified, determined conclusion to the World Series might help even more. Play it. Play hard. Cheer if you can. This Series will never again step entirely straight. And it should not. However, in its proper place—which is in the Bay Area—and in its proper time—which is when the community says it's ready—this World Series can serve a purpose. If only by offering an example of how to meet the road erect.

Angels in Hell

Capt. of the Pequod

ANAHEIM, California, October 7, 1982—

For thirty-eight years, man and boy—and now as silver eminence—Gene Mauch has played, managed and loved the game for the game itself.

Whether he was taking an outfielder and making him a fifth infielder, or issuing an intentional walk with first base occupied, or putting on the suicide squeeze with his cleanup hitter, Mauch's passion for baseball has been primed by a more elevated concept than victory.

Oh, he's burned to win; he's broken clubhouse furniture and thrown more trays of cold cuts against the locker-room wall than any other manager of his era. But above all, Mauch always has meditated upon the game, believed it was worthy of being the consuming passion of a first-rate mind. To him, baseball is the head game.

As a result, Mauch is the only manager in major-league baseball who always pauses to think before he speaks. You can almost see his brain editing words down to their clipped, cryptic nub. Every sentence must be part of the canon.

"That doesn't fit in with my ideal idea of the game," says Mauch when a notion is proposed that strikes him wrong. "I'm not comfortable with that."

For twenty-two years, this approach has unsettled other baseball men. Mauch's apparent arrogance, combined with his perplexing record of turning out fourth-place teams, has made him the most mysterious, most argued-about manager in the game.

Strange, almost perverse, how one week can change the perception of a man's lifelong odyssey. Only seven days ago, Mauch was still the smartest manager who'd never won anything.

Now, his California Angels have clinched the American League West title and, after winning the first two games of their playoff with Milwaukee, could be only hours away from a pennant, too. And in another week or so, given the inauspicious nature of the National League's division winners, the Angels also could be world champions.

So in less time than it took Mauch's 1964 Phillies to lose ten games in a row and complete the worst squandering of a pennant on record, Mauch may win a division and pennant and be on his way to a Series victory.

It's always bothered Mauch that he has had to share the opprobrium attendant on his teams' persistent failures—20 finishes of fourth place or lower in 22 seasons. Mauch knew that, in baseball parlance, he'd usually finished ahead of his teams. If they were bad, they'd probably have been even worse without him.

Now it annoys Mauch that this season's success is being interpreted as an exoneration of unnamed past sins. For a man who has made a career of bringing fifth-place clubs home fourth, and getting criticized in the process, it's hard to swallow praise for managing a first-place team into first place.

In Mauch's eyes, the praise he is receiving now is as cheap, as ignorant of the facts, as the gainsaying he has endured for years. Either Mauch has been doing it right all along or he hasn't. These Angels don't change the past. "I've got so many horses," he said this week, "that I've just hitched 'em up and gone along for the ride."

Many are surprised Mauch isn't having a good time; he's testy and abrupt. Questions about that old Phillie foolishness bring a look to his eyes that make everyone within kill range glad that machine guns aren't allowed in dugouts.

What's forgotten is that this handsome steel-gray man with the level gaze, the cryptic habits of speech, the barely suppressed temper and the blade-edged wit has lived in a sort of purgatory ever since his Phillie ship went down. He has carried the memory, flaring at any mention of the Fold, like a shamed captain who has ignobly survived a wreck in which all other hands were lost.

A world championship may take other Angels to heaven, but not Mauch; he knows there's modest credit at best for managing such a gaudy crew. What he desperately wants is to avoid the hell of another ship foundering under him.

Actually, the Mauch of 1982 is no different than the Mauch of any other year. He's still the same old pick-a-side-and-argue-a-while puzzle. Either the man's ahead of everybody else or he's outsmarted himself again.

Mauch is still jeopardizing potentially big innings with early-inning bunts. He's still juggling his lineup almost every day, running the risk of confusing his players by batting them all in a half dozen positions in the order. He's still a master of impatience in dealing with a pitching staff. Mauch sticks with a hot pitcher, even if it risks burning him out, while losing confidence in those who are slumping; they are quickly consigned to roles in which they can't contaminate the proceedings.

This year, the power-laden Angels led the league, again, in sacrifices (114). This leads other managers, like Baltimore's Earl Weaver, to chortle about how the man who plays for one run ends up losing by one run.

Game 2 of the American League Championship Series was an example. With the bases loaded in the second inning and one out, and with the Angels leading, 1–0, Mauch had Bob Boone squeeze home a run with a bunt. Then, in the fourth inning, with two on and none out, Mauch had Tim Foli attempt a sacrifice bunt. Of two rallies in which five men were on base against a struggling pitcher with only one out, Mauch managed to get two runs.

Did this strategy win the game, since California triumphed, 4–2?

Or did Mauch help defuse two potential blowout innings and thus help Pete Vuckovich remain on the mound and pitch a complete game?

Mauch says, "We play Little Ball at the bottom of the order, but we play Big Ball in the middle of the order with home runs. . . . I appreciate execution, whether it's Foli bunting or Reggie [Jackson] hitting a homer."

The Angels' lineup is Mauch's perverse passion. "In my heart, I don't know the true lineup of the California Angels," he has said. Even that is understatement. Mauch has changed his lineup more than seventy times this year, and some call this making a Mauchery of your lineup. Some call it genius.

Mauch gets uniformly high marks for bringing the Angels' get-no-respect pitching staff home with the second-best ERA in the AL. He had a hand in changing the deliveries of Bruce Kison, Mike Witt and Ken Forsch in spring training, helping them hold runners closer to first. He understood that older pitchers like Forsch and Geoff Zahn (18–8) would follow an ancient pattern of going from great to poor back to good as the hot summer defeated them and the cool autumn restored them.

Whether teaching Zahn a slider or making Luis Sanchez a bullpen ace, Mauch has felt as free to demand that his pitchers try something new as he has been hands-off with his proven stars.

"If there's one thing that drives me crazy," he says, a flash of anger showing, "it's a guy who says, 'I've always done it this way.' Yeah, I can see that. That's probably why you're still a .250 hitter or a .500 pitcher. Why don't we try something new? We can always go back to that."

Finally, with age, Mauch, fifty-six, has become an adept stroker of egos. Doug DeCinces, hypersensitive to Weaver's habit of barking and grumping, has blossomed under Mauch's praise/flattery. Jackson loves to be consulted on cerebral matters; Bobby Grich likes how-does-your-back-feel-today meetings; Rod Carew craves affection; fragile Fred Lynn wants some days off without being bad-mouthed.

Mauch, since he genuinely admires such "special people" and might even be a little star-struck, can keep this gang happy.

An extra bonus is that the famous Angels are rich and confident enough to tease Mauch, cracking his flinty exterior and showing the fine fellow inside. "Nobody beats us," mimics Jackson, flexing every muscle in his neck à la Mauch and cocking his head at a crazy-captain angle, "when we put our 'A' game on the field."

"I don't think I have ever felt pressure in baseball, not after all the years I've been in uniform," Mauch said. "Unless, maybe, pressure is the emotion that I get when I think of the people who care about me and how they'll feel if we lose. I don't lead the world in friends, but I have enough so that I don't want them disappointed."

Take the Money and Walk

KANSAS CITY, Missouri, September 26, 1984—

Who could be on the side of the Angels? They ought to go to the devil.

If one big-league team makes the blood boil, it's the California Angels. They ought to give their fans a rebate.

They're the Me Generation nine.

The next time an Angel cheers for a teammate, they ought to stop the game and give him the ball. This club thinks hustle and morale require inoculation.

Last month in New York, the Angels' third baseman made a fabulous play in a close game. In the same situation, the Royals or Twins would have partied. The California dugout was a still life. No hand applauded. No foot moved. Somebody wanna get up and flip those burgers on the grill?

Five days ago, the Angels looked ready for the playoffs. Luckily, they lost five in a row. Now they can go where they really want to be: the beach. Who wants to risk playing in the World Series in chilly Chicago in October when you know the surf's up at Zuma?

On Tuesday night here, the Angels faced a team crisis. They were about to win a must-win game—something they've never done. Hey, who wants to ruin a perfect record?

Gene Autry's only owned this team since 1961. He's only spent half the gold in California to buy a winner. Why should he go to the World Series?

The Angels passed their crisis as if it were a screen test. Picture this: Bottom of the ninth, Kansas City trails by a run, base hit to left, Royals runner heads home but he misses third base in his haste. Thousands see it, gasp and hold their breath for the appeal that will win the game and keep California in pennant contention.

Nothing happens.

With its season on the line, the whole team is asleep.

How can the Angels be so dead? Oh, that's simple. They got a bad break at home last weekend and they've been using this week in Kansas City to sulk.

On Sunday, the Angels were half a game out of first place. A Texas batter hit a foul pop in extra innings. A teenage Angels fan, at the game on his birthday, tried to get a souvenir and knocked the ball out of third baseman Doug DeCinces's glove. The reprieved batter advanced a runner a vital base, which, in turn, helped the Rangers win, 2–1. Six cops threw the fan out of the park ("for his own safety").

The Angels were mad at that fan.

In response to this tragedy, they followed form.

They quit. Lost a pair the next night by a combined score of 16–4. Now they're four and a half back. And dead. It's almost inconceivable. This whole AL West season seemed to have been concocted so the Angels win at the end.

This team has:

Reggie Jackson—502 home runs.

Rod Carew—seven batting titles.

Fred Lynn—nine-time All-Star.

Bobby Grich—six All-Star games, four Gold Gloves.

Bob Boone—three All-Star games, two Gold Gloves.

Doug DeCinces—All-Star in '83.

Brian Downing—a past All-Star with 70 homers the last three years.

Gary Pettis—46 steals this year and a center field Gold Glove in hand.

Tommy John—255 victories.

Juan Beniquez—hitting .335.

Three quality starting pitchers—Mike Witt, who might strike out 200 this year; steady Geoff Zahn; sturdy Ron Romanick.

Three relievers with a combined 18–9 record, 23 saves and a 2.53 ERA in 206 innings over 115 appearances.

A solid manager: John McNamara.

A top front-office mind: general manager Gene Mauch.

All the money on earth.

And a losing record.

You could say their stars are too old, but they aren't. Carew is hitting .300, when he decides to play. Jackson, Grich, Lynn, DeCinces and Downing have 107 homers—an average of 22 a man.

What we have here is bad karma and bad chemistry.

The bad karma comes from the '82 playoffs, when this bunch cut Mauch's classy heart out for good by blowing the last three games of the season and a trip to the Series. Mauch retired, the ghosts of his Pholdin' Phillies of twenty years before redoubled, not exorcised.

Last year, in one of the all-time give-up performances, these same Angels, knowing they couldn't catch Chicago, lost 92 games and were the disgrace of the sport. Team motto: Take the money and walk.

Next comes bad chemistry.

No matter how much talent you have, baseball still is a battle of one-run games. It's in the nature of the sport. The teams that play better as teams—with hustle, intelligence, cohesion, unselfishness—do better in tight play. The Angels are 21–29 in one-run games. By contrast, the Royals, with a fraction of the Angels' ability, are 25–20. Reverse that and the Angels would be on top.

For the purposes of everyday life, the Angels are extremely bright and friendly. That's what drives people so crazy. Sure, Carew feels persecuted and nurses his injuries. Jackson has a vast vanity. Lynn is as casual as Southern California. Downing is a weight-pumping introvert. Grich is no holler guy. Boone's a thinker, not a screamer.

Up close, the Angels really are angels—hard not to like. Yet perhaps no group of good players has interacted so inertly. What an ironic commentary that the only Angel who could be called a field leader is that supreme individualist, Jackson. It also doesn't help that McNamara lacks charisma.

The Angels' batting order has no internal dynamic. It's just a random collection that constantly changes as one star after another takes a night off against a tough pitcher. Lynn and Carew skipped the nightcap of Monday's desperate doubleheader.

This team has no speed, no spark, no energy arising from fellow feeling or commitment to a goal. Everybody has already made his name and fortune. After a defeat, the Angels munch and withdraw from each other as though consoling themselves with glories in other towns and times.

The Angels have no past, no present and no future. They arrive at the park on time, make sure their uniforms fit nicely, give a passable effort and make sure they get the best table at the best restaurant in town after the game.

It's a heavenly life for them.

But it's hell to watch.

□ □ □ □ □ □ □

Author's note: Team owner Gene Autry and Angels president Buzzy Bavasi telephoned the next day to thank me for writing this piece. "Too bad you didn't write it a month ago," said Bavasi. "It might've helped."

Someone posted copies of this column on all four walls of the Angels clubhouse before the last game of the season.

Mike Witt pitched a perfect game.

A Mauchery of Justice

September 3, 1985—Gene Mauch wears no rings. The wedding band is gone because his wife, Nina, whom he met in junior high, died last summer of cancer. There's no World Series ring because Mauch's forty-year career has been a wilderness of disappointments. No man ever managed so long without a pennant.

About his wife's death, Mauch has nothing to say. He is the most severe, intelligent and formal of men. He loved her his whole life. She knew it. That's that.

About those sixteen years as a player and twenty-four more as a manager —with never a trip to the Series—Mauch also keeps a silence as deep as his wounds.

No team ever collapsed as badly as close to the wire as his '64 Phillies. Ten losses in a row. Mauch can remember every play of "the thing." Those ten defeats are the stigmata of a violent-tempered tactician who, more than any other manager since John McGraw, made baseball into an intellectual's secular religion.

Three years ago, misery repeated itself. Mauch's California Angels made history: the first team to blow a playoff series after leading by two games.

Mauch retired, almost in disgrace. An overmanager, too smart and stubborn for his own good. A dead-ball genius lost in a home run age. He'd won a ring he wouldn't wear.

"I felt like I'd never manage another game. I lost interest in it and everything else about that time," he says. "I was so indifferent that I was indifferent about being indifferent."

Last fall, the Angels' brass, convinced their rich team was fainthearted and brain-dead, asked Mauch to return and inspire them. His job: to make baseball's most careless collection of fading stars care again.

To do that, he had to care again.

"I'm grateful that baseball revived my interest in something. And that has rekindled an interest in everything," Mauch says. "If you don't know what I'm talking about, I can't tell you."

The day the vets reported, Mauch took them to a remote spot to talk. Nobody's leaked yet. But Reggie Jackson, Bobby Grich, Rod Carew, Doug DeCinces, Brian Downing and Bob Boone have been caught doing high-fives in public.

"I don't get involved with that because I can't reach that high," Mauch says with the sort of self-deprecating touch that was utterly beyond him in the old days.

When Mauch left the game, not everyone mourned his going. Vain and hot-tempered in his youth, and only marginally mellowed, Mauch made the worst strategic error an exceptional person can commit: he acted superior.

Not deliberately. Just by nature. Small talk annoyed him. Insincerity was beneath him. The slipshod enraged him.

These days, Mauch gives the kind word, the generous answer to a silly question, even the affectionate pat, that he withheld so long. Mortality teaches humility, they say.

Always the innovative thinker, never the feeler, Mauch finally has learned how to relinquish enough control to admit, "I can't win a pennant by myself, on brains alone. I need you."

In return, the Angels have committed themselves to the uncool goal of hustle and risk. Men who made their names and fortunes in other towns, men who came to Anaheim to kick back and enjoy their last few years, have chosen to fall in love with the high cost of winning one last time. Mauch has shown his heart. They've rediscovered their pride.

The Angels, picked for the pits, are in first place by two and a half games over Kansas City in the American League West. Ask Mauch where he'd wear that Series ring if he gets it this year and he blurts, "Any place but my ear." Putting his guard back up, he adds, "Oh no, that's bush. I didn't say that."

This is a man, you see, with private standards in all matters. When coaching third base, he never shook the hand or patted the rear of a home run hitter in midtrot. "I clapped. It was his home run, not mine."

A self-flagellating perfectionist who kept detailed longhand notebook re-capitulations of all 3,600 games he managed, Mauch, at fifty-nine, finally may have learned to forgive himself. "Nothing could ever tear me up again," he says.

This year's Angels are an ideal testament to Mauch. They've barely out-scored their opponents (by 18 runs), yet they're 17 games above .500. Last season, they were awful in one-run games (22–30). Now, they're the best (28–10). These are classic great-manager stats.

Even Mauch's flaws may be suitable to these particular flawed Angels. True, his team leads the league in sacrifices, but California's strengths—defense and bullpen—make it possible to play close-to-the-vest, low-scoring games. True, he still juggles his lineup constantly, but these aged Angels need rest.

"This is the most delicate thing I've ever done," Mauch says of nursing his old men to good seasons. "As long as they're mad at me about being rested, I know they're not tired."

Mauch has always fostered bullpens built on nobodies. He's done it again. Donnie Moore, thirty-one, was a twelve-season mediocrity, adrift in the compensation pool. Now: 1.62 ERA, 31 wins-plus-saves. Stewart Cliburn, twenty-eight, was released in '82 and even sent to the minors this spring. Now: 1.80 ERA.

Mauch's Angels are a precarious mix of fragile bodies and complex psyches. "If people could see what Doug DeCinces goes through each day to get his bad back ready to play," Mauch says. "Grich and Jackson the same. Players take far better care of themselves now."

Give effort. Get kudos. Done deal.

Even with the stretch-drive addition of three talented bad actors (fatsos Al Holland and John Candelaria, plus George Hendrick), the Angels are a dicey bet to win their division, let alone a pennant. Now that Mauch has, perhaps, the full range of skills to win a pennant, does he have the team?

Will this man, already so tangled up with his long history, cross his own tracks again?

In one of baseball's eeriest recurrences, Mauch faced the same tactical decision in the '82 playoffs that he'd made in the final week of September 1964. After two decades of defending the way he'd used Jim Bunning and Chris Short then, how could he use Tommy John and Bruce Kison differently?

Does a comparable irony await him?

These Angels are a staggering, lurching team, prone to ominous drubbings. They'll fret their fans until the final days. But, for once, Mauch doesn't seem to be among those worrying himself sick.

"There aren't enough hours in the day for me to worry about Gene Mauch," he says. "Either I know what I'm doing or I don't."

Not Again

ANAHEIM, California, October 12, 1986—

In the greatest game ever played—except perhaps for the night before—the Boston Red Sox beat the California Angels, 7–6, in eleven innings this afternoon to send the American League Championship Series back to Fenway Park for a sixth game Tuesday.

Once baseball gets beyond a certain level of excitement, pressure, human drama and glorious improbability, the mind refuses to calibrate degrees of excellence and must satisfy itself with simple exhilaration. That's where this game hovers now, awaiting its place in the sport's history.

Amid myriad central characters and a dozen plots and subplots, Dave Henderson of the Red Sox was this game's linchpin.

With the Angels one strike from their first pennant, Henderson hit a two-run home run off Donnie Moore in the ninth inning to put Boston ahead, 6–5. If the Red Sox, still down, three games to two, in these playoffs, end up in the World Series, that 400-foot blow into the left-field stands will become legendary. As it was, Henderson's leaps of joy, his pirouette as teammates burst from the dugout, even fell to the ground, provided the highlight of this season.

As a denouement, Henderson hit the game-winning sacrifice fly with the bases loaded and nobody out, also against Moore, in the eleventh. What made this all triply improbable and thrilling was that Henderson stood to be the goat. In the game as a mid-inning replacement for injured Tony Armas, Henderson had deflected a Bobby Grich hit over the center-field fence for a two-run homer in the sixth inning to put the Angels ahead, 3–2.

When Henderson stepped to bat in the ninth, when he was down to his last strike—with the Angels' bat boys already popping champagne corks in the clubhouse—he knew that if he made the final out, his defensive misadventure would be entered in the record books as the pennant-winning home run for the Angels.

"I thought I should have had that ball . . . thought I had it all the way," said Henderson, traded to Boston from Seattle just two months ago. "But it hit the heel of my glove, my wrist hit the fence and it went over."

Henderson's homer, on an almost perfect low forkball, was something of a mystery to him. "I was just protecting the plate," he said, remembering a pair of gasping, two-strike foul balls. Then, in a flash, before Henderson knew what he'd done, "it was gone. When I hit 'em like that, they're gone."

Perhaps only two teams with twenty-five past and present All-Stars in uniform would have had the thoroughbred fortitude to take this day to its eventual heights.

Boston heroes were legion. Steve Crawford, the winning pitcher, has a lifetime of tales from two innings' work. With the bases loaded in the bottom of the ninth (and the game-tying run already across the plate), he faced Doug DeCinces and Grich. One popped up the first pitch, the other shattered his bat on a liner back to the mound; that season-in-the-balance escape forced extra innings.

Crawford also survived a harrowing moment in the bottom of the tenth when Gary Pettis hit a ball to the top of the eight-foot fence in left field. Crawford, shoulders drooped, started to head off the field in defeat, sure the season was dead. Somehow, the drive must have had topspin. Jim Rice —the defensive goat of Saturday's defeat when he misjudged a similar drive by Pettis—jumped and snagged the ball two-handed.

Calvin Schiraldi, the other Boston goat in Saturday's 4–3, eleven-inning defeat—a game in which the Red Sox blew a three-run ninth-inning lead, just as California did today—got the save with a perfect 1-2-3 eleventh inning.

"I was just hoping I could get back in there today and make up for last night," said the young hurler, who, with the Angels down to their final strike in the ninth inning Saturday night, hit Brian Downing with a pitch to force home the tying run. "I didn't sleep much last night, but finally the sun rose."

And with it a new day for the Red Sox.

Rich Gedman and Don Baylor rivaled Henderson and Crawford on the honor roll as this day's 234-minute marathon broke the American League playoff record for longest game by four minutes—a record set, it goes without saying, the night before.

Gedman was four for four with a two-run homer off starter Mike Witt. It was fear of Gedman coming to bat that forced Angels manager Gene Mauch to do what he hated most—remove his ace, Witt, with one out to go in the ninth and the Angels' lead down to 5–4.

"If I had left Witt in and Gedman had hit another one, I couldn't have handled that," said Mauch, the much-scarred Ahab of 1964 in Philadelphia and 1982 here.

Gedman was hit by the only pitch thrown by left-handed reliever Gary Lucas, the man who followed Witt. On came Moore, up came Henderson and out went the ball, eight rows into the bleachers.

As if that weren't enough, Gedman's perfect bunt—which started as a sacrifice attempt—loaded the bases for Henderson with none out in the eleventh. Gedman had laid the table so well that Henderson could hardly fail.

In an absolutely fitting touch, Baylor, judge of the kangaroo court, lit the comeback fuse for Boston in the ninth with a two-run homer off Witt. That cut California's three-run lead to 5–4. After that crowd-quieter, anything could happen. And did.

In fact, it was Baylor who was hit by a Moore pitch to open the Boston eleventh. After Dwight Evans's single and Gedman's bunt, Baylor scored the decisive run on Henderson's long liner.

"That was the finest, the most competitive baseball game I've ever seen," said Boston manager Johm McNamara. ". . . The hill is not as steep now."

"This was by far the best game, out of more than 2,200 in my career," said Baylor. "All of a sudden, you felt like a kid once again. The emotion in that dugout was just unbelievable.

"We've been a team all year, but we're closer to each other now," said Baylor, who before the game "gave out more speeches than McNamara."

Even Mauch, who had seen the first pennant of his twenty-five-year career torn from his hands, admitted, "It was a great game."

So great that it may well have repercussions beyond this day. "When Henderson's home run went out, I said, 'We're gonna win this sucker,' " said Crawford. "We'll win it [all] now."

Mauch saw a different side of the truth. There's a distinction between a pressure game and a desperation game. The latter is easier psychologically. As McNamara said: "Nobody had to tell us it was win or 'See ya next February.' "

"I thought they were going to be loose and I wouldn't be surprised if they were loose again Tuesday," said Mauch, inserting a wedge of doubt that the Red Sox had proved themselves pressure-proof this afternoon. "But we'll be loose, too."

The anger of a brutal defeat can cut both ways. Now the Angels may summon their own wounded pride. After all, this was the day when Gene Autry, seventy-nine, might have had a new champion while Mauch, sixty, could have had his first.

With sleep and time, the Angels will remember their own nobility. Bob Boone, who hit a bases-empty homer off starter Bruce Hurst, began the game-tying rally in the bottom of the ninth with his ninth hit of these playoffs.

They won't forget the head-first, fall-away slide that Ruppert Jones used to get around Gedman and tie the game, 6–6, on Rob Wilfong's clutch, one-out hit in the ninth. That slide had to be inspired, because Evans's throw was a knee-high, one-hop work of craft.

As they fly East, how many memories from this game will drift to mind? Maybe they will think of Downing, with the Red Sox already ahead, 7–6, in the eleventh and almost all hope gone, sprinting face first into the left-field fence to rob Ed Romero of what would have been a two-run, game-icing double. Or will they see Wilfong, on the very next play, diving full-length to steal another potential run-scoring hit?

The truth is that this game did not end, any more than the previous night's did. Both masterpieces—perhaps the two finest back-to-back post-season games of this generation—simply stopped with this riveting addendum:

To be continued.

Nothing to Forgive

July 21, 1989—This is for Bill Buckner, Ralph Branca, John McNamara, Tom Niedenfuer, Don Denkinger, Johnny Pesky and Gene Mauch. It's for the '64 Phillies, the '78 Red Sox, the '87 Blue Jays and every Cub since

World War II. In particular, it's for Donnie Moore, who shot his wife, then committed suicide this week.

You, and countless others who get branded as "goats" in sports, didn't do anything wrong. We know it, though we almost never say it. Just once, let's put it in words: The reason we don't forgive you is because there's nothing to forgive in the first place. You tried your best and failed. In games, there's a law that says somebody has to lose.

Many of us wish that, just once, we could be in your shoes and have a chance to fail so grandly. Although, if we really had to live the experience and its aftermath, which sometimes lasts a lifetime, maybe we would not.

We've had our share of sad stories in sports recently. But none approaches Donnie Moore's. Numerous other athletes who're in trouble— taking heat, answering tough questions, hearing catcalls—got themselves in hot water by doing what they knew was wrong. All Moore did was pitch despite a sore arm, throw a nice nasty knee-high forkball and watch it sail over the left-field fence.

Nobody will ever be able to prove that the haunting memory of giving up Dave Henderson's home run in the 1986 American League playoffs led Moore to commit suicide. Maybe, someday, we'll learn about some other possible cause. But, right now, what some people are saying, and many are thinking, is that this "goat" business isn't funny anymore.

Moore was a good little pitcher, a battler, a student of the game, a tough guy with a sensitive inside who was one of Mauch's favorite players. That tells a lot, because Mauch respects Joe DiMaggio and about two other people.

For two seasons, late in his twelve-year career, Moore became a star. He came within one foul tick of pitching the California Angels into their only World Series. But Henderson, off balance, barely tipped the two-strike pitch. With the next swing, Henderson made history. He kept the Red Sox alive so that they could go to the World Series in the Angels' place—and endure miseries.

"Ever since he gave up the home run . . . he was never himself again," said Dave Pinter, Moore's agent for twelve years. "He blamed himself for the Angels not going to the World Series. He constantly talked about the Henderson home run. . . . I tried to get him to go to a psychiatrist, but he said, 'I don't need it. I'll get over it.' . . . That home run killed him."

"You destroyed a man's life over one pitch," exploded the Angels' Brian Downing. "The guy was just not the same after that. . . . He was never treated fairly. He wasn't given credit for all the good things he did. . . . Nobody was sympathetic. I never, ever saw him be credited for getting us to the playoffs, because all you ever heard about, all you ever read about was one pitch."

Moore's wife, Tonya, once said that, after the Pitch, Moore would often come home after games at Anaheim Stadium, where he was booed, and burst into tears.

One of the powerful appeals of sports is its artificially created fairness. Every precaution is taken to ensure a level playing field. In a sense, sports is purely democratic. Almost nothing about you, except the way you play the game, is inspected or judged.

That's why sports are, in a sense, an escape. All the moral ambiguities of daily life are suspended. Somebody wins and is happy. Somebody loses, but gets to play again the next day or season.

Duane Thomas once said, "If the Super Bowl is the 'ultimate game,' why do they play it again next year?" The answer is: "So somebody else can win it. And so whoever loses this year doesn't feel too bad."

Some people get over losing their "ultimate game." Perhaps no manager ever made a bigger blunder than Tommy Lasorda when he had Niedenfuer pitch to Jack Clark with first base open and the Dodgers just one out from reaching the World Series. Clark hit a three-run homer and St. Louis went to the Series—which they lost because of—no, we're not going to blame Denkinger today.

Lasorda wept in the clubhouse, went to the players to apologize, then went on with his life.

At the moment he manages the reigning world champions. Maybe Lasorda coped so well because he'd already gone to three Series and won one.

The flaw in our attitude—perhaps it is even an American predisposition with Puritan roots—is to equate defeat with sin. The unspoken assumption is that those who lose must do so because of some moral flaw.

Sports, especially pro sports, is not a morality play, much as it suits our national appetite to act as if it were. Even some athletes, perhaps including Moore, seem to crush themselves under a burden of self-imposed guilt in areas of life where no cause for guilt exists.

If you work hard enough, sacrifice enough, then you will win. That's what many coaches teach. Or should we say preach? It might be more honest, and healthier, to say that if you work very hard you will become excellent, and because of that excellence, you may do great deeds and win great prizes. Unless, of course, you don't. Because, sometimes, the other player is better or luckier. In which case you simply have to be satisfied with your excellence and the dignity of your effort.

Those of us who are merely fans and critics have a responsibility, too. The right to a raspberry comes with the price of a ticket and the right to an opinion goes with the First Amendment.

Still, before we boo or use words like "choke" and "goat," perhaps we should think sometimes of Donnie Moore.

Not So Bush

Throws Left, Bats Right

CLEVELAND, August 9, 1981—

Lots of politicians throw out first balls at All-Star Games, but perhaps only Vice President George Bush really worries about it.

"I'm going with the slider," said Bush decisively a half hour before the game. "I know there's a lot of risk there, but if I keep it low and outside, I think I'll be all right.

"By the way, who's catching me?" asked Bush. "[Carlton] Fisk?"

The Vice President was told that a thirteen-year-old had been picked out of the center-field bleachers to handle his first pitch.

Bush's face fell. "You mean," he said, "that I'm going to have to take something off?"

To Bush, that's no joke. Every President or Vice President finds some way to claim he was a ballplayer, or at least a softball player.

Bush was rather close to the real thing. He was the first baseman of the Yale baseball team, which doesn't sound like much, perhaps, until you realize that in 1947 and '48 the Elis, with Bush aboard, made it to the final game of the College World Series, losing the national title in the last game of the year both times.

Of his senior-year teammates, five played pro ball and two made the majors. His coach, Ethan Allen, according to Bush, "always claimed that his lifetime batting average in the majors was .301. Since he was the coach, we never disputed him."

And who was the captain of that Yale powerhouse? Bush, of course.

While waiting to do some handshaking in the All-Star dugouts tonight, Bush reminisced about his baseball days, both past and, unfortunately for him, present as well.

"I remember one year in the national finals in Kalamazoo, Ethan Allen walked the eighth hitter to get to the Cal [University of California] pitcher," said Bush. "That pitcher turned out to be Jackie Jensen. He hit a ball that's still rolling somewhere out in western Michigan. We never let Allen forget it."

Was Bush ever tempted by the thought of pro ball, like the majority of his teammates?

"Yes," he said.

After all, Bush can still recall a day against North Carolina State when he hit the easy three-quarters of the cycle: single, double, triple. And, he still says proudly, "I once worked my way up from eighth in the order to fifth."

But Bush was a pragmatist then, as now. "I never could hit, although I will say that I was a great fielder," remarked Bush, who says the word "great" as a cute politician's joke, but, considering the level of his play, probably means it. "I wasn't good enough. I knew my limitations in baseball as I know them in life. I'd have floundered somewhere down in the minors."

Nonetheless, Bush is far more at home with professional athletes than most ersatz politicos who draw a behind-the-back sneer from serious jocks.

Just a few days ago, the fifty-four-year-old Bush ran his daily three miles with the Mets' Rusty Staub. "Let the record show," said Bush, "that Rusty quit after two and a half miles. Maybe I can't hit . . . but I can run better."

Bush flew in with his New England friend, seventeen-time All-Star Carl Yastrzemski. When he walked through the dugouts, he slapped and wrestled a bit with both Nolan Ryan and Tom Seaver, who are both friends and past campaigners. "What the hell's an Eli doing in here?" said Seaver, throwing an arm around Bush from behind as the Secret Service did a collective twitch.

Before this game, Bush had great plans. He said that on the plane he suggested to Yastrzemski that "maybe I should stride up to the plate with a bat, point to left field and take one cut. If you hit it, good. If you miss it, you haven't lost much. . . . The guys thought it was a lousy idea."

Perhaps they had gotten wind of Bush's last batting adventure while on the campaign trail last fall. While jogging with the president of the University of California, Bush spotted a batting cage at a college practice field. "Let's try it," pleaded Bush. Once in the cage against a semiserious college Iron Mike, Bush found out the truth. He still can't hit.

"Whiff, whiff, whiff," he said grumpily. "Then, finally, a couple of foul balls. I was awful, absolutely awful . . . no excuses."

Then Bush noted, "I've now started wearing glasses, so I can see."

Those Iron Mikes better watch out now.

This evening, as Bush was introduced to his thirteen-year-old catcher, Derrick Williams, who was wearing jeans, sneakers, a Police Athletic League T-shirt and the glove of Kansas City's Frank White, the Vice President sized up his battery mate and thought he had spotted an athlete.

Gradually, Bush warmed up with short tosses to him. Then he started spinning the ball in a mini-curve. "It's really breaking tonight," he said playfully to Bob Hope. "Let's try the knuckle-curve."

Finally, Bush had confidence in the child. During the long minutes of ceremonial time wasting, Bush took the boy aside and said, "Well, what are our signals? How about 'one' [finger] for a fastball and 'two' for a curve? If you get nervous about the curveball, just give me a 'one.'"

The kid smiled. Maybe not as much as when he got Yastrzemski's autograph. But it was a smile.

Bush threw out two first pitches. The first was just your basic not-so-fast fastball. But on the second he could not resist. He broke off the slider and the kid had to make a nice lunging snag or the ball would still be rolling somewhere out in western Ohio.

The participants dispersed. Bush hopped back over the railing into his bulletproof, glass-enclosed seat. The crowd gave him the usual bored mixture of unenthusiastic cheers and sarcastic boos that are reserved for Vice Presidents who fly all over the country at taxpayers' expense, making silly ceremonial appearances at games about which they obviously couldn't care less.

The largest crowd in All-Star history figured Bush was bored to tears.

Derrick Williams knew better.

In the milling crowd, Bush caught the little boy's eye. "Well done," said Bush, grinning. "Hey, how'd you like the . . ."

And the Vice President made the universal snapping motion of the wrist to indicate a breaking ball.

Make no mistake, when the Vice President of the United States decides he's going with the slider, that's what it's going to be.

The McQuinn Claw

March 31, 1989—Inside a drawer in the Oval Office sits a handsome old first baseman's mitt that has been oiled and tended so lovingly and so long that it's almost turned black. Though it's nearly fifty years old, the mitt has been rewebbed and is in near-mint condition: good for another million scoops.

As Presidents go, Teddy Roosevelt may have carried a big stick, but George Bush is definitely the glove man. As the first spring of Bush's first term approaches, the South Lawn and the Rose Garden better watch out. If a grandchild wants to play catch, President Bush is an easy sell. "Sure, I get the itch," said the sixty-four-year-old chief executive, who, all his life, has been lured by every tennis racket, golf club, fishing pole, horseshoe, soccer ball, bat or glove that caught his eye.

"This is the very glove I used for three years at Yale. It's the George McQuinn claw," said the President, pulling the old friend from his desk and popping his fist in the pocket as he leaned back in his chair. " 'Trapper' it says here. It's a Rawlings. I remember when this glove came out. It was just wonderful. For a while I think they outlawed this cup [i.e., style of pocket], but now you can use anything."

Every politician and especially every President tries to establish his ties to baseball—the national pastime. Jimmy Carter played softball as cameras clicked. Richard Nixon knew reams of major-league statistics. And Ronald Reagan spent five years broadcasting Chicago Cubs games. Bush does not have to strain to prove his bona fides. He's the real thing—a legit ballplayer —although he habitually soft-pedals it.

In the first College World Series ever played, in 1947, Bush's Yale team played the illustrious University of California, led by Jackie Jensen, in the national championship game. The next year, Yale reached the national finals again, this time against Southern California.

Back in that postwar golden age of baseball talent, no college played a higher level of ball than Yale, which thumped schools like North Carolina and Clemson and, during one eleven-game Bush-era winning streak, outscored its foes by 76–20. The Elis' coach, Ethan Allen, was a career .300 hitter in the majors. Three of Bush's teammates reached the big leagues and others played in the minors. Yale then was Stanford or Miami now.

How good was Bush? Good enough that he never missed a game at first base in three years and, his senior year, was team captain. Good enough that, his last year, he fielded .990 on 190 chances and batted .264 with six doubles, two triples, a home run and 28 runs produced in 25 games. And, finally, good enough that Yale teammate Dick Tettelbach (Yankees and Senators) has seriously compared him with Keith Hernandez as a defensive first baseman. "Absolutely superb. A real fancy Dan."

Of course, presidential mythology grows with the years. Still, recent evidence exists. Eight years ago, Warren Spahn and Bill Dickey needled Bush into playing in an old-timers' game in Denver.

"When Tony Oliva came up," recalled Bush, "the second baseman kept yelling at me, 'Get back.' I said, 'Back? I'm on the damned grass. Whaddaya want?' But the second baseman said, 'Back. This guy can still hit.' And damn if Oliva didn't pull one right down the line."

Though Oliva was forty-four then and Bush fifty-seven, the President's memory of the play is that he just wishes he'd had his McQuinn Trapper. "My excuse on this part is I had a brand-new mitt—knocked the ball down —should have had it clean."

Bush dove to his left, backhanded the smash, then flipped to Milt Pappas for the out on a play that brought the crowd to its feet. Since Bush already had a solid single to center in his only at-bat, he decided to walk right off the field and into a glorious and permanent retirement. Like his old fishing friend Ted Williams, Bush knew when to quit.

"There are still some television clips available of that moment," said Bush. "Seems the demand has slackened a little, but they're there."

Bush the ballplayer and Bush the politician are not entirely dissimilar. Thought to be a lightweight hitter by Yale coach Allen, Bush became such a showman with his glove that he beat out several muscular candidates for the first base job, even though he often batted eighth. Or, as Bush calls it, "second cleanup."

Bush practiced tirelessly and did everything to please. Hit to all fields. Stole bases. Made his more talented teammates look even better than they were by becoming flawless on digging throws out of the dirt. Also, he ingratiated himself effortlessly, whether by singing on train trips, teasing teammates or organizing the team gin game.

Already a war vet (in the same Naval aviation class as Ted Williams), Bush was known as competitive, even hard-nosed. His leadership was understated, yet his eventual captaincy was almost taken for granted.

To this day, Bush's mediocre hitting is a source of presidential humor— with just a hint of self-dissatisfaction tucked underneath. "I only had one 'best memory,' " he said, recalling a single-double-triple day against North Carolina State that had scouts crawling around him (until Allen disabused them).

Actually, Bush was the rarest of baseball freaks—throws left, bats right. And he knows it. "I was all inverted . . . just backwards," he said. "I started to play tennis serving left and then hit ground strokes right . . . but my mother was a bit of a perfectionist. I was about five years old and she said, 'This won't do. Make up your mind.' So I opted for right."

Next, Bush learned golf right-handed and, as any physiologist will attest, he was pretty much doomed as a hitter. Among natural lefties, few (except Cleon Jones) have ever become top righty hitters.

Though Bush had Ivy Leaguer Lou Gehrig (Columbia) as his childhood hero and "memorized all the stats and lineups" for years, he never had illusions about his ability. At the All-Star Game in '81, he said flatly, "I wasn't good enough. I knew my limitations in baseball as I know them in life. I'd have floundered somewhere down in the minors."

Nevertheless, a lot of ballplayer mannerisms cling to Bush. He deflates the great, inflates the small, knows how to needle and be needled. The first time he met George Brett, the Royals star forgot to address Bush properly as Mr. Vice President. Bush responded slyly, "George who?" Yet when a little bald man with a tobacco chaw said, "Hello, Mr. Vice President, I'm Don Zimmer," Bush answered, "Oh, I know. I know. You used to play for the Mets, didn't you?"

Although Bush lacks the time to study box scores and attend games as he once did, he still claims to have a "Walter Mitty" joy in throwing out first balls. In fact, it will take more than a faraway coup d'état to keep him from doing the honors in Baltimore on Monday. He even plans to bring Egyptian President Hosni Mubarak with him.

Nolan Ryan, one of Bush's longtime baseball friends, has filled the President's ear with first-ball advice. "Nolan says throw it high because amateurs get out there, no matter how good they are, and throw it into the dirt. . . . You get more of an 'ooooh' [from the crowd] if you heave it over the [catcher's] head instead of going with the fast-breaking deuce into the dirt."

History notes, and Bush knows, that Ronald Reagan's initial first ball cleared Rick Dempsey's leap by two feet and was met with majestic "ooooohs."

Bush even plots his first-ball strategy for getting to the mound. "I will stride to the mound," he said, "then stop a couple of steps short of the rubber and encourage the catcher ahead of time to [cheat out] in front of the plate. That worked very well last year in Cincinnati."

For that first ball, Bush had a preliminary practice workout at St. Albans School with his Little League grandson. ("He modestly claimed to be hitting .600. We have not authenticated that.") Once in Cincinnati for the momentous occasion, Bush even solved the universal politician's problem in ballparks: how not to get booed.

A twelve-year-old boy and an eight-year-old girl were supposed to precede Bush onto the field. "I said to the little girl, 'Are you nervous? . . . Why don't we walk out together,' thus foiling anybody who would boo an eight-year-old blond kid and a strapping looking Little League guy. . . . It was a little defensive on my part, but it worked."

Thus Bush's soft personal touch and hard political instincts were wedded.

Gerald Ford may have been an All-American football player at Michigan and Teddy Roosevelt shot at least one of every species that could walk, but no President has ever had a wider or deeper interest in games than Bush. Whether he's fly-fishing or pitching horseshoes, playing doubles tennis with Bjorn Borg or getting his golf handicap down to 11, Bush is just a blink away from being a sportsaholic. He still thinks soccer, in which he led Yale to a title as center forward, may've been his best sport.

Once bitten, Bush never loses his love for a sport—except golf, the game he's learned to despise. Yes, he's got the yips bad. "Putting and dancing are two of the things I hate the most," he said. "Putting, I can practice all day and still get it up in the neck—can't bring the club through. . . . It's terrible. Your friends laugh at you. They won't give you a six-inch putt because they know you're apt to stab it into the dirt and it's really been a humiliating experience."

The only time Bush feels more humbled is when he campaigns with Ted Williams. "Up in New Hampshire, for example," said the President, "it's 'Hey, fella, would you get out of the way? Ted, how are you?' A great lesson . . .

"Actually, I think [my putting] is one of the reasons I'm more calm now than I used to be—the discipline that comes from being a lousy putter. [The] ridicule factor . . .

"It's strictly psychological."

Where does baseball rank among all his dozen athletic passions? Bush's answer is simply to hold up one finger. He can't resist the game.

"Baseball is just the great American pastime. I try to figure out what it is. I think it's the joy of feeling a part of [the game] more than other sports— wondering whether the guy's going to walk the hitter on purpose, wondering if the steal sign is on, wondering if he's going to bring in a relief pitcher. . . . The fan somehow feels more a part of the game sitting in the stands.

. . . A lot of them are faster-moving, but in baseball I get caught up in what I'd do if I were managing.

"The game seems to move along pretty good . . . but I don't even mind when it drags."

On Monday in Baltimore, many baseball fans may be tempted to utter a testy little boo when they see yet another politician who seems to be horning in on opening day. President George Bush is different. If his first ball bounces, it was probably a curve. And if he's wearing a glove, it's his own.

FOR THE BEST IN PAPERBACKS, LOOK FOR THE

In every corner of the world, on every subject under the sun, Penguin represents quality and variety—the very best in publishing today.

For complete information about books available from Penguin—including Pelicans, Puffins, Peregrines, and Penguin Classics—and how to order them, write to us at the appropriate address below. Please note that for copyright reasons the selection of books varies from country to country.

In the United Kingdom: For a complete list of books available from Penguin in the U.K., please write to *Dept E.P., Penguin Books Ltd, Harmondsworth, Middlesex, UB7 0DA.*

In the United States: For a complete list of books available from Penguin in the U.S., please write to *Dept BA, Penguin*, Box 120, Bergenfield, New Jersey 07621-0120.

In Canada: For a complete list of books available from Penguin in Canada, please write to *Penguin Books Canada Ltd, 10 Alcorn Avenue, Suite 300, Toronto, Ontario, Canada M4V 3B2.*

In Australia: For a complete list of books available from Penguin in Australia, please write to the *Marketing Department, Penguin Books Ltd, P.O. Box 257, Ringwood, Victoria 3134.*

In New Zealand: For a complete list of books available from Penguin in New Zealand, please write to the *Marketing Department, Penguin Books (NZ) Ltd, Private Bag, Takapuna, Auckland 9.*

In India: For a complete list of books available from Penguin, please write to *Penguin Overseas Ltd, 706 Eros Apartments, 56 Nehru Place, New Delhi, 110019.*

In Holland: For a complete list of books available from Penguin in Holland, please write to *Penguin Books Nederland B.V., Postbus 195, NL-1380AD Weesp, Netherlands.*

In Germany: For a complete list of books available from Penguin, please write to *Penguin Books Ltd, Friedrichstrasse 10-12, D-6000 Frankfurt Main 1, Federal Republic of Germany.*

In Spain: For a complete list of books available from Penguin in Spain, please write to *Longman, Penguin España, Calle San Nicolas 15, E-28013 Madrid, Spain.*

In Japan: For a complete list of books available from Penguin in Japan, please write to *Longman Penguin Japan Co Ltd, Yamaguchi Building, 2-12-9 Kanda Jimbocho, Chiyoda-Ku, Tokyo 101, Japan.*